IDOLS FOR DESTRUCTION

IDOLS FOR DESTRUCTION

*The Conflict of Christian Faith
and American Culture*

Herbert Schlossberg

Preface by
Robert H. Bork

Foreword by
Charles Colson

CROSSWAY BOOKS • WHEATON, ILLINOIS
A DIVISION OF GOOD NEWS PUBLISHERS

Idols for Destruction.

Copyright © 1990 by Herbert Schlossberg.

Preface copyright © 1990 by Robert H. Bork.

Published by Crossway Books
        a division of Good News Publishers
        1300 Crescent Street
        Wheaton, Illinois 60187.

Cover design: Dennis Hill

Art Direction/Design: Mark Schramm

First printing, Crossway edition, 1993.

Printed in the United States of America

ISBN 0-89107-738-3

The Bible text in this publication is from the Revised Standard Version of the Bible, copyright © 1946, 1952, 1971, 1973 by the Division of Christian Education of the National Council of Churches of Christ in the U.S.A. and is used by permission.

01		00		99		98		97		96		95		94		93
15	14	13	12	11	10	9	8	7	6	5	4	3	2	1

*This book is dedicated to the magnificent
woman who made it possible.*

Table of Contents

CHAPTER FOUR / Idols of Nature 140

CHAPTER FIVE / Idols of Power 177

Acknowledgments

I N 1977 I began a serious reading program to learn more about what seemed to me were the most vital and perplexing questions concerning the life of the individual as it relates to the society. These issues had first caught my interest almost twenty years earlier, while I was attending college, but were allowed to lie in dormancy. To my surprise, ideas for a book began emerging from this study and eventually took their present form.

A number of old friends and new acquaintances provided encouragement and criticism, as well as numerous hard knocks, and the book could not have achieved what merit it has without their contributions. Although none agrees with all the ideas expressed here, it is a pleasure to acknowledge the generous help of J.J. Barnett, Richard Johnson, Robert MacLennan, Norris Magnuson, Robert Malcolm, Theofanis Stavrou, Robert Glockner, Guy Chiattello, Michael Gattie, Carl Henry, Ronald Roper, Donald McGilchrist, James Sire, Howard Mattsson-Bozé, Lyman Coleman, Randall Tremba, and Wesley Anderson.

My wife, Terry, deserves special mention and thanks. She not only helped revive flagging spirits but made many important suggestions, typed several drafts of the manuscript, and provided the sole support of our family for more than four years while all this was taking place.

Foreword

Charles Colson

*I*N THE late 1970s, Herbert Schlossberg, who had recently resigned his academic position, found himself with some spare time and a persistent question. He combined the two in the University of Minnesota library, reading everything he could on economics, sociology, philosophy, political science, and ethics, in order to answer his query: How are Christians to discern and influence the culture around them?

Herb had attended an evangelical college whose assumptions led him to believe that Christians were to pristinely separate themselves from culture. Later he became part of a mainline church whose perspective led many of her members to presume that Christians were to merge with culture. He rejected those two extremes of separatism and enculturation, but still the question remained: What *was* the healthy relationship between the believer and the society around him or her?

As the months went by, Herb's search intensified; his notes and his convictions mounted. His wife encouraged him to shape his intellectual and spiritual pilgrimage into a book, so others might profit from his insights. At her urging, Herb agreed to take a year off to write his book.

Five years later, Herb completed his manuscript. One hundred publishers rejected it. Then, in 1983, Thomas Nelson agreed to publish *Idols for Destruction*. Christian readers *did* benefit from Herb's studies; they told their friends about the book, and it became a runaway bestseller.

Now, ten years later, Crossway Books has republished *Idols for Destruction*, and I salute them for doing so.

The bookshelf next to my desk holds Christian classics and books I refer to often. *Idols* sits on that shelf, for Herb's lucid critique has been an invaluable reference for my own writings. It helps believers to understand the ideologies that undergird secular culture, and how they dramatically—and dangerously—differ from the Judeo-Christian view based on adherence to absolute truth.

Over the past decade, the simmering conflict between those two perspectives has escalated into a full-scale war. Tragically, many Christians are fighting that war with the wrong weapons. Some, confronted with the pervasive anti-Christian basis among cultural elites, are tempted to retreat to the sanctuary of their churches and fellowship groups. Others, in an attempt to appear relevant to the culture they seek to win, have donned the characteristics of their opponents, and are now indistinguishable from them. And others are fighting with the world's weapons, wielding the long knives of hatred and hostility with a vengeance.

The call for Christians right now is as fresh as this morning's headlines and as ancient as Christ's command to His disciples of a much earlier era. We must be as harmless as doves, fighting today's culture war with spiritual weapons of love, peace, and hope. And we must be as wise as serpents, judiciously discerning the course of the battle around us, so we might both articulate and demonstrate the gospel to those in such desperate need of it.

So Herb Schlossberg's dilemma, and the answers he explores in *Idols for Destruction*, are as compelling as they were a decade ago. The only difference is that the call for Christians to expose today's idols is even more urgent.

CHARLES W. COLSON
WASHINGTON, D.C.
APRIL 22, 1993

Preface

Robert H. Bork

TO say that American culture is changing rapidly is to state not merely the obvious but the obtrusive. The evidence is thrust at us dozens of times every day. Social, moral, and legal constraints that were effective quite recently are now breached regularly and with impunity. Everyone can cite illustrations. Rock music, in itself degenerate, now comes with lyrics celebrating everything from perverted sex described in graphic terms to anti-Semitism. The United States government funds obscene displays of homoerotic photographs that not long ago would have attracted the attention of the police rather than taxpayers' dollars. It was never reasonable to expect television to be the educational force some predicted, but surely it is surprising that the popular programming slipped so rapidly from Sid Caesar and Imogene Coco to Roseanne Barr, whose form of humor would not have been shown ten or fifteen years ago. A federal judge feels free to rule, which can only be called preposterous, that after two hundred years the first amendment has suddenly evolved so that begging in the subways of New York is protected free speech—and professors of law announce that it would be very difficult to rule any other way.

If these appear to be instances of individualism, or moral relativism, run wild, in yet other areas of life developments seem to be running the other way. When the Supreme Court displayed some mild resistance to the imposition or coercion of racial and sexual quotas where there has been no showing of discrimination, the outcry from politically powerful groups was enormous and there is a strong movement in Congress to put quotas back in place. An increasing number of institutions and local governments punish individuals for choosing not to deal with other individuals who are homosexual. Individual moral choice is not to be allowed in such matters.

There are those, of course, who hail both trends—that of individualism run rampant and that of collective intrusion into individual judgment and morality—as welcome advances in freedom. It may be difficult to see how moral relativism and state-enforced morality can both be gains for freedom, but in the current state of public discourse simplistic, heated, and self-righteous rhetoric is very powerful. It may be apparent by now that I am out of sympathy with these cultural trends. Apparently divergent, they seem to me consistent primarily in being assaults on traditional virtues. Not long ago I heard a thoughtful clergyman, a man not given to violent rhetoric, say that Americans are moving into a "sub-pagan culture." The expression jolted a bit, but a moment's reflection suggested that the point is certainly arguable.

Most of us shake our heads and bemoan the latest outrage but are helpless to understand why our culture seems increasingly degraded. In *Idols for Destruction*, Herbert Schlossberg offers an analysis that seems to me increasingly persuasive. Some few years ago friends whose judgment I greatly respect argued that religion constitutes the only reliable basis for morality and that when religion loses its hold on a society, standards of morality will gradually crumble. I objected that there were many moral people who are not at all religious; my friends replied that such people are living on the moral capital left by generations that believed there is a God and that He makes demands on us. The prospect, they said, was that the remaining moral capital would dwindle and our society become less moral. The course of society and culture has been as they predicted, which certainly does not prove their point but does provide evidence for it.

Schlossberg makes the same point. "After biblical faith wanes, a people can maintain habits of thought and of self-restraint. The ethic remains after the faith that bore it departs. But eventually a generation arises that no longer has the habit, and that is when the behavior changes radically."

To many, this will seem a counsel of despair. Since we live in a rational and scientific age, it will be said, it is impossible to believe the superstitions of religion. If faith is required, then our moral capital is bound to dwindle and cannot be rebuilt. Schlossberg's response to that argument is one of the great strengths of his book. He examines the major belief systems that have replaced religion in our time—*e.g.*, historicism, materialism, scientism—and demonstrates that each of them rests upon premises which the believer must accept on faith: "All alternatives to Christian doctrine are themselves grounded in unprovable assumptions, and in that sense cannot be distinguished from positions of faith. Dogma is inescapable notwithstanding the failure of so many to recognize the pervasiveness and fragility of their own belief systems." Of course that is correct. Nobody lives without some idea of what life is, even if the idea is that life is essentially meaningless and governed by random events. But even that position constitutes a philosophy that cannot be proved correct and thus rests upon an act of faith or, if you prefer, a leap to a premise.

Those who do not accept a God who stands outside of "natural" processes have no more reason for their faith than Christians who believe that Jesus rose on the third day or Jews who believe God made them His chosen people. Many people have a sort of vague idea that one day science will reveal everything, but that rests upon a number of assumptions essentially taken on faith, among them that there is a natural world independent of the mind that purports to observe it and that that universe is ultimately reducible to laws the mind can discover. Perhaps these things will ultimately prove to be true but at the moment they are taken on faith. It is not necessary to that proposition to point out that reports from the front lines suggest to the layman that natural science's difficulties with ultimate reality are increasing rather than diminishing. We are told that nobody understands quantum physics and that some physicists think there may be no reality, or none other than mathematics. At the other end of the spectrum, we are told that cosmology is in grave difficulty and that the more humans peer into the universe, the less they are able to understand how it achieved its present condition. The belief that science will ultimately comprehend the nature of reality at both the micro and macro levels is no less founded on faith than the belief that there is a God and that Jesus was His son.

If that were all, the reader might conclude that this leaves us free to accept on faith any system of comprehending life that appeals to us for any reason. Schlossberg most emphatically disagrees. The book's title is taken from Hosea, who said the Israelites' idolatry had brought their nation to ruin. "With their silver and gold they made idols for their own destruction." The trouble with silver and gold idols is not that they are made of silver and gold but that they are things men put in the place of God. For that reason, "idols" need not consist of graven images. Schlossberg is surely correct, therefore, to classify as an "idol" any value or principle that men substitute for God.

Schlossberg's thesis is that these philosophical idols—historicism, humanism, science, and so on—do indeed lead to our destruction, that they are in themselves pernicious. These demonstrations are, for me at least, the most interesting parts of the book. Schlossberg has read widely and thought deeply in philosophy, economics, politics, religion, and much more in order to explain the destructiveness of the idols of non-religious belief systems. His argument in these areas does not depend on Christian faith but meets the alternative belief systems on their own grounds. A reader need not be in the least religious to find this aspect of the book enormously rewarding.

From what I have said so far, it may be supposed that Herbert Schlossberg has written a book uncritically admiring of religion and its institutions. The reader will be rapidly disabused of that notion by the chapter entitled "Idols of Religion," in which it is argued that the institutions of religion are and always have been particularly susceptible to the hazards of idolatry. Today, "by and large, the religious institutions of the United States do not teach values that are distinctive to their own traditions but rather use religious terminology that ratifies the values of the broader society." Church leaders variously adopt as religious values Marxism, liberation theology, the latest trend in psychology; the secular religions insinuate themselves into the Christian churches and leach them of their distinctive religious values.

> Meanwhile [Schlossberg writes], we are left with a church that to a large extent has chosen to befriend the powers that dominate the world instead of judging them. We should be reminded that the crucifixion of Christ was a joint production, instigated by religious authorities and then carried out by the state. When the state joins forces with historicism and humanism in forging the great brutalities of the future, we should not be surprised to find the representatives of the establishment churches, fuglemen for the idolatries, earnestly assuring us that God's will is being done.

That is why Schlossberg says, "In a society in which idolatry runs rampant, a church that is not iconoclastic is a travesty. If it is not against the idols it is with them."

Perhaps Mr. Schlossberg owes us another book, one that speaks at greater length about the nature of a just society as defined by Christianity. But this book is a marvel as it stands. An emptiness lies at the center of liberal democratic ideology. Vastly superior though it is to alternative forms of government—authoritarianism and totalitarianism, in the various forms this century has shown us—individual freedom and democratic governance leave the question of life's meaning untouched. Yet most people cannot live without assigning meaning of some sort to their existence and, as religious belief has faded, the idols have tried to provide that meaning. At the moment, the most virulent of the idols in America appears to be the belief that political results of a leftist variety are the only things that count; and we are observing the politicization of our culture with consequent damage to institutions and disciplines that once had standards of integrity unrelated to political results. That is today's cultural war, and since the idol of politics rests upon faith quite as much as any other belief system, our cultural wars are religious wars. *Idols for Destruction* is a powerful weapon on the right side of the religious wars and has restated the case for a Christianity unrelated to, indeed ranged against, the secular religions of our time.

. . . they made idols
for their own destruction.
—Hosea 8:4

Introduction

*T*HE technological flowering and economic expansion of the twentieth century has been accompanied by an astonishing growth in pessimism, even despair. The period just before the turn of the century was so charged with a sense of decadence that the phrase *fin de siècle* has come to convey the idea of decline, with a foreboding of doom. Those fears were not groundless, and Europe and the United States plunged into a devastating world war, then a great depression, and then another world war. Those disasters in turn have served to convince many people that Western civilization has entered a period of breakdown from which it may never recover.

The last thirty-five years, though prosperous almost beyond belief, have been visited with social pathologies that reinforce the sourness of those earlier expectations. Our society is now described in such terms as post-capitalist (Ralf Dahrendorf), post-bourgeois (George Lichtheim), post-modern (Amitai Etzioni), post-collectivist (Sam Beer), post-literary (Marshall McLuhan), post-civilized (Kenneth Boulding), post-traditional (S. N. Eisenstadt), post-historic (Roderick Seidenberg), post-industrial (Daniel Bell), post-Puritan, post-Protestant and post-Christian (Sidney Ahlstrom).[1]

Examples abound in which the images of contemporary society have

---

[1] Compiled by Richard John Neuhaus, *Time Toward Home: The American Experiment as Revelation* (New York: Seabury, 1975), pp. 1f.

1

shifted to decline, disintegration, atrophy, and so on. Arnold Toynbee reminisced late in life about his family's expectations around the turn of the century. His scientist uncle was wildly optimistic about the future, anticipating that a golden age was about to be ushered in by science. His social worker father, on the other hand, was rather somber as he contemplated the future. At the time he found his uncle's outlook exhilarating and his father's melancholy. By 1969, however, Toynbee had concluded that his uncle had been naive and his father realistic.[2]

The case of H. G. Wells is more striking because the evolution of his thinking is marked by a trail of books that shows plainly the descending path. His *Outline of History* (1920) was a song of evolutionary idealism, faith in progress, and complete optimism. By 1933, when he published *The Shape of Things to Come*, he could see no better way to overcome the stubbornness and selfishness between people and nations than a desperate action by intellectual idealists to seize control of the world by force and establish their vision with a universal compulsory educational program. Finally, shortly before his death, he wrote an aptly-titled book, *The Mind at the End of Its Tether* (1945) in which he concluded that "there is no way out, or around, or through the impasse. It is the end." In Wells's journey to despair Reinhold Niebuhr saw "an almost perfect record in miniature of the spiritual pilgrimage of our age."[3]

A few examples illustrate the point further. A French Catholic philosopher: "The end of the Roman Empire was a minor event compared with what we behold. We are looking at the liquidation of what is known as the 'modern world.' "[4] A British journalist: "I have to report the affairs of a world which has lost its faith, which is like a fish out of water or a drowning man, desperately thrashing around for lack of oxygen. Since the time of Christ there has been no period in which there has been the same feeling of . . . spiritual impoverishment."[5] A German sociologist: "Civilization is collapsing before our eyes."[6]

William Rees-Mogg, former editor of the *Times* of London, while writing of the hollowness and despair that have gripped Western society, has hope that Americans will escape the general malaise and retain

---

[2]Arnold J. Toynbee, *Experiences* (New York: Oxford Univ. Press, 1969), p. 299.

[3]Reinhold Niebuhr, *Faith and History: A Comparison of Christian and Modern Views of History* (New York: Scribner's, 1949), pp. 162f.

[4]Jacques Maritain, *Christianity and Democracy* (London: Geoffrey Bles, 1945), p. 12.

[5]William Rees-Mogg, *An Humbler Heaven: The Beginnings of Hope* (London: Hamish Hamilton, 1977), p. 2.

[6]Karl Mannheim, *Man and Society: In an Age of Reconstruction* (London: Kegan Paul, Trench, Trubner, 1940) p. 15.

an optimism that will serve to redeem the remainder of the West.[7] But the United States does not lack for observers who disagree with him. In terms strikingly similar to those of Rees-Mogg, William Foxwell Albright, the distinguished archaeologist, said that American society is at an impasse similar to that of the Hellenic world at the time of Christ.[8] Sociologist Robert Bellah believes that the United States is undergoing a third time of trial, which may be even more severe than those of the Revolution and the Civil War.[9] With some exaggeration, perhaps, two social scientists assign the shift to despair to a single decade: the 1960s. Daniel Moynihan, now a United States Senator, believes that at that time a "set of untroubled, even serene convictions as to the nature of man and society, and the ever more promising prospects of the future, of a sudden collapsed. No one any longer really believed it."[10] And Daniel Bell, a sociologist at Harvard University, noticed a plethora of writings in the 1950s on such subjects as a prodigious growth in productivity, superabundance, and the problems of leisure. All that has come to an end. "Paradoxically, the vision of Utopia was suddenly replaced by the spectre of Doomsday."[11]

Now, one might object that this outpouring of pessimism reveals the disaffection with society that one expects from intellectuals, and that ordinary people are far less dissatisfied than those chronic complainers. Crane Brinton, himself a Harvard intellectual, made such an argument two decades ago,[12] but it is hard to believe that he would be so certain of that now. A Roper poll commissioned by the U. S. Department of Labor reported in 1978 that, for the first time since that poll was initiated in 1959, the respondents rated their expectations for the future lower than their assessment of the present.

Of course, all of this evidence is subjective, and one could argue that if objective criteria were examined we would find that everything really is getting better and better just as we used to think, even if nobody believes it. We will have occasion later on to look at some of the objective infor-

---

[7]Ress-Mogg, *An Humbler Heaven*, p. 58.

[8]William Foxwell Albright, *From the Stone Age to Christianity: Monotheism and the Historical Process,* 2nd ed. (Garden City, N.Y.: Doubleday Anchor, 1957), p. 403.

[9]Robert N. Bellah, *The Broken Covenant: American Civil Religion in Time of Trial* (New York: Seabury, 1975), p. 1.

[10]Daniel P. Moynihan, *Maximum Feasible Misunderstanding: Community Action in the War on Poverty* (New York: Free Press, 1969), p. 7.

[11]Daniel Bell, *The End of Ideology: On the Exhaustion of Ideas in the Fifties,* rev. ed. (New York: Free Press, 1962), pp. 460–63.

[12]Crane Brinton, *A History of Western Morals* (New York: Harcourt, Brace, and World, 1959), pp. 391f.

mation at our disposal, but there will not be much to support that rosy view.

Understanding Our Place in History

A society conscious of its place in history is seldom content merely to note changing circumstances with no attempt to evaluate their meaning. Edward Gibbon's history of Rome made spatial analogies—such as rise, decline, and fall—commonplace in evaluating civilizations. In the twentieth century, organic phrases perhaps have become more common, possibly due to Oswald Spengler's influence. Societies are thought of as being born, growing, decaying, dying. Other terms are sometimes drawn from the social sciences or from the requirements of political propaganda. Thus, a society may be said to be coming of age, to be attaining self-consciousness, to be throwing off the chains of oppression, to be entering a dark age, to be entering a golden age.

We make such evaluations because we are not content with mere descriptions of events or recitations of facts and statistics. We want, rather, to be able to understand their meaning, and we cannot do that without having an idea about the end toward which those events are proceeding. Even the most cynical among us, if they have not reached the nadir of complete nihilism, have this teleological orientation. We can say that society is growing up (or regressing) because we have an idea of what a society would be like if it should reach a state analagous to mature adulthood. We can say a society is dying because we think we know what a dead society would be like. Or we can speak about the arrival of a golden age because we have in mind a state of full equality or complete order or extravagant prosperity, or whatever vision would inspire us to use such a phrase.

These teleological visions are agglomerations of values, often having powerful emotional force even if one is not conscious of their components. That is why they have the power to energize people in such extraordinary ways. Men may risk everything, including their lives, for family, for wealth, for country, for class, or for the kingdom of God. Even the cynic who believes he is above all that nonsense has established a hierarchy of values; otherwise he could not identify *those* values as nonsense. We may think his vision crabbed and deformed, but neither we nor he can deny that he has one.

All such visions are freighted with religious content, although this is often not recognized. They contain at least some of the components we expect to find in religions: a theory of knowledge, an authoritative literature, a theory of historical relationships, a cosmology, a hierarchy of values, and an eschatology. To cite an obvious example, Marxism, which some people still insist on calling a science, has every one of those features. What more could anyone ask of a religion? Well, it might be said that a religion should have God as its end. But anyone with a hierarchy of values has placed *something* at its apex, and whatever that is is the god he serves. The Old and New Testaments call such gods idols and provide sufficient reason for affirming that the systems that give them allegiance are religions. The semantic difficulty comes in part from assuming that to call something a religion is to express a value judgment. Those in our own day who are pleased or affronted at being identified with a religion should ask why that is so. The biblical writers did not speak of religion as something to be revered, and there is no good reason for any of us to feel honored or dishonored at being so identified.

Christianity, along with its Hebraic antecedents, is by its nature historically minded. It rejects both cyclical theories of history and notions of the eternality of the universe. The doctrines of creation and of eschatology are explicit statements that history has both a beginning and an end and that it is possible to say something intelligible about both. Events between the two termini are also intelligible, and, being related to them, have meaning. From those relationships we may infer that general evaluations of the state of our society ought to be of great interest to Christians and that Christian faith has insights of close relevance to this discussion.

Idolatry as a Framework for Understanding

This raises the question of what analogy Christians are to use in understanding our society. It is a curious fact that the Old Testament, which describes the beginning, course, and end of a number of societies, never assesses them as being on the rise or decline, as progressing or regressing, as growing to maturity or falling to senescence. One might object that only a failed sense of history could expect an evaluation of society to take the forms that would be common two or three millenia in the future. Yet those particular analogies do not seem anachronistic for the time and place we are considering. The idea of cataclysmic fall as a result of moral failure is common enough in the biblical literature, and analogies relating to the life cycle could hardly have been foreign to nomads, herdsmen, and farmers.

Spatial and biological analogies are incompatible with biblical thinking because they are both quantitatively oriented and deterministic. To say that a society is young is to imply that on a scale between birth and the expected three-score-and-ten, this society is, say, thirty, and when its time has run out it will die. Spatial analogies lead us to expect that what goes up must come down; they imply a trajectory that can be plotted and an apex that is determined by such numerical factors as velocity, weight, and angle. In place of these analogies the biblical explanation of the end of societies uses the concept of *judgment.* It depicts them as either having submitted themselves to God or else having rebelled against him. Far from being a typical nationalistic exaltation of a "chosen people," the Old Testament portrays Israel as having become an evil nation, fully deserving the judgment that God meted to it. Its rebellion against God was accompanied by a turning to idols, and this idolatry brought the nation to its end. "With their silver and gold," said the prophet Hosea, "they made idols for their own destruction" (Hos. 8:4).

Idolatry in its larger meaning is properly understood as any substitution of what is created for the creator. People may worship nature, money, mankind, power, history, or social and political systems instead of the God who created them all. The New Testament writers, in particular, recognized that the relationship need not be *explicitly* one of cultic worship; a man can place anyone or anything at the top of his pyramid of values, and that is ultimately what he serves. The ultimacy of that service profoundly affects the way he lives. When the society around him also turns away from God to idols, it is an idolatrous society and therefore is heading for destruction.

Western society, in turning away from Christian faith, has turned to other things. This process is commonly called *secularization*, but that conveys only the negative aspect. The word connotes the turning away from the worship of God while ignoring the fact that something is being turned *to* in its place. Even atheisms are usually idolatrous, as Neibuhr said, because they elevate some "principle of coherence" to the central meaning of life and this is what then provides the focus of significance for that life. Niebuhr's principle of coherence corresponds to what we referred to earlier as the apex of the hierarchy of values. All such principles that substitute for God exemplify the biblical concept of idol. The bulk of this book is an exploration of the forms these idols take in late twentieth-century America.

Ideas and Action

Our argument, then, is that idolatry and its associated concepts provide a better framework for us to understand our own society than do any of the alternatives. Toynbee was right to say that by the 1950s, "the crucial questions confronting Western Man were all religious,"[13] because of the inevitable dependence of a society's actions on its beliefs. If its actions are destructive, we must ask what it believes that causes it to behave in such a way. Now, to some people such statements are axiomatic, but others would sharply dispute them. Many social scientists, in particular, would quarrel with a formulation that ties behavior to belief, and that is a disagreement we shall have to deal with at some length.

For the moment, however, let us consider another kind of critic, much more numerous in our society. The emphasis on ideas and beliefs in this discussion does not find warm welcome in an age that respects the tough-minded pragmatist who disdains philosophy and insists on the immediate, the concrete, and the practical. But it is impossible for anyone to say that he will avoid philosophies and simply live pragmatically, because that statement is based on a philosophical belief that he has accepted without realizing it. Legions of ordinary people know how to use such ideas as inferiority complex, relativity, and pragmatism, although scarcely any of them have read a page of Freud, Einstein, or Dewey. Those philosophies may come down in transmogrified form, but come down they do. That is the wisdom in John Maynard Keynes's remark that "Madmen in authority, who hear voices in the air, are distilling their frenzy from some academic scribbler of a few years back."[14]

Our anti-philosophers are especially vulnerable in this age, because the media fill our environment with popularized philosophies. Marshall McLuhan was right in saying that environments tend not to be noticed (although he exaggerated the effect). We see many of their explicit contents, but the environments themselves are imperceptible.[15] We do not see the environment, as Os Guinness says, because we see *with* it. That means we are influenced by ideas we do not notice and therefore are not aware of their effect on us. Or, if we see the effect, we find it difficult to discover the cause.

Given our media-saturated existences, we would do well to consider how Keynes's academic scribblers (of whom Keynes was one) affect us.

---

[13]Arnold J. Toynbee, *A Study of History,* abridgement by D. C. Somervell, 2 vols. (New York: Oxford Univ. Press, 1947, 1957), vol. 2, p. 314. This is not to say that the commonly advanced religious answers are of value. Toynbee's repeated portrayals of religion as the goal of civilization come perilously close to making an idol of it.

[14]John Maynard Keynes, *The General Theory of Unemployment, Interest and Money,* p. 383, quoted in Walter Lippmann, *An Inquiry into the Principles of the Good Society* (Boston: Little, Brown, 1937), p. 45.

[15]Marshall McLuhan, *Understanding Media: The Extensions of Man* (New York: McGraw-Hill, 1965 [1964]), p. vii.

Some academic disciplines, especially those in the social sciences, are profoundly anti-Christian in their effect, and it is difficult to counter that effect by dealing with their evidence or their arguments. The evidence is often good and the arguments sound. It is the assumptions we must question. These are statements that are presumed to be true but are not proven. No serious thought can be conducted without assumptions, but recognizing them—in our own thinking as well as in others— is vital if we are to avoid falling into serious error. Assumptions are *beliefs*; if they were proven they would not be assumptions. And they are beliefs so taken for granted that it is not deemed necessary to prove them. That makes them doubly seductive: first, because the careless or untrained are misled into accepting conclusions without recognizing their shaky foundation of unstated beliefs; and second, the very fact that the most dubious beliefs are so taken for granted by experts lends an aura of verisimilitude that beguiles the overly respectful into accepting them without question.

By and large there is nothing insincere about the way these assumptions are held. They function in some respects much the way religious beliefs do, although in academia they are seldom recognized in that way. And that explains the vehemence with which attacks on someone's assumptions are met; they are often attacks on that person's unacknowledged religion.

Although academic disciplines by their nature have wide divergencies of opinion within them, they also have broad areas of common agreement. This book takes issue with some of those agreements, sometimes with the evidence or arguments in their favor, but more often with the beliefs with which the investigations were begun. Soundly designed experiments, complete data, airtight controls, scrupulous honesty, and rigorous logic yield wrong conclusions when the original assumptions are wrong.

Unfortunately, many Christian intellectuals and others who influence ecclesiastical policy have adopted the academic models too uncritically. Peter Berger, a Rutgers University sociologist, has accused opinion leaders in the church of taking their cues increasingly from the "official reality-definers—that is, from the highly secularized intellectual elite."[16] In an earlier essay, Berger had explained what was wrong with that. "Liberal intellectuals are always top candidates for the role of fall guy, for the simple reason that it is of the essence of liberalism to be

---

[16]Peter L. Berger, "A World With Windows," in Peter L. Berger and Richard John Neuhaus, eds., *Against the World for the World* (New York: Seabury, 1976), p. 12.

contemporaneous and of the essence of being an intellectual to know what is contemporaneous."[17] He need not have wasted his sympathy, for their wounds are all self-inflicted. These intellectuals must have been the people W. R. Inge had in mind when he made his famous remark that he who marries the spirit of an age soon finds himself a widower.

Idols of the Left, Right, and Center

The irony in Berger's point is that the churches' intellectuals are falling for intellectual fashions that have used up all their capital and fallen into bankruptcy. It was hard to see that in the nineteenth century when Christians began retreating before the new ideologies. Now American religion is full of the contradictions and paradoxes that come from the attempt to merge a true gospel with the faltering creeds of the surrounding society. The internal clash is reflected in the title of one of Niebuhr's books: *Pious and Secular America.* Elsewhere, Niebuhr described the prevailing national religiosity as a "perversion of the Christian gospel," aggravating the nation's problems.[18]

A pluralistic society heralds the virtues of paths that have no exits. George Forell, a theologian at the University of Iowa, has described the political movements that range across the spectrum from left to right as "rival deck stewards competing with each other about the arrangement of the deck chairs just before the Titanic hits the iceberg."[19] German sociologist Karl Mannheim reveals the intellectual barrenness of thinking that one has said something when he has pasted a label. "Nothing is simpler than to maintain that a certain type of thinking is feudal, bourgeois or proletarian, liberal, socialistic, or conservative, as long as there is no analytical method for demonstrating it and no criteria have been adduced which will provide a control over the demonstration."[20] Those terms have rendered service mainly as polemical devices to smear opponents and as shorthand methods of identifying friends and enemies. (This book will make some small contribution to civility by forbearing

---

[17]Peter L. Berger, "The Liberal as the Fall Guy," *The Center Magazine,* vol. 5, no. 4, July-August 1972, p. 39.

[18]Reinhold Niebuhr, "Religiosity and the Christian Faith," *Christianity and Crisis,* May 28, 1951, reprinted in Reinhold Niebuhr, *Essays in Applied Christianity,* ed. D. B. Robertson (New York: Meridian, Living Age, 1959), p. 65.

[19]George Forell, "Reason, Relevance and a Radical Gospel," in Berger and Neuhaus, eds., *Against the World for the World,* p. 76.

[20]Karl Mannheim, *Ideology and Utopia: An Introduction to the Sociology of Knowledge,* trans. Louis Wirth and Edward Shils (London: Kegan Paul, Trench, Trubner, 1946 [1936]), p. 45.

their use except to identify self-labels. Thus, when someone is called a conservative on these pages, it only means that that is what he calls himself.)

The struggle between Forell's deck stewards may usefully be thought of as a clash of idols, beckoning to us as antinomies: capitalism and socialism, individualism and collectivism, statism and libertarianism, rationalism and irrationalism, nature worship and historicism, conservatism and liberalism, reaction and radicalism, elitism and equalitarianism. The conflicting parties and the media create false dilemmas, and the ecclesiastical leaders lunge at them as if the only response to a dilemma were to impale themselves on one of its horns. The issues of the day are so contrived as to create the illusion that every choice is wrong, that nothing can be done without doing some evil, and that the only question is which course of action is less evil. Reinhold Niebuhr—"the father of us all," George Kennan called him—whose genius did so much to reveal the destructive self-righteousness of the twentieth-century utopias, did not serve us well on this matter. Lesser men who learned from him that there is no course of action without its admixture of evil and that one must choose between evils concluded, naturally enough, that doing evil must not be so bad.

The participants in this struggle, along with their ecclesiastical admirers, insist that we have to choose between left and right on every issue, that there is no third way. But if we are successful in identifying the first two ways as idols, then it is reasonable to conclude that there must be a third way. The final purpose of this book is to make some progress toward finding out what it is.

CHAPTER ONE

Idols of History

*A*LL idols belong either to nature or to history. The whole creation falls into those two categories, and there is no other place to which man can turn to find a substitute for God. Any idol that is not an artifact of the natural world is an artifact of the social world.[1]

In this chapter, *history* is used in a more restricted sense. We are considering here the idolatrous thinking that focuses its attention on the historical process itself, reserving for later a discussion of the outcomes of such thinking, that is, the idols created from within the theater of history. It may suffice to say at this point that idolatry based on history becomes power politics and, finally, one of numerous systems that people use to control other people.

History as a Religious Enterprise

Early in this century German historian Oswald Spengler published

---

[1]William Foxwell Albright objected to this dualism, which he believed was fairly recent in origin. Inasmuch as both nature and history are part of the creation, there is a certain artificiality to the distinction, but that is true of all systems of classification. The danger in Albright's position is that it presents no barrier to a complete naturalism. See *From the Stone Age to Christianity: Monotheism and the Historical Process,* 2nd ed. (Garden City, N.Y.: Doubleday Anchor, 1957), p. 126.

his monumental interpretation of Western civilization, *The Decline of the West*. With equally monumental confidence, he declared that the book "contains the incontrovertible formulation of an idea which, once enunciated clearly, will . . . be accepted without dispute."[2] Spengler probably had in mind, as did many of his contemporaries, the great scientific theories that had received virtually unanimous acceptance, and he hoped his theory of history would have similar success. The book achieved great popularity but never fulfilled its author's expectations. It is little read today, and one would have to search hard to find anyone who found its argument "incontrovertible." Spengler's mistake lay in thinking that theories of history were of the same order as theories of physics or biology. Time, however, is a *religious* concept, and there can be no agreement on a philosophy of history without agreement on religion.

Whether time is important or unimportant, intelligible or absurd, cyclical or linear are questions intimately bound up with the most fundamental of metaphysical, anthropological, and theological convictions. The linearity of Western conceptions of history reflects the conviction that history is what comes between creation and final judgment. But there are other models. Ancient theories of cyclical history were related to religious ideas concerning the periodic nature of redemption. Norman O. Brown, Freud's romantic reviser and popularizer, rightly described secular rationalism, dependent as it is on Newtonian time, as a religion. The new relativist notion of time represents the disintegration of that religion.[3]

What we think of the meaning of history is inseparable from what we think of the meaning of life. "In this sense," says Herbert Butterfield, a Cambridge historian, "our interpretation of the human drama throughout the ages rests finally on our interpretation of our most private experiences of life, and stands as merely an extension to it."[4]

That the question of history has any importance at all is in itself a religious conclusion. The classical view was that reason transcends the facts of history, just as universals transcend particulars. Therefore, historical events—as, indeed, all change—were relatively unimportant. The cycles of history were not drawn to a goal but would keep on recur-

---

[2]Oswald Spengler, *The Decline of the West*, trans. Charles Francis Atkinson, rev. ed., 2 vols. (New York: Knopf, 1926, 1928), vol. 1, p. 50.

[3]Norman O. Brown, *Life Against Death: The Psychoanalytical Meaning of History* (Middletown, Conn.: Wesleyan Univ. Press, 1959), p. 274.

[4]Herbert Butterfield, *Christianity and History* (London: Collins, Fontana, 1957 [1949]), p. 141.

ring endlessly. This notion devalued events and robbed them of significance. Eastern mystics also devalue history, regarding events as particularities in which they have no interest and preferring instead to contemplate the unity from which they believe the particularities derive their meaning. That is why, as G. K. Chesterton said, it is fitting that the Buddha be pictured with his eyes closed; there is nothing important to see.

Western civilization, in keeping with its Christian underpinnings, has always valued history highly. But as it has departed from the faith, that value has been transmuted. Rather than the arena in which providence and judgment meet the obedience or rebellion of man, history is now seen as the vehicle of salvation. Whether in the form of doctrinaire Spencerian evolution (now rare), the Enlightenment type of progress (also rare), Marxism (not so rare) or Western social engineering (the most common form of this cult), it places salvation within the institutions of history and thus fulfills the biblical definition of idolatry. The idolatries of history exalt an age (past, present, or future), or a process, or an institution, or a class, or a trend and make it normative. They place the entire meaning of life *within* the historical process or some part of it, allowing nothing extrinsic to it. Historical events in their relationships exhaust the whole meaning of history. In a word, the meaning of history is wholly *immanent*, and that is a term we shall find occurring repeatedly in our consideration of idolatry. History, to borrow the expression C.E.M. Joad used in a different context, is "the whole show."

The Cult of Historicism

There is general agreement that the modern form of the historicism we have been describing finds its classic expression in the philosophy of Hegel. Karl Popper, whose work is among the most illuminating on this subject, believes that Hegel's aim was to transcend the intractable dualism that Kant had established between phenomena—the realm of particularity, fact, event—and noumena—the world of value, spirit, faith. Hegel's philosophy coalesced the duality of ideal and real, of right and might, finding that fusion in the historical process. This means, says Popper, that all values "are *historical facts*, stages in the development of reason, which is the same as the development of the ideal and of the real." Everything is fact, but some facts are also values.[5]

---

[5]Karl R. Popper, *The Open Society and Its Enemies*, 4th ed., 2 vols., vol. 2, *The High Tide of Prophecy: Hegel, Marx and the Aftermath* (Princeton, N.J.: Princeton Univ. Press, 1963), pp. 394f.

Woodrow Wilson's ideas on law provide an example of how this abstruse philosophical point has come to affect men of power. He believed that laws must be adjusted to fit facts, "because the law . . . is the expression of the facts in legal relationships. Laws have never altered the facts; laws have always necessarily expressed the facts."[6] Walter Lippmann, a determined foe of historicism, nevertheless expressed an idea almost identical to Wilson's, showing how pervasive the doctrine has become. Laws must change, said Lippmann, because they are based on sentiments that "express the highest promise of the deepest necessity of these times."[7]

The disastrous quality in this confusion of fact and value is that it is utterly relativistic; as the facts of history change, values, and consequently laws, will have to change with them. That is the justice in Martin Sklar's remark that *whatever* should happen to evolve in the social system, according to Wilson's theory, would be morally indisputable.[8] For Lippmann, whenever the "sentiments" of society change, the laws must change apace; thus, it is not only events that are normative, but sentiments. We can expect, therefore, that when the sentiments shift from nursing homes to gas chambers as the answer to the problems of the elderly, the laws presumably must comply. Lippmann, of course, would not countenance that application of his idea, but it is the logical outcome of the historicism into which he inadvertently stumbled. And while Lippmann would shrink from that outcome, we shall see further on that others do not. Thus, by the alchemy of historicism, fact is turned into value. In this fashion, says Jacques Ellul, a contemporary French social critic, history "is habitually transformed in modern discourse into a value, a power which bestows value, and a kind of absolute."[9]

History as Lord of the Universe

Dutch philosopher Herman Dooyeweerd, similarly vexed by historicism, showed how its relativism issues forth in determinism. "History has no windows looking out into eternity. Man is completely enclosed in

---

[6]Quoted in Martin J. Sklar, "Woodrow Wilson and the Political Economy of Modern United States Liberalism," in Ronald Radosh and Murray N. Rothbard, eds., *A New History of Leviathan: Essays on the Rise of the American Corporate State* (New York: Dutton, 1972), p. 14.

[7]Walter Lippmann, *An Inquiry into the Principles of the Good Society* (Boston: Little, Brown, 1937), p. 324.

[8]Sklar, "Woodrow Wilson and the Political Economy," p. 10.

[9]Jacques Ellul, *False Presence of the Kingdom,* trans. C. Edward Hopkin (New York: Seabury, 1972), p. 20.

it and cannot elevate himself to a supra-historical level of contemplation. History is the be-all and end-all of man's existence and of his faculty of experience. And it is ruled by destiny, the inescapable fate.''[10] Just
as man cannot understand history by reference to anything beyond it, so
is he powerless to struggle against anything that history has a mind to accomplish. Karl Mannheim, as if to provide an illustration for Dooyeweerd's point, dismissed the possibility that a central planning authority might be avoided. We do not have a choice between planning and not
planning, he said, but only between good planning and bad.[11] In the conclusion to his investigation of the good society, Lippmann declared that
classic liberalism was the culmination toward which history had always
been reaching. Spengler closed his two volumes of doom with perhaps
the best example we could find of the role of fate in historicism: ''We
have not the freedom to reach to this or that, but the freedom to do the
necessary or to do nothing. And a task that historic necessity has set *will*
be accomplished with the individual or against him.''

Historicism, in taking freedom out of the historical experience, parallels similar tendencies in the social sciences that make it impossible to retain the Christian conviction that people are responsible and account-
able for what they do. If there is no freedom to do this or that, how can it
be said that responsibility inheres in the person who does something or
refrains from doing it? Here is a philosophy made to order for a generation of intellectuals infatuated with Niebuhr's teaching that doing evil is
inevitable, that one's choices can do no more than mitigate its severity.

This complex of ideas, like so many others, has not remained the exclusive province of intellectuals, and we can identify examples of its use
by people who do not know its origins. One of the most common is the
saying, ''We can't turn back the clock.'' The progressive connotations
of this saying are wholly illusory. It actually looks *back* and says that the
trend of which the present moment is only the most visible manifestation
is the inevitable one, that anyone who disagrees with it is trying to
squeeze the whole world into a time machine and return to an earlier era.
But in refusing to believe that an identified historical trend may be chal-
lenged, the historicists have divinized history. In any given case, they
have absolutized *this* trend and thereby put history's seal of approval on
this status quo, one, no doubt, that is moving their way. The paradox of a

---

[10]Herman Dooyeweerd, *In the Twilight of Western Thought: Studies in the Pretended Autonomy of Philosophical Thought* (Philadelphia: Presbyterian and Reformed, 1960), p. 63.

[11]Quoted in Karl R. Popper, *The Poverty of Historicism,* 2nd ed. (London: Routledge
and Kegan Paul, 1960), p. 75, n. 1.

moving *status quo* is explained by the function of historical movement in historicist thinking; it plays precisely the same role as the lack of movement to a traditionalist, acting as a standard or value with which one must not tamper.

As a matter of simple historical observation, it would be hard to find a common saying as implausible as "We can't turn back the clock." The reason intelligent observers of the past found the cycle theory of history persuasive is precisely because it seemed as if the clock *had* been turned back. For, if turning back the clock describes the ending of a perceived historical trend and a reversion to the historical configuration that it replaced, we could list examples of this phenomenon endlessly: alternations between democracy and authoritarianism, high and low hemlines, moral permissiveness and prudery, war and peace, and so on. At each turn of the times we might be able to find historicists (witting or otherwise) saying plaintively that we can't turn the clock back. As a polemical device this idea pictures historical trends as juggernauts that cannot be stopped even if one were so foolish as to wish to stop them. These juggernauts, in fact, always do seem to be stopped eventually; and after they are, it is not a convincing explanation of what happened to say that the clock was turned back.[12]

The problem with the clock that cannot be turned back is that it is the wrong metaphor. Only a metaphor having to do with space rather than time will help us out of this blind alley. That seems like another paradox, since the whole discussion is one of historical and not geographical interpretation. The resolution of the paradox lies in the fact that people support or oppose historical trends on the basis of the ends to which they are directed. "This will lead us to the welfare state." "That will lead us to a society based on competition." The analogue of those ends is *destination,* and so we need to speak of taking a path to a place we wish to reach. We take a wrong turn and find ourselves in what appears to be an endless bog. We decide to turn around and retrace our steps to discover the correct route to the destination. However, someone in our party has read his Hegel and tells us that we want to turn the clock back. The reply to that is that to go straight ahead will take us deeper into the bog without knowing how many miles it stretches or what lies beyond, that the des-

---

[12]If we were limited to an immanentist conception of history, the cycle theory would be a very powerful one because it seems to describe what we actually see. As long as historical events are "the whole show" and we keep seeing the same patterns repeat themselves with varying amplitudes, then this ancient model is more persuasive than some of its modern rivals.

tination is elsewhere, and that the only way we shall find it is to discover where we made our mistake. Thus, the turning back has to do with space and not time. Of course, that scenario makes the disagreement of smaller importance than it commonly is. The conflicts to which historicist polemics are applied often center on the identity of the desirable destination. When that is the case, the values of the respective disputants are so fundamentally at odds that the tactical questions are irrelevant. But when that is true, people often still propose the clock metaphor. Their values are up-to-date, they say, and their opponents' values are not.

Getting in Step with History

This application of historicism, like all of them, deifies time, making it an idol. Time will unfold all things, it says, in a way that is inevitably right no matter what happens. But this particular kind of idol could only appear as a distortion of a biblical concept, because systems of thought having other origins do not take history seriously. The evolutionary philosophy of the Jesuit Pierre Teilhard de Chardin is another example of the same heresy: All things work together for good to him that is in tune with the times. Trying to "turn back the clock" becomes more serious than impropriety or stupidity; it is an act of impiety. Historicism is a dogma, Robert Nisbet has said, "that has had greatest appeal to several generations of intellectuals bereft of religion and driven thereby into the arms of the waiting church of historical necessity."[13] This is a church with many branches, all of whose members are on the move. Anyone convinced that X is the wave of the future is tempted mightily to enter the struggle on the victory side. Certain that he is on the team that the future will vindicate, the historicist fights with abandon; tepidity is only for people with doubts.

The ferocity of some forms of historicism, such as Marxism, devalues people and events in favor of apocalyptic visions. J. L. Talmon reached that conclusion in comparing Hegel's historical ideas with some aspects of medieval metaphysics. For Hegel, particular facts were not quite real. They took on meaning only insofar as they could be related to the grand scheme of the movement of history. Within this framework, history assumes the quality of "essence" in medieval thinking, the facts being accidents. People lose all significance, except as fuel for the progress

---

[13]Robert Nisbet, *Twilight of Authority* (London: Heinemann, 1976), p. 235.

of history and as symbols of ideas.[14] As with Hegel so with his disciples, and the dehumanization of mankind in Marxist practice is consistent with its historicist foundation.

Less ambitious forms of historicism do not profess to see what the purpose of history is but, with failed imagination, expect that whatever the trend is will inevitably continue. History is assumed to be going someplace, and if its final destination remains a mystery, at least in the immediate past events we can tell the direction it is traveling. If one is pleased with the way things are going, the result is optimism. If one is displeased, the result is pessimism. Concentrating on the perceived trend locks one into a mindless optimism or a hopeless pessimism. Thus does historicism bring us what Chesterton called those two great fools, the optimist and the pessimist.

Inevitable Progress

Toynbee placed the terminal date of the age of faith at the start of World War I, because that was when expectations of a golden age to be ushered in by science died.[15] But that pronouncement was premature, not only because it overlooked the power of Marxism but also that of the milder ideologies in Europe and the United States. The optimism that even now breaks through the gloom in American liberal political thought bespeaks the nineteenth-century currents to which it is indebted. Sometimes the old faith appears in unlikely places. Jude Wanniski, former editorial page writer for the *Wall Street Journal* who became one of the chief publicists for Arthur Laffer's tax strategies, still takes an avowedly optimistic position, even while writing of the follies and crimes that are destroying the economy. He believes that neither natural limitations nor a foolish electorate will undermine progress; in common with other expressions of the secular faiths, no reason is given, and Wanniski ends up in mystification.[16]

J. B. Bury, who wrote the seminal work on the history of the idea of progress, showed why this idea is properly associated with the Enlight-

---

[14]J. L. Talmon, *Political Messianism: The Romantic Phase* (London: Secker and Warburg, 1960), p. 202.

[15]Arnold J. Toynbee, *Experiences* (New York: Oxford Univ. Press, 1969), p. 307.

[16]Jude Wanniski, *The Way the World Works* (New York: Basic Books, 1978), p. 17. On the flirtation of intellectuals with Marxism and other forms of historicism, see Raymond Aron, *The Opium of the Intellectuals*, trans. Terence Kilmartin (New York: Norton, 1962 [1955]).

enment of the eighteenth century; it was a new faith that could not prosper until the old faith had weakened. "The process must be the necessary outcome of the psychical and social nature of man; it must not be at the mercy of any external will; otherwise there would be no guarantee of its continuance and its issue, and the idea of Progress would lapse into the idea of Providence." In other words, the Christian doctrine of a Lord of history *beyond* history, commonly called Providence in the eighteenth century, could not be reconciled with the idea of progress made inevitable by some teleological principle found *within* history. Thus, as with all idols, the principle of immanence is central to the theory.[17]

There is no way to escape determinism in the idea of inevitable progress. Its exponents do not merely believe or hope that conditions will improve but, rather, hold a firm conviction that because of the very nature of reality progress *must* take place; it is built into the universe. That is why Wanniski, though nonplused by the election results in Massachusetts in 1976, said that everything must have turned out all right. He could not explain why the losers lost, but "for some reason they deserved to lose." That is the faith that leads him to adopt conclusions completely at variance with the evidence he so convincingly marshals in his book. All devotees of progress hold to the same odd kind of determinism. History brings constant improvement, forcing the good to come whether it wants to or not, binding evil, pressing it back to successive retreats until the final inevitable defeat.

La Trahison des Clercs: History As a Polemical Device

Thus far almost everything we have said has stressed the plasticity of history. Instead of the constellation of names, dates, treaties, and other hard facts we learned in school, it now seems that history is apprehended subjectively and used in accordance with the purposes of the moment. Carl Becker contrasted the discontinuities that one finds in eighteenth-century historiography with the continuities in the next century's efforts. In the first period, by no coincidence, the scholars looked forward to revolution, and in the second, fed up with the chaos of a generation of revolution and war, they sought—and found in history—stability.

---

[17]J.B. Bury, *The Idea of Progress: An Inquiry Into Its Origin and Growth* (New York: Dover, 1955 [1932]), p. 5. The Russian philosopher Nicholas Berdyaev also discussed the question of idolatry in the idea of progress but, mistakenly in my view, placed the teleological principle of progress outside of history. I do not believe exponents of inevitable progress commonly explain their position in that way. See Berdyaev, *The Meaning of History,* trans. George Reavey (New York: Scribner's, 1936), p. 186.

Becker described how the Enlightenment philosophers studied history in order to use it for attacks on the church:

> They start out, under the banner of objectivity and with a flourish of scholarly trumpets, as if on a voyage of discovery in unknown lands. They start out, but in a very real sense they never pass the frontiers of the eighteenth century, never really enter the country of the past or of distant lands. They cannot afford to leave the battlefield of the present where they are so fully engaged in a life-and-death struggle with Christian philosophy and the infamous things that support it—superstition, intolerance, tyranny.[18]

Thus, history has always served equally as well those who ransack it for weapons and those who explore it for wisdom. The past is made to fight the battles of the people who are using it.

Peter Berger explains one common way of doing this. "The *past,* out of which the tradition comes, is relativized in terms of this or that sociohistorical analysis. The *present,* however, remains strangely immune from relativization."[19] While Berger describes the "progressive" use of this method, conservatives are adept in using the same technique. All periods are relativized except the one the conservative wishes to have us believe is normative: the first century, the thirteenth, the nineteenth, or two weeks ago. In this thinking, the golden age lies in the past instead of the future. French philosopher Julien Benda excoriated the German historian Von Treitschke and his French counterparts for exalting the power and glory of modern military states, branding them as politicians who used history only as a tool to support their causes. But on the same pages he praised Voltaire and Nietzsche as if they wrote objective history without hidden agendas.[20] Robert Nisbet worries that the historicist fallacy will wreck the university because the scholars cannot seem to keep it out of their advocacy of pet solutions. Not content with supporting a proposal with evidence, they must further declare it to be inevitable. "Failure to hook on to the locomotive of history results, it is said, in being condemned to archaism, in being reactionary or nostalgic."[21]

The ultimate expression of history as a polemical device is found in

---

[18]Carl L. Becker, *The Heavenly City of the Eighteenth-Century Philosophers* (New Haven: Yale Univ. Press, 1959 [1932]), pp. 96f.

[19]Peter L. Berger, *A Rumor of Angels: Modern Society and the Discovery of the Supernatural* (Garden City, N.Y.: Doubleday, 1969), p. 51.

[20]Julien Benda, *The Betrayal of the Intellectuals,* trans. Richard Aldington (Boston: Beacon, 1955 [1928]), p. 56.

[21]Robert Nisbet, *The Degradation of the Academic Dogma: The University in America, 1945–1970* (New York: Basic Books, 1971), p. 112.

nations in which the state—that other idol of Hegel's—controls its writing and dissemination; no totalitarian state can afford to allow such a powerful tool unfettered expression. In Orwell's *1984*, history is what the state says it is, and it changes with every vagary of state policy.

The Historical Profession

It is generally thought that the empirical orientation of Western historiography immunizes it against the virus of historicism. Toynbee attributed the savagery of the attack on him by traditional academic historians to their view that he represented an attempt to disparage the unique event in favor of law or regularity.[22] Except for the Marxists, who are not numerous in the United States, there are few historians who subscribe explicitly to any of the easily recognizable forms of historicism. The profession, in fact, has an odd lack of interest in dealing with the philosophy of history and may even be unique in academia in its unwillingness to consider systematically the meaning of its own work. Budding historians in most graduate programs receive no training in the subject at all. If a philosophy of history is virtually indistinguishable from a philosophy of life, as we argued earlier, then it is understandable that the profession should wish to maintain tranquillity by not emphasizing such a divisive subject.

Yet the empirical nature of academic history should not be overemphasized. A long time has passed since the profession departed from the nineteenth century ideal of "scientific history," and nobody ever says, as Leopold von Ranke did, that he writes history *wie es engentlich gewesen,* as it actually was. Many historians are good students of ideas as well as facts and show considerable sophistication in discerning the assumptions that governed historical writing in other times; historiography is a well-developed aspect of the profession, possibly in compensation for its weakness in the philosophy of history. The philosophical deficiencies, however, make it difficult for the profession to discover its present assumptions. It has as many internal disagreements as any academic discipline, but it is possible to identify at least a couple of assumptions that, if they cannot be called governing ones, can at least be described as prevalent.

One principle that students of history learn early is that of multiple causation. It is now considered dubious to ascribe important historical events to single causes. School children once learned that slavery was

---

[22]Arnold J. Toynbee, *Reconsiderations,* vol. 12 of *A Study of History* (New York: Oxford Univ. Press, 1961), p. 19.

the cause of the American Civil War, yearning for liberty the cause of the Declaration of Independence, and the desire for religious freedom the cause of the early settlements in the New World. The doctrine of multiple causation says that there must be more than one cause and that all causes must be identified: the economic, social, political, religious, cultural, intellectual, and so on. Only then can realistic conclusions be drawn. On one level this is a salutory effort to avoid the polemical purposes that once so marred the professional writing of history. It also reflects the increasing maturity and sophistication of the profession, since it recognizes the complexity of events.

On the other hand, where is it written that, even before we study an event, we know that it has three or five causes? Why is it not possible that a given event should have only one cause? If all historical situations must have several causes, it seems highly unlikely that those causes will be repeated in the same proportions at a later time. If similar occurrences happen later but with their causes in differing proportions, then there are no repetitions of events. If no events are repeated, then there is nothing to learn from them.

The very use of the idea of *cause* conceals philosophical commitments that the profession seldom addresses. If we wish to consider the Babylonian captivity of the kingdom of Judah in 587 B.C., we shall find sufficient documentation and archaeological evidence to speak of the political, economic, social, and military causes of the debacle. But the Hebrew prophets said that it took place because God's judgment had fallen on the Judeans for their idolatry and wickedness. From that perspective, the ''causes'' that the historian's explanation advances are not causes at all, but effects, and are thought to be causes only because of the meta-historical commitments that the historian brings to his evidence. For him history is ''the whole show,'' and therefore nothing lies beyond it to enter the historical stage and cause events to happen. We might call this assumption a proto-historicism because from there it is only a short step to one of the specific forms of historicism. Thus far there are not many in the profession who have taken that step, but intellectual fashions are known to change.

In 1977, David Donald of the Harvard history department wrote an article for the *New York Times,* entitled ''Our Irrelevant History,'' which exemplifies the weariness that comes from engagement in a career that seems to have lost its point. Donald thought that his profession had become irrelevant because American history is comprehensible only in terms of abundance, which has staved off all serious social problems. Now the time of abundance is gone, and hard choices must be made. "The people of plenty have become the people of paucity." This means, Donald says, that the lessons of the past are not only irrelevant for his students, but dangerous. "Perhaps my most useful function would be to disenthrall them from the spell of history, to help them see the irrelevance of the past."

It is hard to imagine how a respected historian could have made such grievous errors on the subject of his own discipline. His belief that past abundance contrasts with present poverty is an exact reversal of the truth. If he is right in believing that our prosperity will be coming to an end, he could more accurately have said that the long history of privation stretching back through the millenia of recorded history might provide valuable lessons on how to cope with hardship. And far from being in the thrall of history, most students have preceded Donald in dismissing it as a source of valuable knowledge and wisdom. His thesis is one that few of his colleagues would agree with, but many share with him what may be a source of his confusion. He hoped that he could render service to his students by making it "easier for some to face a troubled future by reminding them to what a limited extent humans control their own destiny." Where did he learn that? It is the conclusion of a man in despair and has nothing to do with the study of history. Donald's position gives the appearance of devaluing history but in fact is only a disguised version of the Hegelian divinization of history. It dismisses history as a subject of study to exalt it as a principle of inevitability. You do not control your life, he is saying, but are subject to fate or to the inexorable powers that control the universe. Spengler returned from the grave could read those lines and say, "Ah, you see, it is as I taught you two generations ago: 'We have not the freedom to reach to this or to that, but the freedom to do the necessary or to do nothing. And a task that historic necessity has set *will* be accomplished with the individual or against him.' You had to go through two world wars and a depression and enter the inflationary vortex that is disintegrating your society, but at last you see that history is lord of the world."

The modern historical profession is Hegelian in the sense that it assumes that the explanation of history lies within itself. Just as the antithesis lies within the thesis and the synthesis within the relationship between the two, so the meaning of history is thought to be comprehended exhaustively in itself. What the historian is unable to explain must be a matter of defective or incomplete sources or of his own limitations in drawing inferences from them. His failure to acknowledge that the ex-

planation of history may lie outside of history is analagous to the naturalism of the physical and biological sciences, which also sees "the whole
show" in the artifacts of creation. There is no evidence for this point of
view, but being an assumption, it can live without evidence. The historians who hold it—most historians, that is—would express bewilderment that it should seriously be questioned. Even those historians who
explicitly disbelieve it—Christians, for example—write history as if
they do believe it. They are stretching the necessarily artificial boundaries of an academic discipline to encompass all of reality, accepting assumptions as professionals that they do not accept as individuals. An
obvious response to that contention is the affirmation of the need to hold
to strict rules of evidence in order to avoid mystical flights of fancy and a
spineless subjectivism, and it is only by thus disciplining itself that history can be called a discipline. True enough, but these questions should
be posed: Is it possible to confine the working assumptions of the discipline to its own operations? Or is it necessary to extend them to embrace
the entire universe? There is no simple answer to questions such as
those, because they ask if it is possible for the scholar to divide his mind
into separate private and professional spheres and work as if his assumptions were different than they are.

That is the problem of naturalism in general. It may be possible for a
chemist to work with material substances *as if* all reality were material,
even though he does not believe it, without distorting his results. But history is of a different order that will not permit that kind of methodologi-
cal pretense. If the historian works *as if* he believed that the political,
economic, social, and military events are sufficient to explain why ancient Judah fell to Babylon, then his conclusions about causation will be
utterly wrong, if the prophets were right. But the question of whether or
not the prophets were right is not one that the accepted methodology of
the historical profession is prepared to deal with. That is classified as a
matter of faith, and faith is considered, wrongly, to have nothing to do
with scholarship.

Academic history's failure to deal seriously with its own assumptions
makes it seriously deficient in helping people find answers to the larger
questions of life. David Donald's despair was unique in its expression
but may be fairly common beneath the surface. C. Gregg Singer, who
has taught history in colleges for more than thirty years, reports attending a small meeting of prominent historians at the annual convention of
the American Historical Association some years ago. All the scholars
were agreed that history is devoid of meaning and purpose. When Sing-

er asked why they then taught it, there was no reply.[23] The only way the profession can avoid meaninglessness within the framework of immanence is to find for itself practical little tasks to do. That was Donald's conception of history's use, and when he found that the little task could no longer be performed in the way he thought it had been, his profession lost all meaning for him. All of this may signify that the profession has entered a blind alley, and this could account for the general abandonment of the study of history that began in the colleges in the 1960s. Students then turned in greater numbers to the social sciences, which claimed for themselves the ability to contribute to the solution of social problems and thus promised to be more useful to people who wished to make a contribution to society.

The Myth of the Seamless Web

In a highly regarded book, Charles Cochrane wrote of the first century of the Roman Empire's existence as a period of adjustment to the Augustan system, the second as a period of fruition, and the third as a period of disintegration. He drew those generalizations as inferences from the factual information at his command, but then he undercut completely his schema by adding that "distinctions of this kind are largely arbitrary, since the web of history is seamless."[24] The *facts* at his disposal showed him seams—or discontinuities—in history, which he described, but he had a *theory* that history had no seams, and that made him reject what he saw, declaring that it was only an arbitrary distinction. If he really believed that the distinction was arbitrary, why did he first inform his readers of its existence? He wrote successive sentences that were contradictory because that was the only solution he could find to the problem of believing a theory that could not be reconciled with his evidence.

German theologian Dietrich Bonhoeffer thought that the principle of the seamless web had its origin in philosophical idealism, specifically with Hegel,[25] and considering the massive and generally unacknowledged influence of that philosopher, that seems likely. It has become a dominant assumption of the historical profession, although in recent

[23]C. Gregg Singer, "The Problem of Historical Interpretation," *Foundations of Christian Scholarship: Essays in the Van Til Perspective,* ed. Gary North (Vallecito, Calif.: Ross House, 1976), p. 53.

[24]Charles Norris Cochrane, *Christianity and Classical Culture: A Study of Thought and Action from Augustus to Augustine* (Oxford: Clarendon, 1940), p. 114.

[25]Dietrich Bonhoeffer, *Letters and Papers from Prison* (London: Collins, Fontana, 1959 [1953]), p. 78.

years the appearance of radicals has provided a vocal dissent. Insisting on a smooth flow of events, it abhors discontinuity, revolution, or sudden catastrophe. The historical "process" takes place entirely with materials already present within itself. All the elements of history are already there in embryo before a complex of events occurs. Afterwards the historian identifies the elements and tries to explain how they "emerged" in the pattern that he finds took place. The system is closed. It is Hegelian in that nothing happens that does not have its entire explanation in preceding events. Nothing breaks through from the outside because there is no outside. When unwelcome seams appear, the historian who believes in the seamless web stretches the web to cover them. He discovers that events are explained fully by their antecedents, because that is what he assumes before he begins his investigation.

Different assumptions are fully as plausible, and if they seem otherwise it is because current habits of thought cannot accommodate them. The dominant assumption of the historical books of the Old Testament, for example, is that God enters history with blessing and judgment. To the one who holds that opinion, the Hegelian seamless web seems not only pallid and lifeless but at variance with the observed facts of history. The difference is not so much in the facts that are observed as in the religious beliefs that are brought to them. Anyone beginning his study believing in the seamless web will see no seams, or if he does see them he will explain them out of existence as Cochrane did.

The field in which this is most apparent is the history of science, because that is the one in which Thomas Kuhn has done his work. Trained as a physicist, Kuhn shifted almost immediately to the history of science. His main contribution has been to show the domination exercised on scientific thinking by the framework of basic belief into which all facts and theories are fit and from which they receive their coherence. Kuhn calls those frameworks *paradigms*. Philosophies of science demonstrate that any collection of facts can be explained by more than one theoretical system, Kuhn says, but scientists normally do not venture from the reigning paradigm. When they do, it is usually because a crisis has occurred that makes the older paradigm impossible for them to continue with. After a paradigm shift the textbooks are all rewritten in such a way as to obscure the tortuous path of change. History becomes smoothed out; it "evolves" naturally, and progress is enshrined. The desperate twistings, retrogressions, denials, and struggles are omitted, and history is then seen from the point of view of the reigning paradigm. When it changes, the textbooks are again rewritten. In this way, the pattern of "normal science" without revolution remains intact, and "science once again comes to seem largely cumulative," even to the scientist looking back at his own research. This is writing history backwards, Kuhn says, and he believes it to be a perennial temptation.[26]

That cumulative process without revolution is what we have been calling the seamless web. Historians know the history of history better than scientists know the history of science, and they do not make the same mistakes; they look at the sources rather than the textbooks. But they see discontinuities in historical writing that they will not allow in the subject matter. Like the scientists, they have a reigning paradigm, which they do not transcend: that of continuity in which all reality emerges out of what is already there.

The established historical paradigm does what it can to remove anything revolutionary from the upheavals it must explain. It deals with Jacob Burckhardt's famous thesis on the Renaissance, for example, by finding in the Middle Ages features that Burckhardt described as unique to the Renaissance and by seeing in the modern period medieval features that Burckhardt's thesis might lead us to believe had ended in the fifteenth century. Thus the seamless web paradigm has transformed a revolutionary change into . . . well, into a seamless web. Now, the practice of casting doubt upon generalizations by finding exceptions to them cannot be faulted. The question is whether the historian's governing paradigm enables him to do it without distorting beyond recognition what his sources have to tell him.

The Christian View of History

Modern people seriously considering the meaning of history generally conclude either that it has no meaning—"just one damn thing after another" or a more sophisticated equivalent—or that it contains within itself its own principle of teleology, what we have referred to as the historicist fallacy. The Christian faith that once informed Western society had an answer that was different from either, but people who rejected that faith naturally rejected the interpretation of history that was an integral part of it. The biblical view is that history had a beginning and will have an end, and that both the beginning and the end are in God's hands. Therefore, what comes between them is invested with meaning and purpose; the creator is not the prime mover of ancient philosophy,

---

[26]Thomas S. Kuhn, *The Structure of Scientific Revolutions* (Chicago: Univ. of Chicago Press, 1962).

and the terminator is not the bleak exhaustion of resources or the running down of the sun. Will and personality dominate everything and make of history a moral arena.

This conception takes lordship out of history, recognizes God as creator, sustainer, and lord of the universe, and acknowledges history as an artifact of the creation. The dual effect of this revolutionary idea is to de-divinize history, removing it as an idol, and, paradoxically, to acknowledge its vital importance. It is no longer to be idolized but also is not to be regarded as trivial, meaningless, or absurd. It is important but not all-important. It has much to teach but is not the source of knowledge and wisdom. It imposes limitations on the actions of men, but it does not control them. It commands respect but not worship. Taking history down from above the altar, Christian faith also lifts it up out of the pit.

It follows from this that historical facts are neither elevated into values nor denigrated as unworthy of notice. The biblical writers took seriously the individual act, the physical presence, the concrete thing; that is one reason ordinary people who value the particularity are closer to the kingdom than those who seek truth in grand generalizations and vast intellectual constructs. The Bible knows nothing of ghostly entities whose substantiality depends on their participation in higher forms in worlds more real; Platonism has always had a harmful influence on Christianity.

The New Testament writers insisted on the factuality of their message, rejecting a spurious spirituality that has dogged the church down to our own day. When John the Baptist wavered in faith, Jesus vindicated his ministry with the acts he was performing (Matt. 11:2–6). Doubting Thomas believed the resurrection had occurred only after seeing the risen Christ and feeling his wounds (John 20:24–30). The early church denied that its message had anything to do with "cleverly designed myths" but insisted that it was based on verified fact; "we were eyewitnesses" (2 Pet. 1:16). Judas's replacement in the apostolate was to have one qualification: He had to be an eyewitness (Acts 1:22). When Paul spoke of the factuality of the resurrection, he pointed to five hundred people, most of whom were still alive, who were available to attest on the basis of what they had seen. He would not allow this central act of the faith to be spiritualized but said flatly that if it did not take place as he was describing it, then Christian faith was futile, and the believers were to be pitied (1 Cor. 15:3–19).

Taking factuality seriously gives meaning to linear arrangements of events, and that is why the Bible is principally a book of stories and glosses on stories. The poetry and the doctrinal and prophetic books are based on the stories. It is the stories of nomadic wanderings, captivity, exodus, conquest, exile, return, annunciation, birth, teaching, healing, and persecution that provide in the Bible a unique apprehension of reality. Mystical visions, ratiocination, and emotional experiences are not central to the biblical epistemology, but history lessons are. When Samuel gave up the office of judge, he charged the people to remain faithful to God and reminded them, in a history lesson, that God had been faithful in leading them out of captivity (1 Sam. 12). When Stephen the martyr appeared before the high priest on charges of blasphemy, he gave the council a history lesson (Acts 7). Stories in the form of sacred history were such a vital part of the Christian culture of the West that the novel and the short story became characteristic forms of the art of this culture. It may be no coincidence that widespread complaints about the decline of the novel should come at a time when the culture is moving away from the faith that provided the models and the appreciative audience for the novel.

This biblical understanding of history rescues us from an infatuation with historicist idols because it says without equivocation that history's creator is outside of history and gives meaning to it. That knowledge brings with it at least five inestimable benefits.

(1) It distinguishes history from nature, which is the same as saying it distinguishes man from nature, and therefore insists that he is neither an animal nor a machine. This understanding thus launches a frontal attack on any system, such as behaviorism, that reduces history to a category of nature, the supreme reductionism. That is one reason Harvard psychologist B. F. Skinner has displayed such passionate disdain for history.[27]

(2) It restores meaning to events that otherwise would be without value or significance. The present and future also take on new importance in this view because otherwise they, too, enter the past only to be relativized into the historicist oblivion.

(3) It enables us to place means and ends in proper perspective, subordinating the former to the latter. Historicism's focus on process made plausible McLuhan's dictum that the medium is the message, and also made it seem reasonable that revolution should be a goal without knowing what kind of society would emerge from it; if the process is the product the outcome is irrelevant. Means, medium, process are all grist for

---

[27]See, for example, B. F. Skinner, *Walden Two* (New York: Macmillan, 1948), pp. 94, 129, 162, 198f.

the historicist's mill because he is aiming at a moving target. Those who look beyond history are more interested in ends, message, and product.

(4) It provides a basis for understanding change, because there is something that does not change. Change can be explained only by reference to the unchanging. Flux can have no principle of explanation. Only the unchanging can provide a principle of explanation against which all explanations can be judged.

(5) It provides a principle of value against which all values are judged. Without it, as we argued earlier, values change along with fact and sentiment, and everything becomes permissible.

God's Action in History

Christian thinking about God's action in history has sought to provide metaphors that preserve human freedom and responsibility. C. S. Lewis defended the doctrine of God's care for the creation while guarding against historicist extrapolations from past to future. "I do not dispute that History is a story written by the finger of God. But have we the text?" Butterfield suggests that we think of a composer "who composes the music as we go along, and, when we slip into aberrations, switches his course in order to make the best of everything." Toynbee, trained as a classicist, ingeniously preserved cyclical history and combined it with linear biblical history (although his religion was more pantheist than Christian) in picturing the cycles of history as wheels bearing God's chariot forward toward the goal.[28] Formulations such as these reflect the biblical teaching that God has "a plan for the fulness of time" (Eph. 1:10) and that he works out the details of this plan through the course of history. "I am the LORD your God, who brought you out of the land of Egypt, out of the house of bondage" (Ex. 20:2). "Blessed be the LORD, the God of our fathers, who put such a thing as this into the heart of the king . . ." (Ezra 7:27). "So the king did not hearken to the people; for it was a turn of affairs brought about by the LORD that he might fulfil his word . . ." (1 Kin. 12:15). Divine intervention in history, directed toward the goal planned for the fulness of time, is found throughout both Testaments. Jacques Ellul calls attention to Paul's vision to cross into

---

[28]C.S. Lewis, *Christian Reflections,* ed. Walter Hooper (London: Geoffrey Bles, 1967), p. 105; Herbert Butterfield, *Christianity and History* (London: Collins, Fontana, 1957 [1949]), p. 143; Arnold J. Toynbee, *A Study of History,* abridgement by D. C. Somervell, 2 vols. (New York: Oxford Univ. Press, 1947, 1957), vol. 1, p. 556; vol. 2, p. 263. Toynbee's teleological twist, however, is best regarded as a *tour de force* which fails to reconcile two opposing views.

Macedonia to preach and thus extend the gospel to Europe. Through that event, "God changed the course of history and politics and society and civilization by means of a vision that had nothing to do with history or politics or society or civilization."[29] Nobody ever planned an industrial revolution, and those most responsible for the Reformation and the French Revolution maintained that events had gone far beyond what they had intended. Thus, although each person may be said to be a history maker, there is a kind of history-making that, in Butterfield's words, "goes on so to speak over our heads." He quotes Ranke as saying he sometimes felt "as though an occult force were at work in the midst of the apparent confusion."

The conviction that God is active in history makes historicism especially attractive to the church, tempting it to argue that the resurrection guarantees continual victory over the world, that the Christian consequently can enter into the world's works without worrying about the finer points of scruples, that the lordship of Christ over history guarantees that, when one system replaces another, God's will is being accomplished. The chief consequence of such mistakes is that Christians justify evil political, economic, and social forces.

These Teilhardian conceptions ignore the flawed character of history, a consequence of the flawed character of man, which cannot be reconciled with historicism's belief that history is normative. In contrast with the historicist religion of progress, Christianity foresees no improvement in the moral condition of mankind. The apostolic assessment of society's moral stature in the last days (2 Tim. 3:2-5) is almost identical with the description Paul gave of people in his own day (Rom. 1:28-31). And the account of the tribulation given by Jesus (Matt. 24) led Niebuhr to conclude that human defiance of God will reach its height at the end of history.

Just as the Christian refusal to sacralize history accompanies an affirmation of history, so its denial of inevitable progress attends a principle of development or improvement. God's original intention that man "fill the earth and subdue it" (Gen. 1:28) and the New Testament doctrine of sanctification furnish sufficient reason to distrust any institution or party that wishes to freeze history in whatever configuration seems agreeable to its supporters. Declining to sacralize any period or institution (including the church) means that Christians are free to do what is right, regardless of how radical it may seem. And refusing to sacralize

---

[29]Jacques Ellul, *The Betrayal of the West,* trans. Matthew J. O'Connell (New York: Seabury, 1978), pp. 73f.

history itself frees them to do what is right no matter how conservative it may seem. They do not need either to stand fast against change or to go with the tide. There is no movement or ideology, no matter what label it bears, that they are obliged, by custom or by the world's expectations, to support or to oppose. Their norms come from outside of history, and they do not submit to the judgment of those whose faith they consider to be wrongly placed. That conviction was well expressed by Ranke in his famous statement that eternity is equidistant from all points in time. None of those points is worthy of being invested with sacred aura. That freedom from contingent systems should be regarded as a foretaste of the freedom from bondage and decay, toward which Paul looked, when the whole creation would obtain "the glorious liberty of the children of God" (Rom. 8:21).

Desacralizing history and its elements relativizes all human institutions and values, but only with respect to the absolute beyond history. There is no ideology, party, movement, or organization that may declare itself to be the absolute judge and arbiter of history. The Christian is free to regard each of them in the light of the absolute that is outside of history, that relativizes and judges them, and provides a point beyond which relativity is not permitted. That absolute, and the judgment it implies, is unacceptable to a generation that seeks to relativize everything without limit, but it is the only bar to Wilson's and Lippmann's attempts to make facts and sentiments, respectively, govern the relations between human beings and thereby render everything permissible. There can be no mercy without judgment because only judgment can pronounce the final NO! to relativism's blessing on barbarity and provide people with the motivation and courage to oppose it.

Judgment

Historicism always implicitly carries within itself an immanent and secularized form of the doctrine of judgment. It sees value in historical events and institutions—and indeed in people—only in their quality of "leading up to" the real focus of the historicist's interest: whatever it is he says history is progressing toward. After something is finished leading up to the next step in the process, there is no further use for it, and it becomes expendable. Thus, paradoxically, the historical event or institution is first idolized and then dumped into what Marx called the trash can of history. Marx only made explicit what was already in the historicist thinking he adopted. Any system of historical thinking that believes history is going some place, and that means biblical thinking and its heresies, needs something like a trash can. Anyone who says we must do something in order to keep in step with the times has a trash can in mind for those who fail to do it. Who or what gets thrown into it depends on who or what controls history. To a Marxist who believes that economic relationships control history, capitalism, as an outmoded economic system, will have to go. Ultimately, historicism throws everything into the trash can because it thinks history is moving on to ever greater things. The only escape it provides from that is when through the process of mystification, it explicitly elevates something to a pinnacle of importance beyond history. That is what Hegel did to the state, Marx to the classless society, and Lippmann to classical liberalism. Those idols tend to be a means of controlling others, because control is needed to "stop" history and give it the stability and significance that historicism otherwise takes from it.

Niebuhr believed that without the concept of judgment, biblical faith degenerates into a Platonism that reduces events to insignificance or else sinks into illusions of utopia as the outcome of human effort. This suggests rightly that meaning in history is inseparable from perceptions of moral integrity and justice. Historical events—crimes, natural disasters, wars, and so on—appear "senseless" when no connection is perceived between the event and any antecedent event that could be called a cause. But there may be causes that are not apparent because the perceiver implicitly has declared beforehand that he would not consider them. A man who said a priori that he would not consider causes that could not be seen would miss entirely the connection between moon and tides because gravity cannot be seen, thereby making tides "senseless." To reject the idea of judgment is to accept a moral void in the universe and to make unintelligible any notion of justice, except in a purely instrumental sense based on convention. A catastrophe occurs, and to the one who believes that ultimate justice and judgment are illusions, it is senseless or meaningless, taking him a step nearer to nihilism.

Catastrophe, of course, is another nail in the coffin of the seamless web. Butterfield has said that the power of Old Testament history lies in its ability to infuse cataclysm with meaning. In good times, stable times, improving times, or gently declining times the seamless web may appear to cover the observed facts, but when catastrophe occurs and the discontinuities become so striking as to be completely disorienting, belief in the seamless web leads to despair. This disorientation is especially acute because people believe a theory that cannot accommodate sudden and unexpected shocks. Jesus used Old Testament examples of such shocks to teach his followers what they should expect (Luke 17:22–36). When Isaiah warned Judah of the judgment to come, he said it would be on them as quickly as

> a break in a high wall, bulging out, and about to collapse,
> whose crash comes suddenly, in an instant;
> and its breaking is like that of a potter's vessel
> which is smashed so ruthlessly
> that among its fragments not a sherd is found . . . (Is. 30:13f.).

The popular view of judgment—rewards and punishments that come, finally, from a ledger of good and bad acts—is a serious distortion of the biblical faith, but it does at least bear a similarity to the biblical insistence that human acts have moral meaning and entail consequences that transcend historical contingencies. Judgment comes because men have broken moral laws and have defied God. Babylon was to be destroyed because "the LORD is a God of recompense,/he will surely requite" (Jer. 51:56). Jeremiah said that God would destroy Judah both for its idolatry and for the wickedness it did in shedding innocent blood (Jer. 19:3–9). Tyre, that Phoenician city of great beauty and power, would be destroyed because in its pride it said, "I am a god" (Ezek. 27; 28:2).

The Christian view of judgment gives meaning to history but does not solve every problem, nor does it provide a formula that would enable us to make predictions about the future. The biblical records show us that God's judgments may be very different from ours. Does it seem just to bring judgment on an evil nation by destroying it with a nation even more evil? The Judeans had great difficulty accepting this, and that may have contributed to their hatred of the prophets who warned them about it. Retribution for evil is the principle, but it is not necessarily applied on the scale of values we would use nor by the method we would think appropriate nor by the timetable we would judge most suitable. The instruments of divine judgment in the Old Testament themselves became the objects of judgment as they fell into pride and self-worship; their modern counterparts do the same. They "forget that they are also under judgment," Niebuhr says, "and thereby they increase the measure of new evil which attends the abolition of traditional injustice."

Judgment and Mercy

Earlier we suggested the connection between judgment and mercy, and it is time to develop this theme further. The common understanding of divine judgment seriously misstates the biblical position, often drawing false distinctions between the wrath of the Old Testament God and the love of the New Testament God; there is wrath and love enough in both Testaments because the two are connected. The judgment pronounced against Israel was intended to bring the nation back to God. "And my eye will not spare you, nor will I have pity; but I will punish you for your ways, while your abominations are in your midst. Then you will know that I am the LORD" (Ezek. 7:4). The picture we are given is that of a grieving parent pleading with his children to refrain from evil and thereby save themselves from disaster. " 'Yet I persistently sent to you my servants the prophets, saying, "Oh, do not do this abominable thing that I hate!" . . . Why do you commit this great evil against yourselves . . . ?' " (Jer. 44:4,7). Judgment is the means for bringing repentence and restoration.

> Therefore the LORD waits to be gracious to you;
>   therefore he exalts himself to show mercy to you.
> For the LORD is a God of justice; blessed are all those who wait for him.

> Yea, O people in Zion who dwell at Jerusalem; you shall weep no more. He will surely be gracious to you at the sound of your cry; when he hears it, he will answer you. . . . Then you will defile your silver-covered graven images and your gold-plated molten images. You will scatter them as unclean things; you will say to them, "Begone!" . . . Moreover the light of the moon will be as the light of the sun . . . when the LORD binds up the hurt of his people, and heals the wounds inflicted by his blow (Is. 30:18,19,22,26).

The Judean prophet does not forget the ancient enemy and portrays the same divine judgment and mercy on Egypt. "And the LORD will smite Egypt, smiting and healing, and they will return to the LORD, and he will heed their supplications and heal them" (Is. 19:22). Judgment thus rescues catastrophe from the curse of pointlessness and its victims from anomie. The vision of judgment's purpose shows it to derive from love and compassion and not malevolence.

Consequences of the Christian View of History

If Nicholas Berdyaev was correct in saying that catastrophic periods are especially ripe for the elaboration of philosophies of history, we may be entering an era of renewed vitality for this neglected subject. Catastrophe also may help us discern better the deficiencies in our common historical thinking that do not readily accommodate such breaks in the seamless web. In his inaugural address at Cambridge University in 1954, C. S. Lewis described the study of history as a kind of psychological purge.

> In the individual life, as the psychologists have taught us, it is not the remembered but the forgotten past that enslaves us. I think the same is true of society. To study the past does indeed liberate us from the present, from the idols of our own market-place. But I think it liberates us from the past too. . . . The unhistorical are usually, without knowing it, enslaved to a fairly recent past.[30]

The liberation of which Lewis speaks is the kind that keeps us from thinking that in the case of *our* object of interest or affection, the movement of history will stop. Other cultures may have withered but not ours. Other nations have crumbled but not this one. The Christian is in a better position than most to see the weakness in that conception. Insofar as history is the portrayal of the entrance and departure from the scene of man's creations, we should expect it to record the end of this favored civilization (nation, party, organization). Even the chosen nation of God was not spared judgment when it fell into idolatry, and the line separating the inordinate adoration of man-made institutions from idolatry is too fine to risk flirting at the margins. For one who believes that history has a living judge, all those institutions are relativized.

Relativization has its own special hazards, and important distinctions must be preserved. Historicism's rejection of transcendence subjects its followers to the same dizzying loss of stability that Einsteinian physics created for categories of time and space. The time-space dimensions in modern physics become vertiginous to the observer because nothing has the stability needed to measure the position of other entities. Everything is in flux, and such categories as *up* and *down* lose all objective reference. Everything is relativized because there is nothing transcending the flux that could provide the stability needed to position everything else. Historicism analogously relativizes everything in the moral universe and sends history careening over the same rootless, wandering course on which Einstein sent the cosmos. It relativizes everything, that is, except for the idol that the historicist miraculously extracts from the flux with the forceps of mystification—the state, the

---

[30]C.S. Lewis, *De Descriptione Temporum* (London: Geoffrey Bles, 1962), p. 23.

proletariat, the national honor, the liberal society, the fact or sentiment. Without that mystifying process, historicism has no way to speak of truth beyond the flux and would offer no common ground for discourse. Similarly, it would have no unifying principle to stand against the complete atomization of society; therefore it cannot provide for community except by coercion. That is why, as we shall see further on, modern societies ruled by the historicist mentality are ruled also by the polarities of individualism and statism.

The kind of relativization that can be affirmed, in contrast, is that which places human values under the judgment of the transcendent God. "You shall not make for yourself a graven image . . . you shall not bow down to them or serve them" (Ex. 20:4f.) is an absolute injunction against which human loyalties are judged and relativized. "You shall not steal" (Ex. 20:15) is an absolute injunction against which economic relationships are judged and relativized. Such passages bespeak the judgment that relativizes Woodrow Wilson's "facts" and Walter Lippmann's "sentiments," and refuses them the normative status that historicism bestows on them. Thus, deprived of divinity, history resumes its creaturely status and is rendered subservient to God.

But in the late twentieth century, bereft of the biblical limitations by a generation that has turned away from Christian faith, history pursues its mad career, running amuck with saviors making rules that they crown with divine status. History thus dechristianized has no moral limitations. "Right" is a moving target, propelled by the march of facts and sentiments. Theft, homosexuality, pornography, genocide, and torture were wrong yesterday, but tomorrow who can say? Perhaps we shall find compelling national, social, or economic interests that require us to do things that would not have been contemplated without horror a short time ago, and perhaps we shall find that they are "right." A society that cannot tolerate a judge beyond history will find that it can learn to tolerate anything else.

In the Christian conception, the unconditioned acts on the conditioned, the absolute on the contingent, the outside on the inside, creator on the created, God on history. The action beyond history makes history what it is but is absent from the accounts of history. That is why Niebuhr concluded that "history does not solve the enigma of history." It will be objected that this conception of history depends on the faith of the observer, and so it does. But the rival conception, immanent history, is no less dependent upon belief. As with most pairs of diametrically opposed convictions, incompatible faiths confront each other. That is why Butterfield said that our

> final interpretation of history is the most sovereign decision we can take, and it is clear that every one of us, as standing alone in the universe, has to take it for himself. It is our decision about religion, about our total attitude to things, and about the way we will appropriate life. And it is inseparable from our decision about the role we are going to play ourselves in that very drama of history.[31]

It was also Butterfield who said that the great task of the prophets was to show Israel that God was still active in history, just as he had been in the time of Moses. Without that, their denunciations of evil in the two kingdoms would be little more than an exercise in finger-wagging. Judgment for them was not an intellectual activity but a word denoting God's action against evil. The church, too, is custodian of the prophetic message that, after twenty-five hundred years, God is still active in history and still makes himself known in blessing and judgment. The message is as unpopular now as it was then, and there are many places in which the church is faithless to its charge, preferring to preach on popular themes that find ready acceptance among those who have rejected the first principles of Christian faith. But churches are no less subject to judgment than are other institutions, and they will learn this truth as did the faithless prophets who were contemporaries of Amos and Isaiah.

The church's paramount message about history, of course, is that the dividing line between B.C. and A.D. is not just a convention, and that the coming of Jesus Christ into history is the manifestation of eternity into time. He is the ultimate reason that immanent history is an idol, attempting to crown its own saviors and to screen history from its creator. And since he is the object of God's "plan for the fulness of time" (Eph. 1:10), he is the starting place in our quest for historical understanding.

---

[31]Butterfield, *Christianity and History,* p. 39.

CHAPTER TWO

Idols of Humanity

Human Beings as Gods

*E*VE was the first humanist. Centuries of religious art and, in recent years, hundreds of cartoons of naked women, apples, and snakes have served to distract us from the meaning of the Fall in Genesis 3. The temptation was not the desire for a piece of fruit, for the tree of the knowledge of good and evil was in the garden before we are told anything about a temptation. The garden was full of good things to eat, and the serpent, who was "more subtle than any other wild creature that the LORD God had made," could not have expected to succeed in tempting the woman with anything so common. He drew her to rebel against God by telling her of this attraction: "God knows that when you eat of it your eyes will be opened, and you will be like God, knowing good and evil." *You will be like God*. The serpent tempted her with a religious argument. She could be like God, having knowledge and power. She could be wise apart from God. The physical attraction of the fruit clearly was intended to be ancillary. What was to be fed was her pride, and what would grow was her appetite for self-worship.

The same human propensity for self-worship is behind the incessant biblical injunctions against pride. Tyre was struck down "Because your heart is proud, and you have said, 'I am a god' " (Ezek. 28:2). Habakkuk wrote of "guilty men, whose own might is their god!" (Hab. 1:11). The judgment at the Tower of Babel was evidently of the same order; those who wished to "make a name for ourselves" built their tower having "its top in the heavens" as a declaration of independence from God (Gen. 11:4). Surveying civilizations across the whole span of history, Toynbee concluded that self-worship was the paramount religion of mankind, although its guises are numerous and diverse.[1]

Sometimes we have revealed to us what most people learn to camouflage. Assur-Nasir-Pal, ruler of ancient Assyria, in a long and exultant boast of his conquests, his execution of captives with fire and sword, the enemies he skinned alive, and the general devastation he wrought, gave a theological explanation of his actions.

> And now at the command of the great gods, my sovereignty, my dominion, and my power, are manifesting themselves; I am regal, I am lordly, I am exalted, I am mighty, I am honored, I am glorified, I am preeminent, I am powerful, I am valiant, I am lion-brave, and I am heroic. (I), Assur-Nasir-Pal, the mighty king, the king of Assyria, chosen of Sin, favorite of Anu, beloved of Adad, mighty one among the gods. I am the merciless weapon that strikes down the land of his enemies. . . .[2]

The king here speaks of the gods and himself in such a way as to blur the distinction between them. The brutality of which he was so proud, unsurpassed even by the barbarities of the twentieth century, is indeed what we might expect from one who believed that he was lordly, exalted, honored, glorified, and preeminent, all terms used in the Bible when speaking of God. When once a man lavishes theological distinctions upon himself, he is less likely to suspect that there exists a standard of behavior more exacting than his own or that a righteous judge is observing his actions. That is why Assur-Nasir-Pal's association of his cruelty with the intimations of his god-likeness reveals a sound instinct: the former follows from the latter.

Exalting mankind to the status of deity therefore dates from the fur-

---

[1] Arnold Toynbee, *Reconsiderations,* vol. 12 of *A Study of History* (New York: Oxford Univ. Press, 1961), p. 488.

[2] Quoted in Crane Brinton, *A History of Western Morals* (New York: Harcourt, Brace, and World, 1959), p. 48.

thest reaches of antiquity, but its development into an ideology embracing the masses is a characteristic trait of modernity. Renaissance humanism concentrated its attention on the literary, philological, and grammatical studies essential to the revival of classical literature, rather than on philosophy; to be a humanist then was to be a student of the humanities. But it was impossible to study the great classical literatures without absorbing something of the pagan assumptions that underlay them. When the Italian humanists in the fifteenth and sixteenth centuries compared the ancient writings to the dregs of late-medieval scholasticism, it was natural for them to judge their own immediate Christian heritage unfavorably. Their interests gave a secular turn to high Renaissance culture in all its varieties, but there was no open break with the Christian past.

Succeeding centuries, however, saw that break. English deism in the seventeenth century all but openly rejected Christian faith. And the Enlightenment of the eighteenth century came completely out of the closet and launched vigorous, skillful, and sustained attacks on Christianity. Humanism by now had achieved its modern identity as the opposition to Christian faith.

Unifying the various forms of humanism is their rejection of the Christian view of mankind, however muted this might have been in the neo-pagan Renaissance years. Auguste Comte, the nineteenth-century French philosopher who gave sociology not only its name but also its major assumptions, was one of the most influential of the theorists who deified the human race. His Religion of Humanity, as he called it, advocated the worship of the Great Being, defined as humanity past, present, and future. This religion had a catechism, sacraments, a sacred calendar, a priesthood, prayers, and something imitative of the Trinity. It also had a social system of which Comte was the chief planner. The Religion of Humanity, as a visible institution, for a time had great vitality. Comteans formed positivist societies for the worship of great people, and their churches spread even to South America. George Eliot was a member of the movement and penned these lines in celebration of the new deity:

> O May I join the choir invisible
> Of these immortal dead who live again
> In minds made better by their presence.[3]

---

[3]Roland N. Stromberg, *An Intellectual History of Modern Europe* (New York: Appleton-Century-Crofts, 1966), p. 268.

For Comte and his immediate followers, humanity was, as one historian put it, "a mystical as well as a positivist phenomenon, not alone the subject of meticulous research but the object of religious worship, a substitute, as it were, for the Christian God."[4] That is not an overstatement, and the ideology of modern humanists shows them to be faithful disciples of the master. "No deity will save us," says the second Humanist Manifesto; "we must save ourselves."[5] The source of salvation and the object of worship are one, in the humanist religion as in the Christian.

The idea of humanity as a deity is seldom avowed openly but rather is expressed by ascribing to man attributes of God: sovereignty (or autonomy), complete rationality, and moral perfection. Those combined attributes went far toward explaining the spread of the idea of inevitable progress during and after the Enlightenment.[6] Jude Wanniski affirms that his work in economic analysis is founded on a "soaring faith in mankind . . . the idea that from the beginning of civilization the community of man has moved rationally, purposefully toward a unity, and that it can be delayed but not deterred."[7] The writers of the second Humanist Manifesto looked back from the vantage point of 1973 to the work of their predecessors and concluded that the first manifesto, written during the great depression, had been "far too optimistic." Here, then, is their new, sober assessment of humanity's future:

The next century can and should be the humanistic century. Dramatic scientific, technological, and ever-accelerating social and political changes crowd our awareness. We have virtually conquered the planet, explored the moon, overcome the natural limits of travel and communication; we stand at the dawn of a new age, ready to move farther into space and perhaps inhabit other planets. Using technology wisely, we can control our environment, conquer poverty, markedly reduce disease, extend our lifespan, significantly modify our behavior [B.F. Skinner was one of the signatories], alter the course of human evolution and cultural development, unlock vast new powers, and provide humankind with unparalleled opportunity for achieving an abundant and meaningful life.[8]

---

[4]Carlton J. H. Hayes, *A Generation of Materialism: 1871–1900* (New York: Harper and Brothers, 1941), p. 118.

[5]"Humanist Manifesto II," *The Humanist,* Sept.-Oct., 1973, vol. 33, no. 5, p. 6.

[6]Brinton summarized Enlightenment ethics as "the late-eighteenth-century belief in the power of right thinking to change rapidly and completely the conduct of large numbers of men . . . . " *A History of Western Morals,* p. 17.

[7]Jude Wanniski, *The Way the World Works* (New York: Basic Books, 1978), p. xii.

[8]"Humanist Manifesto II," p. 5.

The manifesto does not neglect to point out dangers ahead, particularly from traditional religion, but few observers will find the new note of realism convincing. The humanists wanted to avoid the unwarranted optimism of the 1933 document, but they believed nevertheless that "an affirmative and hopeful vision is needed." They could see the mistake in the earlier forecast, but they could not see that since they had not repudiated the view of mankind that had informed it, they would make similar mistakes.

Such exuberance in humanist statements comes, in part, from the sense that men and women have thrown off the shackles of tradition and of obligation and thereby gained freedom. "What a comfort," reflected the hero of Aldous Huxley's utopia, "to be in a place where The Fall was an exploded doctrine!"[9] John Cage recalls a lecture in which the New York painter Willem de Kooning responded to a questioner by saying, "The past does not influence me; I influence it."[10] Daniel Bell has concluded that the idea of liberty that developed in the nineteenth-century enabled one "to be free of the ascriptive ties of family, community, or state; to be responsible for oneself; to make or even remake one's self in accordance with one's ambition." Whereas formerly a person perceived his identity in terms of his family, as we can see in the Russian use of patronymics, or in names like Johnson and Anderson, now he believes: "I am I, I come out of myself, and in choice and action I make myself." This new definition of identity, says Bell, is the mark of modernity.[11]

The Ethics of Antinomianism

Modern humanists are hostile to any notion of law that is external to the legislative organs under human control, and this means that morality cannot be predicated on universal codes. The Humanist Manifesto characterizes ethics as being "*autonomous* and *situational,* needing no theological or ideological sanction."

For the more powerful examples of humanist thinking, we turn to the church intellectuals. "Nothing is inherently good or evil," says Joseph Fletcher, the publicist of situation ethics, "except love (personal concern) and its opposite, indifference or actual malice."[12] Much earlier the

---

[9]Aldous Huxley, *Island* (New York: Harper and Brothers, 1962), p. 250.

[10]John Cage, *Silence* (Middletown, Conn.: Wesleyan Univ. Press, 1961), p. 67.

[11]Daniel Bell, *The Cultural Contradictions of Capitalism* (New York: Basic Books, 1976), pp. 224, 89.

[12]Joseph Fletcher, *Moral Responsibility: Situation Ethics at Work* (Philadelphia: Westminster, 1967), p. 38.

young Reinhold Niebuhr had said something very similar in a widely quoted and very influential book. "Nothing is intrinsically immoral except ill-will and nothing intrinsically good except goodwill."[13] Those expressions place the locus of good and evil in sentiment, just as we saw Walter Lippmann do. But not just any sentiment: Lippmann said that law must be based only on the sentiments that "express the highest promise of the deepest necessity of these times," and Fletcher and Niebuhr gave their approval to whatever stems from love or goodwill. But Lippmann's principle gives us no guidance in deciding which sentiments serve higher ends and which serve lower ones; he placed his moral system in a universe that has no "higher" or "lower," because it has no fixed moral reference point against which to judge those directions. To assign such values in a system that has no objective standard must either be the arbitrary judgment of a sovereign elite or else a matter of mere social convention. In either case they are subjectively ascertained and may be changed at any time.

Fletcher and Niebuhr gave us no more help than Lippmann in this matter. If good and evil are purely a matter of sentiment, then no action can be judged, since sentiments remain opaque to outside certification. Only the motive counts, not the action. In this way sentiment, not reason or law, is determinative of right and wrong. That kind of assertion led Bertrand de Jouvenel to say that it is only a bad habit of modernity that uses the term "just" to describe whatever is thought to be emotionally desirable.[14] Once the primacy of sentiment is granted, that habit cannot be disputed and human autonomy is affirmed. When autonomy is affirmed, there can be no complaint when the grossest brutalities are committed in the name of serving the poor, the nation, the purity of the race, the supremacy of a religion, or other values that are deemed to be "high." Nobody apparently does anything merely because he wants to dominate others or to have their property, and therefore nothing anybody does is subject to judgment.

For an example of how moral decisions are actually made when based on the teachings of King Sentiment, we need look no further than Fletcher's exegetical work. He examines the encounter between Peter and Ananias, and in particular Peter's statement:

---

[13]Reinhold Niebuhr, *Moral Man and Immoral Society: A Study in Ethics and Politics* (New York: Scribner's, 1952 [1932]), p. 170.

[14]Bertrand de Jouvenel, *The Ethics of Redistribution* (Cambridge: Cambridge Univ. Press, 1951), p. 15.

"Ananias, why has Satan filled your heart to lie to the Holy Spirit and to keep back part of the proceeds of the land? While it remained unsold, did it not remain your own? And after it was sold, was it not at your disposal? How is it that you have contrived this deed in your heart? You have not lied to men but to God" (Acts 5:3f.).

Fletcher says that Ananias's sin was that he kept back part of his property and not that he lied, exactly the opposite of what the text says. His reason is that "selfishness is sin in greater depth than deceit." This is a statement utterly without meaning. What is meant by the "depth" of one sin compared to another? And why is selfishness deeper than deceit? Only because it seems so to Fletcher. He does not seem bothered by Peter's acknowledgement that the property was Ananias's and at his disposal before it was sold, but says that Peter meant that "it was *disposable* and dispersible." This interpretation is fully in keeping with humanist ethical thinking on three counts: (1) It is intellectually dishonest. (That is not a serious problem for Fletcher because "nothing is inherently good or evil.") (2) It is based wholly on sentiment, since Fletcher refers to no other standard to provide normative guidance. (3) It is directed toward the solution of an ethical problem completely extraneous to it; Fletcher contends that people's goods should be expropriated by the state and distributed to others. Therefore he does not like the idea that Peter said that Ananias could legitimately have kept his property. There is always a hidden agenda in humanist ethical thinking because the sentiment is never neutral but reflects the value of the person making the judgment. Humanist thinking holds no monopoly on rationalization, but in refusing to base moral judgments on objectively understood law, it hides its source of value, using sentiment as a front.

The function of law is shown clearly in the second table of the decalogue. Man is strictly enjoined there to hold inviolate his neighbors' rights against being victimized by killing, adultery, theft, false witness, and covetousness (Ex. 20:12–17). The law erects a fence around the neighbor that protects him from the malevolence that people would otherwise direct against him with impunity. Like any other fence, it can be breached; but there are penalties for doing so, and they were spelled out in the pentateuchal statutes. The statutes recognized mitigating circumstances and the role of motive in the contravention of the law, but they did not negate the law's purpose of restraining man's proclivity to damage his neighbor. The Lutheran *Formula of Concord* (1580) interpreted the law correctly in saying that its first purpose was to ensure "that certain external discipline might be preserved, and wild and intractable men might be restrained, as it were, by certain barriers." The law's efficacy in performing that function is dependent upon the way society attends to the first table of the decalogue that tells man to turn away from idols and serve the living God.

Humanism raises sentiment to a level of command that is wholly inappropriate to its nature. In so doing, it bases its ethical structure on sentimentality, which is the doctrine of the primacy of sentiment, its elevation into a principle of truth. Humanism thrives on sentimentality because few religions are more dishonest in their doctrinal expressions. Unable to withstand dispassionate analysis, which would reveal its lack of foundation, it stresses feeling rather than thought. That is what makes sentimentality so vicious. People can get good feelings from almost anything; "sadism" refers to a philosophy that elevates feeling into a moral principle.

As Fletcher acknowledges, this system is one of moral relativism. With all norms (sentiments) driven from the universe (individual autonomous person) by successor norms (sentiments) there is no principle of justice that transcends the expediency of the hour, and the hidden value takes charge. Niebuhr said that a political policy "cannot be intrinsically evil if it can be proved to be an efficacious instrument for the achievement of a morally approved end." That justifies Fletcher's intellectual dishonesty that was directed toward an end that had Fletcher's approval. It leaves the decision open for sentiment to make, because no means is so horrible as to be called evil if sentiment decides that the end is good. And it locates the moral decision in a chain, potentially infinite in length. As means succeed means, the final moral judgment recedes continually, along with the end, making it impossible ever to say, "This is wrong." J. Allen Smith of the University of Washington, one of many crusaders against the old morality, used to worry about where it would all lead. "The real trouble with us reformers," he said, "is that we made reform a crusade against standards. Well, we smashed them all and now neither we nor anybody else have anything left."[15] He no longer had any justification for saying that an action was morally wrong.

The love Fletcher holds to be the guiding sentiment is a "social attitude," having nothing to do with "abstractions such as 'laws' or general

---

[15]Quoted in Eric Goldman, *Rendezvous with Destiny: A History of Modern American Reform* (New York: Vintage, 1956 [1952]), p. 240.

principles."[16] That typifies the opposition of humanist love to law. Any conception that has love without law as its ethical principle will be relativistic and self-serving and without any means of arranging a priority between rival goods. There is no action so evil that it cannot and will not be said to be motivated by love. Antinomian love goes perfectly with autonomous man; neither can stand the shackles of law. They both epitomize lawlessness. Humanist anthropology does not need law because it has a high view of man's moral stature. Not being encumbered by a propensity to sin, he has no need for external restraint or correction.

The Function of Law as Ethical Foundation

Laws are always theologically based, whether or not they are so acknowledged. In the societies of the ancient Near East, laws were always associated with deity. The famous Hammurabi stele, for example, shows the sun god Shemash giving the Babylonian laws to the king.[17] The laws had to have ultimacy, or they could not work as intended. When law loses what only the conviction of ultimacy can bestow, it degenerates into pragmatism, and that means that breakdown is near. Right and wrong become questions of risk versus reward, and morality then is purely a matter of calculation. In his attempt to elevate sentiment over law as the principle of ethics, Bishop John Robinson said that to the man who rejects the transcendent God, objectively understood moral value, or law, "has no compelling sanction or self-authenticating foundation."[18] That is perfectly true, whatever we might think of the inferences he drew from it. Nobody who rejects the first four commandments' call to reject idols and worship the true and living God can be expected to recognize any ultimate significance in the last six commandments' ethical requirements. Bishop Robinson's theology is of one piece with his ethics. For the same reason, Norman St. John-Stevas was unable to find an alternative to Christian faith as a basis for the sanctity of

---

[16]Fletcher, *Moral Responsibility,* p. 34. Elsewhere, Fletcher tried to show that situation ethics were not antinomian. But the final appeal to sentiment makes that a futile attempt. See Joseph Fletcher, *Situation Ethics: The New Morality* (Philadelphia: Westminster, 1966), pp. 17–37: "Nevertheless, in situation ethics even the most revered principles may be thrown aside if they conflict in any concrete case with love."

[17]James Muilenberg, *The Way of Israel* (New York: Harper and Brothers, 1961), p. 64. Cf. Jacques Ellul, *The Theological Foundation of Law,* trans. Marguerite Wieser (New York: Seabury, 1969 [1960]), p. 18: "In its origin law is religious. This is confirmed by almost all sociological findings. Law is the expression of the will of a god; it is formulated by the priest, it is given religious sanction, it is accompanied by magic ritual."

[18]John A. T. Robinson, *Honest to God* (London: SCM Press, 1963), p. 113.

life. He decided finally that common law would have to serve the purpose.[19] But all laws are conceived, obeyed (or not obeyed), and enforced on the basis of faith in their legitimacy. If the Christian faith that bolstered the legitimacy of the common law loses credibility, common law will not long retain its own persuasiveness. No law can survive the hegemony of sentimentality and human autonomy. Only force remains.

Theologians of sentiment find encouragement in the New Testament teaching that salvation comes from faith and not from doing the works of the law. Love then is taken to be the opposite of law, which encourages subjective judgments about good and evil. There are manifestations of this on left and right, and we can find both those who want to kill infants for their own good and those who want to kill a Commie for Christ. Basing those antinomian sentiments on the New Testament strains the texts in the same way that Fletcher's socialist manifesto did the Ananias story. Faith and law are opposed only as principles of salvation, not as principles of conduct. Paul could hardly have made the point more clear than he did in the midst of one of his main passages on the primacy of faith: "Do we then overthrow the law by this faith? By no means! On the contrary, we uphold the law" (Rom. 3:31). This understanding of law stands as the main barrier to the harm done by the rationalizations of sentimental love, thereby earning for itself the hostility of humanism.

If faith may not be opposed to law, neither may love. Sentimental love negates the law by asserting priority over it. But Paul linked the performance of the duties of Christian love with the keeping of the law. Christian love, he said, sums up the commandments of the second table of the decalogue, the "thou shalt nots." That is the sense in which "love is the fulfilling of the law" (Rom. 13:8-10). The antinomian idea that Christian love can be used to nullify the requirements of the law and so free autonomous man to determine good and evil for himself repeats the serpent's blandishments.

Law also brands as idolatrous the proclivity of humanist sentiment to act as the autonomous giver of statutory law. Humanist law can function as an autonomous standard only when faith in God's law is absent. That was what the serpent told Eve: "You will be like God, *knowing good and evil.*" There can be no plainer description of the humanist delusion or clearer explanation of the idolatrous nature of humanist antinomianism, theological or avowedly secular. The biblical view is that God informs humanity about what is good and what is evil, and the form this

---

[19]Norman St. John-Stevas, "Law and the Moral Consensus," in Edward Shils *et al.*, *Life or Death: Ethics and Options* (Seattle: Univ. of Washington Press, 1968), pp. 40-58.

information takes is law, which means that there are normative and judgmental aspects to it. The alternate view is in the temptation, succumbed to by Eve and her humanist descendants, to make autonomous judgments about good and evil and so to be like God. That is why no statement that describes humanist teaching as "secular" can be allowed to pass unchallenged.

Is there anything that cannot be justified when sentiment replaces law? There is no bar to a Hitler in sentiment, for the nation is not a contemptible thing whose interests are to be given no consideration. There is no bar in sentiment to killing some people if it benefits others. Can it be denied that the insane, the aged, and the crippled constitute a drain on society? Are the rights of the producers to be trodden into the ground? One may object that this line of argument assumes that humanist ethics cannot discern when the means are disproportionate to the end. But that bootlegs value in by the back door after sentiment has elbowed it away from the front door; sentiment yields no information about value that it does not create out of thin air, and nobody can predict what value it will be.

Many people place their hopes in political institutions to prevent the excesses that might otherwise occur. If we can maintain democratic institutions, they seem to believe, that will save us. But that repeats the original humanist error about the natural goodness of man. It imputes wisdom and goodness to the collectivity that are not present in the individual. Idolizing democratic government as the antithesis to a Hitler or a Stalin ignores the fact that a tiny handful of people cannot rule without the tacit agreement of the masses. If democracy were restored, what assurance would there be that the multitudes would not insist on doing the same things done in one-party states? The unconstitutional repression of minorities in the United States, using the legal apparatus, has been a fact at least since the Civil War. That is almost undisputed now, but those who believe that democracy is the answer to political repression do not draw the right inferences from such examples.

Subjective Pragmatism

In practice, the hallmark of the humanist ethic is pragmatism. The fact that politicians describe themselves as pragmatic in order to induce people to vote for them is a telling indication of the values of our society. The pragmatic politician portrays himself as a realist who looks at the facts to tell him what to do rather than seeking a wise course of action in theory, in principle, or in ideology. All of that is illusory. Facts never told anyone what to do. Facts are always interpreted according to principles and values, and the pragmatist hides his, possibly even from himself. The ethical result of this is worse than the means being justified by the end, because the pragmatist explicitly elevates means over ends; the means justify themselves. And the values remain hidden because to speak of them, except in the most general and meaningless sense, is to lose one's credentials as a pragmatist.

All forms of humanist sentimental ethics have one common characteristic: subjectivism. Humanists decide for themselves what is right and what is wrong without any external entity to instruct them. Sentiment judges each situation on its merits. It may decide in one case on a subsidy, in another case on a fatal injection, in another on incarceration, in another on a state of permanent dependence. It is answerable to no one and nothing. Sentiment rules. In all these cases, of course, sentiment will be serving the interests of state, class, agency, corporation, university, or individual, but that is seldom admitted. What rules is what Niebuhr called goodwill and Fletcher called love. Others will have different masks for it, but the reality will always be the same: Subjective emotional responses are the determinants of right and wrong.

As Niebuhr recognized in other contexts, our capacity for self-deception and self-justification is almost infinite. That is the reason sentiment as an ethical principle must lead to disaster. The law of God is the only hedge against that. "Now if I do what I do not want," wrote the apostle, "I agree that the law is good" (Rom. 7:16). That is, if he recognizes that he has no self-righteousness, that the humanist delusion is fraudulent, then he needs the law to identify and restrain the evil that he might do. But the law of God only serves such a purpose if statutory law and the citizens recognize it. If lawmaking, however, is considered an expression of human autonomy, it will be idolatrous and eventually tyrannous. Statutory law then will be used to justify anything.

Humanitarianism

If humanism is the theological arm of the Religion of Humanity, the ethical arm is humanitarianism. This term is usually thought simply to mean the practice of doing good for people who need help, and in recent years it has attracted the support of Christians to diverse humanitarian projects that seemed to have the same goals that the Christian church has always espoused. That is an unfortunate example of the way changing linguistic practice can obscure the truth. Once we penetrate the surface resemblances, it becomes apparent that to link humanitarianism with Christian social action is wholly untenable. They are completely at odds with one another, as we should expect: two systems of thought that have opposing views of what man is must have very different theories of how he is to be served.

Humanitarianism was the term originally applied to the followers of a group of eighteenth-century theologians who affirmed the humanity but denied the deity of Christ. It was later used when speaking of the Religion of Humanity, and it carries the subsidiary meaning of the worship of the human race. It is only recently that humanitarianism has come to imply almost exclusively the doing of good deeds that help people. That recent usage should not be allowed to obscure the origins and motivations of humanitarianism. It is above all a religious term.[20]

Ressentiment

The twisted path from humanism's soaring tributes in honor of the human divinity to the consequences of modern humanitarianism is best explained by the concept of *ressentiment*. When Nietzsche wrote his celebrated attack on Christianity, he transliterated this word from the French because he could find no German equivalent. Max Scheler, a German sociologist, built on and corrected Nietzsche's work and again used the French word. When Scheler's book was translated into English the same practice was followed, because "resentment" is too weak to convey the meaning he intended. *Ressentiment* begins with perceived injury that may have a basis in fact, but more often is occasioned by envy for the possessions or the qualities possessed by another person. If the perception is not either sublimated or assuaged by the doing of some injury to the object of the feeling, the result is a persistent mental condition, stemming from the repression of emotions that are not acceptable when openly expressed. The result is hatred and the impulse to spite and to say things that detract from the other's worth.[21] One of the most common secret elements to be repressed is *Schadenfreude,* the rejoicing at another person's misfortune; vengeance is the principle manifestation of *ressentiment.*

This phenomenon differs from mere envy or resentment because it is not content to suffer quietly but has a festering quality that seeks outlet

---

[20]See the *Oxford English Dictionary,* vol. 5, p. 445; also *Encyclopedia Brittanica,* 11th ed., 1911, vol. 13, p. 872.

[21]Max Scheler, *Ressentiment,* ed. Lewis A. Coser, trans. William W. Holdheim (Glencoe, Ill.: Free Press, 1961 [1915]), pp. 45f.

in doing harm to its object. *Ressentiment* has its origin in the tendency to make comparisons between the attributes of another and one's own attributes: wealth, possessions, appearance, intelligence, personality, friends, children. Any perceived difference is enough to set the pathology in motion. *Ressentiment* "whispers continually: 'I can forgive everything, but not that you *are*—that you are *what* you are—that I am not what you are—indeed that I am not *you.*' "[22] The other's very existence is a reproach. "There is no vice of which a man can be guilty," said an English newspaper more than a century ago,

> no meanness, no shabbiness, no unkindness, which excites so much indignation among his contemporaries, friends, and neighbors, as his success. This is the one unpardonable crime, which reason cannot defend, nor humility mitigate. "When heaven with such parts blest him, have I not reason to detest him?" is a genuine and natural expression of the vulgar human mind. The man who writes as we cannot write, who speaks as we cannot speak, labours as we cannot labour, thrives as we cannot thrive, has accumulated on his own person all the offenses of which man can be guilty. Down with him! Why cumbereth he the ground?[23]

Ressentiment does much to explain the existence of crimes that otherwise are thought of as "senseless." They are senseless from a materialist perspective because the criminal does not gain anything tangible from his action. But if he is striking at the object of *ressentiment,* his crime is as rational as if he had made off with the crown jewels. He has gained what he desired. *Ressentiment* values its own welfare less than it does the debasement or harm of its object. Many crimes of vandalism, brutality, and murder might be explained in that way. Even anti-intellectualism is described by Richard Hofstadter in *ressentiment* terms, being "a resentment and suspicion of the life of the mind and of those who are considered to represent it; and a disposition constantly to minimize the value of that life."[24]

In attacking the sources of its irritation, Scheler says, *ressentiment* uses third parties as foils. "The formal structure of *ressentiment* expression is always the same: A is affirmed, valued, and praised not for its own intrinsic quality, but with the unverbalized intention of denying, devalu-

---

[22]*Ibid.*, pp. 52f.

[23]*Times* of London, October 9, 1858, quoted in Helmut Schoeck, *Envy: A Theory of Social Behavior,* trans. Michael Glenny and Betty Ross (London: Secker and Warburg, 1969), p. 171.

[24]Richard Hofstadter, *Anti-Intellectualism in American Life* (New York: Knopf, 1963), p. 7.

ating, and denigrating B. A is 'played off' against B." Therefore, what appear to be positive affirmations of the worth of others are really disguised attacks on still others. Altruism has its source in this poisonous brew. The word was invented by Auguste Comte, who thought that self-love was immoral. In common with other forms of *ressentiment*, altruism glories in the praise of the weak and base, even at its own expense, if that will also debase the strong and good.

> Thus the "altruistic" urge is really a form of hatred, of self-hatred, *posing* as its opposite ("Love") in the false perspective of consciousness. In the same way, in *ressentiment* morality, love for the "small," the "poor," the "weak," and the "oppressed" is really disguised hatred, repressed envy, and impulse to detract . . . directed against the opposite phenomena: "wealth," "strength," "power," "*largess*." When hatred does not dare to come out into the open it can be easily expressed in the form of ostensible love—love for something which has features that are the opposite of those of the hated object. This can happen in such a way that the hatred remains secret.[25]

Altruism is thus best interpreted as a counterfeit of Christian love, informed by the ideology of humanism and powered by *ressentiment*. It permits demeaning the successful, or those who display any form of superiority, by pulling over that act the mask of concern for the poor and weak. Scheler believed that the counterfeit is often good enough to fool the astute, and he concluded that Nietzsche confused Christian love with its imitator. Of course, by the time Nietzsche wrote, the church was sufficiently infused with humanism to make his mistake understandable.

Christian love, says Scheler, does not help the weak, sick, and helpless because it values those attributes but because of concern for the person who lies beyond them. There is none of "the exposure of social misery, the description of little people, the wallowing in the morbid—a typical *ressentiment* phenomenon." The fake love of altruism perverts the sense of values so that sickness and poverty approach the status of virtues. Christian love seeks to help the person but refuses to elevate the problem by giving it ontological status and worth. It also avoids helping the weak as a means of causing harm to the strong. In this it heeds the apostle's admonition that love "does not rejoice at wrong, but rejoices in the right" (1 Cor. 13:6). That is the meaning of Goethe's statement that "against another's great merits, there is no remedy but love." Christian love is directed toward persons who need help and not at abstractions

---

[25]Scheler, *Ressentiment*, p. 96.

such as humanity or the general welfare. It is action and movement and not primarily feeling or "psychical contagion." It is concerned for the other person and is not preoccupied with such internal experiences as empathy.

The *ressentiment* penchant for creating wards in order to strike at enemies is illustrated in humanitarianism's treatment of class in Western nations. So effusive has been its praise of the lower class that Jacques Ellul protests what he calls "the divinization of the poor."[26] When Judas criticized the use of expensive ointment to anoint Jesus, it was ostensibly due to his concern for the poor (John 12:5f.). In general this phenomenon praises the worthiness of what is unsuccessful or debased while expressing contempt for the exceptional and successful. Along with the exaltation of the poor comes the abasement of the middle class; "bourgeois" has become an epithet of hatred among those who chortle at H. L. Mencken's lampooning of the "booboisie." Michael Harrington recalled that in his youth in Greenwich Village the chief moral stricture in the midst of a dissolute life was, "Thou shalt not be bourgeois." Thus the poor are foils through whom *ressentiment* can strike at the successful while hiding its evil intentions under a mask of goodwill.

A common humanitarian complaint is that the poor are not sufficiently interested in their own welfare, making it necessary for the humanitarian gospel to be preached among them. B.F. Skinner's behavioral controller explained that they would not speak out on their own behalf because the environment had implanted a system of beliefs within them that inclined them toward compliancy. John Kenneth Galbraith is offended by what he thinks is indifference of people toward their own economic improvement, and thinks that only trauma or education will bring them to their senses. Helmut Schoeck, a German sociologist now living in the United States, finds it ominous that equalitarians are striving with greater urgency to whip up among poor people a keener sense of resentment against their neighbors.[27] Galbraith and others complain of their difficulty in this task; perhaps that is because some of the poor can recognize when they are being used as tools.

---

[26]Jacques Ellul, *The Betrayal of the West,* trans. Matthew J. O'Connell (New York: Seabury, 1978), p. 132.

[27]B. F. Skinner, *Walden Two* (New York: Macmillan, 1948), p. 122; John Kenneth Galbraith, *The Nature of Mass Poverty* (Cambridge: Harvard Univ. Press, 1979), pp. 61ff., 93, 100f.; Schoeck, *Envy,* p. 209. Cf. Ellul, *Betrayal of the West,* p. 78: "When the 'gospel of the poor' is preached today, the purpose is to rouse the poor to rebellion, violence and hatred."

Equalitarianism

The dual effort to raise the lower classes and debase the higher has long been called "leveling," and in recent years has grown into the movement with the awkward name of *equalitarianism* (often used in the French form, *egalitarianism*). Equality in its original meaning in the United States required that immutable privileges of birth and position be uprooted from the new nation. There was no longer to be king or nobility; hereditary offices were abolished, and people were to reach whatever station in life their qualities and their efforts earned for them. Equality of opportunity and equality before the law were realized only imperfectly but remained worthy ideals for most Americans. The new equalitarianism is not a development or fruition of the old, as humanitarians argue. It is, in fact, the opposite. For equality of opportunity guarantees inequality of results because people are unequal in motivation, ability, and will, and their values are so varied that they direct their energies toward different goals. Humanitarianism, thoroughly materialistic, can measure equality only in monetary terms.

It has often been said that the rich are getting richer and the poor poorer and that, as the disparity increases, the poor will rise against the rich in a revolution. The old socialist idea was that the great dissatisfaction of the poor masses could only be assuaged by a socialist redistribution of wealth. The dissatisfactions, however, have grown with the increase of *equality,* exactly the opposite of those expectations. This is what Alexis de Tocqueville predicted when he visited the United States 150 years ago, and more recently observers have been calling this odd social phenomenon the Tocqueville effect. As society erases social distinctions and moves toward a leveling of income differentials, the demand for equality is not satisfied, but intensified. People do not envy a Rockefeller his millions as much as they envy their neighbor a ten percent differential in income. All inequalities, monetary or otherwise, are more galling to the envious when they are nearby, when the advantage is held by those whom one knows and when it is seen daily. The leveling movement has nothing to do with justice, because its impulse is not to raise those who are down but to topple those who are up; *ressentiment* is the motive.

Christopher Jencks, a Harvard social scientist and one of the best-known proponents of equalitarianism, shows how it works. Jencks disputes the common practice of computing the cost of living by adding up the prices of a basket of essential goods and services. The true cost of living for him "is the cost of participating in a social system," and it varies, depending largely on what other people are spending. Anyone who falls far below the material level of other people, regardless of how well he lives, suffers deprivation. "It follows that raising the incomes of the poor will not eliminate poverty if the incomes of other Americans rise even faster." This novel definition of poverty accompanies a novel definition of wealth. Steaks and yachts do not make the rich, says Jencks. What sets them apart is that they can afford to buy people's time. He wants income disparities reduced so that fewer people can afford to have servants. It may be true that those servants would prefer to be servants than to be unemployed, but Jencks wants it his way because it "will lower the living standards of the elite somewhat." He believes that we should consider educational resources in the same way. Therefore, he says, "it makes more sense to think of poverty and ignorance as relative than as absolute conditions." Jencks's argument, with its frank determination to bring down the successful, is an excellent example of the modern use of *ressentiment*.[28]

Thus we have come a long way from equal opportunity, and the simple quest to eliminate inequity takes odd turns. In 1966 James Coleman of Johns Hopkins University directed a massive study of four thousand schools and six hundred thousand children, under the sponsorship of the U.S. Office of Education. Working under the mandate of the Civil Rights Act of 1964, he was charged with the task of determining the disparities between the respective resources used to educate black and white children. He found little measurable difference between predominantly black and white schools in physical facilities, curricula, or other obvious determinants of educational quality. Coleman was shocked by the wholly unexpected results—as were many others when they became public. The real differences seemed to come from family background and were already present by the first grade; they could not be changed significantly by schooling. When his conclusions did not reveal that black students suffered from discriminatory educational practices, Coleman changed the terms of his study. He refused to produce results that did not show great disparity between black and white opportunities, and the focus had to shift, in his words, from "equal schools to equal students."[29] Thus, opportunity is not enough. For *ressentiment*, the chance to learn is unimportant; the gap is all-important.

[28]Christopher Jencks et al., *Inequality: A Reassessment of the Effect of Family and Schooling in America* (New York: Basic Books, 1972), pp. 5–7.

[29]Daniel Bell, *The Coming of Post-Industrial Society: A Venture in Social Forecasting* (New York: Basic Books, 1973), pp. 429–31.

The Misuse of Guilt

It is only natural to ask why the equalitarians have been so successful. One reason seems to be their ability to use guilt feelings to effect property distribution. Observing this process in Europe and the United States, Ellul describes "a vast procession of flagellants who slash at each other and themselves with the most horrendous of whips. . . . We even scourge ourselves hysterically for crimes we did not commit." One of the most effective of the early publicists of the New Left, who later turned against it, concluded that the movement grew out of "self-hatred and self-contempt."[30] Jencks frankly wishes to exploit those feelings. Not content with fanning the flames of envy at the bottom end of the gap, he says that those at the other end "must begin to feel ashamed of economic inequality." Fletcher also speaks of the "shameful gap." Galbraith wants rich countries to feel guilty because poor countries exist.

Politicians are sometimes able to exploit irrational guilt feelings when they fail to elicit sufficient support by rousing envy. Jean-François Revel, a French commentator, concluded that there is a kind of helper that needs someone helpless to assist. After the Six Days War such people deserted Israel because the Israelis were insufficiently downtrodden. During the period of widespread strikes and rioting in France in 1968, students surprised striking workers by asking them if they were hungry. To say that the position of blacks in the United States has improved in the last generation is impermissible for that frame of mind.[31] The victims must remain victims.

It is ironic that those who have denied the existence of any objective reason for believing in guilt should be the ones to accomplish their ends by fanning guilt feelings. They have already established that sentiment is the final arbiter of right and wrong. What makes them so sure that my sentiments will conclude that it is wrong to exploit others, even if I were to accept the dubious conclusion that wide income differentials were prima facie evidence that I had? And what obligates me to conform to the sentiments belonging to Niebuhr, Jencks, and Fletcher? If I am bound by their sentiments there is something external to my own sentiments that places a moral obligation on me. But that is exactly what they said was not true. By their own principles, I conform to my own definitions of goodwill or love and go my way without bothering about any

---

[30]Norman Podhoretz, *Breaking Ranks: A Political Memoir* (New York: Harper and Row, 1979), p. 361.

[31]Jean-François Revel, *Without Marx or Jesus: The New American Revolution Has Begun*, trans. J. F. Bernard (Garden City, N. Y.: Doubleday, 1971), p. 222.

kind of external restraint, including the external restraint of humanist sentiments. If I succumb to the humanist delusion, the ultimate egoism of believing that my own sentiments have the force of supreme law— that is if I succumb to the serpent's temptation by declaring myself a god who determines good and evil—I can do anything at all with confidence in its legitimacy. The supreme lawgiver—I, myself—has ruled. With all the confidence of being on the side of the supreme god, I can go on a bloody rampage as Assur-Nasir-Pal did, and exult in my divine attributes.

That is the fraud in the humanitarian arousal of guilt feelings while building a moral system on sentimentality. Radio Hanoi early in 1980 interpreted the Soviet invasion of Afghanistan in these words: "This is an action of generosity and love to humanity." Humanitarians have no basis for disputing that statement, for it is perfectly in keeping with their principles. Soviet and Vietnamese humanitarians are responsible to their own sentiments, not to the sentiments of Western humanitarians who have a larger residue of unacknowledged Christian principle.

The paradoxical inclusion of guilt feelings in a system that has no place for guilt because of the absence of any law to break probably finds its resolution in the envy and *ressentiment* that are central to the humanitarian ethic. Humanitarian behavior is not a characteristic peculiar to modernity. Examples abound of primitive societies in which to express admiration for the property of another is to be given it. Nothing is withheld. Such behavior is often believed to be generous and loving, but its real motivation is fear. People correctly consider the power of envy so great that it is worthwhile to lose almost anything rather than invoke its malevolence against themselves. There is no reason to engage in productive economic activity, because that increases wealth and thereby elicits envy. Thus the society remains primitive. The kind of "generosity" that gives under those circumstances can be called humanitarian but not for the reasons usually assumed.

Schoeck disputes the conventional belief that the guilt feelings of those who have what others do not is a Christian quality. That belief, he says, overlooks "the New Testament's remarkable religious, psychological and historical achievement in freeing believers from precisely this primitive, pre-religious, irrational sense of guilt, this universal fear of one's neighbors' envy and of the envy of the gods and spirits." Nineteenth-century socialism, he continues, revived primitive notions of envy and made them normative instead of recognizing the pathology. Guilt feelings coming from the real or imagined envy of others have nothing whatever to do with the Christian understanding of guilt.[32] P. T. Bauer, an economist at the London School of Economics, has argued that contemporary feelings of guilt about the economic privations of others are primarily group phenomena, centering around class or nation, and do not concern what individuals have done or failed to do. They are not concerned, then, with a sense of personal moral failure requiring repentence and restitution. "Collective guilt has replaced a sense of personal sin."[33] Bauer's insight explains why humanitarians tend to deprecate the charitable action of individuals in comparison with that of the collectivity. Fletcher contemptuously dismisses the former as "microethics" while he lauds the charity based on taxation and distributed by the state.

The Poverty Issue

To understand how humanitarian ethics affect the larger society, we shall consider two issues of current importance and widespread public interest. The first of these is poverty. Much of the discussion on this subject is not about poverty at all but about something else. If poverty were still considered the lack of means to procure sufficient food and protection to sustain health, the range of disagreement would be far narrower than it is. As wealth increases, however, people redefine poverty. The need for food, clothing, and shelter is taken to mean the need for meat, new clothing, and a house with indoor plumbing, and then again to mean steak, stylish clothing, and a house with still more amenities. William Ryan, a psychologist at Boston College who has written one of the most influential of the recent books on poverty, is very frank about this. In the preface to the second edition (1976) of his book, he says that in the six years following the first edition he "enlarged" his vision of the victims of American society. He no longer considers only the 15 percent of the population that is below the federal poverty line to be deprived. "At least two-thirds, perhaps three-fourths of us are relatively poor compared to the standards of the top 10 or 5 percent."[34] He could, of course, have used a ratio of 80–20, 60–40 or 99–1. Any arbitrary division will do because his concept has nothing to do with poverty but with *ressentiment*. That is the nature of equalitarian discussions, and Ryan acknowledges his membership in that camp.

---

[32]Schoeck, *Envy*, pp. 257 ff.

[33]P.T. Bauer, *Dissent on Development: Studies and Debates in Development Economics* (London: Weidenfeld and Nicolson, 1971), pp. 21f.

[34]William Ryan, *Blaming the Victim*, rev. ed. (New York: Vintage, 1976), p. xiii.

Humanitarian ethics finds it necessary to "upgrade" the poverty minimums in such a way as to prevent the number of poor people from declining. According to the Bureau of Labor Statistics, an adequate living standard in New York City in 1947 required an income of $4000 for a family of four. In 1961 it had risen to $5200, and was projected to rise to $7000 by 1975. (These figures are all expressed in 1961 dollars and are not affected by inflation.)[35] Eugene Smolensky, an economist, has calculated that no matter what the improvement of living standards might be, about 20 percent of the population is always considered below the poverty level. Irving Kristol of New York University concludes from this that poverty is a function of ideology and not of science. He suggests that a society that continually improves the lot of the poor while denouncing itself for not having done so is neurotic.[36]

Our thinking about poverty is badly distorted because the statistics relating to it are often used either incompetently or dishonestly. Poverty literature ritually includes tables showing the grossest disparities in the distribution of income. But Kenneth Boulding, an economist at the University of Colorado who favors humanitarian policies, has shown that when the figures are not corrected for age they are badly misleading. He wants the statistics adjusted to account properly for the very young and very old who earn and need far less than do others. When that is done, the inequalities are far less imposing.[37] Statistics on the ownership of common stock present analagous pitfalls. About 2 percent of individual stockholders own 66 percent of stocks held by individuals. But about 35 percent of shares are held by pension funds, insurance companies, mutual funds or profit-sharing plans, and therefore are beneficially owned by millions of individuals. The Sears and Roebuck pension plan, to cite one example, owns 20 percent of the company's

---

[35]The figures were compiled by an official of the Bureau of the Census, Herman P. Miller, *Rich Man, Poor Man* (New York: Crowell, 1964), cited in Bell, *The Coming of Post-Industrial Society,* p. 319.

[36]Irving Kristol, *Two Cheers for Capitalism* (New York: Basic Books, 1978), p. 217. Cf. Michael Harrington, *The Other America: Poverty in the United States* (New York: Macmillan, 1962), p. 179: "Poverty should.be defined absolutely, in terms of what man and society could be. As long as America is less than its potential, the nation as a whole is impoverished by that fact." He says absolutely, but he means relatively, because the nation's potential is always changing. For other examples of the statistical legerdemain employed by the poverty theorists to support their views, see Martin Anderson, *Welfare: The Political Economy of Welfare Reform in the United States* (Stanford, Calif: Hoover Institution Press, 1978), pp. 22–39.

[37]Kenneth E. Boulding, *The Economy of Love and Fear: A Preface to Grants Economics* (Belmont, Calif.: Wadsworth, 1973), p. 50.

outstanding shares. The Bureau of the Census borders on the fraudulent in its use of poverty statistics. They show that the wealthiest 20 percent of the population receives 40 percent of the national income, and the lowest 20 percent receives 5 percent. But these figures consider cash income only. If in-kind transfer payments are included, the two groups would be shown to receive, respectively, 33 and 12 percent of the national income. And those figures are not corrected for age and therefore are still badly skewed.[38]

Recent studies by Harry Schwartz of the Columbia University medical school show that, contrary to the poverty literature, the poor receive medical attention equal or superior to other groups. They receive more hospital care, for example. Families earning less than $5,000 accounted for 1,541 days of hospital care per thousand persons in a recent year. For families earning more than $25,000 annually the corresponding figure is 679. Schwartz concludes that the poor in the United States "get more care from physicians and hospitals than any other group of Americans."

The humanitarian definition of poverty shows it to be relative. This means that nobody can be content with what he has because someone else has more. We should all be consumed with envy, it says, and seek ways to have other people's possessions. What kind of definition of the good life must lie behind the conception that one is oppressed if he only has meat twice a week, if his plumbing does not come up to the modern code, or if he does not have a color television set or a car? He may be oppressed with or without those things, but the fact that he is without them gives no information about the presence or absence of justice or guilt. Being poor is the greatest evil, in humanitarian thinking, because having material possessions is the greatest good. It is fitting that the war on poverty should come at the same time as the apogee of materialism. Modern materialism is not only an ethical philosophy that places a high value on money and possessions but a social philosophy that says that human relations are determined by material factors. Social pathology, in this thinking, requires a material cause, and that sets the stage for finding culprits on whom to inflict guilt. The readiness of humanitarian politics to exploit that philosophy leads the British historian C. Northcote Parkinson to conclude that all modern politicians are Marxist in orientation, inasmuch as they believe that all problems are primarily economic.[39]

[38]Kristol, *Two Cheers,* pp. 196f., 239.

[39]C. Northcote Parkinson, *Left Luggage: A Caustic History of British Socialism from Marx to Wilson* (Boston: Houghton Mifflin, 1967), p. 49.

Poverty and Culture

Insofar as the humanitarian literature on poverty recognizes cultural factors, it is usually in the context of something called "the unbreakable cycle of poverty." Poor people are said to be locked into their status, generation after generation, because they are so oppressed by material deprivation that they have sunk into apathy and despair. This means that they cannot find relief except when an outside agency changes material conditions. Culture, in this use, implies environmental determinism and is closely associated with metaphysical materialism. Michael Harrington, who wrote the most influential—and probably the best—book on the humanitarian view of poverty, recognized that culture had a broader meaning, one that does not lend itself well to the usual humanitarian argument. He called attention to the fact that, in the past, poor people lived in a way that was very different from what is now thought of as the culture of poverty. Their diet and housing may have been bad, but they were not impoverished, because they had will, vitality, and aspirations. The immigrant culture, in particular, had these characteristics and built from them a strong family life and social cohesiveness that enabled them to move into a central role in American life. They "found themselves in slums, but they were not slum dwellers." Intellectuals without much money have similar attributes. Other observers have pointed out numerous instances in which having little money is associated with *virtue,* and not with the pathology that comes with modern poverty.[40]

It does not take Harrington long to forget what he has said about the compatibility of being poor and living in dignity. He begins to speak of the will being warped because of poverty, and so transforms the healthy culture living well without money into the familiar culture of poverty. He thus retreats from his earlier idea that poverty is a cultural phenomenon that has no direct correlation with the amount of money available. Losing his serious consideration of culture as a determinant of the quality of living, he slips into the crass material determinism common to the humanitarian ethic. The environment then becomes an external force trapping people into behavior patterns they cannot change.

But a culture is a network of shared beliefs as well as institutions and relationships. It has internal aspects under the control of people who are

---

[40]Some examples may be found in Robert Nisbet, *Twilight of Authority* (London: Heinemann, 1976), pp. 62f., 93.

in the culture. They can change some of its features or they can abandon the culture for another; countless people have done that, including many millions still living. Jencks was somewhat bewildered to discover "an enormous amount of economic mobility from one generation to the next." In fact the differences in income between brothers are almost as great as in the population at large. This means there is no reason to treat people as helpless pawns of the environment, and it also recognizes that changes in the environment have only limited power to change the culture. Max Weber, in his classic study on Calvinism, refuted the common assumption that the material environment was the only determinant of social action. Material and nonmaterial factors, he concluded, both shape social institutions.[41]

In his study of poor nations, P. T. Bauer concludes that economic progress depends more on human abilities and attitudes, on the social and political institutions, shared values and historical experience than on the material factors that are often the only considerations mentioned. It is these, and not poverty, that cause prolonged economic stagnation. Bauer lists a number of cultural properties that make it likely that people will be and remain poor: resignation; disinterest in material goods; lack of self-reliance; high preference for leisure; lassitude; the prestige of a passive or contemplative life compared with an active one; the prestige of mysticism; renunciation of the world's goods; acceptance of determinism; fear of change; belief in the occult; pantheism; a mystical view of nature. Theodore White calls the cultural requirements for economic well-being "the law of invisible social capital," which is the mirror image of the cultural deficiencies about which Bauer writes. The physical destruction of Germany in World War II was erased in a few years because the Germans retained skill, will, and determination.[42] Without that kind of capital, financial credits disappear down a bottomless hole.

We do not lack examples of the impact that such personal traits have on the social world. Daniel Moynihan points out that a sexual ethic that places a low premium on chastity, and therefore has a high rate of births outside of marriage, is "predisposed to dependency."[43] Edward Banfield, a social scientist at Harvard University, finds that poverty is related to time orientation. The lower classes tend to be present-oriented,

---

[41]Max Weber, *The Protestant Ethic and the Spirit of Capitalism*, trans. Talcott Parsons (London: George Allen and Unwin, 1930).

[42]Theodore H. White, *In Search of History: A Personal Adventure* (New York: Harper and Row, 1978), p. 322.

[43]Daniel Patrick Moynihan, *The Politics of a Guaranteed Income: The Nixon Administration and the Family Assistance Plan* (New York: Random House, 1973), p. 40.

less willing to forego present benefits in order to secure future ones. Thus, they choose a way of living that finds little value in work, self-improvement, or self-sacrifice. Banfield believes this is the most realistic explanation of class, but, whether or not that is so, it is a reasonable explanation of why some people are poor.[44] Harrington concluded that only the federal government was capable of bringing an end to slums, and that it should undertake a massive new housing program. But a few pages earlier he had shown that moving slum people into new housing creates new slums instantly. That is a graphic example of how culture is more than, and more powerful than, material circumstances.

Poverty and Work

Discussions of the culture of poverty usually consider the relationship between poverty and work. The Proverbs are full of material on the subject, teaching that sloth and poverty are cause and effect. "A slack hand causes poverty, but the hand of the diligent makes rich" (Prov. 10:4). Now, humanitarian literature is studded with contempt for such an outlook and for all manifestations of the work ethic or the "Puritan" ethic. Yet, outside of the back-to-nature movement, it is seldom true that a critic will be as contemptuous of the fruit of the work ethic as of the ethic itself. Harvard theologian Harvey Cox in his festive incarnation—after he found the gray flannel suit of *The Secular City* a bit tight but before he donned the robes of an Eastern guru—showed that curious affinity for the result while deprecating the cause. He wants the prosperous nations of the West to recover their lost sense of festivity and fantasy and stop trying "to inflict their worship of work on the rest of the world." But in the next sentence he berates their insensitivity "to the enclaves of poverty in their midst and the continents of hunger around them."[45] It is difficult to see how he could write two consecutive sentences like those and not reflect on the possibility that dedication to work has produced prosperity and dedication to fantasy has produced poverty. Cause and effect relationships are understood rationally, but those who deal in fantasies and *ressentiment* guilt-trips prefer other kinds of epistemology.

Humanitarian poverty literature is almost unanimous in denying

---

[44]Edward C. Banfield, *The Unheavenly City Revisited* (Boston: Little, Brown, 1974), pp. 53f., 235.

[45]Harvey Cox, *The Feast of Fools: A Theological Essay on Festivity and Fantasy* (Cambridge: Harvard Univ. Press, 1969), p. 13.

that people are unemployed because they prefer not to work. Harrington says that he does not believe such people exist. To link the rejection of the work ethic with poverty is to invite harsh rejoinders that speak of reaction and racism. But that response is wholly inappropriate. Leisure is an economic good, and it is clear that many prefer it to other economic goods, such as cash or luxuries. The redistributive incentive systems that *ressentiment* tends to foster make such tradeoffs prevalent.

Sweden, which was long the showcase of social democracy before falling into economic decrepitude in the 1970s, exemplifies such a system. A Swedish father of four children who earns $25,000 per year does not suffer a drop in spendable income if he stops working and collects welfare benefits. It is no surprise that absenteeism is one of Sweden's major economic headaches. A European study done in 1979 showed that Swedish workers have the highest absentee rates in the industrialized world. The average Swedish worker was absent 16 days in a recent year compared with 1.9 days in Japan and 3.5 days in the United States.

The massive unemployment in Great Britain between the world wars, which stimulated Lord Keynes to write the *General Theory of Unemployment, Interest and Money,* accounts in large measure for the conversion of so many influential people, including much of the ecclesiastical establishment, to Labour Party socialism. From 1921 to 1938 the unemployment rate averaged 14 percent and never fell below 9.5 percent. Two University of Washington economists recently concluded after an exhaustive study that those high figures were caused by a social insurance scheme that made it pay to be unemployed. Benefits began immediately, without a waiting period. By 1931, the weekly benefits were often more than half the former worker's wages, and if he had ever made thirty weekly contributions to the fund, there was no time limit after which benefits expired. Since benefits were not related to wages, lower-paid workers found it more beneficial to stop working; hence they had the highest unemployment rates. The study concluded that the government's policy added between five and eight percent to the unemployment rate. "The army of the unemployed standing watch in Britain at the publication of the *General Theory* was largely a volunteer army."[46]

Harvard economist Martin Feldstein, who is also president of the National Bureau of Economic Research, has reached a similar conclusion about the current American unemployment. He calculates that unem-

---

[46]Daniel K. Benjamin and Levis A. Kochin, "Searching for an Explanation of Unemployment in Interwar Britain," *Journal of Political Economy,* vol. 87, no. 3, June 1979, pp. 441–78.

ployment compensation has pulled about one million people out of the work force. In 1979 the General Accounting Office of the U.S. Congress completed a study that reached the same conclusion. Benefits were set at 50 percent of gross wages in 1935 when Congress began the unemployment insurance program. At that time there was little difference between gross pay and take-home pay. Now, however, the "tax wedge" intrudes between the two and causes a great difference between them. Consequently, about 25 percent of those drawing unemployment compensation receive more than 75 percent of the take-home pay earned when they were employed, and about 7 percent have *more* spending money than they would have were they working. The GAO study found that jobs were available for many of the recipients of federal checks but that they preferred not to work. Martin Anderson has concluded that the preference for leisure rather than work under those circumstances is a rational one. A person on welfare who takes a job loses benefits at a rate that makes the effective tax on his income higher than those earning more than $100,000 annually. The marginal tax rate can be as high as 85 percent. In that way the welfare system erects "a *poverty wall* of high taxation" around the poor person who otherwise might become self-supporting.[47]

Sar Levitan, an economist at George Washington University, recognizes that welfare recipients have incentives to avoid work but seeks the solution to that difficulty in another humanitarian policy. As long as work rewards remain low in relation to welfare rewards, there is little hope of avoiding voluntary unemployment. As of the summer of 1979, he calculates, a family of four would need a full-time job paying at least four dollars per hour to equal the return from assistance programs available to the unemployed. The solution to that, he says, is to keep work rewards high by means of a rising minimum wage law. But it is those same minimum wage laws that have caused unemployment to rise so high, especially among the black youths about whom such humanitarian hand-wringing goes on. Thomas Sowell, a black economist at The Hoover Institution, is one of many in his profession who have pointed out that those laws price unskilled labor at higher levels than their value to employers, ensuring that jobs do not open up for the least skilled. Andrew Brimmer, another black economist formerly on the Federal Reserve Board, has criticized the minimum wage as a leading cause of

---

[47]Anderson concludes that the institution of a guaranteed income, the object of a concerted humanitarian drive for at least the last fifteen years, could reduce the work of low-income people by as much as 50 percent. In support, he gives details of the disastrous effects of the famous Speenhamland experiment of the late eighteenth century.

black teen-age unemployment. Sowell believes the main beneficiaries of such legislation are the labor unions, whose members are able to negotiate pay scales at higher levels than they could without the laws. It is no coincidence that union officials, including those who show no inclination to proclaim minority rights within the unions, have been the most vocal supporters of minimum wage laws. Racism as the cause of black teen-age unemployment is a red herring, according to Sowell; the real cause is humanitarian social policy. The Province of Quebec learned the same lesson. A government favoring redistribution of wealth through legislation raised minimum wages to the highest level in Canada. In 1978 the Quebec Minimum Wage Commission sponsored a report by Laval University economist Pierre Fortin. To his own surprise, Fortin concluded that at least twenty-five thousand jobs, and perhaps as many as forty-two thousand, were wiped out by the higher minimum wage. Levitan knows that minimum wage laws destroy job opportunities, but he is locked into the search for solutions within the humanitarian framework.

Thus do humanitarian policies create situations that humanitarian theorists find intolerable, blame on the wrong causes, and then supplement with an elaborate new set of destructive humanitarian policies. High levels of welfare payments, concluded George Gilder after immersing himself in the life of the black slums, "only demoralize and deprave the poor, destroying their families, draining their energies, and stultifying their lives."[48]

Poverty and Dependency

Poor people who live admirable lives are very different from those in the modern culture of poverty. The mere absence of money gives no explanation for this disparity, and in fact those in the latter group often have much more of the world's goods than those in the former. They may have adequate housing and diets but are sunk in the social pathologies of crime, delinquency, family disintegration, and addiction. Most of all, they are dependent. Moynihan concludes, as do many others, that dependence is the distinguishing mark of the culture of poverty. "To be poor is an objective condition; to be dependent, a subjective one as well." He argues that dependency is a creation of the welfare system itself. France, which has no institutional structure to create and maintain dependency, does not have a problem even remotely like ours. There are

[48]George Gilder, *Visible Man: A True Story of Post-Racist America* (New York: Basic Books, 1978), p. 245.

dependents but not the vast bureaucracy that feeds on and maintains dependency. One of the governing assumptions in France is that people are responsible for taking care of themselves.

Dependency does not become a problem beyond the point where provision is made for it to continue. Moynihan contends that the custodial quality of the welfare system is to be found nowhere but in the United States.[49] This suggests that humanitarian policies do not alleviate the pathologies of the culture of poverty but create and then exacerbate them. Moynihan recalls that by the late 1950s welfare had all but vanished as a political issue. During the next decade, poverty diminished sharply, especially in the non-white population. From nearly 25 percent of the population in 1959, the poor declined in number to 12.2 percent ten years later. Yet in that period, during which the War on Poverty was launched, funded, and staffed, both welfare and dependency increased dramatically. In 1959 two-thirds of poor black families were headed by men. In 1969 more than one-half were headed by women. In the twelve-month period ending June 30, 1970, the number of Americans on welfare increased by 20 percent. After 1970, says Moynihan, the rule became that welfare dependency increased even as poverty declined.

There is other evidence that the source of the problem is in its putative solution. The subjective nature of modern poverty suggests that the feelings that engender dependence are fostered by the public debate in which humanitarians engage. Banfield believes that the constant attention paid to income differentials has increased the feelings of deprivation. As we have seen, humanitarian publicists bring about that effect by intention. Harrington writes movingly of the plight of the lonely and poor aged in his call for an expanded social security system that will "support a dignified old age." But the social security system helped break the family ties that once provided old people with both financial security and companionship. Humanitarian policies now try to deal with the pathologies stemming from the replacement of the extended family by the nuclear family. But it was humanitarian policy that fostered that destructive change. Harrington's warning that we should not turn the poor into wards of the state has a hollow ring because the policies he advocates do that very thing. Inasmuch as humanitarian policy has the tendency to classify more and more of us as poor, as Ryan's conception does, then nearly the entire population faces that bleak future.

---

[49]Cf. Ivan Illich, *Deschooling Society* (New York: Harper and Row, 1970), p. 4: "Nowhere else is poverty treated at greater cost. Nowhere else does the treatment of poverty produce so much dependence, anger, frustration, and further demands."

The Curse of Ontological Victimhood

Ryan's major contribution to the literature of poverty, and a very influential one, is the concept of victimhood. Those who are part of the culture of poverty, in this view, have been victimized by society. There are only two ways to interpret a situation in which poor people are struggling with difficult circumstances: either blame the circumstances or blame the victim. He writes, for example, of a group of welfare workers discussing the problems of unmarried mothers and considering how they could be helped to adjust to the circumstances. Those welfare workers, in Ryan's words, were "Blaming the Victim." Since he has defined the situation in terms of a dilemma, and since the workers did not blame the circumstances, there can be no other conclusion but the one he reached. The argument rests on the assumption that anything one says under those conditions must be considered a word of blame.

But the main assumption in Ryan's reasoning is that what happened *had* to happen, given the circumstances. There is no recognition that the "victim" may have had some role in creating the circumstances, and thus is an accomplice. That, he says, would be blaming the victim. But did those babies arrive after acts of immaculate conception? That is not a question of middle class moralism. It is rather an insistence that circumstances often do not just "come" but are made. If to say, "Why did you do *this* instead of *that?*" is to blame the victim, then everything is determined by circumstance. The victim is a machine producing outputs that can only match the inputs. It is senseless to waste sympathy on a machine; the only course of action is to change its environment. The humanitarian refusal to hold poor people (and everyone else) responsible for their actions keeps them dependent, renders them impervious to challenge and therefore change, and places every obstacle in the way of their betterment. Insofar as it is directed toward blacks and other minorities it is racist, because it says they are not capable of assuming responsibility for their actions the way "normal" people are.[50]

Humanitarianism thus changes victimhood from accident to essence. It expands the category of victim until it swallows the entire person. It takes away the poor person's humanity and gives him in its place the ontological status of victim. The sheltering arms of humanist sentimental-

---

[50]Midge Decter writes of the damage done to blacks by white sympathizers who are convinced of their supposed inferiority, and hence make allowances they would make for no other people. She calls it a "very liberal and very racist idea: that being black is a condition for special moral allowance." See "Looting and Liberal Racism," *Commentary*, vol. 64, no. 3, Sept. 1977, p. 54.

ity shower altruism on the poor person and refuse to allow any criticism to fall on his behavior. Blame instead falls on circumstance. The universe is said to have arrayed its forces implacably against the victim, who understandably feels resentment and self-pity because of the fate that circumstance has arranged for him. He was born out of circumstance, molded by circumstance, determined by circumstance. That hard taskmaster will never release its hold on him, will always keep him in the thrall of ontological victimhood.

But the agents of circumstance must be made to pay, first by an unbearable guilt for which no atonement will ever be sufficient and second with a never-ending stream of resources extorted out of them by *ressentiment* politics. The same humanitarian destiny that perpetuates victimhood on one imposes permanent guilt and material loss on the other. *Ressentiment* enjoys its double triumph in the public celebration of humanitarianism: It exalts categories of weakness, sickness, helplessness, and anguish into virtues while it debases the strong and prosperous. In the country of ontological victimhood, strength is an affront. Denying the possibility of strength for the weak keeps them weak. Being freed from dependence would bring the victim back into the human family, responsible for himself and others. How much better to remain a victim, shielded from trouble and responsibility by altruism. Imposing a load of false guilt on the strong, *ressentiment* elicits a countering resentment that blinds them to the need of repentance for their real sins. Both poor and rich need to be made whole, but nobody can be made whole with a humanitarian understanding of his life. Poor and rich need to be reconciled, but altruism accentuates the self-righteous hypocrisies of both. Even the ontological division of humanity into rich and poor is a *ressentiment* stratagem that exploits differences so that it can use strife for its own purposes.

The Poor Countries

P. T. Bauer's extensive work on economic development in poor countries reveals that all the issues dominating discussions of domestic poverty extend to them as well. There is the same false treatment of the unbreakable cycle of poverty; the equalitarian definitions that ensure the envy-producing gap; the misleading statistics that hide economic progress in poor countries, obscuring the fact that the gap is shrinking. Bauer examines in detail the work of economists informed by humanitarian ideology—Gunnar Myrdal, Paul Samuelson, Ragnar Nurkse—and shows how their conclusions cannot be sustained by empirical investigation.[51] So prevalent is that ideology that Bauer calls their conclusions "the new orthodoxy."

Bauer's analysis of the role of cultural determinants in economic development parallels what we have seen to be the case in domestic poverty. The material considerations that are the main, sometimes the sole, determinants in humanitarian thinking are secondary, in Bauer's thought, to attitudes, mores, and institutions. John Kenneth Galbraith's recent book on this subject, *The Nature of Mass Poverty*, although in many ways typical of humanitarian efforts, recognizes lack of aspiration as a major reason that poor countries remain poor. (But the book's status as a propaganda tract rather than a serious work of scholarship is confirmed by the fact that Bauer, the most formidable intellectual challenge to Galbraith's ideas, is not even mentioned). Support for Bauer's contention could be cited almost endlessly by referring to the reports of informed observers. The French leftist agronomist René Dumont found in India a complete disdain for reality among those with whom he worked.[52] Ellul calls attention to the attitude that, until relatively recently in the West, considered work to be not a virtue but a punishment. Where that attitude prevails, lower consumption is a small price to pay for the release from labor.[53] This value position is one that Galbraith might have considered in his critique of the low aspirations of the population of poor countries, instead of seeing in them an opportunity for the stimulation of envy through "education." Schoeck exposes the disadvantages that many cultures impose on those who would otherwise be innovative and productive. The ubiquitous fear of envy destroys economic incentive, for anyone who receives what his neighbors do not have makes himself vulnerable. This is not an environment that fosters innovation. Agricultural improvements come at a glacial pace, confined to the limits set by the fear of envy. Such are the reasons that lead to Bauer's conclusion that economic development "requires modernization of the mind." It requires, that is, changes that are cultural and therefore religious in nature, not those that are primarily technical.

Statements that relate national poverty to culture say, usually only implicitly, that the culture of the West is superior. Humanitarianism is

---

[51]Bauer, *Dissent on Development*, pp. 25–68. For other examples of the gap in this context see Illich, *Deschooling Society*, p. 7 and Donella Meadows *et al.*, *The Limits to Growth*, 2nd ed. (New York: Universe Books, 1974), p. 44. For another explanation of how the statistics are misused see Wanniski, *Way the World Works*, p. 67.

[52]Jean-François Revel, *The Totalitarian Temptation*, trans. David Hapgood (Garden City, N. Y.: Doubleday, 1977), p. 262.

[53]Jacques Ellul, *The Technological Society*, trans. John Wilkinson (New York: Knopf, 1964), p. 65.

driven to a frenzy by such a position. *Ressentiment,* as we have seen, insists on the opposite, in its elevation of weakness, impotence, and dependence to positions of moral superiority. Bauer finds it paradoxical that the supporters of increased foreign aid extoll the moral superiority of people in poor countries while maintaining that they cannot make their way in the world without outside help. Such views reflect the reigning ideal of global cosmopolitanism, impelled by a sentimental extension of the idea of toleration beyond its proper limits, and reinforced by altruistic self-hatred.

Cultures are equal in value only if there is no standard against which to judge them. The culture of the West, infused as it is with Christian values, is superior to any other, and all the valid charges against the West are indications that it has betrayed its own heritage. It is not superior because it is wealthy; it is wealthy because it is superior, because it believes that work is a calling, that matter is important, that reason is a gift of God. This culture, God's gift, transmits its material blessings along with its interpretation of reality. Animist cultures, to cite one example by way of contrast, are not likely to produce large numbers of skilled engineers as long as they believe that physical objects have spirits. Therefore, the West cannot export prosperity without also exporting the culture that makes it possible. But to spread the culture of the West now means also to spread the destructive accretions that in recent years have altered it so, and that apparently is what the Muslim world has begun to resist so fiercely. To their credit, some Islamic leaders recognize they may have to choose between prosperity and keeping their own culture. In that, they are far ahead of the U.S. government, burdened as it is with the delusions of humanitarian sentimentality.

Destructive policies combine with cultural factors to keep poor countries poor. Walter Heller of the University of Minnesota and Nicholas Kaldor of Cambridge University have long urged these countries to tax their citizens at high levels in order to provide funds for investment. Kaldor, in particular, complained that they were not taking his advice seriously enough when the promised results did not come. Gunnar Myrdal, in *Asian Drama,* followed Kaldor's line and won the Nobel prize largely on the strength of that book. In fact, however, many poor countries have extremely high tax rates. Wanniski blames those rates for the poverty of the Indian sub-continent; risky investments are uninviting when people cannot receive rewards for them. The same is true elsewhere. Many low-tax countries, such as the Ivory Coast, are prosperous. Bauer calls Myrdal's book—one million words in three volumes—"primarily a political tract," rather than the treatise on economics it purports to be. He finds particularly offensive Myrdal's grievances against the economically successful and his transformation of helplessness into virtue. Although Bauer makes no use of the concept of *ressentiment,* its application to his description of Myrdal's work is obvious. He finds the emphasis on central planning in poor countries to be inhibiting to the initiative without which economic development cannot take place. He also writes of many cases in which they retard their own development by excluding or discriminating against the most productive people, usually foreign ethnic groups, such as Chinese, Europeans, and East Indians.

The relationship between poor countries and rich ones is extremely important, as most of the disputants recognize. The role of foreign capital is an especially thorny issue, with charges of neocolonialism coming from critics of various points of view. But most agree that outside capital is essential for investment. Long ago, the great Austrian economist Ludwig von Mises pointed out that poor countries were destroying their opportunities to procure foreign capital by inflicting grievous damage on the international capital market. After recklessly wiping out the investments of foreign entrepreneurs, they continue to seek additional infusions of capital from them.[54]

The misuse of foreign aid by the poor countries is told in innumerable stories. The government of Bangladesh admitted that all the relief food received for a whole year had been sold in India for the profit of the officials who were to distribute it to their own people. In India Jean-François Revel saw cooking oil being sold in the markets, still bearing the label, "Not for sale. Gift of the American People." The broader questions of foreign aid, like the growth of the domestic welfare establishment, have not been favored with informed debate; humanitarian moral fervor has swept the field. Yet Bauer presents forceful evidence that ought to place the burden of proof on the proponents of foreign aid. He shows that aid can obstruct economic development, that destructive national policies are often subsidized from outside sources, that centralization is increased at the expense of individual liberties, and that it tends to encourage the false beliefs that benefit can be obtained without paying for it and that rich countries are so because they exploit poor countries.

There are other parallels between the domestic and foreign versions of the humanitarian ethic toward the poor. Bauer calls attention to the

---

[54]Ludwig von Mises, *Omnipotent Government* (New York: Arlington House, 1969 [New Haven: Yale Univ. Press, 1944]), p. 255.

patronizing belief that nobody should expect the standards of poor countries to be as high as those in the West. Myrdal's work is full of that attitude which is, of course, the awarding of the status of ontological victimhood to whole nations.[55] At the same time he spreads the blame for the plight of the poor countries on those who have the effrontery not to be poor. The leaders of poor countries find it convenient to play on these *ressentiment* themes in order to extricate themselves from the consequences of their own policies. President Nyerere of Tanzania, a country whose economy he has wrecked on the shoals of socialist centralism, often says that the West should send money to poor countries as a matter of justice and not of charity. The imposition of guilt feelings is a tool of redistribution in the international sphere as in the domestic.

Domination by Classification

Shifting our attention from the humanitarian conception of poverty to the humanitarians themselves, it is only natural to inquire further why they should engage in such a destructive set of policies toward people they claim to be helping. The *ressentiment* motif is so prevalent in their public statements that there can be little doubt about its importance in the explanation. But there is more. Sentimentality, as we have seen, finds expression in autonomous, pragmatically based decisions on right and wrong, and in the refusal to declare absolute standards on all matters, including poverty. What sometimes seems to be an intellectual vacuity in humanitarian polemics is associated with this trait, which we may think of as the propensity to *define* or to *classify* rather than to make judgments. As long as the conception of poverty is relative to what others have, the humanitarian retains his freedom to declare poor whomever he wishes. We have seen that Ryan included 15 percent of the population in that category in 1970 but 75 percent in 1976, and the reason he gave is that he enlarged his vision. Sixty percent of the population became poor at a stroke of the pen because, on the basis of his subjective, sovereign act he classified them so. They are poor by definition. If he declared them poor by an act of judgment instead, he would have to justify that judgment by a rational process that would be subject to the critical

---

[55]Old-fashioned Marxism can be healthier and more humane than the sickness of humanitarianism. One American Marxist protested the views of Gunnar Myrdal and Michael Harrington with their emphasis on the impotence of the poor and oppressed. He thought, rather, that "they possess a tremendous as yet largely untapped capacity for action." Hyman Lumer, *Poverty: Its Roots and Its Future* (New York: International Publishers, 1965), pp. 66f.

judgment of others. By avoiding all objective criteria, humanitarians rely on the act of classification to preserve their freedom to think and act arbitrarily.

When observers use classification or definition rather than judgment to place people in categories, they exercise power over those people. Thomas Szasz, a maverick psychiatrist, has described this process in the determination of psychiatric disorders. Szasz shows how classifying people changes them into the image that accords with the classifier's assumptions or his desires. In that way, "classification is like a lever: it gives one a purchase on whatever it is one wants to move." To classify people psychiatrically, Szasz believes, is to establish control over them.[56] To classify people by their culture, as the humanitarians do, is by extension to establish control over whole populations. To the extent humanitarian policies become national policy, a whole society falls under the power of the classifiers. As Szasz says, the process of classification serves the classifier. Since classification is a process of will more than of reason, the arbitrary nature of sentimentality is perfectly suited to the exercise of this kind of power. It creates in people their ontological nature in the way one wishes, just as God created man, and at the same time sets the stage for exercising domination over them. Or, as Szasz says, to get the lever on them and move them.

The Exercise of Power

The power behind the lever of modern humanitarianism is the state, that savior through which the apostles of ontological victimhood find a poor man in the slums and shower compassion on him in the form of other peoples' property. That ensures that he will remain in the slums living off others, despising himself for it, and beholden to his humanitarian benefactors. He remains a ward of the compassionate ones and their political and bureaucratic allies. Humanitarianism is not content to break the shackles of job discrimination, bars to voting, impediments to education. Those obstructions to normal civic life, once destroyed, no longer hinder a person from taking his normal place in society. He is free to be responsible for himself and his family, free to play it safe in a job with security, free to take wild risks in the hope of building something big, free to live penuriously while getting an education, free, in short, to live like a human being released from the clutches of humanitarian sen-

---

[56]Thomas S. Szasz, "The Psychiatric Classification of Behavior: A Strategy of Personal Constraint," in Leonard D. Eron, ed., *The Classification of Behavior Disorders* (Chicago: Aldine, 1966), pp. 136, 155f., 165.

timentality. But he can reject that freedom by attending to humanitarian propaganda, reveling in his own victimhood, drowning in self-pity, inciting the guilt of those taken in by *ressentiment,* demanding that the state indemnify him with the property it has seized from his fellow citizens. In so doing, he cooperates with humanitarianism to ensure his own debasement.

The humanitarian aim is to exercise power. Whether the ideology acknowledges this openly or not, all the policies converge on it. Ryan says as much when he urges us to stop the fruitless tinkering with the victim and focus on "the real targets—redistribution of money and power." Christopher Jencks agrees. He wants to "establish political control over the economic institutions that shape our society." The ultimate recipients of that money, power, and control will be Ryan and Jencks and their friends, the ideologues who wish to reshape the whole society and everyone in it, along with the bureaucrats and the political, business, and educational leaders who can profit from the process.

Some of the black leadership has begun to dissent loudly from the humanitarian assumption of power in defense of blacks. Thomas Sowell has protested bitterly against those with a "vested interest in victimhood and its rewards." Another black economist, Walter Williams of Temple University, has declared that blacks do not need the help of saviors or of any type of paternalism that suggests that blacks are unable to maintain themselves in the same economic environment that others do. Jesse Jackson has worked to persuade blacks—and poor whites as well—that their future lies in learning, working, producing, and performing rather than seeking to live on the labor of others. Of late the NAACP has been taking similar positions, bringing on itself predictable charges of Uncle Tomism. John Perkins, a black man who founded and directed for many years a wholistic ministry to poor people in Mississippi, has recently described the humanitarian gospel of redistribution as a guilt-ridden ploy that has kept blacks under control. "This made us dependent on the government and gave us a welfare mentality. Consequently we were not able to communicate to our own people a philosophy of spiritual self development and indigenous power and leadership." These currents in the black community express determination to insist upon the humanity of black people and are daggers in the heart of humanitarianism, which wants its victims docile.

Puzzling over the contradictions between the claims and the performance of humanitarianism, Daniel Bell concluded that they could be understood by examining the difference between Christian love and its humanitarian imitator. Christian love, which has always emphasized caring for the poor, accepts them as worthy without romanticizing them and giving them qualities they do not possess. Humanitarianism, especially in its mainstream Protestant manifestations, "corroded" that vision, leading to the "erosion" of Christian love. The result is the humanitarian counterfeit of love. Perhaps that is why George Bernard Shaw, that famous publicizer of Fabian humanitarianism, said, "I hate the poor."[57]

Issues of Life and Death

A second subject on which Christian and humanist positions are currently locked in public policy battle is that of life and death. Abortion is the most visible component of this complex of issues, but that is only the tip of the iceberg. The basic problem for old-fashioned humanists is that they wish to keep the fruits of Christian doctrine while jettisoning the doctrine itself. University of Chicago sociologist Edward Shils, for example, correctly associates perceptions that life is sacred with Christian teachings. He rejects those teachings but wishes nevertheless to retain the conviction about the sacredness of life. He thinks that Christianity had such persuasive power because of a "powerful impulse" that he would like to recapture without, however, accepting Christianity itself.[58]

The practical results of a system of belief are products of the beliefs themselves, and that is why Shils is seeking a phantom he will never find. The doctrine is the thing he seeks without knowing it, and without it there is no "powerful impulse" available to sanctify life unless the process of mystification creates one. But that could only be an ephemeral advantage, unable to withstand any significant test. Catholic lay theologian Michael Novak wrote in 1968 that "atheists retain the chief moral imperatives of Judaism and Christianity."[59] He should have known better even then, but that is the kind of mistake that is much less likely to be made even in the few short years that have passed, so quickly is the scene changing.

Modern humanism has a view of both life and death that are diametrically opposed to the Christian view. Shils could not find within the humanism of the dominant culture any justification for the sanctity of hu-

---

[57]Quoted in de Jouvenel, *Ethics of Redistribution*, p. 17.

[58]Edward Shils, "The Sanctity of Life," in Shils *et al.*, *Life or Death*, pp. 37f.

[59]Michael Novak, "The Secular Saint," *The Center Magazine*, vol. 1, no. 4, May 1968, p. 51.

man life because such sanctity can be persuasive only when derived from a transcendent source. If God created man in his own image, then the law that says, "You shall not kill," has meaning; there is a logically persuasive nexus between the stated reality and the ethical injunction that is derived from it. But if man is a product of chance and time, as the modern materialist scientisms have it, then killing is an action, like any other, that must be judged on pragmatic grounds. We are entitled in that case to compare benefits with risks and costs and to decide if killing is warranted. In humanitarian theory and practice, the decision is more likely to be made on the basis of sentiment than on cost-benefit studies, but either is possible.

Scheler wrote long ago that *ressentiment* reverses the normal hierarchy of values by placing utility above life itself. The life of human beings or nations must be judged according to their usefulness for the wider community. Joseph Fletcher validates that judgment by advancing the argument that the quality of life supersedes the right to life. He says this places quality over quantity.[60] This theory supports his earlier contention that imperfect newborn babies and suffering adults may both be considered "monsters" whom doctors should not allow to continue living.

To the natural response that killing innocent human beings is murder, one possible defense is to argue that some people cannot really be considered human beings, and it is therefore legitimate to kill them. Michael Tooley, a philosopher at the Australian National University, has taken just that position. Tooley believes that some people must be considered "non-persons," and that to say that newborn babies are persons is "a wild contention." The right to life inheres only in those who are self-conscious, and those who lack that quality he prefers to call homo sapiens rather than human. Adult homo sapiens have a right to life that the ape does not have because "there are certain psychological properties which the former possesses and the latter lacks." Tooley acknowledges that he is unable to specify exactly what they are. But— startling contradiction—he believes that some adult animals possess the faculty of self-consciousness that many homo sapiens lack. It follows, then, that while there is no moral difficulty in killing either unborn children or infants after birth, it may be "morally indefensible" to kill

---

[60]Joseph Fletcher, "The 'Right' to Live and the 'Right' to Die," *Beneficent Euthanasia*, ed. Marvin Kohl (Buffalo, N.Y.: Prometheus, 1975), pp. 46ff.

animals because when we do so "we are in fact murdering innocent persons."[61]

Since Tooley has established a principle—self-consciousness—for distinguishing between life that is to be considered inviolate and life that is not, it would seem that he has departed from the typical humanist reliance on utility in favor of an absolute. But that is not so. He is unable, he says, to specify the criteria for determining self-consciousness. That would be a standard to which he would be obliged to refer his decisions. He has specified a psychological determinant that he cannot explain, and that suits his purpose perfectly. It gives him the right to classify all life into either the category that must be preserved or the category that may not be, and to place a dog in the first category and a human being in the second. He retains sovereignty, as in any system that rests on classification.

It is a fact that in hospitals over much of the Western world newborn infants apparently considered nonpersons because of some imperfection are starved deliberately in order to cause their deaths.[62] Modern humanitarianism has gone far beyond the old campaign to allow euthanasia—a good death—for those suffering from incurable and painful diseases. In all those arguments the assumption was that acts of mercy killing were done for the sake of the person being put to death. Now people speak openly of killing for the sake of those being kept alive. Yale Kamisar describes the progression of events:

> Miss Voluntary Euthanasia is not likely to be going it alone for very long. Many of her admirers . . . would be neither surprised nor distressed to see her joined by Miss Euthanatize the Congenital Idiots and Miss Euthanatize the Permanently Insane and Miss Euthanatize the Senile Dementia.

---

[61]Michael Tooley, "Abortion and Infanticide," *Philosophy and Public Affairs,* vol. 2, no. 1, Fall, 1972, pp. 41–65. See also Michael Tooley, "Decisions to Terminate Life and the Concept of the Person," *Ethical Issues Relating to Life and Death,* ed. John Ladd (New York: Oxford Univ. Press, 1979), p. 66.

[62]Philippa Foote, "Euthanasia," in Ladd, *Ethical Issues,* p. 37. C. Everett Koop, when surgeon-in-chief at Children's Hospital in Philadelphia, said in public lectures that physicians and nurses in England who allow infants to die of starvation jocularly say they are being put on a lo-cal diet. During one period of less than three years, forty-three babies at the Yale University Hospital were allowed to die after physicians consulted with the babies' parents. R. S. Duff and A. G. M. Campbell, "Moral and Ethical Dilemmas in the Special Care Nursery," *New England Journal of Medicine,* vol. 289, no. 17, Oct. 25, 1973, pp. 890 ff.

And these lasses—whether or not they themselves constitute a "parade of horrors"—certainly make excellent majorettes for such a parade.[63]

The parade has now gone far beyond the stage that Kamisar wrote about. James D. Watson, winner of the Nobel prize for discovering the structure of the DNA molecule, has suggested that we change the legal definition of "person" to be applicable only to infants older than three days. That would give time for parents to decide if they wanted the baby kept alive or killed.[64] Francis Crick, who shared the Nobel prize with Watson, calls for a new ethical system, featuring abortion and infanticide, which would make it mandatory for all persons over eighty years of age to be put to death. In a textbook on ethics written for college students, philosopher Millard Everett envisioned that the early euthanasia laws might be followed by others that would require the deaths of all persons suffering social defects that would make life difficult. He urged that "no child should be admitted into the society of the living who would be certain to suffer any social handicap—for example, any physical or mental defect that would prevent marriage or would make others tolerate his company only from a sense of mercy."[65] So perverted has the sense of morality become that for this humanitarian professor of ethics, the evocation of mercy is a sin meriting the death penalty.

Humanism's pragmatic orientation now stresses the economic benefits to be had when people are not permitted to go on living. Walter Sackett has been introducing euthanasia bills into the Florida legislature since 1969 and argues his case on the basis of the billions of dollars to be saved by obviating the need for costly medical and custodial care. Tooley believes that the cost of keeping a person alive is a valid consideration in deciding whether or not to kill him. Glanville Williams, an old warrior in the long struggle to legalize euthanasia, says it is not necessary to consider involuntary euthanasia yet, because the cost of maintaining the elderly is tolerable. Later on, however, he expects worsening conditions to make mandatory killings more acceptable.[66] Williams's remark draws

---

[63]Yale Kamisar, "Some Non-Religious Views Against Proposed 'Mercy Killing' Legislation," *Minnesota Law Review*, vol. 22 (May 1958), p. 1031, quoted in Jerry B. Wilson, *Death by Decision: The Medical, Moral and Legal Dilemmas of Euthanasia* (Philadelphia: Westminster, 1975), p. 59.

[64]*Prism*, vol. 1, no. 2, May 1973, in C. Everett Koop, *The Right to Live: The Right to Die* (Wheaton, Ill.: Tyndale, 1976), p. 69.

[65]Millard Spencer Everett, *Ideals of Life* (New York: Wiley, 1954), pp. 346ff.

[66]Glanville Williams, "Euthanasia Legislation: A Rejoinder to the Non-Religious Objections," in Tom L. Beauchamp and Seymour Perlin, eds., *Ethical Issues in Death and Dying* (Englewood Cliffs, N.J.: Prentice-Hall, 1978), p. 239.

our attention to the fact that the population is aging and fewer workers will be available to support more retired people under the humanitarian welfare system. His arguments will be increasingly persuasive to a generation determined to consume ever more material goods but decreasingly constrained by laws and values to support their elders. Even now, as Philippa Foote says, many people would like to be rid of aged relatives or even husbands and wives. That is one reason that the suggested safeguards against abuse of euthanasia are worthless; there are too many candidates for the death selection committees who will profit from the whole process: relatives, doctors, and government officials.

In this subject as in all the rest, humanitarian ethics have the same disability as does all pragmatism. The pragmatist, as Hilaire Belloc said, suffers from "an inability to define his own first principles and an inability to follow the consequences proceeding from his own action."[67] He cannot define his first principles because he is not interested in first principles; that is what makes him a pragmatist. The ultimate consequences of what he does escape him because he focuses his attention on the immediate ones. He lives by Lord Keynes's remark that in the long run we are all dead.

Alfred North Whitehead warned presciently that while the Religion of Humanity might in principle favor human happiness, it could provide no bar to "The Humane Extinction of Inferior Specimens."[68] It may kill some because their inferiority makes them consumers rather than producers; that is intolerable for humanists in power who see human beings only as useful tools for social goals. But it may also kill those who are superior, because they are offensive to *ressentiment* mediocrity. Humanitarianism idolizes the one and tolerates the other with its present level of power and residue of Christian ethics, but its instrumental pragmatism may dispose of them later on. If their intelligence or strength or manual dexterity are low, their "social responsibility" suspect—that is if they do not share the humanitarian values of the power elite—or if they prefer leisure over production, there is ample reason to be rid of them. Humanitarian regimes not subject to transcendent law, controlled by gods determining right and wrong for themselves, have proved the logical consequences of this utilitarian view of life in Germany, the USSR, and countless other places. The culture of Western nations in which humanitarian thinking is dominant is a *rentier* living off the moral capital accumulated by its predecessors and giving no atten-

---

[67]Hilaire Belloc, *The Servile State* (New York: Henry Holt, 1946 [1912]), p. 131.

[68]Alfred North Whitehead, *Adventures of Ideas* (New York: Mentor, 1955 [1933]), p. 45.

tion to replenishing it. When it runs out, the horrors begin in earnest.

It is no coincidence that humanitarian policy has reached the zenith of its influence at a time when death propaganda is so much in evidence. The arguments in favor of abortion, infanticide, and euthanasia reveal that the humanitarian ethic wishes to restrict the right to live and expand the right to die—and to kill. Humanism is a philosophy of death. It embraces death, wishes a good death, speaks of the horrible burdens of living for the baby who is less than perfect, for the sick person in pain. It is intolerable to live, cruel to be forced to live, but blessed to die. It is unfair to have to care for the helpless, and therefore merciful to kill. Those who wish to go on living, it seems, are guilty and ungrateful wretches dissipating the energies of the "loved ones" who have better uses for the estate than paying medical bills.

The Christian view of death—as of life—is very different from humanism's. Death is a consequence of sin, and sin is "the sting of death" (1 Cor. 15:56). The church has always rightly emphasized knowing how to die, but that does not make death a friend. In the absolute sense, there are no good deaths. Death is the enemy, the last enemy to be destroyed (1 Cor. 15:26). The good-death people know nothing of life, have small regard for it, and embrace the enemy as if it were a friend. But in Christian perspective the only comfort in death comes from the assurance of resurrection.

The Degradation of Humanity

The hatred that George Bernard Shaw expressed for the poor is not an isolated case. Humanist idolatry, which begins by elevating humans to the status of gods, ends by pouring hatred and scorn on them. The creature cannot act like the creator, and those who expected him to do so fall into disillusionment and worse. As Rosalind Murray said, it is the Enlightenment man—the "good pagan"—and not the Christian who is surprised at the barbarism that results when Christian principles are despised.[69] Gunnar Myrdal, in his eightieth year in 1979, spoke to an interviewer about the lifetime of collaboration between himself and his wife. "Alva and I have always been Enlightenment philosophers," he said. "Now we see that the world is going to hell, now that we're going to die." Following Nietzsche and Freud, Norman O. Brown speaks of "the disease called man." Jean-Paul Sartre described man as the "intelligent, flesheating, cruel species, which knows how to hunt and out-

---

[69]Rosalind Murray, *The Good Pagan's Failure,* 2nd ed. (London: Fontana, 1962), p. 18.

wit the human intelligence, and whose precise aim is the destruction of man.'' Brinton tells of the ambivalence of Enlightenment people toward humanity that dates back to the eighteenth century and is especially evident now. They cannot reconcile the love that their tradition tells them they ought to have with ''the compound of fear, distrust, and contempt for the common man that brews somewhere inside them.''[70]

Notwithstanding the contradictions inherent in its assumptions, humanism continues to affirm the old platitudes. The Humanist Manifesto says that *''the preciousness and dignity of the individual person* is a central humanist value.''[71] Another humanist tract speaks of ''the gracious framework of belief in the dignity of man.''[72] At the same time we are treated on every side to the depersonalization and dehumanization that are inherent in humanism. Most striking is the degradation that humanitarians impose on those about whose welfare they profess to be most concerned. Bauer is right to speak of Myrdal's projection of helplessness and victimhood on poor people as a process of dehumanization. Daniel Bell has noticed that equalitarians, although they speak of the meritocracy, seldom mention personal merit. Merit is a peculiarly human quality that any depersonalizing system will tend to avoid. In its refusal to acknowledge will and responsibility in those over whom it establishes its protection, humanitarianism could be speaking of cocker spaniels or Chevrolets rather than people.

This view of humanity is a twisted and deformed travesty. It is ironic that for humanitarians only poor people, minorities, and those who have run afoul of the law are assumed to be shaped by the iron grip of circumstance. If we look at the villains instead of the victims—the police, politicians, social workers, businessmen—we find that the humanitarians have given them free will. They do not speak about the industrialist's tyrannical father, the loan shark's miserable childhood in an orphan home, the politician's neurotic mother. Those people are responsible for their acts, and therefore are human. Humanism thus awards its enemies the status of human beings while taking that status from its wards.

---

[70]Brinton, *History of Western Morals,* p. 312.

[71]''Humanist Manifesto II,'' p. 6. One may always question the sincerity of those who advocate policies that go counter to their avowed values. One of the signatories of ''Humanist Manifesto II'' is famous for his full-scale attack on the concepts of freedom and dignity that the Manifesto purports to defend. See B. F. Skinner, *Beyond Freedom and Dignity* (New York: Vintage, 1972 [1971]).

[72]Howard Mumford Jones, *American Humanism: Its Meaning for World Survival* (New York: Harper, 1957), p. 108.

The Irrationality of Humanism

Humanism is fundamentally irrational. Although naturalistic in most of its forms, it nevertheless professes belief in the special worth and dignity of human beings, a position for which there can be no support in naturalism. That basic irrationality accounts for most of its contradictions. Elevating the will to a position of eminence in *determining* good and evil, it insists on its impotence in *doing* good and evil. Exalting human beings to divine status, it nevertheless is willing to kill them for their own good or that of others and is even able to place some of them below the status of animals. While stressing the special worth of human beings, it says they must not be kept alive if that would cost too much. Deeming people worthy of support and help when they are needy, humanism reduces their actions to automatic responses to the environment, like those of animals and machines. Since its naturalism is irreconcilable with its anthropology, it confers special status on human beings by the irrational process of mystification. Hostile to reason, it glorifies as virtues irrational and destructive forces like envy, greed, and the lust for power. Like the gnosticisms of old, it speaks as if possessing ''a light not given to others, one not subject to the scrutiny of reason.''[73] When its analysis runs into the ground because of faulty assumptions, it takes refuge in irrational substitutes for explanations.[74]

It is characteristic of this kind of idol to lay its pernicious eggs within the human psyche. The current craze for the pop psychologies that encourage narcissism is typically humanist in its emphasis on sentimental introspection.[75] Therapy, the attempt to manipulate a sense of well-being rather than seeking it in convictions about truth and reality, is a re-

---

[73]Thomas Molnar, *Utopia: The Perennial Heresy* (New York: Sheed and Ward, 1967), p. 10. In his attack on humanism, Rutgers University biologist David Ehrenfeld charges it with being *too* rational. He stresses its failure to recognize its own assumptions, its propensity to take action without anticipating the consequences, its *hubris,* and the general failure of its policies. All of his main points are in agreement with the present study, but it seems more sensible to say that they add up to irrationality rather than rationality. David Ehrenfeld, *The Arrogance of Humanism* (New York: Oxford Univ. Press, 1978), ch. 4.

[74]Jencks, *Inequality,* p. 8, bewildered by his inability to explain income differences on the basis of equalitarian assumptions, attributes them to ''luck.'' In other words, he does not know but will not acknowledge it.

[75]Cf. Christopher Lasch, *The Culture of Narcissism: American Life in an Age of Diminishing Expectations* (New York: Norton, 1978), p. 235: ''In a dying culture, narcissism appears to embody—in the guise of personal 'growth' and 'awareness'—the highest attainment of spiritual enlightenment.'' See also Paul C. Vitz, *Psychology as Religion: The Cult of Self-Worship* (Grand Rapids, Mich.: Eerdmans, 1977), pp. 120–25.

lated aspect of the same phenomenon.[76] When people are cut off from reality by humanist delusions, and are therefore suffering from anomie, they call for Dr. Feelgood. The sense of purposelessness that leads to such pervasive ills as hedonism and workaholism comes from the removal of a final end from the life, and leads to nihilism. "It is a matter of unquestioning surrender to the moment," says German theologian Helmut Thielicke, "to the immediate activity, the immediate duty, the immediate pleasure."[77]

Humanism and the Future

We cannot now see what kind of world it is that the forces of humanism are bringing us to, especially since history has a way of bringing the unexpected. A great catastrophe may lie in our future. Or, perhaps a Ninevah-like repentance of the whole society, with a general healing of the ravages caused by humanism. But if the present progress of humanism should continue, the immediate future will not be bright. "If God is dead," said Dostoyevsky, "everything is permitted." The humanist insistence that its sentiment will not be hobbled by any outside restraint brings us the world he had in mind. Everywhere it is dominant it brings us "higher" morality, which never seems to work out as promised. The Enlightenment smuggled in teleology and ethics to its machine world, and it ended up in the blood bath of the 1790s. Why was that? Because, said Toynbee, the Enlightenment ethic was based on "Mephistophelian maladies of disillusionment, apprehension and cynicism," rather than the Christian virtues of faith, hope and charity. Toynbee saw the same features growing in our own society.[78]

Humanism's misuse of "love" is especially troublesome because it borrows Christian terminology, befuddling much of the church. Denis de Rougemont gives numerous examples of the romanticization of love as something that justifies evil, concluding finally that "deified love is not the God Who is Love. It does not elect a man to save him, but in order to exalt him in the direction of his ruin."[79] It is a short distance from the appearance of compassion to tyranny.

---

[76]Philip Rieff, *The Triumph of the Therapeutic: Uses of Faith After Freud* (New York: Harper and Row, 1966), p. 13.

[77]Helmut Thielicke, *Nihilism: Its Origin and Nature With a Christian Answer,* trans. John W. Doberstein (New York: Schocken Books, 1969 [1961]).

[78]Arnold J. Toynbee, *A Study of History,* abridgement by D. C. Somervell, 2 vols. (New York: Oxford Univ. Press, 1947), vol. 1, p. 553.

[79]Denis de Rougemont, *Man's Western Quest: The Principles of Civilization,* trans. Montgomery Belgion (New York: Harper and Brothers, 1956), p. 66.

Herbert Read once remarked that "a society does not dethrone its flatterers."[80] After the vision of human perfectability was incorporated into the democratic faith, the biblical view of man as sinner began to fade in the popular consciousness. But now that the masses have been comfortable for several generations with that flattering portrait, it is about to be replaced by one they can hardly imagine. There are clues aplenty in the nihilism of the visual arts, the film, stage and fiction, but soon it will be plainer. F. A. Voigt has described how the crimes of National Socialism were all prefigured in the literature, stage, and film of inter-war Germany. "The transition from things imagined to things real is a very easy one, and men, no less than children, will suit action to fantasy."[81]

In one of Tolstoy's stories, a hermit exclaims in amazement, "Others were at least ashamed of being brigands; but what is to be done with this man, who is proud of it?" The prophet must have faced the same kind of problem when he promised judgment on "those who call evil good and good evil" (Is. 5:20). A society exchanging Christian principles for humanist ones begins praising things it once would have condemned. A Nobel prize winner, as we have seen, says it is rational and compassionate to kill people.

The plunge is not sudden, for the habit of centuries is strong, built into the revered documents and the surviving institutions. Marriage, the ideal of love, respect for other persons, for the law, for work, for reason, the self-limitation on human autonomy, all remain. But cut off from the theological and moral foundations, these moral principles are gradually seen to be hanging in midair. People who are interested in ideas—the intellectuals—see this first. Perhaps what is now happening is that large numbers of people are realizing they believe in nothing fundamental that prohibits serial marriage, theft, and the taking of life. Finally, with the remnants of Christian principle entirely gone, sentiment will rule completely. We will have forced sterilization to improve the breeding stock. Infanticide will be practiced openly as it was in the paganism of antiquity; then geronticide to relieve financial pressures; and then anyone may be killed when sentiment wills it. In time, there should be no

---

[80]Introduction to Julien Benda, *The Betrayal of the Intellectuals,* trans. Richard Aldington (Boston: Beacon, 1955 [1928]), p. xviii. Pepsi Cola has drawn almost even with its famous competitor largely because its advertising agency understood that. A spokesman for Batten, Barton, Durstine and Osborne said recently that when two or more brands have little to distinguish them from each other, "the brand that says the more desirable things about the user will have the greater chance of success."

[81]F. A. Voigt, *Unto Caesar* (New York: Putnam's, 1938), p. 267.

longer any need to speak of compassion. Without the overriding ethical requirements that the creator and sustainer of the universe expressed in normative statements, all of that will make sense.

Paul Johnson, a former editor of *The New Statesman,* writes that if the biblical understanding of evil is driven from the field, "then the Christian legitimation of social order, law, and communal self-restraint cannot be maintained very long either."[82] Morality based on individual sentiment means anarchy and the disintegration of society. Humanists cannot have this, and their writings are filled with fervid arguments in favor of a powerful central state. Autonomous man, they find, needs leadership, and strong leadership is the hallmark of humanist society. Whether embodied in a committee or personalized in a leader, the elite dominates. Thus, far from bringing liberation, the anarchy of humanism brings enslavement.[83] The better educated he is, the more likely the humanist is to believe that people are like machines and need to be programmed, and the more likely he is to believe that he should be one of the programmers. Given their premises, the logic of their position is invincible: Gods without power and wealth are an absurd contradiction.

Humanitarianism is saviorhood, an ethic perfectly suited to the theology that divinizes man. But the theology that divinizes man, it turns out, only divinizes some men. The objects of humanitarian concern become less than men, so that the humanitarian can exercise the prerogatives of a god.

The god that failed is man.

---

[82]Paul Johnson, *Enemies of Society* (New York: Atheneum, 1977), p. 245.
[83]A later chapter in this book is devoted to the idolatry of the modern state.

CHAPTER THREE

Idols of Mammon

WHEN Jesus told his disciples they could not serve both God and mammon, the reason he gave was that the two were rival loyalties and that if one were loved the other would be despised (Matt. 6:24). This admonition came in the midst of a portion of the Sermon on the Mount that warned against the preoccupation with wealth and material possessions. It did not say, as some varieties of the ascetic tradition teach, that material things are bad, but rather that they must not be sought as ends in themselves, as if they had everlasting life and significance. Instead, the disciples were to seek the kingdom of God first, and whatever material goods they needed would be given to them as well. The mammon described here as the rival of God, therefore, is the idolatrous elevation of money and the material possessions it will buy as the goal of life. The common expression that describes such a value system as "the pursuit of the almighty dollar" is soundly based in the recognition that the exaltation of possessions to the level of ultimacy is the end of a religious quest, one that seeks and ascribes ultimate meaning. Like all idolatries, it finds ultimate meaning in an aspect of the creation rather than in the creator. And like all idolatries it finds outlet in destructive pathologies that wreck human lives.

Those pathologies cannot simply be subsumed under such labels as liberal, conservative, or radical. The ideologies common to American politics all have a share in them; none has clean hands. Although we must defer our consideration of the economic and political policies that are most compatible with the values of Christian faith until a later chapter, it will be evident from the pages that follow that our position contends that great areas of the social fabric are legitimately free from government constraint. That is a position that is completely antithetical to the dominant American political ideologies. If that contention seems odd, it is only because political rhetoric, the media, and the educational establishment have badly distorted the political and economic landscape, making it appear that the only alternatives to liberal idols are conservative idols.

Covetousness and Theft

Those whose loyalty is to mammon quite naturally cast anxious eyes on the property belonging to others, and that is why the apostle called covetousness a form of idolatry (Col. 3:5; Eph. 5:5). This vice is a strong desire to have the possessions of others. So disastrous is it that the last of the Ten Commandments prohibits it, the only prohibition in the second table that concerns an attitude rather than an action. It often accompanies envy, which is a discontent at or resentment of another's good fortune. Envy precedes covetousness and is itself the object of severe biblical censure. The chief priests demanded that Jesus be condemned because they were envious of him (Mark 15:10). In the long list of wicked acts by which Paul described the conduct of the reprobate, envy comes directly before murder (Rom. 1:29).

In search of an outlet envy may strike at those who are envied in an effort to destroy their superiority. This is the action of *ressentiment,* as we saw in the preceding chapter. On the other hand envy may act in a more straightforward, less devious, way by simply striving to take what it desires from those it envies. In most cases, this action is associated with the idolatry of mammon, and it accomplishes its end by practicing one of many forms of theft. That is why the command "You shall not steal" (Ex. 20:15) is not only an ethical injunction but also a warning against practicing the idolatry of mammon.

Stealing calls to mind such felonies as robbery, extortion, and burglary. People do not commonly realize that it has more subtle and respectable forms. We may understand this better if we consider why money is useful for the conduct of economic affairs. The shoemaker accepts money in exchange for his product, even though he has no direct use for it, because he knows that it can be exchanged for articles he values. Money serves him as a medium of exchange and thus, although it is perfectly useless as a commodity, permits him to transcend the barter system and to engage in a specialized economic function. Secondly, it serves as a store of value, permitting the shoemaker to save rather than consume, and so accumulate capital for investment. Without capital investment there can be no prosperity, a fact that is true of all economic systems. To steal from the shoemaker the fruit of his labor, one can take his product or the money he has received for it. Or else one can so tamper with the monetary system that the money will not serve to purchase economic goods equivalent to the product the shoemaker provides. Outright stealing is widely recognized for what it is, but the economic crime that accomplishes the same thing through debasing the money is not. Yet the motive and the effect are the same.

The Alchemist as Thief

Alchemy, which is usually considered to be a bizarre scientific error, is really an attempt to commit the kind of economic crime that takes wealth from the shoemaker, and all of society's workers, and puts it in the alchemist's hands. It gives the illusion of creating wealth where none existed before. But all it actually does is redistribute the wealth that is already present in the world. The alchemist, with his newly created gold, is able to buy the production of his fellow citizens that otherwise would go to other purchasers. He has increased the supply of money in the world but not of the things that money buys. If he is a surreptitious experimenter working in a basement laboratory, his actions will not be noticed. The only effect they will have on others is to increase prices by an insignificant amount. The effective demand for the products he buys is increased, because of the additional gold, while the supply is not. The successful alchemist is not a harmless experimenter or crank; the relatively small harm he does is a function of the small scale of his operations. He is a thief who has transferred wealth from others to himself while providing nothing of primary value in return.

Why do we say that the alchemist provided nothing in return for his absorption of a part of the world's production when he created and provided a quantity of gold that the world would not otherwise have? The reason is that a medium of exchange does not have intrinsic utility, and creating more of it does not add to the store of the world's wealth; only the production of houses, wheat, and wool does that. Gold's value consists in the willingness of people to accept it for those items. It is a rationing device for the distribution of scarce articles of real wealth. Like all media of exchange it keeps its utility unimpaired only as long as it remains scarce. The alchemist accomplishes his immediate purpose of commanding the market to deliver its products to him, but his success is sustainable only as long as his formula succeeds while his rivals' fail. If all would-be alchemists should discover the correct formula, the world would be flooded with gold. Being no longer scarce it could not serve to ration scarce goods, and therefore would lose its monetary worth. The world would have to devise a substitute for it or else resort to a barter system. A gold supply augmented only by the laborious processes of digging and refining could not destroy the monetary system in that way.

Inflation

Counterfeiting is the modern equivalent of alchemy. When gold and silver were the only money, technology could not meet the challenge of imitating it. But when paper was given the power to command economic goods, people could mimic the official press with the unofficial one. This modern form of theft, like all others, comes from envying the possessions of other people and the coveting that impels one to obtain them. To understand the modern American economic system, as well as that of other Western nations, we must consider how alchemy has been brought up to date. Whether in the form of changing base metal to precious metal, or of counterfeiting government banknotes on clandestine presses, this process, like all theft, transfers purchasing power from its real owners to other people. It does so simply by inflating the supply of money. This is the original economic meaning of "inflation" before it was distorted to signify a general increase in prices. When we understand that there is no *economic* difference between flooding the nation with money from counterfeiters' presses and doing the same thing with money from the official press, then we begin to comprehend the nature of modern inflations.

Inflation is an economic trauma that leads people to ignore its obvious causes in order to place the blame elsewhere. During the inflation that devastated Germany after World War I, successive governments, the central bank, and the preponderance of economists, official spokesmen, and journalists attributed the difficulty to the fact that the balance of payments was in deficit.[1] John Kenneth Galbraith has been saying for many years, in the face of considerable evidence to the contrary, that firms operating in concentrated industries subvert the market by banding together to administer prices and are therefore unconstrained by market forces. A British politician, serving as chairman of the National Board for Prices and Incomes, writes that the main cause of rising prices is the increase in wage costs at a faster rate than the increase in productivity.[2] More recently, American politicians have blamed the international oil cartel for the high rate of price increases in the United States.

The recent emergence into prominence of the monetarist school of economics has brought back into public discussion the truth about rising price levels that earlier economists and historians knew perfectly well: rising prices result from increases in the supply of money without corresponding increases in the supply of goods for it to purchase. The additional money is used to bid for scarce economic resources, forcing prices to rise correspondingly. Legal tender laws make it illegal to have substitute currencies, and the fact that the official currency is considered valid solely on the basis of government declaration has caused it to be called "fiat money." The chief advantage of this for the government is that it may pay its debts and further the ambitions of its leaders by means of a printing press.

This modern version of alchemy is what Ludwig von Mises used to call "the philosophy of stones into bread," referring to the temptation of Jesus. That is the alchemist's trick of creating something of value without work. Whether the wizard mutters incantations, mixes formulas, or runs printing presses, he attempts to produce bread without bothering to plow, sow, reap, grind, and bake. He tries to create value *ex nihilo* and imitate the creative power of God. What he really accomplishes is the taking of someone else's bread.

In the ancient world, before the invention of coinage, there were two ways in which purchasing power could be manufactured fraudulently, and the Old Testament prophets sharply denounced both of them. Gold and silver were the media of exchange, and people used them by weighing on scales the amount that buyer and seller had agreed upon. Isaiah denounced the Judeans for mixing impurities in their silver (and for wa-

---

[1]Constantino Bresciani-Turroni, *The Economics of Inflation: A Study of Currency Depreciation in Post-War Germany*, trans. Millicent E. Sayers (London: George Allen and Unwin, 1937 [1931]), p. 42.

[2]Aubrey Jones, *The New Inflation* (London: Andre Deutsch, 1973), p. 30.

tering their wine), defrauding the people with whom they dealt (Is. 1:22).[3] The other monetary fraud was the use of either false weights or rigged scales to apportion the price. There was to be no acquittal, said the prophet, for "the man with wicked scales and with a bag of deceitful weights" (Mic. 6:11; Prov. 20:23).

The advent of coins in Asia Minor in the seventh century B.C. should have provided relief from those two frauds because the recipient of a coin knew exactly the weight and fineness of the metal that comprised it. Unfortunately, that was not to be. Photographs of ancient coins reproduced in modern textbooks invariably show them to be out of round. The shaving of coins for their metal content was endemic in the ancient world, and was simply another method of theft.

But the weight of metal was not as great a problem as its fineness, which was dependent entirely on the trustworthiness of the issuer of the coinage. Late in the fifth century B.C., Athens, reeling under the financial strain of the Peloponnesian War, replaced its silver coins with coins of bronze plated with silver. That was the start of a plague that persisted throughout antiquity. In the late Roman principate, debasing the coinage became the measure of decline. The wars, building programs, subsidies, doles, and a vast expansion of the military and civil bureaucracies were more than Septimus Severus could pay for in the early third century. He depreciated the silver content of the coinage so that he was provided with an additional 20 percent of spending money. (He also confiscated the wealth of his political enemies, which was only a more visible form of theft.) In the middle of the century Gallienus reduced the silver content of the Antoninianus to 2 percent; the rest was copper.

M. I. Rostovtzeff described the process of wholesale depreciation as a break with the ancient Romans' custom of using real money with a worth corresponding to the weight and purity of the metal, in favor of "a new system of fiduciary money, which had almost no real value at all and was only accepted and circulated because of its recognition by the state." The flood of fiduciary or fiat money sent prices soaring. During most of the first two centuries A.D. the price of wheat remained stable at eight drachmae for each *artaba*. In the first half of the third century the price fluctuated between twelve and twenty drachmae. By the reign of Diocletian in the late third century the price had reached 120,000 drachmae. The issue of depreciated coinage was accompanied by wild specu-

---

[3]For an exposition of this point see Gary North, *An Introduction to Christian Economics* (Nutley, N.J.: Craig Press, 1973), pp. 4–6.

lation, and worked serious hardship, at times making it impossible to buy necessities.[4]

Of course, recalling the coinage and reminting it of cheaper metals in order to increase the quantity is very difficult compared with the modern process. Modern fiduciary money, given monopoly status by legal tender laws, is depreciated by printing ever more of it. Disastrous experiences from this practice are found in the histories of most countries; especially bad were the French inflations of the eighteenth century and the German inflations in the twentieth. The United States had a serious inflation at the time of the Revolution and again during the Civil War. Theodore White recalls his early journalistic career in China during the 1930s when Western bankers taught the Chinese how to pay their debts by printing money. This the Chinese government learned to do with enthusiasm, and the value of the money fell to nothing. "It was like teaching an adolescent how to shoot heroin."[5]

The Role of Banking in the Inflationary Process

Even the printing press has proved incapable of supplying sufficient currency to feed the voracious appetite of modern inflations. The great German inflation after World War I, made infamous by stories of wheelbarrows full of money required to buy a few groceries, saw currency being printed on one side only, the presses working night and day, with ever more zeros added to the nominal value of banknotes. Today the monetary system makes such difficulties unnecessary. Of the basic money supply in the United States, consisting of checking accounts and currency in the hands of the public, less than 30 percent is in the form of currency.[6] If all money is considered, including savings accounts and certificates of deposit, the percentage held in the form of currency is much smaller. Most money now exists in the form of computer entries only.

In modern states, the money supply is regulated by central banks, such as the Federal Reserve System in the United States. The System has in its possession large quantities of debt instruments—bills, notes, and bonds—of the U.S. Treasury. When the government spends more

---

[4]M.I. Rostovtzeff, *The Social and Economic History of the Roman Empire*, 2nd ed., 2 vols. (Oxford: Clarendon, 1957 [1926]), vol. 1, pp. 470-72.

[5]Theodore H. White, *In Search of History: A Personal Adventure* (New York: Harper and Row, 1978), p. 75.

[6]Computed from information supplied by the Federal Reserve Bank of St. Louis, *U.S. Financial Data,* Nov. 19, 1982, pp. 4f.

than it collects in taxes, the Treasury sells this debt to the public to raise the necessary cash for it to continue its operations. Should the public decline to lend sufficient money to the Treasury, the Federal Reserve buys the remaining securities and credits the Treasury's account on its own ledgers; that money is then available for the Treasury to spend. Where does the Federal Reserve obtain the money to buy the Treasury debt? It creates it. The dollars that the System pays to the Treasury in return for the debt instruments come into existence with that transaction, and are available to the state, and then to its suppliers, to compete with the dollars that others spend in the marketplace. The technical term for this monetary inflation is "monetizing the debt."

The Federal Reserve is charged with the task of regulating the quantity of money in circulation in accordance with the government's economic policy. It does this through the promulgation of regulations that control how commercial banks conduct their business and also through what it calls *open market operations*. When the System desires to reduce the money in circulation, it sells Treasury securities from its own account to commercial banks and collects from the banks by debiting their accounts at the Federal Reserve. If it wishes to increase the money supply, it buys Treasury securities from the banks and pays for them by crediting their accounts. That new money in the reserves of the commercial banks is part of what is known as the monetary base—also called by some economists "high-powered money" because of its capability of being multiplied. Subject to reserve requirements that the System changes periodically, commercial banks make loans against their accounts at the Federal Reserve. Those funds in turn are placed in other accounts where they form the basis for further loans. That process is repeated through numerous stages. With a fifteen percent reserve requirement, every newly created dollar the Federal Reserve places in circulation through open market operations can become almost seven dollars in the hands of the public.[7]

When those newly created dollars enter the marketplace, they have the same effect as the debased silver coins that Gallienus loosed on the Mediterranean world in the third century and the American continentals and French *assignats* that came from eighteenth century printing

---

[7]The process summarized here can be studied in any economics textbook. A convenient explanation is in the free publication distributed by the Federal Reserve Bank of Chicago, *Modern Money Mechanics: A Workbook on Deposits, Currency and Bank Reserves*, rev. ed., 1968.

presses. They compete for a relatively static supply of economic goods, forcing prices denominated in the inflated monetary units to rise. The price rise is a function of the increase in monetary units in relation to the supply of economic goods.

In the later stages of an inflation, prices rise much faster than the money supply. This happens because people realize that holding on to the currency even a short time entails loss of purchasing power. Therefore they spend it as soon as they get it. Economists call this a rise in the velocity of money. Since it is changing hands so rapidly, a given quantity of money can do the work of a much greater quantity at a lower velocity. With the velocity exercising more effect than the quantity of money, there is nothing the state can do to slow down the rate of price increases. At this stage, the inflation is essentially out of control, as people frantically get rid of their money in exchange for almost anything. Moreover, for the government to summon the will to end the inflation is virtually impossible. The delay between levying taxes and spending the money means that the tax collecting mechanism is rendered ineffective, and the government is impoverished. For it to go on at all, it must continue to print money.

Politics and Inflation

John Maynard Keynes is usually thought of as the architect of modern inflationary policies designed to prevent economic deflations, but before his depression-era work he had made more clear than anybody else, perhaps, why governments embark on inflationary policies. They have discovered what the Roman emperors who debased the coinage knew: such policies are profitable to governments. Keynes asked us to imagine a government that increases the stock of money from nine million to twelve million currency notes without other conditions being changed. In taking this step, it has transferred from the public to itself an amount of resources equal to three million currency notes "just as successfully as if it had raised this sum in taxation." Who paid the inflation tax? Those who hold the original nine million notes, because each of those notes will purchase 25 percent less than before the inflation. The inflation of currency means its depreciation in value. "The burden of the tax is well spread, cannot be evaded, costs nothing to collect, and falls, in a rough sort of way, in proportion to the wealth of the victim. No wonder its superficial advantages have attracted Ministers of Finance." That is why, said Keynes, the currency notes of a country that is inflating its money supply are the equivalent of income tax receipts of a country that has honest money.[8]

Governments that tax incomes using progressive scales—most modern governments that is—rely on inflation to elevate taxpayers into higher income brackets, and so increase revenues, even when their real income does not rise. Officials in the U.S. Office of Management and Budget frankly projected in 1979 that budget deficits would decline in the next two years just because of this phenomenon. That same year an advisor to the mayor of New York City credited inflation with saving the city's politicians from financial disaster. "The real threat to the city's budgetary stability for the next three to five years," he wrote, "lies in the risk that the rate of inflation will be brought under control."

The progressive income tax is only one reason government profits from inflation. The other is the fact that all debtors benefit from currency depreciation, and in modern societies, government is the chief debtor. Borrowing valuable dollars and returning them after they have lost much of their value benefits the debtor at the expense of the creditor. Inflation ruins creditors. That is enough in itself to commend it to those who foster *ressentiment* politics.

Inflation as Redistribution

If the state were the only beneficiary of inflation, it could not be continued for long. The standard work on the catastrophic German inflation of the early 1920s tells of "a vast net of interests vested in the maintenance and continuation of the depreciation . . . and which, therefore, are assiduously opposed to the return of normal monetary conditions."[9] Some humanitarian social theorists conclude that the poor are not hurt as badly as others by inflation and therefore think it is benign.[10] An entire nation can cheat other nations by inflating, if its currency is the generally accepted medium of world trade. A senior officer of a major New York bank testified before Congress in 1978 that, contrary to common belief, the United States was able to import OPEC oil without paying fair value for it. Rather than having to pay for oil imports by reducing its

---

[8]John Maynard Keynes, *Monetary Reform* (New York: Harcourt, Brace, 1924), pp. 47, 63, 69.

[9]Bresciani-Turroni, *Economics of Inflation,* p. 104.

[10]See, for example, Robinson G. Hollister and John L. Palmer, "The Impact of Inflation on the Poor," *Redistribution to the Rich and the Poor: The Grants Economics of Income Redistribution,* eds. Kenneth E. Boulding and Martin Pfaff (Belmont, Calif: Wadsworth, 1972), pp. 269f.

consumption of other products, as other nations do, "the United States has simply financed its trade deficits, in effect, by printing dollars which were transferred to the rest of the world." He made it clear that domestic politics were responsible for this financial trickery. "The domestic money supply has been permitted to expand so as to assure that the rise in personal income would be more than adequate to offset the income transfer effect of higher oil prices." French President Charles de Gaulle continually complained of American economic domination through the power to issue the world's major reserve currency.[11]

By far the most important reason for inflation is the ancient one that politicians benefit from laws that cancel debts. When Solon became archon of Athens late in the sixth century B.C., he consolidated his power by giving in to the cry for the cancellation of debts. Catiline, a nobleman with fortune dissipated, tried to gather Rome's political power into his own hands in 63 B.C. with the same promise. Keynes believed that along with the propensity of governments to spend more than they have, the main driving force of inflation is "the superior political influence of the debtor class." Barry Bosworth, in the aftermath of his resignation as director of the Federal Council on Wage and Price Stability late in 1979, said that the typical middle class family buys a house with no intention of paying for it because of the effect of inflation. "They are, in effect, betting for inflation. They have a vested interest in inflation." Bruce Gardner, an agricultural economist at Texas A & M University, has concluded that a sudden decline in inflation could devastate the financial position of farmers, who are heavily mortgaged because of land-buying for expansion.

The debt forgiveness that makes inflation attractive to borrowers has another effect. Every debt that appears as a liability on one person's balance sheet appears as an asset on another's. The inflationary act that wipes out one's debt, at the same time destroys the other's wealth. In this way it transfers wealth from one to the other. Inflation is a process of redistribution. With personal and corporate debt setting new records each month during the inflationary cycles of the economy, the built-in constituency that demands the advantages of inflation grows stronger. A few years ago banks began experimenting cautiously with car loans over a four-year period. Now there are five-year loans. Debt leverage is available in almost every kind of investment. This means that reducing

---

[11]The argument may be followed best by reading de Gaulle's senior economic advisor, Jacques Rueff, *The Monetary Sin of the West,* trans. Roger Glemet (New York: Macmillan, 1972).

inflation will hurt ever more people who do not want to pay for what they have. It becomes harder all the time to stop inflation. People demand an end to higher prices, but at the same time they want inflation's advantages. They need a flood of cheap and ever-cheapening dollars with which to satisfy their creditors and thereby enrich themselves at their creditors' expense. Andrew Dickson White, founding president of Cornell University and economic historian, discovered the same phenomenon in revolutionary France: "The outgrowth was a vast debtor class in the nation, directly interested in the depreciation of the currency in which they were to repay their debts . . . . Before long, the debtor class became a powerful body extending through all ranks of society."[12]

The creditors are those with savings accounts, life insurance policies, annuities, pension plans, certificates of deposit, and government and corporate bonds. Millions of retired people live on the proceeds of such investments and are in the process of being consigned to a penury from which only death will remove them. They are victims of the policies of their government. The middle class is the one that saves, and it is the middle class that is wiped out in typical inflations, doing incalculable harm not only to them but to the whole society.

The Consequences of Inflation

Inflation has both moral and economic consequences. It discredits whatever economic system it is part of because it removes any perception of justice that might otherwise be present. Instead of rewarding enterprise and punishing indolence, it "bestows affluence here and embarrassment there," as Keynes put it, "and redistributes Fortune's favors so as to frustrate design and disappoint expectations." Since it permits the accumulation of profit without the need for productive effort, inflation discredits enterprise. Wealth is obtained by plunging into debt, using borrowed money to buy commodities of real value that tend to rise in value at a rate faster than the currency is depreciating. People thus receive wealth without producing anything of value.

Popular governments habitually justify inflation on the grounds that it brings prosperity. Mirabeau told the French that, if they would permit the issue of paper money, the disasters that occurred in the earlier inflation of the eighteenth century would not return. This time the paper

[12]Andrew Dickson White, *Fiat Money Inflation in France* (Irvington-On-Hudson, N. Y.: Foundation for Economic Education, 1959 [1912]), p. 51; for an excellent analysis of the role of debt see Robert Lee, *Faith and the Prospects of Economic Collapse* (Atlanta: John Knox, 1981), especially ch. 3.

would bring wealth with it. After the *assignats* began flooding the markets, the increased economic activity gave the feeling of prosperity. But each injection of fresh currency produced a shorter period of euphoria before the inevitable letdown set in. Andrew Dickson White compared the inflationary binges to the draughts of a drunkard, requiring ever more alcohol and producing shorter highs and more prolonged lows. So deceptive was the early part of the German inflation in that respect that foreigners were envious of what they thought was the prosperity in Germany.

In 1978, representatives of the leading economic nations of the West, meeting as the Organization for Economic Cooperation and Development (OECD), radically changed their recommendations for dealing with the growing stagnation. After many years of advocating faster monetary growth, as the economic orthodoxy had dictated, the OECD now said that economic growth ''cannot be achieved simply by injections of additional purchasing power.'' This change has had no effect on policies of the organization's member states. It was, nevertheless, evidence that the bankruptcy of the current policy was at last becoming apparent to establishment economists.

Figures compiled by the Tax Foundation show that inflationary policies have also failed for families. The average U.S. family of four earned $18,467 in 1979, 66 percent more than in 1972. During that period, however, prices increased 75 percent, federal income taxes 82 percent, and social security taxes 142 percent. The family's purchasing power therefore declined by 8 percent.

With productive work and investment yielding unsatisfactory returns, people turn their efforts and their capital elsewhere. Gambling and speculation become more attractive. There is little doubt that the spread of gambling in Britain and the United States in recent years is part of the complex of events related to inflation. In Germany, as the old wealth tied to productive enterprise was destroyed, new fortunes were made by speculators. Slowly, ordinary people learn about havens that protect them from the inflation tax. A survey in late 1979 by R. H. Bruskin Associates found that 5 percent of American households had investments in commodities, 2 percent in gold, and 3 percent in silver. Surprisingly, one percent of households earning less than $10,000 per year had switched some of their assets to silver coins. All those inflation hedges make sense in an economy that destroys savings, but they do not provide the investments needed to increase the productive capacity of the nation. Stashing silver coins in a mattress may help the family protect its reserves, but it does nothing to help produce food, clothing, and other products. With the capital of the nation increasingly being used for unproductive purposes, the general level of prosperity is bound to decline. Bresciani-Turroni concluded from the German inflation that this decline in productive investment exacerbates the price increases by reducing the supply of products for the increased amount of currency to purchase. This combines with the increasing velocity of the money to give a frenzied appearance to the activity of the markets.

Thus saving and investing are proved to be foolish in an inflationary environment. Gambling and speculating seem more sensible. And spending before prices rise, preferably on credit, is a way to beat inflation. Observing all this during the massive Chinese inflation, Theodore White called it "the haunting pestilence of the middle classes," ruining those "who try to plan, to save, to be prudent," obliterating all loyalties, "denying all effort except to survive."

A society that inflates its currency tampers with a moral value. If the economic system lacks the basic honesty that permits economic transactions to reward both seller and buyer, lender and borrower, there can be no sense of justice. It seems right then to seek advantage at the expense of others. Henry Wallich, a member of the Federal Reserve Board, which has proved itself incapable of providing honest money, recently said that prices expressed in dollars no longer mean what they say. "Inflation is like a country where nobody speaks the truth." He compared the use of the inflating dollar with the making of contracts in which the measures of quantity frequently shrink. The Hebrew prophets denounced those changeable weights and measures as a form of oppression that merited judgment. Yet the title of the Federal Reserve Act reads, in part, "to furnish an elastic currency." Only an anthropology that borrows the Enlightenment myth of human perfectibility would trust people with the power of an elastic currency or changeable weights and measures.

Milton Friedman and Anna Schwartz have described the modern monetary system as a useful fiction: useful because there is great value in having a common money; a fiction because it rests on nothing more than the promise of responsibility by those who are the source of the fiction—government officials. And they are the ones who have the incentive to inflate the currency for their own benefit.[13]

But it is an error to think that venal officials simply take advantage of a

---

[13]Milton Friedman and Anna Jacobson Schwartz, *A Monetary History of the United States* (Princeton: Princeton Univ. Press, 1963), p. 696.

helpless public. The willingness of government officials to buy support from voters with printing press money cooperates with the willingness of the citizens to profit from it. Those dishonesties combine to foster a moral climate in which other excesses take place. A cheapening currency requires higher interest rates to provide incentives for lenders. In his monumental history of interest rates, Sidney Homer agreed with the Austrian economist Eugen Böhm von Bawerk's conclusion that the cultural level of a nation correlates inversely with its interest rates. The higher the moral and intellectual strength, the lower the interest rate and the greater the financial strength.[14] The inflation in revolutionary France was accompanied by rampant gambling and speculation, the abandonment of thrift, a contempt for simplicity in living and for work, a demand for luxury, and the prevalence of corruption and cynicism. With astonishing frankness for a government official, Alfred Kahn said when beginning his new job as President Carter's anti-inflation czar in late 1978: "Inflation is a symptom and a reflection of a society that is, in some degree, in a state of dissolution—one in which the social limitations, the bounds that an orderly society has to accept, in large measure voluntarily, on individual action, are in the process of weakening." As George Lukacs put it: "The inflation of society ran ahead of the inflation of money."[15] The moral state-of-affairs gives rise to the policy.

Inflation is both a cause and effect of moral decline. The citizens like it because they perceive that it gives them something for nothing. Like many of the policies of the modern social democracies, it transfers wealth from some people to others. People will tolerate increasing prices because their paychecks seem to increase apace. The value of their houses and other hard assets goes up, while their load of debt becomes less burdensome. The benefits they receive are visible—the state makes certain of that, since if they were not visible nobody in the state apparatus could profit by providing them—while the costs are as invisible as political and bureaucratic genius can make them. As long as people think they are advancing economically, the pressures to continue inflating outweigh those for stopping. When a society becomes pragmatic, the moral considerations seem less important than the economic ones.

Envy and Economics

Economists and government spokesmen habitually consider eco-

---

[14]Sidney Homer, *A History of Interest Rates,* 2nd ed. (New Brunswick, N.J.: Rutgers Univ. Press, 1977), pp. 3f.

[15]George P. Lukacs, *The Passing of the Modern Age* (New York: Harper and Row, 1970), p. 87.

nomic problems solely in technical and political terms, making serious errors because they do not take adequate notice of the moral elements. Charles Curran, observing the technical debates about inflation, concluded that they resembled a dispute between doctors concerning a patient who did not exist. Their basic mistake lay in discussing inflation without considering the role that envy plays in producing it. Curran said in 1957 that "if the politics of envy triumph they will pretty certainly turn [England] into an impoverished co-operative ant-hill, with no room for differential abilities to flourish."[16] Helmut Schoeck, observing the conduct of economic affairs in the modern social democracies, calls this "the age of envy." By that he means that fewer people than ever are ashamed of being envious, apparently believing that the fact of their envy is proof that social injustice has been done. "Suddenly it has become possible to say, without loss of public credibility and trust, 'I envy you. Give me what you've got.' "[17]

Although this attitude is usually associated with ideologies of the left, it is fully compatible with those on the right. The Nazi party platform included such items as a limitation on income to one thousand marks per person and the total elimination of unearned income. Peter Drucker was approached separately in the 1930s by a wealthy German industrialist, high in the Nazi party, and by an Italian banker, one of the early supporters of Mussolini. They told him they were attempting to keep their sons out of the respective compulsory youth organizations because there they would suffer from the envy of both peers and commanders, carefully cultivated by the authorities. This envy was not invented by those repressive regimes, but it was there for them to exploit.[18]

It has become a common assertion that envy is fostered by inequality and can be ended by equalitarian redistribution. British economist E. J. Mishan believes that feelings of deprivation that cause envy will be eliminated in the process of equalization, and that the progressive income tax is the best way to accomplish that task. "Ideally . . . the tax should suffice to cover all the initial and subsequent claims necessary to placate everybody in the lower-income groups, and the stronger is this envy of others, the heavier must be the tax." One of the most influential of eco-

---

[16]Charles Curran, "The Politics of Envy," *The Spectator,* December 6, 1957, pp. 780f. Earlier, Dorothy Sayers, detective novelist and essayist, had written that England had entered a "squirrel-cage of economic confusion . . . by acquiescing in a social system based upon Envy and Avarice." *Creed or Chaos* (New York: Harcourt, Brace, 1949), p. 46.

[17]Helmut Schoeck, *Envy: A Theory of Social Behavior,* trans. Michael Glenny and Betty Ross (London: Secker and Warburg, 1969), p. 148.

[18]Peter Drucker, *The End of Economic Man* (London: Heinemann, 1939), pp. 131f.

nomists in the past generation, Abba P. Lerner, also wished to tailor social policy to meet the demands of envy, which he called "the canalizing of man's emulatory instincts in the accumulation of wealth and the spending of income."[19]

Those views are erroneous not only in their elevation of a monstrous evil to a position of normative judgment but also in their ignorance of the nature of that evil. Envy cannot be assuaged any more than cancer can be; they are both pathologies whose very being requires expansion to their neighbors' territory. There is no fence that will ever be respected, no limitation that will be recognized as legitimate, no sense of proportion or humility sufficient to smother a sense of inferiority. By its nature, envy is expansive regardless of the realities it encounters.

L. P. Hartley's satire *Facial Justice* (1960) captures the utter irrationality of this impulse. The dictator who controls society after World War III believes that only envy causes social distress and is determined to eliminate its causes. When the ordinary social and economic inequalities are expunged, it is found that envy persists; there are still such inequalities as differences in grammar and accent. This requires that language be placed into the hands of the state and rigidly controlled. But people still suffer envy's pangs in the contemplation of the physical beauty of others. There follows from this the necessity of enforced requirements for plastic surgery, in some cases to reduce and in others to enhance attractiveness. There must be no grounds for perceived superiority.[20]

Hartley's invention is a graphic presentation of the truth that envy by its nature cannot be assuaged. Its unappeasable appetite may even be sharpened by feeding it so that people become more conscious of the inequalities that always remain: a perceived difference in intelligence, in health, in personality, in the quality of relationships, in special skills, in the deportment of one's children, in the general satisfaction with life. This may explain the Tocqueville effect. The Soviet dissident Vladimir Bukovsky, observing the institutionalization of the equalitarian ideology that caters to envy, concludes that it can only lead to a bloody end. As Bukovsky describes the process, the top layer is continually expropriated by the layer below it, which is thereby itself exposed to despoliation.

[19]E. J. Mishan, "A Survey of Welfare Economics, 1939–1959," *The Economic Journal* (London), vol. 70, June 1960, pp. 247f., quoted in Schoeck, *Envy*, p. 30; Abba P. Lerner, *The Economics of Control* (New York: Macmillan, 1944), p. 41. Lerner acknowledged that in catering to "emulatory instincts," what people call *needs* are greatly exaggerated.

[20]Schoeck, *Envy*, pp. 150–54.

"Is it really surprising," he asks, "that whenever you get striving for equality and fraternity, the guillotine appears on the scene?"[21]

One of the most influential recent works in ethical theory, by Harvard philosopher John Rawls, is an elaborate philosophical brief for equalitarian policy. His thesis, however, is entirely dependent on the "special assumption" that rational people do not suffer from envy. One reason this assumption seems reasonable to him is the fact that envy has a deleterious effect on the entire social environment, and therefore is collectively disadvantageous.[22] Herman Kahn and his colleagues at the Hudson Institute have a similar perspective. In their optimistic refutation of the neo-Malthusianism of the Club of Rome, they predict that after affluence spreads throughout the world the national economies will reach a steady-state posture, thus minimizing environmental degradation. This happy turn of events will take place because people will say "enough is enough."[23]

Many of the Austrian school economists—Friedrich Hayek, Ludwig von Mises, and Murray Rothbard, for example—whose work in explaining the inflationary policies of modern states has been so valuable, make the same Enlightenment mistake, supposing that a technical solution, such as the return to the gold standard, will eliminate the evils they have identified. Since they think the environment caused the evil, they expect it to be uprooted by a change of the environment. Their conclusions are exactly the opposite of the equalitarians', but their basic assumption is the same.

The Tenth Commandment is based on a far wiser understanding of human nature because it recognizes that the covetousness that demands what its neighbor possesses is a personal failure that affects the environment, exactly the opposite of the Enlightenment view. And in saying, "you shall not covet your neighbor's wife . . . or anything that is your neighbor's" (Ex. 20:17), it shows that the field for envy is far wider than the constricted vision of modern materialism understands.

---

[21]Vladimir Bukovsky, *To Build a Castle: My Life as a Dissenter*, trans. Michael Scammell (New York: Viking, 1978), pp. 106f.

[22]John Rawls, *A Theory of Justice* (Cambridge: Harvard Univ. Press, 1971), pp. 143f. Robert Nozick, who does not agree with Rawls's work, nevertheless describes it in these words: "It is a fountain of illuminating ideas, integrated together into a lovely whole. Political philosophers now must either work within Rawls' theory or explain why not." Robert Nozick, *Anarchy, State, and Utopia* (New York: Basic Books, 1974), p. 183.

[23]Herman Kahn, William Brown, and Leon Martel, *The Next Two Hundred Years: A Scenario for America and the World* (New York: William Morrow, 1976), pp. 49f.

Morality and Economics

The effect of such humanist views is to separate the conduct of public institutions from the moral state of the people who control them. Daniel Bell, for example, in trying to salvage something from the remains of classic liberalism while avoiding the ill effects of materialism, arrives at an indigestible amalgam that he calls the "public household." Why was this necessary? Because, says Bell, bourgeois society dropped the Protestant ethic. Since "only the hedonism remained . . . the capitalist system lost its transcendental ethic," and therefore its legitimacy.[24] But if the hedonism remains in the place once occupied by the Protestant ethic, it is bound to infect the public household or any other system one uses to replace capitalism. What, then, is gained? Where can the legitimacy of a successor system be found when the society is consumed with hedonism and lacks that transcendental ethic? Bell seeks to expunge the effects of moral failure by the legislative fiat that creates a new system. This is only another version of the Enlightenment delusion. In an earlier work he had shown that such phenomena as the Tocqueville effect and the growth of *ressentiment* were causing social strife, but he did not then claim that a technical fix could solve the problem.[25]

Avarice and envy do not come from a system; they are put into the system and change it. Conceptions that blame systems for the failures of people confuse cause and effect. Peter Drucker, who was forced out of Austria by the advance of Hitler's forces, has called it a contradiction to ascribe anti-Catholic or anti-Semitic measures to the pressure of governments on the unwilling masses. He does not believe it possible for totalitarian regimes to act against the will of a people determined to oppose them. Similarly, Aleksandr Solzhenitsyn has refused to absolve the Russian people, including himself, from the crimes that occurred under Stalin (or those that still occur). Resistance has always been possible, he says, and with enough participants, may be effective. It is even more clear that the citizens in democracies cannot be absolved from the crimes and stupidities of their leaders. There is no refuge in the cry that the system is responsible.[26]

---

[24]Daniel Bell, *The Cultural Contradictions of Capitalism* (New York: Basic Books, 1976), p. 21.

[25]Daniel Bell, *The Coming of Post-Industrial Society: A Venture in Social Forecasting* (New York: Basic Books, 1973), *passim.*

[26]Drucker, *End of Economic Man*, p. 205; Aleksandr I. Solzhenitsyn, *The Gulag Archipelago, 1918-1956: An Experiment in Literary Investigation*, trans. Thomas P. Whitney (New York: Harper and Row, 1973), vol. 1, p. 13. Solzhenitsyn concludes: "We purely and

Materialism

Bell's point about the hedonism of the dominant society is true enough, but the seeds of that development go back a long time. Materialism cannot be inferred simply from the formal shape of the economic institutions. Writing from the standpoint of English socialism, R. H. Tawney concluded that modern capitalism had become materialistic, but he acknowledged that most of capitalism's critics accepted the same assumptions "with hardly less naiveté."[27] Bertrand de Jouvenel observes the grandiose claims of both capitalism and socialism and concludes that we are expected to choose between them on the basis of which is better able to increase our level of consumption. "Nothing quite so trivial has been made into a social ideal."[28] The relative merits of capitalism and socialism as economic systems may be debated, but not on the basis of which is materialistic. Materialism is inherent in neither of them. But modern societies of both types exemplify advanced stages of the disease.

As it is commonly used, materialism is thought to signify the desire for consumer goods, the meaning that led Huxley to refer to the Sears, Roebuck catalog as the "Newest Testament." The legitimacy of such desires may be judged in part by our ability to satisfy them. All true needs—such as food, drink, and companionship—are satiable. Illegitimate wants—pride, envy, greed—are insatiable. By their nature they cannot be satisfied. In that sense materialism is the opium of the people. Enough is never enough. Greater quantities are required for satisfaction, and each increment proves inadequate the next time. That is the horror of the giant in John Bunyan and the wicked witch in C. S. Lewis who give their victims food that causes greater hunger. The idolatries

---

simply deserved everything that happened afterward." Cf. Bukovsky, *To Build a Castle*, p. 102: "Everyone was guilty: Those who did the actual killing, those who gave the orders, those who approved the results, and even those who kept silent. Everyone in this artificial society had carried out the role assigned to him, for which he had been rewarded." Also Frank H. Knight, *Freedom and Reform: Essays in Economics and Social Philosophy* (New York: Harper, 1947), p. 21: "The first business of a political leader is to keep on being a political leader, and his acts and words are to be appraised solely from the point of view of their effectiveness to that end. Rather to be criticised is the familiar habit of criticising politicians for playing good politics. This is palpably stupid. For a politician to do what the voters do not like is neither possible nor conformable to democratic ideals."

[27] R. H. Tawney, *Religion and the Rise of Capitalism* (New York: Harcourt, Brace, 1937 [1926]), p. 286.

[28] Bertrand de Jouvenel, *The Ethics of Redistribution* (Cambridge: Cambridge Univ. Press, 1951), pp. 46–8.

that promise wealth without end draw adherents as the tavern draws alcoholics. Ivan Illich calls this "the ethos of nonsatiety."[29] That is the sense in which the love of money is the root of all evils (1 Tim. 6:10).

The extent to which this has been built into the fabric of society justifies Bell's belief that the revolution of rising expectations, which has been dominant for the last twenty-five years, "is being transformed into a *revolution of rising entitlements* for the next twenty-five."[30] How does an economy produce all that is needed to satisfy a populace convinced that it is entitled to ever more resources? The common answer is economic growth. If desires are insatiable, the source needed to supply them must be infinite, with production graphs curving sharply upward ad infinitum. That leads us to what Gary North calls "the theology of the exponential curve." Such curves always collapse after their meteoric rise. He cites the calculations of the biologist Garrett Hardin who asks us to imagine the thirty pieces of silver that Judas received for betraying Jesus drawing 3 percent interest ever since that time. If they were silver dollars, there would now be more than $300,000 for every person on earth. Since that is far in excess of the real wealth on earth, the dollar wealth would be illusory.[31]

In a world of scarcity, which is the one in which we live, compound interest without end and growth without end are in the same category as entitlements without end; they are illusions. But illusions in which people place their faith take on a certain sinister reality. When they are cashed in without sufficient resources to pay everyone off, then a process of allocation must be devised to settle claims. That process often is violence.

Redistribution

The success of those who favor redistribution of wealth by the state may be judged by these figures. In 1958 transfer payments to individuals accounted for about 21 percent of the federal budget; the comparable figure for fiscal year 1981 was about 50 percent. Even growth of such magnitude is understated because the federal budget as a proportion of the total national income has also grown dramatically. This means that one of the main functions of government is taking resources from some people and giving them to others. Environmental determin-

---

[29]Ivan Illich, *Deschooling Society* (New York: Harper and Row, 1970), p. 113.

[30]Bell, *Cultural Contradictions of Capitalism,* p. 233.

[31]North, *Introduction to Christian Economics,* pp. 86–9; see also E. J. Mishan, *Growth: The Price We Pay* (London: Staples Press, 1969), p. 4 and *passim.*

ism adds its own argument to the leveling impulse of *ressentiment*. If a person is poor because society made him that way, then it is a matter of simple justice that society should idemnify him for what it has done.

More recently, the popularity of neo-Malthusian ideas has accustomed people to believe that the structure of the universe requires increasing poverty for humanity. Since this means death for those on the bottom end of the economy, it seems inhumane to refuse to redistribute resources. It need hardly be said that such arguments rest on assumptions that have serious deficiencies. Nevertheless, only such formulations can sustain the fiction that says redistribution furthers a quality called "social justice."

Kenneth Boulding calls the redistributory process the "grants economy," to distinguish it from ordinary economic activities that feature exchange, and he associates it with the doing of justice. "The car of justice, shaky and broken down as it usually is, nevertheless must ride on the road of the dynamic process of the grants economy if it is to get anywhere."[32] The assumption is that injustices are righted by the wise and benevolent hand of those who manage the grants economy, taking from the rich who unjustly have seized what should belong to others and giving to the poor who are more deserving. Yet Boulding was coeditor of another book on the same subject, entitled *Redistribution to the Rich and the Poor*. Clearly he knows something more about the subject than is conveyed by his image of the broken down car rattling down the road of the grants economy.

Redistribution to the Rich

What Boulding knows is that the redistributory process that determines who gets what is one in which the car of justice is shunted down a dead-end trail to the town dump by those who run the grants economy, while the limousine of self-interest hogs the road. Joined to the misconception that redistribution directs aid to the needy is another that sees redistribution only as the giving of cash and services. Fully as potent is the kind of government intervention that changes the rules of economic life so that some individuals and businesses are enriched at the expense of others.

Former Secretary of the Treasury William Simon has calculated that if we consider only the *increase* in federal social welfare expenditures between 1965 and 1975, and divide that by the twenty-five million people

---

[32]Kenneth E. Boulding, *The Economy of Love and Fear: A Preface to Grants Economics* (Belmont, Calif.: Wadsworth, 1973), unpaginated preface.

who were officially defined as poor in 1975, $8,000 per person would be available each year. This means an income of $32,000 for each family of four to be derived from only that increase of expenditures. Why were the benefits actually received by the poor so much less than that munificent sum? Simon believes that most of the money was, in effect, redistributed to the middle class people who administered the programs of redistribution. Using 1966 figures, Benjamin Okner of the Brookings Institution calculates that the distribution of social welfare expenditures between the poor and the nonpoor was close to fifty-fifty.[33] In 1980, Congressman Ron Paul estimated that the poor actually receive less than 20 percent of social welfare expenditures, with the remainder absorbed by administration, fraud, and waste. Robert Nozick concludes that those in charge of the redistribution process find it cheaper to buy off the middle class with public subsidies than to have them join the lower class in expropriating the upper. That is oversimplified, however, because this process does not work along simple class lines. Simon's analysis shows that the publicly employed middle class uses the redistribution process to despoil the privately employed middle class.

The schemes by which people get economic benefit at the expense of others are almost endless in variety. There are many kinds of credit assistance, for example, and it is widely considered that they are conferred at no cost. But that is not true. Credit is a valuable and scarce commodity, and when it is subsidized by loan guarantees, such as those given to veterans to help them purchase houses, or to Lockheed to bail it out of the consequences of gross mismanagement, that credit is taken away from individuals and companies who are better risks and would receive preference from lenders. Further, it stimulates demands from those deprived sectors for similar subsidies.[34]

Bernard Frieden, an economist at M.I.T., studied the process by which Marin County, north of San Francisco, induced the federal government to buy land on the seashore for a national park with a proviso against urban development. After Washington bought the land, the local government decided it was too fragile to permit its use for recreational purposes. Accordingly, the county blocked the road construction and

---

[33]Benjamin A. Okner, "Transfer Payments: Their Distribution and Role in Reducing Poverty," *Redistribution to the Rich and the Poor: The Grants Economy of Income Distribution,* Kenneth E. Boulding and Martin Pfaff, eds. (Belmont, Calif.: Wadsworth, 1972), p. 65.

[34]Murray Weidenbaum, *Government-Mandated Price Increases: A Neglected Aspect of Inflation* (Washington: American Enterprise Institute for Public Policy Research, 1975), p. 79.

recreational development that would have attracted visitors. Frieden concluded that by freezing local land development, the fourth wealthiest county in the United States had been able to charge the whole nation for the preservation of its scenery, refusing to allow outsiders to visit the land their money had bought. All along the California coast, wealthy communities have used the preservationist movement to restrict the right of others to build while, not incidentally, driving up the value of their own properties.[35]

The federal energy program contains many examples of redistributive policy masquerading as something else. The misnamed windfall profits tax (which is really an excise tax to be paid irrespective of profits) provides the vehicle by which the government, by exciting the envy of the populace, turns the general distress at high energy costs into an enormous windfall for the officials who promulgated the tax and spend the money it raises. It is not generally known that among those who pay the tax are the thousands of people on whose land the oil produced by the big companies is found. Since the tax is levied at the wellhead, and not on profits, it comes out of their pockets. Part of the benefit of the tax goes to the foreign oil cartel because the tax restricts the development of U.S. oil, raising the demand for foreign oil. This is one example of many that could be cited wherein the government buys support by placating the anger of the populace with the property of the unpopular or the weak. Such actions are invariably accompanied by moral fervor and much noise about protecting the public.

Redistribution to Business and Industry

This luxuriant variety in the garden of redistribution suggests that we must not think that it is only money and services that grow there. Beyond those simple transfers, Boulding describes a vast array of public policy measures, which he calls "implicit grants." He defines those grants as "redistributions of income or wealth that take place as a result of structural changes or manipulations in the set of prices and wages, licenses, prohibitions, opportunity or access; they are anything, in fact, that is not an explicit grant yet leads to economic redistributions." There is nothing new about those activities. Jonathan Hughes, an economist at Northwestern University, found the American economy to be full of government interventions going back to colonial times. They even predate the earliest settlements, because they were brought to the new

---

[35]Bernard J. Frieden, *The Environmental Protection Hustle* (Cambridge: M.I.T. Press, 1979), pp. 5f. and *passim*.

world from the experience of European mercantilism that Adam Smith decried so strenuously.[36] During and after the Civil War, influential businessmen profited from high tariff walls and immigration and financial policies tailored expressly for their needs, and this in the heyday of what people still call laissez-faire. The original federal minimum wage laws were supported by northern textile manufacturers who wanted protection from the competition of southern manufacturers benefiting from low-cost labor.

From the avidity with which businessmen seek to avoid having competitors, we can infer that competition is at least as distasteful to capitalists as it is to socialists. They may praise it on the lecture tour, but when it comes to questions of public policy, they seem to believe that it works well only in other industries. Tariffs are always popular with the protected industries because they reduce the threat of foreign competition. And if tariffs are reduced by negotiation, then nontariff barriers may work as well: quotas, standards, and irrelevant requirements can protect a domestic industry as well as a tariff.[37] Widespread publicity surrounding the multinational trade conferences of recent years has led many people to accept the belief that protectionism is receding. That is not so. In the United States, as in other Western countries, industry has manipulated the laws for its own benefit, including those ostensibly designed to protect consumers. Robert Bork's ground-breaking work on antitrust policy concludes, surprisingly, that some antitrust laws *curtail* competition: "During the past twenty years or so, the protectionist anticompetitive strain in the law has undergone a spectacular acceleration."[38]

Redistributive schemes favored by business are not limited to the curtailment of competition. Government expenditure provides an immediate payoff if it can be directed into the appropriate channels. Military spending is only the most obvious area in which this is true. With the

---

[36]Jonathan R. T. Hughes, *The Governmental Habit: Economic Controls from Colonial Times to the Present* (New York: Basic Books, 1977), chs. 1 and 2. Students of classical history know of innumerable instances of redistribution that are different only in detail. There were debt cancellations, confiscation and redistribution of land, grain distributions, and public circuses. The ancient politicians, like the modern ones, maintained power by buying public favor with the property of others.

[37]For the relative incentives of tariff and nontariff barriers for protection from foreign competition see Melvyn B. Krauss, *The New Protectionism: The Welfare State and International Trade* (New York: New York Univ. Press for the International Center for Economic Policy Studies, 1978), pp. 13–17.

[38]Robert H. Bork, *The Anti-Trust Paradox: A Policy at War With Itself* (New York: Basic Books, 1978), p. 7.

surge of foreign aid after World War II, the theory was advanced that wealth would come to poor countries through the building of an economic infrastructure—roads, bridges, schools, and dams—and the big U.S. firms that would get the contracts became enthusiastic advocates of this doctrine. Roadbuilding, hot lunch and milk distribution programs in schools, higher education, food stamps, public transportation, and environmental protection are only a few fields in which government expenditures are supported by business people who profit from them.

A few examples taken from recent newspaper articles suggest the range of implicit grants by which the federal government redistributes to business:

—The steel industry, aided by the unions, successfully lobbied for a trigger price mechanism by which the government restricted steel imports. This raised prices for the industry's customers and, because their costs were raised, made them more vulnerable to foreign competitors who were able to buy cheaper steel.

—Chrysler Corporation was able to survive by generating political support for federal loan guarantees, without which it could not have borrowed enough to stay in business.

—Not content with receiving the money that otherwise would have gone to more credit-worthy businesses, Chrysler demanded that the government restrict the importation of Japanese cars, which customers preferred to their own.

—Florida tomato growers continued efforts to tighten federal restrictions that already limited the importation of vine-ripened Mexican tomatoes that customers preferred to the gas-ripened Florida product.

—Major corporations induced Congress to pass special legislation that freed them from their legal difficulties with regulatory agencies.

—New oil import quotas reduced the competition that domestic energy producers would otherwise face. Similar quotas existed long before there was an energy shortage to provide justification.

—The trucking industry fought bitterly to prevent deregulation, striving to maintain the status of a cartel, protected by the Interstate Commerce Commission from the horrors of competition. Estimates of the additional cost to the public ranged as high as $15 billion per year.[39]

It is surprising to some that business and labor should cooperate in their influence on federal policy, since so much is made of their adver-

---

[39]John Semmons, "Regulation of the Truckers, by the Truckers, for the Truckers," *Reason*, March 1979, pp. 26–29; see also E. Scott Royce, "The Hauling Cartel," *Inquiry*, April 7, 1980, pp. 16–20.

sary relationship. In fact, they frequently work together for common goals. Friedrich Hayek pointed out long ago that when they do that they have no difficulty arriving at a way to divide the spoils.[40]

Far from being an inconvenience to business, massive federal intervention, long before the New Deal, was welcomed as a means for increasing profits. During World War I, Woodrow Wilson staffed the War Industries Board, which had quasi-dictatorial powers over the American economy, with corporation executives who went back to their old jobs after the war. Their new vision for the post-war economy included a system of trade associations that would coordinate planning, production, and advertising. Cooperation would be the watchword in the new economic order.

Herbert Hoover, amazingly referred to even by historians as a partisan of laissez-faire, energetically supported this conception. All through the 1920s, when he was Secretary of Commerce, Hoover advocated the idea of a powerful central state that would coordinate the efforts of business. Finding competition offensive, he had a major part in making the federal role in the nation's economic life an ideological principle. Hoover was ideally suited to play this part because his service as food czar during the war had given him a taste for power from which he never recovered. He transformed the entire food production industry of the country into a giant cartel. Like any cartel, it kept prices higher than they would have been otherwise, and Hoover dealt harshly with firms that cut prices below the prescribed minimums. The executives of the protected businesses saw the advantage of the arrangement and tried to continue it after the war in the form of business and trade associations. Franklin D. Roosevelt became president of one of the largest of the government-sponsored business associations designed to curb competition, the American Construction Council. The meeting in which he was elected to that post was chaired by Hoover himself.[41]

A corollary error to that of the supposed infatuation of big business with competition has been the idea that modern American liberalism has been a restraint on big business. There is considerable evidence to show that the New Deal and its successors have cooperated actively with

---

[40]Friedrich A. Hayek, *The Road to Serfdom* (Chicago: Univ. of Chicago Press, 1944), p. 77.

[41]Murray Rothbard, "War Collectivism in World War I," *A New History of Leviathan: Essays on the Rise of the American Corporate State,* eds. Ronald Radosh and Murray N. Rothbard (New York: Dutton, 1972), pp. 84f.,100; Eric Goldman, *Rendezvous with Destiny: A History of Modern American Reform* (New York: Vintage, 1956 [1952]), pp. 237ff., 252ff.

the goals of big business.[42] The 1978 Congressional elections provided a good illustration of that, as the political action committees (PACs) of big businesses overwhelmingly supported Democrats. The Federal Elections Commission, which monitors the PACs, reported that corporate giving to Democratic incumbents was about five times as great as to Republican challengers. Presumably they knew where their political advantage lay. With this in mind, it is no surprise that industry has captured the federal agencies that are supposed to be regulating them.

The range of government programs that subsidize the middle class is so vast that there is virtually nobody who does not believe he profits in some way from them. To cite a few examples, these include loans from the Small Business Administration, engineering projects that subsidize house-building in fragile coastal areas, land maintenance by the Bureau of Land Management, which assists livestock grazing on public lands, low-interest mortgages that are made possible by the issuance of tax-free bonds, and federal assistance that lowers the cost of higher education. Bernard Frieden calls our attention to the Bay Area Rapid Transit system in which the capital and operating costs are paid for by the residents of three counties, but the riders are mostly middle and upper class suburbanites. "The poor are paying," he concludes, "and the rich are riding."

The Political Payoff

Why do we have a political system in which people of every class and circumstance crowd up to the trough of the public treasury for their living? Bryce Harlow, advisor of presidents from the 1950s to the seventies, told an interviewer in 1976 what any politician knows. Politics is a business, he said, and not a hobby. "The bottom line is not profit and loss, it's votes. A congressman's profit is more votes than a competitor

---

[42]Radosh and Rothbard, eds., *New History of Leviathan,* p. vi; Ronald Radosh, "The Myth of the New Deal," in *Ibid.*, p. 157. Radosh and Rothbard demolish the tendentious arguments of Arthur Schlesinger, Jr., in *The Vital Center.* The confusion on this subject is often so complete that writers sometimes refute their own positions without realizing it. Here is a defense of state interventions on free markets: "Witness the fixed agricultural subsidies in the United States whose grotesque workings penalize the customer three times over. This kind of market-economy irrationality vies with the irrationality of war." Lewis Mumford, *The Transformations of Man* (New York: Harper and Brothers, 1956), p. 213. The policy Mumford attacks here is the product of the state system he is defending, and the only defense against it is the free market he finds so distasteful. Far from being irrational, it is the purposeful outcome of negotiations between legislators and agricultural producers, serving the interests of both at the expense of the public. The only irrationality is Mumford's.

can get. That puts him in the black. So whatever contributes to his getting profit in the next election instead of a deficit, which is fatal, is a motivator for him." William Simon, out of office, declared that his party was as bad in this respect as were the Democrats. Other social democratic countries have the same political forces working. When conservative governments replaced socialist predecessors in Sweden and Britain, the pattern of redistributive policies continued. The change in party fortunes tends to affect the identity of the beneficiaries and victims more than it does the level of transfers. As Thomas Sowell puts it, balancing the budget was normal until the politicians "discovered the political magic of winning votes with giveaways without losing votes with tax increases." The damage done by control mechanisms on the energy industry led University of Michigan economist Edward Mitchell to conclude that "quotas and price controls offer the political sector the benefits of a perceived lack of responsibility for price hikes and a bundle of wealth to be distributed to supporters. These are awesome forces for economic logic to overcome."

In recent studies, Edward Tufte of Yale University plotted the provision of federal benefits against the incidence of elections and found striking correlations. The money supply, for example, increases more rapidly in the two years that precede presidential elections than in the two years following. As the president sees election time approaching, he finds that the illusion of prosperity is more advisable than the restraint of credit curbs, unemployment, and recession. The rate at which real disposable income increases during years when an incumbent president runs for reelection is about double that of other years. The months before the election become the liberal hour, government checks flowing with abandon. Tufte even found that the date recipients receive the November transfer payment checks depends on whether the election is early or late. The administration apparently times the checks to arrive just before the voters depart for the polls. As Tufte says, "A bribe to the voters is, after all, a bribe to the voters."[43]

The Politics of Pressure Groups

A corollary of a generalized ethic of redistribution is the dominance of pressure groups or constituencies. The major question in such a society is what Hayek called "Who, whom?" This comes from Lenin's state-

---

[43]Edward R. Tufte, *Political Control of the Economy* (Princeton, N.J.: Princeton Univ. Press, 1978), p. 50.

ment: "Who plans whom, who directs and dominates whom, who assigns to other people their station in life, and who is to have his due allotted by others? These become necessarily the central issues to be decided solely by the supreme power." The whole purpose of joining people with the same interests in order to form pressure groups is to ensure that we become "who" and others in society become "whom." We know that a despoliation will take place, that government will give money and privileges to some at the expense of others. That means that we are in a struggle to capture the state for our benefit at the expense of our rivals. Redistribution thus ensures that society is divided into adversary groups. Because pressure groups do not appear in constitutionally based descriptions of the political process, their influence is often underrated. Joseph Schumpeter described their effect in modern democracies as "battering rams," fully as powerful as that of political parties.[44] Their predominance in a society is the clue that power has replaced justice as the principle of order.

In the redistributive government there is no such thing as impartiality. Everyone in the pressure group and everyone in politics has something to gain. The bureaucracy, too, is full of people grinding axes, usually by allying themselves with one of the pressure groups.[45] Some pressure groups even derive a substantial part of their budgets directly from federal grants.

So successful have the politicians been in coopting people into the redistributive system that it is difficult to see how it can ever be ended short of complete economic collapse. A. Gary Shilling, an economist, has tabulated the number of people dependent upon government largesse, including employees at all levels of government, private employment that depends heavily upon government spending, and recipients of transfer payments and pensions. In 1977, 53.5 percent of the population was in some way a government dependent, up from 42.3 percent in 1960. More than half the population, therefore, perceives that its economic well-being is dependent on the public treasury.

As we see below the surface of the modern political-economic system, it becomes clear that to associate redistribution with the doing of justice is a sham. The principle that determines the actions of both those who

---

[44]Joseph A. Schumpeter, *Capitalism, Socialism and Democracy*, 5th ed. (London: George Allen and Unwin, 1976), p. 382.

[45]"In fact, the agency may organize the clientele in the first place. The agency may then offer to fulfill the demand it has helped to create. Indeed, congressmen often urge administrators to make a show of their clientele." Aaron Wildavsky, *The Politics of the Budgetary Process* (Boston: Little, Brown, 1964), p. 67.

seek money and favors from the state and those who distribute them is self-interest. Justice has little to do with the process, except to serve as a cover. In his defense of a libertarian society as an alternative to both anarchy and oppression, Robert Nozick makes the Enlightenment error of assuming that people will demand a just society. It is impossible to understand the modern social democracies within the context of that assumption. In our society, people call the arrangement that meets their demands "just." When Irving Kristol, editor of *The Public Interest*, asked a number of outspoken proponents of greater equalization of income to describe for publication an income-distribution curve that was just, he could find nobody who would accept the challenge. That is an impossible task, because redistribution is determined by the principle of interest, not that of justice. Some want resources to be taken from the prosperous and given to those who are not. Others want the welfare cheats off the rolls but are happy with federal schemes that confer privileges on themselves or that restrict their competition. Justice is a stranger to all of this.

Since government produces no goods, it can distribute only what it takes from others. This process is indistinguishable from theft. When an election, or in some countries a coup, changes the identity of plunderers and plundered, yesterday's injustice becomes today's justice. In a redistributive society, the law is a thief.

The Power of the State over Economic Life

Modern idolatries of mammon rely largely on the enhancement of the power of the state in economic affairs in order to attain their ends. Along with historicist perspectives that speak of the inevitability of this development,[46] we are given arguments that purport to show the dire consequences of hesitating to give economic authority to the state. The young Arthur Schlesinger, Jr., raised the Communist bogeyman in 1949 to justify the arrogation of power by the federal government. We are to be grateful to the New Deal, he said, because without it communism would have appealed to the masses after "orthodoxy" failed to end the depression.[47] Thirty years later he wrote an article for the *Wall Street Journal* repeating the same fatuous arguments, this time in order to tout the presidential aspirations of Sen. Edward Kennedy. Now the enemy was

---

[46]See Hayek, *Road to Serfdom,* p. 43, for a description.

[47]Arthur Schlesinger, Jr., *The Vital Center: The Politics of Freedom* (Cambridge, Mass.: Riverside, 1962 [1949]).

inflation, he insisted, and once again we were to rely on state power to save us. Galbraith's position has been that executives of concentrated industries are able to administer prices through collusion, thus circumventing the restraints of competition and requiring a powerful state as a "countervailing power."[48] The most recent arguments for the expansion of state power are based on neo-Malthusian perceptions of extinction through resource exhaustion and worldwide pollution.[49]

Whatever rationale is used to justify expanding the role of the state in economic life, the inescapable outcome will be the increase of coercion. Legal scholar Ronald Dworkin says that "a more equal society is a better society even if its citizens prefer inequality." In other words, a people so foolish as to ignore what the elite say are their own interests must be forced to change. There is nothing new about the connection between equality and coercion. As Hannah Arendt has stressed, equalization of condition "has been one of the foremost concerns of despotisms and tyrannies since ancient times."[50] The tyranny of Sparta was an equalitarian one. C. Grayson Jackson, Jr., ruefully reflecting on his experience as President Nixon's chief price controller, somewhat belatedly writes of his fears that our economic system is steadily shifting away from private enterprise toward state control.[51] This turn of events is often associated exclusively with the coming to power of leftist regimes, but that is erroneous. The Fascist and Nazi regimes of the 1930s strictly controlled all decisions of economic importance—prices, production schedules, hiring, firing, investment, profits, dividends. The bureaucrats and politicians made all the decisions, but the system was still said to be capitalist because the principle of private ownership was not formally repudiated. The state took the profit, and the "owner" was left with the risk.

The question to be asked is whether the economic controls that are

[48]Galbraith's position is based largely on the work of Gardner Means, which has suffered serious damage from critics. Means published his arguments in *Pricing Power and the Public Interest: A Study Based on Steel* (New York: Harper and Brothers, 1962). For a review of the evidence see William H. Peterson, "Steel Price Administration: Myth and Reality," *Central Planning and Neo-Mercantilism*, ed. Helmut Schoeck and James W. Wiggins (Princeton, N.J.: D. Van Nostrand, 1964), pp. 155–78; for additional arguments against the administered price theory see Bell, *Post-Industrial Society*, p. 156 and Schumpeter, *Capitalism, Socialism and Democracy*, p. 84.

[49]See, for example, Jeremy Rifkin with Ted Howard, *The Emerging Order: God in the Age of Scarcity* (New York: Putnam's, 1979).

[50]Hannah Arendt, *The Origins of Totalitarianism*, new ed. (New York: Harcourt, Brace, and World, 1966), p. 322.

[51]C. Grayson Jackson, Jr., with Louis Neeb, *Confessions of a Price Controller* (Homewood, Ill.: Dow Jones-Irwin, 1974), p. 199.

always present in the totalitarianisms of left and right can, in other kinds of societies, coexist with the protection of individual freedom. Daniel Bell maintains that they can, that political liberty and economic liberty can be "sundered." He associates the acquisition of private property with bourgeois materialism and accepts Galbraith's idea that the state's possession of a piece of property is more moral than its ownership in private hands. He recognizes the potential for coercion but believes that if society retains political liberalism it will assure the individual of just rewards and also protection from coercion. Increasing the power of the state to control property, says Bell, "does not necessarily mean the expansion of the governmental economy or the administrative sector." There is considerable wishful thinking in Bell's formulation. He does not tell us why we should believe that the expanded powers of government will not be used in ways he considers illiberal. If he knows of good reasons for that belief he should inform his friend and colleague Irving Kristol, who is unable to find a single example in history "of a society that repressed the economic liberties of the individual while being solicitous of his other liberties."[52]

We do not find individual liberties respected when the state controls the economy because in that situation politics replaces economics. In other words, coercion replaces free choice. In the free economy, mutual service is the ruling principle because buyer and seller must both be satisfied or there is no transaction. There must be value given in return for value received. When politics replaces economics, people are no longer permitted to do what seems advantageous to them. Or, to put it another way, the advantage of avoiding fines or imprisonment (or execution in some parts of the world) outweighs the advantages of alternative courses of action. When people are permitted to think economically, it means freedom has been retained. When they are forced to think politically, it necessarily means, as Hayek put it, "the substitution of power from which there is no escape for a power which is always limited." A multi-millionaire who employs you has less power over you than the third secretary in a bureaucratic agency. Privately exercised power can be coercive but, barring physical force, is not exclusive or inescapable.

Even when the worst does not happen, state controls make citizens timid. Milton Friedman thinks controls mean the end of free speech because taxpayers fear reprisals by the IRS, business people worry about antitrust suits or legal actions by regulatory agencies, professors are

---

[52]Bell, *Cultural Contradictions of Capitalism*, pp. 297f. Irving Kristol, *Two Cheers for Capitalism* (New York: Basic Books, 1978), p. xi.

concerned about the renewal of government grants. Galbraith, who thinks our salvation lies in a society dominated by the state, agrees. He doubts that we will ever again see the head of the Ford Motor Company castigate the government as did the original Henry Ford.[53] Recent studies of federal financing of higher education have reached similar conclusions. Partially funded by Washington, "private" colleges and universities find their independence slipping away.[54]

Bureaucratic Domination

Assessing a system that fails to achieve most of its purported goals requires that we consider who profits in the midst of failure: the old question, *cui bono,* to whose advantage? In his disillusionment after President Nixon's price control bureaucracy broke up in failure, C. Grayson Jackson concluded that the gainers were the members of "an elitist group planning for others." Kristol popularized the phrase "the new class" to refer to the intellectuals who ride to power on the coattails of the welfare state: The lawyers, bureaucrats, and social scientists who gain nothing from private action but much from the continuation of social problems that can be said to require their ministrations. P. T. Bauer sees in the worldwide march to centralization the creation of positions of power for politicians and bureaucrats to which they could not aspire in a society without an intrusive state apparatus.[55] Sociologist Lewis Feuer surveyed "new class" people who visited the USSR in the 1920s and 1930s and found that they liked what they saw. "In practically all cases, what they saw was power and status in the possession of their own kinds of people."[56]

The nature of bureaucracy belies the old idea that it is apolitical, dependent entirely on the legislative documents brought into existence by

---

[53]John Kenneth Galbraith, *The New Industrial State* (Boston: Houghton Mifflin, 1969), p. 397.

[54]See, for example, Chester E. Finn, Jr., *Scholars, Dollars, and Bureaucrats* (Washington, D.C.: The Brookings Institution, 1978).

[55]P. T. Bauer, *Dissent on Development: Studies and Debates in Development Economics* (London: Weidenfeld and Nicolson, 1971), p. 92.

[56]Kristol comments on the same phenomenon in the West: "The simple truth is that the professional classes of our modern bureaucratized societies are engaged in a class struggle with the business community for status and power. Inevitably, this class struggle is conducted under the banner of 'equality'—a banner also raised by the bourgeoisie in *its* revolutions." *Two Cheers,* pp. 176f. We should add to Kristol's observations that the boundaries are often not that precise. It is not hard to find businessmen coopted by the bureaucrats.

the political authorities.[57] The administrative rules carried in the Federal Register are many times more voluminous than the legislation from which they derive their authority, and that reflects the truth that the interpretation and enforcement of the law carries with it enormous power. In some countries bureaucratic discretion includes the power of life and death. In the social democracies it carries the power to award economic prosperity or penury or to force people to depend on the goodwill of those who wield the power of the state. One apologist for the administrative state, Emmette Redford of the University of Texas, cautioned that, wherever possible, policy should be "self-executing," that is, without the necessity for bureaucratic discretion. But two pages later he dropped the mask and admitted that, however desirable, such an ideal solution would seldom be possible. He thus ended up a defender of bureaucratic "flexibility," which means that within very broad limits officials should do as they please.[58] Bernard Frieden has noticed that, in contrast to the old-line regulatory agencies that are captured by the major industries they are supposed to be regulating, the newer ones exercise domination. Hostile to compromise, they thrive on compulsion. That imperial mien is likely to be the exclusive style of state officials in the future.

To a large extent, the new class dominates in matters of value. Not content to claim competence only in technical matters too arcane for ordinary people, the redistributive and regulatory mechanisms insist on affecting every area of life, the elite being secure in the superiority of their values. The wishes of people expressed in the marketplace must be frustrated if the planning and control mechanisms are to make any sense. As Ernest van den Haag says, central direction makes sense only insofar as its purpose is to thwart the wishes of the citizens. For if the markets produce what people want, "trivial (sinful) things will be produced—too little education, too much beer." The political authorities and their mentors of the new class consistently and deliberately fail to say that their policies are intended to exercise their will over the masses.[59] "Who, whom," again. Two hundred years ago a group of

---

[57]Since shortly after World War II, students of bureaucracy have accepted the fact that administration and politics are inseparable. It is no longer possible to regard bureaucrats as faceless technicians, merely following the rules, as Max Weber's ideal type portrayed them. This revolution in interpretation was led by Paul Appleby, *Policy and Administration* (University, Ala.: Univ. of Alabama Press, 1949).

[58]Emmette S. Redford, *Democracy in the Administrative State* (New York: Oxford Univ. Press, 1969), pp. 185ff.

[59]Ernest van den Haag, "The Planners and the Planned," *Central Planning*, eds. Schoeck and Wiggins, pp. 21, 36.

royal subjects believed themselves to be oppressed by a king living across the ocean. Among their complaints was this one: "He has erected a multitude of new offices and has sent hither swarms of officers to harass our people and eat out their substance." Americans should reread the Declaration of Independence and consider if Thomas Jefferson would think the Revolution had accomplished much.

Public confidence that government bureaucracy could solve major problems probably hit the high water mark in the 1960s. Daniel Moynihan, who was in a position to know better, thought the econometric revolution of Keynesian theory combined with powerful computing capability had solved the problem of managing a modern industrial economy.[60] Jacques Ellul, in what is perhaps his most widely quoted book, said that while planned societies cannot be free they are nevertheless inevitable because they are the most efficient.[61]

Yet, there is scarcely a field of endeavor in which the modern centralized state has come close to achieving the avowed purpose of a major initiative without also bringing into existence destructive, usually unanticipated, side effects. Welfare, urban renewal, and macroeconomic policies are only the most visible of a long list of unacknowledged disasters. Even the Federal Reserve System, now two-thirds of a century old and almost without fundamental challenge as to its powers, has failed utterly to achieve its basic purpose. It was supposed to ensure monetary stability, but its establishment was followed by a period of instability greater than any since the Civil War and possibly than any period of American history after the Revolution.[62] Planned economies, far from being efficient, are notable for their inability to match supply and demand with anything like the effectiveness of the free market system. The Soviet economy retains what meager efficiency it has only because of an unofficial network of middlemen, called *tolkatchi,* who link buyers and sellers in a way that the planners cannot.[63] Thus, in spite of statist ideology, only a truncated and clandestine free market rescues the state system from complete breakdown.

---

[60]Daniel P. Moynihan, *Maximum Feasible Misunderstanding: Community Action in the War on Poverty* (New York: Free Press, 1969), p. 25.

[61]Jacques Ellul, *The Technological Society,* trans. John Wilkinson (New York: Knopf, 1964), p. 183. For other expressions of faith in the efficacy of state interventions see Reinhold Niebuhr, *Moral Man and Immoral Society: A Study in Ethics and Politics* (New York: Scribner's, 1952 [1932]), p. 33; John C. Bennett, *The Christian as Citizen* (London: Lutterworth, 1955), p. 42; Joseph Fletcher, *Moral Responsibility: Situation Ethics at Work* (Philadelphia: Westminster, 1967), p. 205.

[62]That is the conclusion of Friedman and Schwartz, *Monetary History,* p. 698.

[63]For an extended account of this phenomenon see Joseph S. Berliner, *Factory and Manager in the USSR* (Cambridge: Harvard Univ. Press, 1957).

It is a serious error to suppose that activities of the state are directed toward their avowed ends. *Cui bono* is no less a principle in public life than it is in private, but political realities require it to be overlaid with a covering of hypocrisy. Paul Craig Roberts's characterization of American energy policy—made before he became an official in the Reagan administration—can be made of activities throughout the government: "Once you get an energy department you are in for it, because you have a policymaking body with no interest whatsoever in abundant, reasonably priced energy." A problem solved gives an agency new difficulties justifying its existence. In the economy of the omnicompetent state, nothing succeeds like failure.

One reason the state fails to accomplish even simple tasks within its purview is that people work actively to thwart it. In recent years the cash economy, which leaves no records, has grown to what federal officials consider epidemic proportions. Robert D. Laurent, an economist at the Federal Reserve Bank of Chicago, estimates that the currency in circulation equals about $600 for each adult, which means that many people have more than $10,000 in hand. Peter Gutmann, an economist at the City University of New York, believes that the unofficial economy, which remains unreported, may be equal to one tenth of the gross national product. He thinks people participate in the underground economy because they are contemptuous of the tax and regulatory mechanisms. Robert Heilbroner, an economist who believes it proper that government should control people's behavior, complains about the failure of its policies. The trouble is that "every new policy is an intrusion that sets into motion activity designed specifically to recapture the former state of affairs by avoiding, evading, or overcoming the new policy element."[64] The increasing price of gold, for example, is a vote of no-confidence in government monetary policies. It is evidence that people have taken a "short" position against any currency in which the gold price is rising, in an attempt to escape the policies of the monetary authorities. This trait is widespread enough that economists have invented a name for it: the "rational expectations model." It explains how economic policy fails because people do everything they can to withdraw from its zone of effectiveness.

Price Controls

The futility of government economic controls could be demonstrated

---

[64]Robert L. Heilbroner, "The Missing Link(s)," *Challenge,* March–April, 1978, p. 17.

with endless examples. For illustrative purposes let us consider one of the more beguiling of these policies, price controls. This form of control dates back at least four thousand years; the Hammurabi Code had strict price ceilings on a wide variety of commodities. The best-known price control system of antiquity was the one inaugurated by Diocletian's Edict of 301. After fruitlessly issuing calls for self-restraint and denouncing the public's avarice in the midst of accelerating price increases the imperial government sent forth this draconian edict, which incorporated severe penalties, including death, for infractions of the price limitations. In the exhortations, the blaming of the populace, and the ineffectiveness of their measures, the modern controllers imitate Diocletian. They have learned nothing from history. Modern controls are issued for the same reasons as the ancient ones: they serve to hide the reason for the price increases. Diocletian's problem with rising prices came from the fact that he was depreciating the money by issuing large amounts of debased coins. Given that, prices *had* to rise. People could not comply with the law, which eventually fell into disuse after causing great hardship and many deaths.[65]

Our chief price controller during World War II, John Kenneth Galbraith, thinks the controls worked and advocates their use today. But even with the help of wartime patriotic fervor, the controls did not accomplish what their supporters expected. The price increases took concealed forms. There were deteriorations of quality and service; production was concentrated in lines in which the controlled prices were higher, causing shortages of other products; there was considerable legal and illegal evasion of the controls that did not show up in the official indices. The shortages that are inevitable during price controls were managed by long lines in front of shops or else by ration coupons. Different categories of people received differing coupon entitlements, which means that political pull was the real rationing principle.[66]

Price controls cause shortages because capital then flows into more profitable areas. Rent controls, for example, redistribute money from landlords to tenants, reducing whatever incentive there was to become a landlord. That is why jurisdictions that have rent controls, like New York City, have housing shortages. Now that such controls are spreading across the nation, as tenants use political means to remove the pressures of inflation from themselves and place them on apartment owners,

---

[65]Robert L. Schuettinger and Eamonn F. Butler, *Forty Centuries of Price Controls: How Not to Fight Inflation* (Washington, D.C.: The Heritage Foundation, 1979).

[66]Friedman and Schwartz, *Monetary History,* pp. 557–61.

we can expect a nationwide shortage of rental housing.[67] For the same reason, the United States, with incomparably more energy resources than Western Europe, has had a far more serious energy crisis. Insisting on the enforcement of artificially low prices that did not reflect the scarcity of energy—a policy of redistribution—Washington stimulated consumption and discouraged production. Our most recent flirtation with generalized price controls, President Nixon's program in the early 1970s, caused severe dislocation and considerable hardship. Yet in a 1979 study for the National Bureau of Economic Research, two Princeton University economists, Alan S. Blinder and William J. Newton, concluded that by early 1975 prices were slightly higher than they would have been without the controls.

Autonomous Officialdom

The basic assumption justifying the extension of government power over economic life is the Enlightenment conviction that people have the goodness and wisdom to control other people. Much has been made in recent years over the debates between Keynesian and monetarist economists, but this is just a family feud. Both agree that the state has the right to control economic relations. This means that politics replaces economics, and compulsion replaces freedom. That is the meaning of Ludwig von Mises' remark that the "outstanding fact of the intellectual history of the last hundred years is the struggle against economics."[68] One of the conditions of a society in which politics replaces economics is that wealth is obtained not so much from production as from pull. Robert Bork concludes that antitrust law cannot be enforced uniformly because the damage done to the economy would overwhelm it. But if the law cannot be enforced uniformly, then it cannot be enforced justly; the selectivity of its enforcement makes the law a weapon. State officials decide against whom it is to be used. That is not the kind of power that anyone can be expected to handle with justice.

Trusting officialdom with control of our economic destiny is the foundation for both tyranny and economic futility. In the midst of his early masterful explanation of the cause and effects of inflation, Keynes insisted that we make that error. He wanted us to "free ourselves from the deep distrust" of government officials in controlling monetary systems. Yet his entire book was a vivid demonstration that no good could come

---

[67]Thomas W. Hazlett, "The New York Disease Heads West," *Inquiry,* May 26, 1980, pp. 12–18.

[68]Ludwig von Mises, *Bureaucracy* (New Haven: Yale Univ. Press, 1946 [1944]), p. 82.

from taking that advice. In fact, his concrete recommendations included the coordination of monetary policy by British and American authorities, because neither one acting alone could be trusted—as if two thieves working together are more trustworthy than one acting independently. Keynesians and monetarists alike oppose the gold standard because it is a brake on their capacity to print money. Raymond Aron, reflecting on President Nixon's decision to stop exchanging gold for the dollars we were sending all over the world in place of goods, concluded that by that action, "the authorities of the United States were rid of the final constraint on their freedom."[69] They were rid, that is, of the last major obstacle in the process of creating dollars with which to buy votes. That is why Hayek described gold as "a device for scaring politicians."

The Failure to Invest

The last few years have seen an astonishing reversal in our expectations of the nation's economic future. Norman Podhoretz, the editor of *Commentary,* recalls that in the 1960 presidential election he and his friends sought to elect a man who could deal with the extraordinary promise of abundance just over the horizon. Midway through the next administration, Philip Rieff concluded that the "old culture of denial has become irrelevant . . . to a world of infinite abundance."[70] Those views were typical of the fifties and sixties, and it scarcely seems possible that the new orthodoxy is dominated by the laments and forbodings of neo-Malthusians of various types. Somehow President Kennedy's main task was to help us grope our way through a material prosperity of such staggering dimensions that it was a major national problem, whereas President Carter's difficulty lay in coping with a planet whose resources were being depleted so rapidly that even the present generation would have to tighten its belt. And all this happened in less than twenty years. Where now is Rieff's "infinite abundance?"

If we consider the problem to be one of the earth's physical resources, there is no explanation for the sudden reversal in perception except to say that one party or the other was foolish. It is incomprehensible that those resources were actually abundant in 1960 and scarce in 1980. Yet, there is considerable objective evidence to support both the optimism of

---

[69]Raymond Aron, *In Defense of Decadent Europe,* trans. Stephen Cox (South Bend, Ind.: Regnery/Gateway, 1979), p. 191.

[70]Norman Podhoretz, *Breaking Ranks: A Political Memoir* (New York: Harper and Row, 1979), p. 97; Philip Rieff, *The Triumph of the Therapeutic: Uses of Faith After Freud* (New York : Harper and Row, 1966), p. 254.

the earlier period and the widespread pessimism of the later. We feel poorer now because our expanding economy first stopped expanding and then slowly began to contract. But if that was not caused by a sudden scarcity of natural resources where else can we look for an explanation?

It is only a slight oversimplification to say that prosperity is largely a matter of saving and investment. The enemy of saving is consumption. What is consumed cannot be saved, and what is not saved cannot be invested. Resources that are not invested cannot be used to replace machinery that is worn out or to increase productivity. Keynes, showing his superiority to the intellectual flabbiness of so many of his materialist followers, explained why the nineteenth century was a period of such extraordinary economic growth. ''The morals, the politics, the literature, and the religion of the age joined in a grand conspiracy for the promotion of saving,'' and consequently for the creation of wealth. (Once again Marx's world is turned upside down as the cultural substructure provides a foundation for the material superstructure.) Those who are preoccupied with the conditions of the depression warn against oversaving, usually in order to advocate that the state seize the funds in order to ensure their investment.[71] But that has not been our problem for a long time, if it ever was.

The failure in the oversaving thesis is part of a more general problem of misinterpreting economic processes. Daniel Bell says that before modern technology was developed, obtaining wealth was a zero-sum game in which every gain implied a loss, making exploitation inevitable. B. F. Skinner had a character in *Walden Two* say that when people have things it is only ''at the expense of poverty, disease, and filth for many more.'' But only redistributive processes are zero-sum games: protective tariffs, mortgage subsidies, and armed robberies all transfer wealth forcibly from one person to another. Economic transactions are voluntary exchanges, which means that both parties perceive themselves as benefitting. A given economic transaction is zero-sum only if one party has miscalculated or been deceived. The principle of redistribution is exploitation and the principle of economics is cooperation. Applying zero-sum theory inappropriately to economic thinking has reinforced the damage done by making envy a normative principle. Both assume that economic activities are analogous to a series of feuds in which every winner implies a loser.

As Christopher Jencks puts it, justice requires that we change the

[71]That was Niebuhr's position in 1932; see *Moral Man and Immoral Society,* p. 89. There was less excuse for Galbraith to take the same position in 1969; *New Industrial State,* p. 35.

rules "so as to reduce the rewards of competitive success and the costs of failure."[72] But penalizing success and rewarding failure means there will be less success and more failure. That is a prescription for producing irresponsibility in people, governments, and businesses. We will end up with more slum dwellers, New Yorks, and Chrysler corporations. That is why the redistributive societies have begun to make stagnation and crisis continuing features of their economies.

The Role of Profit in the Economy

No discussion of incentives can ignore the role of profit in the economic system. One of the poisonous fruits of the great depression was the increasing respectability of the idea that capital investment, and especially profit, was opposed to the Christian gospel. Christian socialism became the dominant theme among a number of thinkers gathered around the leadership of the Archbishop of Canterbury, William Temple. In a typical remark, one of the clergymen in this group asked this question: "Does not the greed and self-seeking implicit in the profit-motive on which Capitalism rests flout the whole substance of Christ's teaching?"[73] Reinhold Niebuhr, whose depression-era writings were not far from Temple's position, later disputed that conclusion vigorously.

> I never spoke of socialism as bringing in a society in which "motives of service" would supplant the "profit motive." This was a complete confusion between systems and motives, unfortunately popular in Christian circles. It invested a collectivist system with a moral sanction it did not deserve. It further obscured the fact that the so-called "profit-motive" can hardly be eliminated under any system, particularly since it is usually none other than concern for the family, as contrasted with the total community.[74]

Greed and self-seeking find abundant avenues for expression in all economic systems, and profit, regardless of the name under which it may disguise itself, is present in any system that is not collapsing. Profit is the incentive for investment. Without the prospect for profit it would

---

[72]Christopher Jencks, *et al., Inequality: A Reassessment of the Effect of Family and Schooling in America* (New York: Basic Books, 1972), pp. 8f.

[73]S. J. Marriott, "The Soul of Man," in *Towards a Christian Order* (no editor) (London: Eyre and Spottiswoode, 1942), p. 13.

[74]Reinhold Niebuhr, "Communism and the Clergy," *Christian Century,* August 19, 1953, reprinted in Reinhold Niebuhr, *Essays in Applied Christianity,* ed. D. B. Robertson (New York: Meridian, Living Age, 1959), p. 122.

be irrational for people to save and invest rather than consume. The current attack on profits as "obscene"—and lately, even "pornographic"—by political demagogues demonstrates the extent to which the power of envy has gripped American life.

The evidence suggests that those obscene profits have actually been far too low to encourage a healthy amount of investment. From the mid-1960s, when the politics of envy began to dominate our society, to the late-1970s, the rate of return on invested capital fell about 50 percent. During the same period, the proportion of corporate profits in the GNP was reduced by 20 percent. Yet, the nominal profits have been vastly overstated because inflation has brought about illusory inventory profits and caused the depreciation of capital assets to be grossly understated. In turn, the overstated levels of profit have been the basis for inflated income tax payments, further reducing the real rate of return to investors.[75] It is no wonder that the stock market is down substantially even from the nominal levels of 1966. Adjusted for inflation, American equity investments have been disastrous during the past fifteen years, an accurate reflection of the decline of profitability. John Paulus, when he was chief economist at the Federal Reserve Bank of Minneapolis, studied the corporate earnings reports that roused such political fury at the end of 1978. With the effects of inflation factored out, he found that instead of the 26 percent gain in profit over the previous year that was so well publicized, the real gain was 2.4 percent. Paulus concluded that this was far too low to support the level of economic growth that would permit creation of sufficient jobs in the future.

With profitability reduced by envy-driven regulatory and tax policies, the inevitable consequence is that people do other things with their money than invest it productively. According to figures released by the Federal Reserve Board, corporations were able to raise only slightly more than $2.1 billion in new capital in 1978 and slightly more than $3 billion in 1979. As recently as 1976 new capital raised totaled $10.8 billion.

The Onset of Poverty

If capital is not invested, what is done with it? Capital that is not invested is consumed, in one way or another. Keynes wrote that one of the evils of a depreciating currency is that it confuses the distinction be-

---

[75]Richard W. Kopcke, "The Decline in Corporate Profitability," *New England Economic Review*, May–June, 1978, pp. 36–60. Kopcke is an economist at the Federal Reserve Bank of Boston.

tween income and capital, making it likely that people will live on the latter while thinking they are living on the former. "The increasing *money* value of the community's capital goods obscures temporarily a diminution in the real quantity in the stock."[76] A family that borrows against the increased equity in a house in order to buy a car is living on capital. A city in which the roads, buildings, and parks are deteriorating is doing the same thing. And so is a business that is not depreciating its machinery sufficiently because accounting procedures and tax laws do not fully recognize the effects of inflation.

Capital that is neither invested nor spent voluntarily is taxed away and consumed anyway. When capital is taxed by the state, it is diverted from an investment role to a consumption role. The social democracies specialize in this, but it is an ancient practice. The rulers of the late Roman Empire, desperate for funds and having already taxed income unbearably, resorted to taxing capital, with disastrous results.[77]

David Smith, a former official in the Bank of England, studied nineteen countries between 1961 and 1972 and concluded that each 5 percent increase of state spending reduced the growth rate about 1 percent because it reduced investment.[78] When the system skims off the illusory profits that are overstated by inflation, the taxation of capital is accelerated. The effect of this is suggested by industrial surveys that show that American metal-cutting machinery is older than that of any other major industrial country.

An economy living on capital rather than income resembles a body deprived of nourishment, living off its own tissues and wasting away. But this is not an organism that is starving because of the pressure of external factors beyond its control. It is, rather, suffering from an infantile inability to discipline itself and provide for its future. The irresponsibility of a government that behaves as ours does reflects the irresponsibility of its electorate. "There is a bias," concludes Edward Tufte, "toward policies with immediate, highly visible benefits and deferred, hidden costs—myopic policies for myopic voters."[79] This is the mentality that refuses to plant a tree, that consumes the seed corn. The point of the proverb that warns against killing the goose that lays the golden eggs is that capital must be preserved in order to provide income. If you enjoy roast goose today, you cannot have golden eggs tomorrow. The present

---

[76]Keynes, *Monetary Reform*, p. 33.

[77]Rostovtzeff, *Social and Economic History of the Roman Empire*, vol. 1, p. 392.

[78]Robert Bacon and Walter Eltis, *Britain's Economic Problem: Too Few Producers,* 2nd ed. (London: Macmillan, 1978), p. 106.

[79]Tufte, *Political Control of the Economy,* p. 143.

consumption of capital—often capital accumulated by previous generations—bears ominous tidings for the future, when people will seek income from capital that is no longer there. That is why the outcome of greed is poverty.

Several years ago, Peter Berger concluded that the process of delegitimation, which was overturning the values on which the political order had been founded, had not yet dislocated severely the economic life of the nation.[80] That error came in part from taking literally the official figures that described economic activity. But those figures included purchases of bureaucratic activity, legal and accounting services required by regulatory and tax policies, and myriad other costs chargeable to restrictions, controls, and standards imposed by bureaucratic fiat rather than the demands of people who valued those services and products. If one insists on taking the official figures at face value, they still show that our economy combines stagnation and inflation in a way once thought impossible.

Even during the depression, Walter Lippmann could see that the redistributive state would bring us to this end by raising visions of a cornucopia as part of the vote-buying process and by simultaneously removing the incentives for production. "Thus, on the one hand the state raises the people's expectations, and on the other hand, it reduces their productivity. The state is expected to perform the miracle of providing everyone with a large and stable income . . . by universalizing the privileges of not producing as much wealth as efficiently as possible."[81] British economists Robert Bacon and Walter Eltis sought to discover why prosperity has not followed from the increasing productivity made possible by technological advances. Their conclusion is that redistribution has made refraining from work more attractive than working, since it provides a decent living. The workers are more productive, but there are fewer of them to support greater numbers of the indolent.

Taxes reduce the production of what is taxed: industry, profitability, thrift, and investment. Subsidies increase the production of what is subsidized, and in the redistributive society that means idleness and parasitism. It also means cynicism, because redistribution is invariably done in the name of justice. It is not an ideological preference to say that a state-directed economy tends to reduce wealth and a free one to increase

---

[80]Peter Berger, *Religion in a Revolutionary Society* (Washington, D.C.: American Enterprise Institute for Public Policy Research, 1974), p. 14.

[81]Walter Lippmann, *An Inquiry into the Principles of the Good Society* (Boston: Little, Brown, 1937), p. 130.

it. It is, rather, a matter of observation. That was also the experience of the Roman Empire. The first two centuries were prosperous ones, buoyed by the unfettered opportunities for private initiative. After that the heavy hand of the state brought both poverty and oppression.[82] People that choose wealth over freedom can have neither.

Irving Kristol has described one facet of our present array of economic relationships as the struggle between the new class and the business and commercial classes. The intellectuals dislike the vulgarity of commercial activity and disparage those who engage in it.[83] Jean-François Revel sees that phenomenon as "a hatred in principle" which would persist even if it should be proved that people in the commercial civilization were better off in every way.[84] The media, populated with new class people, have made the vilification of entrepreneurs a major theme of countless films, books, and television programs.[85] One of the socialists in the group around Archbishop Temple referred to businessmen as "some little gang that directs their resources contrary to the will of any substantial majority."[86]

Freedom and Coercion

The hatred revealed in such statements is all that can be expected in a society that has institutionalized envy and uses the term social justice to describe a system of legalized theft. That should alert us to the cant in the old fraud that property rights can somehow be separated from hu-

---

[82]Rostovtzeff, *Social and Economic History of the Roman Empire,* vol. 1, pp. 54-8, 170-74, and *passim.*

[83]Hayek speaks of "the deliberate disparagement of all activities involving economic risk and the moral opprobrium cast on the gains which make risks worth taking but which only few can win . . . . The younger generation of today has grown up in a world in which in school and press the spirit of commercial enterprise has been represented as disreputable and the making of profit as immoral, where to employ a hundred people is represented as exploitation but to command the same number as honorable." *Road to Serfdom,* pp. 130f.

[84]Jean-François Revel, *The Totalitarian Temptation,* trans. David Hapgood (Garden City, N.Y.: Doubleday, 1977), p. 263.

[85]For numerous examples see Ben Stein, *The View from Sunset Boulevard* (New York: Basic Books, 1979). John Elsom, theater critic for *The Listener,* has commented on the flood of antibusiness plays appearing throughout the West, often with the financial support of governments: "A certain radical rabies is infecting much Western theater . . . sending whole companies and councils mad with good intentions and poor art. It is like watching some sub-Christian cult, with its fanatics and martyrs, taking over sedate city squares and frightening the horses. Authorities treat these new madmen with respect, for nobody knows whom they will bite next, or what the consequences will be."

[86]Sir Richard Acland, "What Shall the New Order Be? The Case for Common Ownership," *Toward a Christian Order,* p. 146.

man rights and are inferior to them.[87] There are no societies that are cavalier toward property rights but which safeguard human rights. The state that lays its hand on your purse will lay it on your person. Both are the acts of a government that despises transcendent law.

Those who think they will replace the competition of capitalism with the cooperation of socialism know nothing of either.[88] The novels in C. P. Snow's *Strangers and Brothers* series illustrate that the rapacity, hatred, and back-stabbing that are endemic in academic and bureaucratic settings are fully as destructive as those that take place in commercial life.

Another of Archbishop Temple's colleagues contended forty years ago that when capitalism was replaced by socialism it would mean the end of the reign of greed and the start of a new order based on cooperation. He looked forward to the "comradeship and the zest for efficient public services" that would follow, and cited the Soviet experience as evidence for the soundness of his expectations.[89] He used a good example; Soviet "cooperation" cost by 1959 some 110 million lives.[90] The alternative to free economic activity is not cooperation but coercion. The alternative to economic exchange is pull; that is the driving force of the grants economy which has enveloped us. Greed has driven purposeful economic activity on the defensive and is replacing it with political power in order to get what it wants. The modern redistributive society has made factual Spengler's remark that every modern election "is a civil war carried on by ballot-box." Redistribution is absolutely incompatible with peace. Accepted as a norm for civic life, it means that social strife is inevitable.

Those who bought stock in the redistributive state before it began its dizzying rise have done well. Professors of the social sciences, powerful business executives, high government officials, successful politicians, recipients of tax money and implicit grants in an almost infinite variety

---

[87]That is the position, to cite one example, of William Stringfellow, *Dissenter in a Great Society: A Christian View of Crisis in America* (New York: Holt, Rinehart, and Winston, 1966), p. 33.

[88]For example, Richard Bube, a Stanford University scientist writing from a conservative Protestant perspective, described the method and goal of the free enterprise system as competition and profit and the corresponding facets of socialism as cooperation and service. Richard H. Bube, *The Human Quest: A New Look at Science and the Christian Faith* (Waco, Tex.: Word, 1971), p. 235.

[89]Sidney Dark, "Socialism: The Only Way to Democracy," in *Toward a Christian Order,* p. 189.

[90]The figure is taken by Solzhenitsyn from the Russian statistician Ivan Kurganov. Aleksandr I. Solzhenitsyn, *Warning to the West* (New York: Farrar, Straus, and Giroux, 1976), p. 129.

of forms, heads of research institutes, lecture-circuit gurus, international consultants, humanitarian leaders with well-watered reputations for benevolence—they all radiate the aura of wisdom belonging only to those who buy at the bottom and ride their investment up a one-way escalator. It is only now that the exterior is rotting away that ordinary people can see that the foundations are lacking, and the general shabbiness of the position belies its former glory. It is becoming ever more difficult to cover up the fact that redistribution is a Ponzi game that can pay off old victims only by producing new ones. The moral justifications fade and are replaced by force. As the claims to be championing justice appear increasingly ludicrous, Hayek's warning that the recipients of redistribution can be a racial elite, a party, or an aristocracy, will be seen to be prescient. The nightmares of the nineteenth-century French philosopher and politician, Frederic Bastiat, have come true: The law is converted "into an instrument of plunder."[91] The spectacle of a whole society busily living off the labors of others, in turn stealing and being stolen from by the redistributive powers of the elite, brings us what Hilaire Belloc, some seventy years ago, called the "servile state."[92]

The Evasion of Evil

In the late-twentieth century, most of the competing socio-political systems embody one version or another of the Enlightenment mindset, which cannot understand the nature of evil. Only that kind of error could place the powers in the hands of officials that we have placed there and expect anything good to come of it. Those, on the other hand, who see all our troubles in the modern state and think they will be solved by a libertarian solution make the same error. Both ideologies are environmentalisms that place the blame for social malfunction everywhere but where it belongs: on man himself. The apologists for modern capitalism distorted Adam Smith's vision to mean that when people do evil, those acts are somehow not permitted to bear their evil fruits. The invisible hand solves the problem of evil by taking from it all its consequences.[93]

---

[91]Frederic Bastiat, *The Law*, trans. Dean Russell (Irvington-on-Hudson, N.Y.: Foundation for Economic Education, 1950 [1850]), p. 12.

[92]"That arrangement of society in which so considerable a number of the families and individuals are constrained by positive law to labour for the advantage of other families and individuals as to stamp the whole community with the mark of such labour we call THE SERVILE STATE." Hilaire Belloc, *The Servile State* (New York: Henry Holt, 1946 [1912]), p. 16.

[93]Smith's statement about the invisible hand was more benign than its popular form. He said that a person who invests his money "intends only his own gain, and he is in this,

Kristol was correct in saying that the evolution of capitalist apologetics from Smith's time to our own entails a gradual "liberation" of capitalism "from its Judeo-Christian moorings—most such apologetics being the work of economists, who do not know how to think in moral terms." Philosophies that preach stones into bread are preaching sin without tears. And ideologies that take the invisible hand to mean a preordained guarantee that good will result from every freely undertaken action, no matter how evil or senseless, are folly. Neither the messianic state nor autonomous man can escape the consequences of evil.

For every grantor there is a grasper, and that is the moral meaning of the modern social democracies. Western societies have succumbed to what R. H. Tawney called the "unbridled indulgence of the acquisitive appetite." For one with that appetite, said Max Weber, money is not so much a means of securing goods and services as "an end in itself . . . . Man is dominated by the making of money, by acquisition as the ultimate purpose of his life."[94] Emmette Redford, in his apologia for the expansion of state power, says frankly, although without any understanding of the moral implications of his position, that people demand such expansion because they desire benefits that they cannot have without it.

The Failure of Mammon

It is the constant claim of ideologies of the left that capitalism has not satisfied people. That is perfectly true, because it is not in the nature of economic systems to satisfy anyone. Economic ideologies ranging across the entire political spectrum promise a cornucopia of material prosperity that will wipe away all tears. In so doing, they become idolatrous. The Christian position from the beginning has been that people are satisfied by becoming reconciled with God, not by acquiring wealth.

---

as in many other cases, led by an invisible hand to promote an end which was no part of his intention. Nor is it always the worse for the society that it was no part of it." Adam Smith, *An Inquiry into the Nature and Causes of the Wealth of Nations,* ed. Edwin Cannan (New York: Modern Library, 1937), p. 423. Nevertheless, he set the stage for others to carry his meaning further. He made liberal use of Bernard de Mandeville's *Fable of the Bees,* the subtitle of which was *Private Vices, Public Benefits,* a perfect complement to the libertarian use of the invisible hand.

[94]Max Weber, *The Protestant Ethic and the Spirit of Capitalism,* trans. Talcott Parsons (London: George Allen and Unwin, 1930), p. 53. Reinhold Niebuhr believed that American materialism had its roots in the fusion of the Jeffersonian idea that virtue stems from prosperity with the Puritan idea that prosperity stems from virtue. But that explanation does not account for the similarities of American materialism with that in other Western countries. See Niebuhr, *The Irony of American History* (New York: Scribner's, 1952), p. 53.

Idolatries of mammon are in fundamental disagreement with the warning of Jesus that "a man's life does not consist in the abundance of his possessions" (Luke 12:15). The ethical injunction that has to accompany such a position is contentment; therefore, the apostle says that "if we have food and clothing, with these we shall be content" (1 Tim. 6:8). And again, "Keep your life free from love of money, and be content with what you have" (Heb. 13:5). That is why Marx called religion the opium of the people; he rightly saw that Christian faith is antithetical to the envy, the grasping for more, on which his revolution depends.

What of those who reject that counsel? "But those who desire to be rich fall into temptation, into a snare, into many senseless and hurtful desires that plunge men into ruin and destruction" (1 Tim. 6:9). People who are thus described naturally disagree, too, with the statement of Jesus that "it is more blessed to give than to receive" (Acts 20:35). Jeremy Seabrook, in a book subtitled *Why Hasn't Having More Made People Happy?*, tells a horrifying tale of the misery of modern Britain, a pioneer on the road now entered upon by the United States. All his hopes of a socialist heaven on earth have been disappointed, but he has learned the wrong lessons from his experience. Materialism is good, he is still convinced, but has been subverted by evil people. He cannot see that the dehumanizing and exploitive effects he deplores are inseparable from the system he champions.[95]

Idolatries of mammon are unanimous in their insistence that it is more blessed to receive than to give; their ethic therefore is one of taking. Political economies that follow them are inflationary and redistributive. They elevate respectable forms of stealing into principles of virtue, putting themselves in the position of those whom the prophet denounced: "Woe to those who call evil good and good evil" (Is. 5:20). That is why it is not the worst elements of society that are the most dangerous but those whom society has judged most worthy of respect and trust, just as in the Old Testament: the objects of the prophets' wrath were the princes, judges, and religious leaders.

There is another aspect to the idolatry that leads to redistribution. Both testaments speak of God as the great redistributor who brings judgment upon exploiters and rescues their victims. As the Magnificat puts it:

. . . he has put down the mighty from their thrones,
and exalted those of low degree;

---

[95]Jeremy Seabrook, *What Went Wrong? Why Hasn't Having More Made People Happier?* (New York: Pantheon Books, 1978), pp. 14 and *passim*.

he has filled the hungry with good things,
and the rich he has sent empty away (Luke 1:52f.).

Just as idolatries of mammon imitate the creation of value out of nothing by policies of inflation, so they imitate the redemptive process with redistributive schemes.

Judgment falls in ways that are appropriate to the evils that provoke it. Our policies of greed have brought an end to the increase of wealth to which we have become accustomed, and we have begun to destroy the capital resources that have taken three centuries to build. In so doing, we have spurned the biblical principle that we are stewards of the material goods entrusted to us and not their masters. The ancient kingdoms of Israel and Judah committed similar deeds, and the prophetic voices raised at that time warned that their crimes would call forth judgment that would shatter their economic well-being.

Though they build houses,
they shall not inhabit them;
though they plant vineyards,
they shall not drink wine from them (Zeph. 1:13).

"You have sown much, and harvested little; you eat, but you never have enough; you drink, but you never have your fill; you clothe yourselves, but no one is warm; and he who earns wages earns wages to put them into a bag with holes" (Hag. 1:6).

Shall I acquit the man with wicked scales
and with a bag of deceitful weights?
Your rich men are full of violence;
your inhabitants speak lies,
and their tongue is deceitful in their mouth.
Therefore I have begun to smite you,
making you desolate because of your sins.
You shall eat, but not be satisfied,
and there shall be hunger in your inward parts;
You shall put away, but not save,
and what you save I will give to the sword.
You shall sow, but not reap;
you shall tread olives, but not
anoint yourselves with oil;
you shall tread grapes, but not drink wine
(Mic. 6:11–15).

The prophets did not prescribe a technical fix for the economic desolation that comes from greed and idolatry. Only repentence and faith would serve. Our own economic difficulties seem to bear no relationship to those times, but the differences are only superficial. Idols of mammon invite us, too, to place our hopes on wealth, tell us that taking is better than giving, tempt us to covet what our neighbor has, convince us that we have been wronged because we do not possess as much as we desire, and, finally, pervert the sense of justice that alone can preserve peace. If we continue to worship them, the unrest and discontent that mark our society now are only a sample of the destruction that is to come. Insatiable greed placing infinite claims on finite resources can have no other end.

CHAPTER FOUR

Idols of Nature

Nature and History

IN the continuing struggle between opposing idols, nature is the enemy of history. Historicism flowered as part of a reaction against the domination of nature. Here is the way Hegel's contemporary, Goethe, put it:

The Godhead is effective in the living and not in the dead, in the becoming and the changing, not in the become and set-fast; and therefore, similarly, the reason (*Vernunft*) is concerned only to strive towards the divine through the becoming and the living, and the understanding (*Verstand*) only to make use of the become and the set-fast.[1]

Goethe's statement is a classic expression of the warfare between history—the "becoming and the changing"—and nature—the "become and set-fast." Such ideas came as a breath of fresh air to those fed up with the preoccupation with nature that had captivated European intellectuals since the Enlightenment. Their reaction set the stage for the growth of historicism in the nineteenth and twentieth centuries. Spengler said of Goethe's passage that it "comprises my entire philosophy."

To a degree, this dispute appeared to be another replay of the classical

---

[1]Quoted in Oswald Spengler, *The Decline of the West,* trans. Charles Francis Atkinson, rev. ed., 2 vols. (New York: Knopf, 1926, 1928), vol. 1, p. 49.

arguments between those who sought meaning in stability (Parmenides) and those who sought it in change (Heraclitus). In the nineteenth century, however, the gap between historical change and natural stability was bridged by a reinterpretation of nature that permitted science to accommodate the idea of change within the naturalist cosmology. Biological evolution is the most visible manifestation of this innovation. It enabled science to deal with the realities of change, instead of leaving them to the exclusive jurisdiction of history; to interpret natural change as progressive rather than cyclical; to make possible the notion of teleology, something that could not be contained within a static view of nature.[2] This development might have paved the way for the reconciliation of history and nature as aspects of the creation but instead made nature more beguiling for people whose search for meaning led them into idolatry. Those who sought to incorporate an explanation for change into their vision of reality now could turn either to history or to nature.

This modern struggle between history and nature has counterparts in the biblical literature. Butterfield describes the Israelite religious odyssey as an early manifestation:

> The God who brought his people out of the land of Egypt . . . was to be celebrated in the Old Testament pre-eminently as the God of History. It seems to have been when the children of Israel lapsed into idolatry—gave themselves over to the worship of Baal, for example—that they turned rather to the God of Nature, glorifying the forces of the physical universe and the fertility of the earth.[3]

In its idolatry, Israel rejected the pentateuchal insight that there is one God, the God of both nature and history.

Nature as the Whole Show

So disastrous have been the effects of historicist idols that it is only to be expected that naturalist idols should benefit from renewed attention. Just as historicism denigrates nature in the belief that significance is comprehended entirely within the realm of history, so naturalism assumes that nature comprises "the whole show."[4] There is a kind of one-

---

[2] R.G. Collingwood, *The Idea of Nature* (New York: Oxford Univ. Press [Galaxy], 1960 [1945]), pp. 9–16.

[3] Herbert Butterfield, *Christianity and History* (London: Collins, Fontana, 1957 [1949]), p. 9.

[4] The phrase is from C.E.M. Joad, *Guide to Modern Thought,* new ed. (London: Faber and Faber, 1948).

eyed theology that pursues the same course. Michael Novak believes that Albert Camus's advocacy of nature over history is one reason that he has attracted such an avid following among young people. Novak applauds this development and urges that the West abandon what he calls the German preoccupation with history, to embrace instead the Mediterranean passion for nature. Turning away from the biblical emphasis on the distinction between man and nature, he is attracted by Eastern mysticism, which views man as a part of nature.[5]

Although Spengler fell into the opposite error, he saw clearly that to collapse the world of history into the status of a part of nature is to confuse the principles belonging to one realm with those of another. "It was assumed that a rigid culture existed [in history] just as electricity or gravitation existed, and that it was capable of analysis in much the same way as these."[6] This error plunges man into complete irrationality, because mind, reason, will, thought, and knowledge can have no ontological existence in such a world. They are epiphenomena, mere shadows of the only world that exists, the world of matter. Everything that distinguishes man from nature disappears in this outlook, and that can only mean that man himself disappears. That is why C. S. Lewis was right to call the triumph of such a conception "the abolition of man."

Science as Religion

For historicism, the study of history and related disciplines is the key to unlocking the secrets of the universe. For naturalism, the study of the natural sciences serves that function. We can see the evidence in the religious language routinely used for the scientific enterprise conceived within that framework. The early years of the twentieth century were the heyday for this exuberant conception. Toynbee recalled that his uncle Percy Frankland, an eminent chemist and bacteriologist, believed that science would cure all evils and solve all religious and political questions. "In Uncle Percy's vision, science was the irresistible force that predestination was in Calvin's vision, and historical necessity in Marx's."[7]

---

[5]Michael Novak, *A Theology for Radical Politics* (New York: Herder and Herder, 1969), pp. 92–109.

[6]Spengler, *Decline of the West,* vol. 1, p. 49.

[7]Arnold J. Toynbee, *Experiences* (New York: Oxford Univ. Press, 1969), p. 297. Poet John Crowe Ransom concluded that the interwar generation worshiped science as other people did a god. John Crowe Ransom, *God Without Thunder: An Unorthodox Defense of Christianity* (New York: Harcourt, Brace, 1930), p. 185. The distinguished astronomer Sir Bernard Lovell thinks that for the people of that era, science and technology

The intellectual power inherent in scientific formulations swept before it and threatened to relegate to obscurity and impotence all other means of obtaining knowledge. Reinhold Niebuhr, whose powerful intellect had a sure instinct for unmasking the hidden assumption or the *non sequitur* in the historical and theological literatures that were his forte, submitted meekly to the pretentions of an arrogant scientism that went far beyond the evidence at its disposal.[8] Toynbee, too, even though he recognized that science was continually changing its views, decided that he would have to accept the reigning cosmologies "on trust." John Dewey adopted the same position, complacently enumerating scientific advances and the theological ideas they supposedly outmoded. He thought, for example, that biology cast into doubt the doctrines of sin, redemption, and immortality.[9]

Such ideas sound odd today. People now are more likely to agree with Huxley that science is "that wonderfully convenient personification of the opinions, at a given date, of Professors X, Y, and Z."[10] Charles Raven, biologist and theologian, believed that the arrogance so prevalent among scientists early in the century has been replaced with a humility that extends so far as to question whether science can say anything with certainty.[11]

Our uncritical faith in science has diminished largely because we understand better the limitations under which scientists must do their work. Logical positivism gained widespread influence by insisting that the validity of any form of knowledge is dependent upon its conformance with the standards set by the natural sciences. It is losing its hold on the philosophy departments partly because science itself cannot meet the prescribed criteria. As Karl Popper says, anyone who refuses to lend credence to a proposition because it cannot be demonstrated by argument or experience is advancing a theory that cannot meet its own test.[12]

All systems of thought rest on assumptions or beliefs. An assertion

---

"became the God through which man was seeking the road to economic and intellectual salvation." Sir Bernard Lovell, *In the Center of Immensities* (New York: Harper and Row, 1978), p. 157.

[8]See, for example, Reinhold Niebuhr, *Christian Realism and Political Problems* (New York: Scribner's, 1953), pp. 197ff.

[9]John Dewey, *A Common Faith* (New Haven, Yale Univ. Press, 1934), p. 31.

[10]Aldous Huxley, *Brave New World Revisited* (New York: Harper Colophon Books, 1960), p. 80.

[11]Charles E. Raven, *Christianity and Science* (London: Lutterworth Press, 1955), p. 38.

[12]Karl R. Popper, *The Open Society and Its Enemies,* 4th ed., 2 vols. (Princeton, N. Y.: Princeton Univ. Press, 1963), vol. 2, p. 230.

about God is not logically different from a physicist's assumption that the physical world actually exists apart from anyone's mind.[13] There can be no simple appeal to the "facts," for factuality cannot be considered apart from a philosophy by which the facts are interpreted. The inductive method of the sciences ensures a certain tentativeness to all their findings because the patient addition of new instances supporting the generalization does not provide any logical necessity for it. No matter how many instances support it, a single experiment or observation to the contrary destroys it.

Scientific advances do not follow the "normal science" model as conceived by the general public, the patient addition of fact upon fact. Rather they tend to come after a "gestalt switch" or what the scientist perceives as a flash of light.[14] University of London philosopher C.E.M. Joad has described science as a form of art, "an imaginative picture constructed by the human mind."[15] Far from maintaining an objectivity denied to other pursuits, science is subject to the same array of personal vagaries as any human enterprise. As James Watson describes the scientific coup that led to his winning of the Nobel Prize for discovering the structure of DNA, the chase was composed of ambition, envy, political maneuvering, luck, and intrigue—as well as the intellectual brilliance we expect.[16] Milton Friedman recalls being seated next to the great geneticist R. A. Fisher at a dinner at Cambridge University. Fisher regaled him with story after story that illustrated the fact that he could infer his colleagues' scientific views on genetics from their political opinions.[17] D.M.S. Watson, known to the public for his B.B.C. talks popularizing the Darwinian notion that human beings descended from primates, declared in an address to his fellow biologists at a Cape Town conference: "Evolution itself is accepted by zoologists not because it has been observed to occur or . . . can be proved by logically coherent evidence to be true, but because the only alternative, special creation, is

---

[13]Paul Meehl *et al., What, Then, Is Man?: A Symposium of Theology, Psychology, and Psychiatry* (St. Louis: Concordia, 1958), p. 24.

[14]Thomas S. Kuhn, *The Structure of Scientific Revolutions* (Chicago: Univ. of Chicago Press, 1962), p. 121.

[15]Joad, *Guide to Modern Thought,* pp. 115ff.

[16]James D. Watson, *The Double Helix: Being a Personal Account of the Structure of DNA* (New York: Atheneum, 1968).

[17]Milton Friedman, *Tax Limitation, Inflation and the Role of Government* (Dallas: The Fisher Institute, 1978), p. 83.

clearly incredible."[18] Similarly, the great British astronomer Sir Arthur Eddington, brooding about cosmological theories that appeared to support creation, said in 1931, "The notion of a beginning is repugnant to me." The scientific scabbards fall away to reveal ideological swords.

Thomas Kuhn concluded that at a given time any scientific community will always have in its structure an element that is more will than intellect, a product of personal history. He thinks it inevitable, therefore, that a scientific group will practice its craft with a "set of received beliefs." C. S. Lewis argued that those beliefs affect the perceptions of the observer so powerfully that they control his interpretation of the empirical information he uses.[19] That was evidently Spengler's meaning when he wrote that there "is no natural science without a precedent Religion."[20]

Natural science, therefore, shares an important feature with historical studies. They both have noses of wax, to be twisted whichever way the scholar's assumptions and personal predilections impel him. Science does not possess an objectivity denied to other investigative activities, because scientists cannot fully insulate their critical faculties from the other aspects of their personalities. In fiercely denouncing his fellow intellectuals, Julien Benda made the common mistake of supposing that, as a class, they were capable of rising above the selfishness, prejudice, and party spirit that afflicts ordinary mortals; he could not help but fall into disillusionment, because no group of people in the world could have lived up to his expectations.[21]

Studies in the history and philosophy of science in recent years have made increasingly dubious the old dream of objective science searching for and drawing ever closer to the truth. Kuhn thinks the Darwinian model is appropriate for understanding science, as long as it lacks a tel-

---

[18]Douglas Dewar and L.M. Davies, "Science and the B.B.C.," *The Nineteenth Century and After,* April, 1943, p. 167. C.S. Lewis responded to Watson's remark: "Has it come to that? Does the whole vast structure of modern naturalism depend not on positive evidence but simply on an *a priori* metaphysical prejudice? Was it devised not to get in facts but to keep out God?" C.S. Lewis, *They Asked for a Paper* (London: Geoffrey Bles, 1962), p. 163.

[19]"We can always say we have been the victims of an illusion; if we disbelieve in the supernatural this is what we always shall say. Hence, whether miracles really have ceased or not, they would certainly appear to cease in Western Europe as materialism became the popular creed." C.S. Lewis, *God in the Dock,* ed. Walter Hooper (Grand Rapids: Eerdmans, 1970), p. 25.

[20]Spengler, *Decline of the West,* vol. 1, p. 380.

[21]Julien Benda, *The Betrayal of the Intellectuals,* trans. Richard Aldington (Boston: Beacon, 1955 [1928]).

eology. Science has evolved and will continue to do so, he says, but without any goal "set by nature in advance." Thus, no scientific paradigm may be absolutized, as if science were to be frozen or disallowed from introducing successor paradigms. Those paradigms are themselves, in part, the product of religious presuppositions that can be traced and identified; they are not to be considered the last word.

Popper, considering the same question from the philosophical rather than the historical point of view, concludes that we can say nothing of a scientific theory except "that it explains this or that; that it has been tested severely, and that it has stood up to all our tests." He believes it can be shown mathematically that all such theories have the same probability: zero. Science, therefore, "has nothing to do with the quest for certainty or probability or reliability," but only with testing theories in an effort to devise better ones.[22]

We have come full circle. Natural science, which seemed to have credentials of objectivity and reliability that other forms of learning did not, gained credibility that the others lost. It took over the consideration of questions that formerly were reserved for philosophy, and metaphysics fell by the wayside as a serious means of ascertaining the nature of reality.[23] Now science, too, has been found to have some of the same disabilities as its rivals: reliance on unproved assumptions, subjectivity, and the propensity to make pronouncements on questions that lie outside its field of competence.

Social Science and Philosophical Materialism

The newfound humility among natural scientists, compared with their predecessors of two generations ago, is not matched by that of their counterparts in the social sciences. B. F. Skinner advocates a science of human behavior as the means of solving social problems that otherwise remain intractable and says that it must adopt the strategies of physics and biology.[24] This is consistent with his view, and that of many other psychologists, that psychology is a biological science. Human beings are simply a part of nature, in that conception, and a science of human behavior must study them in that light. Such a science produces the

---

[22]Karl R. Popper, *Conjectures and Refutations: The Growth of Scientific Knowledge* (London: Routledge and Kegan Paul, 1963), pp. 192, 229.

[23]See for example, R.G. Collingwood, *Essay on Metaphysics* (Oxford: Clarendon, 1940).

[24]B.F. Skinner, *Beyond Freedom and Dignity* (New York: Bantam/Vintage, 1972 [1971]), p. 175.

technology that will enable people to control human behavior and there-by permit humanity to survive. Thus, in the behaviorist view, the science of human behavior serves the same high purpose that natural science did for Toynbee's Uncle Percy and his contemporaries.

But behaviorism does not stop at adopting ideas about the purpose and potential of science that were in vogue three quarters of a century ago; it repeats substantive assumptions that were current then and re-jected long since. When Skinner says that the science of human behavior must follow the strategies of natural science, he means that it must be wholly materialist. He sees no hope of ever solving the old philosophical problem of how mind and matter interact and follows the common prac-tice of assuming that one of them does not exist, the monist position. For behaviorists, everything is material, and therefore qualities we have been accustomed to attribute to mind or spirit are merely epiphenomena of material origin. They are successions of mental events that find co-herence only in their identification with the nervous tissue of a particu-lar organism. "All differences are physical," says Frazier, Skinner's alter ego. "We think with our bodies, too."[25] That is why Skinner insists that to speak of human behavior in terms of aims, purposes, intuitions, or goals is to betray an understanding of man which is "prescientific."

The Eclipse of Materialism

Mind has to be a prescientific concept for a metaphysic that believes all reality to be material. *Matter* has the commonsense meaning we are all familiar with: something tangible, solid, and possessing the quality of reality that is not found in nonmaterial entities. But that all reality is matter is common sense only to laymen who happen to have been born in the hundred years or so prior to the middle of the twentieth century. For physicists, that certainty was gone before Skinner went to college.

Matter is now thought to be indistinguishable from energy. Even the old certainties about the measurement of matter have fallen by the way-side. Following discoveries by German physicist Werner Heisenberg, modern physicists believe that the act of observing subatomic particles imparts to them sufficient energy to alter their movement; thus they conclude that they can measure precisely either the location or the veloc-ity of a particle but not both. Many physicists have become monists un-der the impact of such discoveries, but they have become idealists who believe that *mind* is the ultimate reality with *matter* being the epiphenom-

---

[25]B.F. Skinner, *Walden Two* (New York: Macmillan, 1948), p. 104.

enon. As Max Planck put it: "I regard consciousness as fundamental. I regard matter as derivative from consciousness." And Sir James Jeans said that things seem objective due to their "subsisting in the mind of some eternal spirit." Philosopher Mortimer Adler has even predicted that immaterialism will become the new scientific orthodoxy.[26]

This abrupt rejection of materialism has been interpreted by R. G. Collingwood as a switch away from a temporary aberration in intellectual history and a return to the mainstream of European thought. When Skinner speaks of the nonmaterialist view as prescientific, he is advancing a scientific conception that was current for a short time but is now largely abandoned outside his own field. Spengler's interpretation of that conception was much shrewder. Writing at a time when materialism was at its zenith, he called it "the effective religion of the time."[27]

Determinism

Usually accompanying materialism, although some have denied that the connection is logically necessary, has been determinism, the idea that people act as they do solely because of antecedent experiences. They do things because they must do them. They have no freedom to do otherwise. This interpretation of human action has ancient roots, going back at least as far as Babylonian astrology in the third millenium before Christ. Enlightenment thinking, especially that derived from Rousseau, found in determinism a welcome substitute for the Christian anthropology it was discarding. For if evil were not to be explained by something inherent in man, then it was natural to look to circumstances for the explanation. Objective conditions, a corrupt society, and bad teaching account for man's destructive actions, and one need look no further to understand them. Scientific research accustoms people to think in determinist categories because it proceeds as if each event has a cause that fully determines it. If that is true when observing a chemical reaction, why not when observing an example of human behavior? Analogies like this, of course, are far from constituting proof, and those few physicists and many social scientists who accept determinism do so by an act of faith.

---

[26]Mortimer J. Adler, *The Difference of Man and the Difference it Makes* (New York: Holt, Rinehart, and Winston, 1967), p. 294.

[27]Collingwood, *Idea of Nature*, pp. 155f.; Spengler, *The Decline of the West*, vol. 2, p. 308; see also Tibor R. Machan, *The Pseudo-Science of B.F. Skinner* (New Rochelle, N.Y.: Arlington House, 1974).

If man is all matter and his actions completely determined by events over which he has no control, we may ask wherein lies his uniqueness. The obvious answer to that question comes from another product of the Enlightenment, French physician Julien La Mettrie, who wrote a book in 1748 entitled *Man the Machine*. He argued that human beings were small machines connected to the large machine we call nature. At death those small machines stop and disintegrate. Although seldom expressed so plainly, this kind of thinking is not uncommon, and it accounts for G. K. Chesterton's remark that determinists do not pretend to be human beings.[28] By this he meant that man, in the traditional meaning of the word, could not exist in the world of determinism. That is, man who freely chooses, responsibly makes moral decisions, and possesses freedom and dignity is swallowed up in the behaviorist machine and simply reacts mechanically to stimuli in accordance with prior patterns of reinforcement. Skinner meets this criticism head on and says, in effect, good riddance to a man so described. "His abolition has long been overdue."

Since human beings, along with everything else, are assumed to be all material—"we think with our bodies"—their behavior results purely from external contingencies, not on any supposed sense of moral value. There can be no free choice in the world of behaviorism because there is no human faculty that may be said to "choose." The organism simply acts as the prior contingencies have programmed it (him) to act. Moral categories, therefore, are superfluous in understanding human behavior. They may serve a useful function only as they become tools for the shaping of behavior by the controllers. The moral life, in short, is a delusion, and it often functions only as a hindrance to the survival of the human race. Determinism, like other manifestations of naturalism, may best be interpreted as a denial of one of the aspects of the creation. Genesis speaks of three separate creations: that of the cosmos (1:1), life (1:21), and man (1:27). Determinism erases the gulf between the first and third, just as evolutionism does between the second and third. If man cannot be distinguished ontologically from other forms of matter, then materialist determinisms are logical inferences from the observed facts of nature. But empirical observations alone yield no information about ontology. Skinner tells us repeatedly that human beings may not survive if they do not accept behavioral engineering, but nowhere does he explain why that should bother us. Human survival—the sanctity of human life—is a value, and there is no way he or anyone else can derive

---

[28]G.K. Chesterton, *Orthodoxy* (London: Collins, Fontana, 1961 [1908]), p. 36.

value from material facts.[29] Materialists almost invariably use language that is value-laden, even though their avowed epistemology does not allow for values. Mystification covers the logical gaps. The only ethical framework compatible with materialism is nihilism, defined as living without values.

The irrationality of determinism has yet a more basic aspect. When we consider allowing a controller to rescue us from extinction by conditioning us to behave in ways compatible with survival, we shall want to know if the controller is himself free or determined. If he is free, then determinism cannot be true. If he is determined, then there is no point in talking about the rationality or wisdom of the plan; since its contents and its outcome are both inevitable, we can only discuss cause and effect. That is why rationality and determinism cannot fit in the same system. Lenin solved this problem by saying that the vanguard (that is, Lenin and his lieutenants) is exempt from the general law of determinism. But if that is true, determinism cannot be a general law. Lenin had to resort to mystification to allow himself freedom in the grim world of determinism. The behaviorist form of determinism has a related difficulty because it identifies ideas with material substance. If that is true, the ideas of the behaviorists, as well as those of their opponents, are only a function of their bodies. "To ask which of the different theories is true is as meaningless as to ask which of the various blood pressures of the theorists concerned is true."[30]

In his fictional account of the behaviorist utopia, Skinner shows why he finds determinism indispensable. Frazier tells his guests that the main interest the utopian experiment has for him is not the improvement of mankind but *"to make possible a genuine science of human behavior!"* That goal is compatible only with determinism. "If man is free, then a technology of behavior is impossible. . . . I deny that freedom exists at all. I must deny it—or my program would be absurd. You can't have a

---

[29]Cf. C.S. Lewis, *The Abolition of Man* (New York: Macmillan, 1947 [1943]), p. 20: "From propositions of fact alone no practical conclusion can ever be drawn. . . . The Innovator is trying to get a conclusion in the imperative mood out of premises in the indicative mood: and though he continues trying through all eternity he cannot succeed, for the thing is impossible."

[30]Joad, *Guide to Modern Thought*, p. 61; also C.E.M. Joad, *The Recovery of Belief: A Restatement of Christian Philosophy* (London: Faber and Faber, 1952), pp. 142ff.: "Determinism itself is a complex set of thoughts. Why . . . should we suppose it to have any epistemological reference to a state of affairs external to the series of thoughts in which the theory of Determinism consists? . . . it can have only causal reference and can, therefore, give information only about the conditions prevailing in the body and the brain of the determinist."

science about a subject matter which hops capriciously about. Perhaps we can never prove that man isn't free; it's an assumption."[31] Thus the main assumption of the behaviorist, on which stands the legitimacy of his control over other people, is intimately bound up with his perception of his self-interest. Elsewhere Skinner acknowledges that the measures the controller takes are going to be those that accommodate his own interests. "He will select goods or values which are important to him and arrange the kind of contingencies to which he can adapt." "To some extent he will necessarily design a world *he* likes."[32] "To some extent" is superfluous, since the determinist conception allows the controller to plan for others only those contingencies that will be reinforcing to himself.

The determinist faith has an aspect that is self-fulfilling in that it causes the impotence it assumes. Anyone placed in a difficult situation that calls for courage, steadfastness, or integrity, if he is convinced he can do nothing of his own volition but instead must simply act out the implications of his conditioning, will tend to take the easy way out. He believes he *does* only what he *is,* and what he is cannot be altered by determinants within himself, for that would be what Skinner calls prescientific. It is not to be expected that he will make a great effort to deflect the inevitable. Much more sensible to bend with the tide, which is to say, accept what must be. That is why cowardice is one of the natural results of determinism. Machines do as they are programmed, and it is idle to complain that a machine is timid. Skinner is perfectly consistent to say that ethical lapses require treatment and not punishment. Mechanical responses do not have moral content. When they malfunction, only a technical fix is required. Thus social pathologies, such as crime and alcoholism, come from the environment, and only by changing the environment can we effect a cure.

Social Science as Ideology

Naturalistic assumptions about human beings proceed to the conclusion that human behavior follows laws that can be used to predict the organism's future actions. Niebuhr called this a "naive belief" and rightly held that it pervaded the social sciences. It all stems, he said, from the assumption that history is not very different from nature; therefore, the methods that work in the natural sciences are fully as valid when study-

---

[31]Skinner, *Walden Two,* pp. 242, 213f.

[32]Skinner, *Beyond Freedom and Dignity,* pp. 164, 156.

ing human actors.[33] For his study of the decline of the family in modern America, Christopher Lasch read mountains of social science material on the subject and was appalled by its one-sided focus on abstract social "process," which is incapable of discerning the struggles of flesh-and-blood human beings. That blindness makes plausible the "laws" that society is said to follow, the claims about which Lasch calls "the overriding mystification of social science."[34]

Lasch found that social science theory tends to follow popular prejudice and shifts along with the dominant trends. When the popular view turned against the notion of romantic love in favor of the socialization function of the family or toward the therapy function, the theoretical studies followed. The same is true of such topics as privatism, "togetherness," and feminism. Lasch concluded that the claims of scientific detachment and the ability to work out theoretical positions apart from the push and shove of popular polemics is an absurd pretention. Such criticisms have become increasingly common. Harvard psychiatrist Leon Eisenberg has railed against the conjuring up of "pseudo-scientific support for a priori social ideologies that are projected onto" the subjects being studied.[35] This tendentious scholarship has been prevalent in such fruitful areas for humanitarian activity as poverty studies and development economics. There is a general unwillingness to distinguish, as P. T. Bauer puts it, "between the advancement of knowledge and the promotion of policy, often accompanied by the subordination of the former to the latter." Literature that gives all appearances of being objectively academic shows systematic errors reflecting the advancement of unacknowledged objectives.[36] Thus, social and political propaganda comes disguised as research. It is no wonder that attention is being focused on the use of social science ideas as determinants in the social disasters that masquerade as public policy.[37]

---

[33]Reinhold Niebuhr, *The Irony of American History* (New York: Scribner's, 1952), pp. 80f.

[34]Christopher Lasch, *Haven in a Heartless World: The Family Besieged* (New York: Basic Books, 1977), p. xv. British Sovietologist Robert Conquest has said that the urge in the social sciences to make sweeping generalizations without adequate support is not a higher development but rather "a sure sign of primitivism."

[35]Leon Eisenberg, in *Science,* vol. 176, April 14, 1972, no. 4031, p. 125.

[36]P.T. Bauer, *Dissent on Development: Studies and Debates in Development Economics* (London: Weidenfeld and Nicolson, 1971), pp. 19f. For an extended discussion of such systematic errors see Martin Anderson, *Welfare: The Political Economy of Welfare Reform in the United States* (Stanford: Hoover Institution Press, 1978), pp. 98-127.

[37]See, for example, Irving Kristol, *Two Cheers for Capitalism* (New York: Basic Books, 1978), p. 234: ". . . a major reason the social reforms of the 60's were so ill-conceived

Reductionism and the Sociology of Knowledge

To say that many social science ideas are biased derivatives of their originators' values is not to say that all ideas are so tainted. But the common social science assumptions bring to us a conclusion nearly that extreme. This is only to be expected from disciplines that assume that mind is a product of material origin or that human behavior is completely contingent on prior experiences. In the context of those beliefs, it is logical that ideas should similarly be degraded to contingencies of previous experience or dismissed as reflections of "deeper" sources. We find this conclusion chiefly in the subdiscipline known as the sociology of knowledge. Such thinking, refusing to take an expressed idea at face value, assumes that it is determined wholly by the context in which it is formulated, its social habitat. That habitat accounts for the opinions of the thinker and explains why his ideas are different from those of another person who lives within a different habitat. Each believes unquestioningly in the respective system, since people tend not to question the environments in which they feel at home. Each socially determined system is known as a total ideology.

Typically, the sociology of knowledge is used as a debunking device. For example, one of its best-known practitioners, German sociologist Karl Mannheim, does not believe in absolutes. He says that people who do are merely exhibiting "a sign of the loss of and the need for intellectual and moral certainty . . . unable to look life in the face."[38] We may question how he learned that, but there will be no satisfactory answer. Erich Fromm believed that any thought that is not merely conventional

---

was that they were shaped so powerfully by the thinking of contemporary social scientists." Also, Daniel P. Moynihan, *Maximum Feasible Misunderstanding: Community Action in the War on Poverty* (New York: Free Press, 1969), p. 191: ". . . social science is at its weakest, at its worst, when it offers theories of individual or collective behavior which raise the possibility, by controlling certain inputs, of bringing about mass behavioral change. No such knowledge now exists. . . . Enough snake oil has been sold in this Republic to warrant the expectation that public officials will begin reading labels."

[38]Karl Mannheim, *Ideology and Utopia: An Introduction to the Sociology of Knowledge,* trans. Louis Wirth and Edward Shils (London: Kegan Paul, Trench, Trubner, 1946 [1936]), p. 77. Mannheim, ironically, describes Freudian psychology in terms that could as easily be used against the sociology of knowledge. For those who mastered the technique, "the unmasking of the unconscious had a terrific advantage over their adversaries. It was stupefying for the latter when it was demonstrated that their ideas were merely distorted reflections of their situation in life, anticipations of their unconscious interests. The mere fact that it could be convincingly demonstrated [whether true or not] to the adversary that motives which had hitherto been hidden from him were at work must have filled him with terror and awakened in the person using the weapon a feeling of marvellous superiority." *Ibid.,* p. 37.

is simply a product of needs and interests, regardless of formal reasons adduced for it.[39] Similarly, he said that the idea of God is derived from political structures dominated by powerful tribal chiefs or kings.[40]

Peter Berger calls attention to the personal disturbance experienced by someone who is confronted with a sociology-of-knowledge explanation for his beliefs. "A person holding certain moral convictions does not take kindly to the suggestion that they can be accounted for, or even very much related to, the fact that he comes from a lower-middle-class background."[41] Elsewhere, in a work on religious sociology, Berger gives an example of that methodology. Lower class churches, he says, reflect older ethical ideas while middle class churches are more up-to-date in their mores. But that is not to say that the beliefs came prior to the affiliation in the respective churches.[42] The sociology of knowledge always has the environment precede the idea, even when it cannot provide evidence for that order.

In its debunking role the sociology of knowledge has analogues in related disciplines. The Freudian who dismisses an opponent as merely working off a repression or the Marxist who interprets social and political opinions as simple expressions of class interest are examples of the same kind of process. C. S. Lewis believed this tendency to be the dominant habit of twentieth-century thought and coined for it the name "Bulverism."

As in the case of other reductionist thinking we have examined, the sociologist of knowledge finds it necessary and therefore possible to escape the otherwise inescapable net of his own limitations. The behaviorist controller is somehow able to free himself from the iron grip of necessity in order to plan rationally; Lenin, in promoting himself to the vanguard, lifts himself and his comrades out of the masses conditioned by their social status; and the sociologist of knowledge is able to make a similar leap into an objectivity denied ordinary mortals. Berger, for example, willing to ascribe opinions to class status, nevertheless affirms the possibil-

---

[39]Erich Fromm, *Escape from Freedom* (New York: Holt, Rinehart, and Winston, 1963), p. 64.

[40]Erich Fromm, *You Shall be as Gods: A Radical Interpretation of the Old Testament* (New York: Holt, Rinehart, and Winston, 1966), p. 18.

[41]Peter L. Berger, *The Precarious Vision: A Sociologist Looks at Social Fictions and Christian Faith* (Garden City, N. Y.: Doubleday, 1961), p. 49.

[42]Peter L. Berger, *The Noise of Solemn Assemblies: Christian Commitment and the Religious Establishment in America* (Garden City, N. Y.: Doubleday: 1961), p. 49.

ity of a value-free social science.[43] Without that mystification he would be unable to say why his ideas should not be considered merely the rationalizations we might expect of a middle-class intellectual addled by years of immersion in an environment full of social science theory. Karl Popper argues that there is no way in which mystification can rescue the sociology of knowledge from the hook on which it impales everyone else:

> For is not their description of an intelligentsia which is only loosely anchored in tradition a very neat description of their own social group? And is it not also clear that, assuming the theory of total ideologies to be correct, it would be part of every total ideology to believe that one's own group was free from bias, and was indeed that body of the elect which alone was capable of objectivity. . . . But we could even ask whether the whole theory is not simply the expression of the class interest of this particular group; of an intelligentsia only loosely anchored in tradition, though just firmly enough to speak Hegelian as their mother tongue.[44]

The power that enables sociology of knowledge arguments to pulverize opponents who do not know how to deal with them lies in its relativizing function. To persuade someone that his opinions are purely a function of his class status is to let all the wind out of his sails. Berger is fully aware of the trickery in that procedure and warns elsewhere about those who relativize the past by socio-historical analysis while preserving the present from the same process.[45] Yet he exempts the sociology of knowledge from the same culpability. He thinks that sociology's advantage lies in its ability to free us from "the tyranny of the present," just as other disciplines are able to free us from the past. "Once we grasp our own situation in sociological terms, it ceases to impress us as an inexorable fate."

But although this perspective relativizes what oppresses us, it relativizes everything else as well, including what liberates us. We may also wonder if the sociological terms with which we "grasp our own situation" will not turn out to be the familiar environmental reductionism we

---

[43]Peter L. Berger, *Pyramids of Sacrifice: Political Ethics and Social Change* (New York: Basic Books, 1974), p. 100.

[44]Popper, *Open Society and Its Enemies,* vol. 2, p. 216; cf. *Ibid.,* p. 243: "The socio-analyst claims that only certain intellectuals can get rid of their total ideology, can be freed from 'thinking with their class;' he thus gives up the idea of a potential rational unity of man, and delivers himself body and soul to irrationalism."

[45]Peter L. Berger, *A Rumor of Angels: Modern Society and the Discovery of the Supernatural* (Garden City, N. Y.: Doubleday, 1969), p. 51.

use to escape our responsibilities by blaming circumstance for our action. Mannheim is caught up in a similar contradiction. He tells us that relativism comes out of a sociological procedure that binds all thought to the concrete position of the thinker, that there is no point in trying to discover absolute or unchangeable ideas, and yet he thinks somehow that the sociology of knowledge can serve as an antidote to relativism.[46]

Beyond the obvious point that these relativisms cannot withstand their own methodology is the fact that they so conceive the nature of argumentation as to render themselves impervious to refutation. We may be helped by the analogy of insanity that Chesterton used in his critique of determinism. If the madman is convinced there is a conspiracy against him, there is nothing you can say to dissuade him. All the evidence you use to show that the meter reader is just a meter reader and not an assassin, he takes as further evidence of the cleverness of those diabolical plotters. The all-inclusiveness of the system makes it invulnerable to refutation, regardless of the evidence adduced. It is thus with the psychological "explanations" for faith and the sociological "explanations" for convictions on social and economic matters. All arguments are turned back as further evidence that the speaker is bound by the determining influence. The technique provides what Mannheim admits is a "means for side-stepping the discussion." Attention is then focused on the alleged motivations or determining experiences of the adversary. This is little more than a sophisticated form of the logical fallacy that beginning students of logic are taught, the argument *ad hominem.* Such imperviousness to refutation, far from being a sign of strength, is further evidence that these disciplines are not the sciences they claim to be.

If we should ask our sociologist of knowledge how he knows that our convictions "can be accounted for" by our social class, the answer is likely to be statistical. But there can be no logical conclusion about the cause of *our* opinion inferred from the fact that 63 percent of an arbitrarily drawn class structure of which we are said to be a part have similar opinions. There is an enormous logical gap here that we must not allow the sociology of knowledge to paper over with statistical legerdemain. The same is true of Freudian put-downs based on anecdotal material. Moreover, even if the debunker correctly identifies the motivation behind his adversary's position, that says nothing about the validity of the adversary's argument or the truth of his conclusion.

It is ironic that sociology, which had its origins in an attempt to treat

---

[46]Mannheim, *Ideology and Utopia*, pp. 70,77,237.

the study of social phenomena in the rational way that the natural sciences were studying nature, has fallen into the service of irrationality. Even a half century ago, Walter Lippmann was complaining about the "host of learned ignoramuses [who] argued that no ideal had validity if any class in the community prospered by upholding it."[47] The mindlessness of public debate in the present day can hardly be unrelated to the spread of this assault on rationality, largely through the educational system. Lewis's warning that under those conditions "reason can play no effective part in human affairs" is increasingly verified. And so is Popper's prediction that the various manifestations of the cult "clearly destroy the basis of rational discussion, and they must lead ultimately to anti-rationalism and mysticism."[48]

Reason as Lord of the Universe

Any appeal to rationality is bound to be blunted by the exaggerated claims for reason that have been current since the Enlightenment. Kant's influence in particular has cast a pall over the succeeding generations of Western philosophy, setting it up for a subsequent period of reaction, especially in the English-speaking countries. For Kant had worked out an epistemology whereby reason was more than merely a tool for discerning nature's configuration, accommodating itself to her; it became for him and his followers a legislative faculty forcing nature to accommodate herself to its requirements. On this showing, reason not only reflects nature but also determines its essence and meaning. Rational categories within the mind are determinative of natural consequences. Such an interpretation fits perfectly the entire Enlightenment tradition, which assumed that man constituted the central meaning of the universe.[49] That is the justification behind Ellul's remark that reason "became the god of this world." It should have meant the operation of a precious faculty, unique to man, enabling him to discern reality and

---

[47] Walter Lippmann, *An Inquiry into the Principles of the Good Society* (Boston: Little, Brown, 1937), p. 380.

[48] Lewis, *God in the Dock,* p. 274; Popper, *Open Society and Its Enemies,* vol. 2, p. 215. In an unpublished paper advancing the cause of the sociology of knowledge, Os Guinness says that "its method is 'dialectical,' and not 'deterministic,' and 'interpretative,' and not 'reductionist.' " There can be no objection to a discipline practiced in that way and it is, in fact, the way many historians do their work. But that is not the dominant method of the disciplines criticized here.

[49] See the explanation of Kant's influence in this respect in J.L. Talmon, *Political Messianism: The Romantic Phase* (London: Secker and Warburg, 1960), pp. 175–79.

measure his actions in accord with it. But it degenerated into a blind rationalism, "incapable of accepting reality as norm and measure."[50]

Almost as if to illustrate the physical law that actions have equal and opposite reactions, the most serious difficulties we face today are associated not with the cult of rationalism, but rather with that of irrationalism. Popper is right to conclude that the struggle between reason and irrationalism is the intellectual issue of our time, with profound moral consequences. The irony is that Kant's enormous shadow lies over the irrational just as it did the idolization of reason. For if, as Kant said, human reason is able to exercise its omnipotent will over the objects of the phenomenal world—objects discerned by our physical senses—it is nevertheless impotent to discover anything about the noumenal world of the spirit. Reason deals with the facts discernible by the senses, then stops at the frontier that guards other kinds of reality. But to offer facts in place of meaning is to offer stones to a world crying for bread. That is why Norman Brown labels the Kantian logic a form of repression.[51]

The Triumph of the Irrational

To discern meaning and value, therefore, the Kantian logic requires the use of the irrational. Harvey Cox, the theologian of fashion, exemplifies to perfection the shift away from reason. He wrote *The Secular City* in the early 1960s, when the Whiz Kids were in charge of the Pentagon and everyone knew that human reason, combined with powerful computers, could solve every problem that faced us, from poverty to guerillas in the jungle. This book exalted the cool and secular rationality that was emancipated from the superstitions of the past, while slighting the noumenal. Half a decade later that world was shattered, and Cox, who can detect a changing trend faster than almost anybody, wrote *The Feast of Fools,* in which he joined Brown in glorious freedom from the "repression" of reason. As Gary North puts it, he "jumped out of Kant's phenomenal frying pan into Kant's noumenal fire."[52] Other trendy theologians were right with the nimble Cox. The same year *The Feast of Fools*

---

[50]Jacques Ellul, *The Betrayal of the West,* trans. Matthew J. O'Connell (New York: Seabury, 1978), pp. 149,164.

[51]Norman O. Brown, *Life Against Death: The Psychoanalytical Meaning of History* (Middletown, Conn.: Wesleyan Univ. Press, 1959), p. 321.

[52]Gary North, "The Epistemological Crisis of American Universities," *Foundations of Christian Scholarship: Essays in the Van Til Perspective,* ed. Gary North (Vallecito, Calif.: Ross House, 1976), p. 20.

was published, Michael Novak wrote that the "fundamental American myth . . . is the myth of the head, of the mind, of the importance of words, rationality, and impersonal logic. The ordinary white American seems to imagine himself as a consciousness encased in a bag of skin."[53] Thus reason is portrayed as a culturally derived and defective mechanism that imprisons us. We are advised to seek deeper meaning in play, festivity, and emotional and physical release. As North says, "The psychedelic baby eats the cybernetic monster."

There is considerable evidence for the generalization that a society that values reason tends to idolize it and, finally, turns against it. Greek rationality, which graced the Mediterranean world in the sixth century before Christ, broke down in the fourth century and later into a bizarre farrago of wild cults and superstitions.[54] The Age of Reason, long before it had reached the end of the Enlightened century, began to be impressed by reason's *weakness* and turned increasingly to the study of what was practical rather than what was true. When people forsake reason they have a tendency to become what Philip Rieff wants us to call "factualists." Turning to facts rather than striving for meaning, they lose the ability to construct coherent syntheses. Regardless of whether they are of the left or the right or try to maintain a scientific neutrality, they labor in self-contained boxes, constructed by themselves. "Being anti-theoretical, they are anti-critical."[55]

Behaviorism is another example of an attempt to undertake rational explanation that ends in irrationality. Skinner emphatically denies that goals have anything to do with behavior. "Behavior is *followed by* reinforcement; it does not pursue and overtake it." This means that when behavior is explained as the purposeful organization of activity designed to attain certain ends—in other words when it is thought of as being rational—the behaviorist replies that that is a prescientific understanding. Rationality can only be understood in connection with freedom and, as we have already seen, Skinner acknowledges that if freedom exists then a science of behavior cannot. Of late, behaviorists in university psychology departments have been forced to make room for what Paul Vitz calls "selfist" psychologies, emphasizing emotional satisfactions

---

[53]Michael Novak, Introduction to Helmut Thielicke, *Nihilism: Its Origin and Nature with a Christian Answer,* trans. John W. Doberstein (New York: Schocken Books, 1969 [1961]), pp. 11f.

[54]Gilbert Murray, *Five Stages of Greek Religion* (New York: Clarendon, 1925).

[55]Philip Rieff, *The Triumph of the Therapeutic: Uses of Faith After Freud* (New York: Harper and Row, 1966), p. 165.

and mystical states that can only be called religious. In all this, the irrational is not only tolerated but cultivated as beneficial.[56]

Our whole century has manifested the same irrationalities that today are increasingly celebrated. Chesterton thought it an ominous sign that the visual arts had begun to defy reason and that people declined to provide explanations for their position, instead referring to the ineffable, the unexplainable, the unutterable, the undefinable.[57] Many novelists, such as D. H. Lawrence, have deplored reliance on the intellect because it degrades the accomplishments of instinct and intuition. Psychoanalysis glorifies what is savage and primitive, unconsciously imitating the Enlightenment attachment to the "noble savage" rather than to the civilization that had produced the learned philosophers themselves. Marshall McLuhan's popularity shows that he has struck a responsive chord with his teaching that decisions are made not by thinking seriously about evidence but by responding to sensations. And here is Cox, reveling in the rebirth of fantasy and feeling rather than intellect.[58]

Beyond the pop intellectuals pandering to changing public moods, there are disquieting signs that something of crucial importance for the well-being of society's intellectual inheritance is eroding. Students' cheating in the colleges, amid plunging academic standards, is no longer news, but now we learn that respected scholars and scientists have been faking evidence. Even a generation ago, University of Chicago sociologist Louis Wirth was alarmed by an academic environment in which the search for truth was being shunted aside by the scholars' drive for personal self-aggrandizement.[59]

There are corrosive currents in the academic world that have still to bear the bitter fruit inherent in them. Perspectives that borrow from the sociology of knowledge have not yet done all the damage of which they are capable. If it should become widely believed that intellectual positions are all concealed derivations of class or of other external determinants, it is difficult to see how academic work can continue. Already some scholars question whether it *should* continue. Geneticist Gunther Stent of the University of California at Berkeley thinks that academic

---

[56]Paul C. Vitz, *Psychology as Religion: The Cult of Self-Worship* (Grand Rapids: Eerdmans, 1977).

[57]G.K. Chesterton, *A Miscellany of Men,* 3rd ed. (London: Methuen, 1920), pp. 145-51.

[58]Harvey Cox, *The Feast of Fools: A Theological Essay on Festivity and Fantasy* (Cambridge: Harvard Univ. Press, 1969).

[59]Louis Wirth, Preface to Karl Mannheim, *Ideology and Utopia,* p. xiii.

progress in most fields—including his own—is near its end. There is little hope of dramatic payoff remaining, and society has small incentive to continue funding such work indefinitely. He believes that science has intrinsic limits and that they are fast being reached. What is more, the findings of science are often at such variance with commonsense observations that people will find continuing estrangement from reality too much to bear and cease to strive further.[60]

Assault from the East

In the 1960s, speculation about the religion of the future was dominated by Dietrich Bonhoeffer's thesis, popularized by John A. T. Robinson and others, that in the twentieth century man would not need religion as a shield to explain or to protect him from the unknown and would shun the churches that did not come to terms with the new situation. That was the outlook from which Cox's *Secular City* sprang.[61] No sooner had this thesis gained general acceptance than it was proved wrong, and Cox's celebration of the irrational in the *Feast of Fools* showed him to have better powers of recovery from an untenable position than the social scientists who were paid to foresee such shifts. Cox, wetted finger still feeling for the shifting wind, now heralds the blossoming of oriental religion in the United States.[62]

Pantheism is an ancient philosophy and probably has always been present, even in the West during the years when it was officially banished by the hegemony of Christianity. Materialism enjoyed perhaps its greatest acceptance when the physical sciences agreed with commonsense notions of the "hardness" and ultimacy of physical matter. With the revolution in physics, however, that support vanished. Commenting on the shift toward the religious mysticism so evident in his paintings, Salvador Dali told an interviewer that he was influenced by the spirituality of the new physics. "I realized that science is moving toward a spiritual state." Spengler could call materialism the religion of his time, but his contemporary, German historian Ernst Troeltsch, gazing at the harbingers of a new world just over the horizon, described pantheism as "the secret religion of the educated classes." German Protestant-

---

[60]Gunther S. Stent, *The Coming of the Golden Age: A View of the End of Progress* (Garden City, N.Y.: Natural History Press, 1969), pp. 110–15.

[61]Cf. Berger, *A Rumor of Angels,* p. 32: "An impressive rediscovery of the supernatural, in the dimensions of a mass phenomenon, is not in the books."

[62]Harvey Cox, *Turning East: The Promise and Peril of the New Orientalism* (New York: Simon and Schuster, 1977).

ism, in particular, drawing on such sources as the remnants of neo-Platonism, romanticism, and mysticism, led the West in switching out of materialism.[63]

Pantheism erases the sharp lines of distinction that are peculiar to biblical religion and its derivatives. Radically monist, just as materialism is, it does not recognize any ontological difference between man and other living beings; between the living and the nonliving; between God and the universe. It insists on immanence, and sees the divine nature in all things and all people. Dali, pondering the implications of quantum physics and Teilhardian biology, concluded that "man in his constant evolution is coming closer and closer to a oneness with God." When the devotee of Eastern pantheism chants *Atman is Brahman,* he means that the soul of each person is the same as the soul of the cosmos. There is no distinction between man and the cosmos, between God and the cosmos, between God and man.[64] In Huxley's pantheist utopia the hero, in drugged ecstasy, experiences union with the universe: ". . . a knowledgeless understanding, only union with unity in a limitless, undifferentiated awareness. . . . Poured upward from union into completer union, from unpersonality into a yet more absolute transcendence of selfhood."[65]

The soaring vistas of pantheism, the undifferentiated cosmos promising an infinitude of experience, the absence of limitations, feelings of harmony, and the promise of profound religious experience are powerful attractions to many people. For Huxley, "the non-dualist calls the vasty deep into his spirit or, to be more accurate, he finds that the vasty deep is already there." When Julien Benda berated the intellectuals of his day for taking up the cause of petty nationalisms, it was in the name of a universal loyalty that was much higher, one that he associated with the pantheist unity. He assumed that *universal* was synonymous with good and *particular* with evil. Compared to pantheism, Christianity has struck many people as being too bounded or too materialistic. Many of the heresies of the church have been pantheistic, and the mystical tradition especially has a tendency to veer in that direction.[66]

---

[63]Ernst Troeltsch, *The Social Teachings of the Christian Churches,* 2 vols., trans. Olive Wyon (New York: Harper Torchbooks, 1960 [1931]), vol. 2, p. 794.

[64]See James W. Sire, *The Universe Next Door: A Basic World View Catalog* (Downers Grove, Ill.,: Inter-Varsity Press, 1976), pp. 131ff.

[65]Aldous Huxley, *Island* (New York: Harper and Brothers, 1962), pp. 309f.

[66]See Adolph Harnack, *History of Dogma,* trans. Neil Buchanan, 7 vols. in 4 (New York: Dover Publications, 1961 [1900]), vol. 6, pp. 104f., 179; vol. 7, pp. 121ff.; Denis

Dutch theologian W. A. Visser 't Hooft, former general secretary of the World Council of Churches, believes that modern pantheism is a rising tide in the Western world, filling the media with subtle messages of immanentism and relativism and constituting a new paganism. He quotes philosopher Jean Brun to the effect that environmental degradation may be a result of the "dualism" of Christianity, separating creation from deity. Brun speculates that we may need some form of nature worship to counter those effects.[67] Nature worship comes naturally to those who already are attracted to the notion that all reality is ultimately one, because the deity is found everywhere. Some manifestations of the environmental movement apparently derive from that view. Jean-François Revel has described Earth Day in the United States as a pantheistic feast.

If pantheism becomes as influential in the West as some observers expect, the effects are likely to be baneful. Troeltsch, observing its influence on German Protestantism, concluded that its propensity to mysticism had the effect of destroying community and fellowship; communing with the "vasty deep" within oneself makes ethics and concrete forms of social life superfluous. Its reverence for animal life, supposedly touched with divinity along with the rest of nature, may have serious consequences for many aspects of economic life.[68] Pantheism is not impressed by such consequences because it does not place high value on community or on economic life, or on anything that seeks to assuage desires. It finds its rewards, rather, in quietism, in surrender and union with the all-pervasive divinity that permeates nature. As Chesterton said, the worshipers of such a divinity have populated Asia for centuries "and have never dethroned a tyrant." Introspection, self-isolation, and indifference derive naturally from such a theological position.

Surprisingly, pantheism ends up in a dehumanization of mankind that is not very different from that of behaviorism, despite the dissimi-

---

de Rougemont, *Man's Western Quest: The Principles of Civilization,* trans. Montgomery Belgion (New York: Harper and Brothers, 1956), p. 123. Cf. Joad, *The Recovery of Belief,* pp. 246f.: Many intellectuals have found attractive Huxley's idea that the world is a "unity of spiritual consciousness" because "denying the reality of time, it refuses to limit the world as Christianity does, to the unfolding of a drama in the time series. . . . The attraction which this kind of view has for the modern mind springs precisely from its denial of limitation, from its escape from arbitrariness."

[67]W.A. Visser 't Hooft, "Evangelism in the Neo-Pagan Situation," *International Review of Mission,* vol. 63, no. 249, Jan. 1974, pp. 81ff.

[68]For the effects of pantheism on the economic life of poor countries see P. T. Bauer, *Dissent on Development,* pp. 327ff.

larities in other respects. In Huxley's utopia, the hero recalls a momentary delusion in which the teeming streets of London appeared to him to be filled with crawling maggots rather than people. Huxley intended this as a metaphor of modern civilization with its remnant of Christian transcendence. But the vision more logically relates to his pantheism because there is in it no essential difference between men and maggots. Only an *illusion* of differentiation exists between the various elements of the cosmos. In his sympathetic survey of the modern religious scene, Jacob Needleman describes the Buddhist anthropology in terms that a behaviorist would have little difficulty accepting: ". . . everything in human nature is in flux, and a man is nothing but a serial bunch of sensations, thoughts and feelings, one proceeding from another with nothing to hold them together in life or death."[69] That kind of dehumanization accounts for the particularly brutal nature of pantheist activism when it finally bestirs itself out of contemplation to action; since the individual personality is illusory, killing it is small loss.[70] Thus spirituality and cruelty accompany each other in perfect harmony.

Nature as Lord of the Universe

Idolizing nature, whether we think it all material or all spiritual, leads us down the blind alley of the Kantian dualism. Those of an older generation usually choose the phenomenal fork and end up in one of the scientisms, such as behaviorism. In this view, life began by chance chemical encounters in the rich primordial soup that once covered the earth; developed into higher forms through the genetic selection of characteristics that enhanced survival; produced the human species; and eventually will pass into extinction.[71]

This picture is drawn entirely from materialist premises, without the interposition of spirit or mind. It depends, however, on rational inferences from the observed facts. Yet it gives us no cause to believe that reason exists except as a fortuitous advent in the continuous and meaning-

---

[69]Jacob Needleman, *The New Religions* (Garden City, N. Y.: Doubleday, 1970), p. 26.

[70]Denis de Rougemont contrasts the culpability of Western brutality with the "innocent" nature of that of the East, a necessary consequence of the respective anthropologies of Christianity and pantheism. "No 'wisdom' clears us; on the contrary, we stand condemned by our faith. An Oriental's cruelty is as though fated, and hence without restraint, without sin, without contradiction or remorse. It is divine, and we are criminals." *Man's Western Quest,* p. 20.

[71]That is the view, for example, of Nobel prize winner George Wald, "The Origin of Life," *Scientific American,* vol. 19, no. 2, Aug. 1954, pp. 44–53.

less flux, one that may disappear soon, to be replaced by another biological event. Reason is thus discredited as a reliable interpreter of reality by a system whose very formulation depends on the rational process. This is a theory that destroys itself.[72]

If the noumenal path is chosen, we end up in the miasma of mysticism, merging with the cosmos, teasing gods and demons out of the subsconscious, deliberately cultivating the irrational. This is the murder of reason. It should be no surprise that our age is filled with the recrudescence of superstitions that the scientific revolution was thought to have conquered with the proud victory of phenomena. Society is awash with witchcraft, astrology, reincarnation, magic, alchemy, and hallucinatory drugs. Bookstores do a land-office business in the occult, as the flight from reason accelerates.

The Effects of Naturalist Irrationality

Irrationality is the prelude to destruction. It is difficult to imagine an antiutopia that values reason, and the fictional ones we have portray societies that exalt the irrational. The *Brave New World* uses a drug to provide "a holiday from the facts," and the new society's controller declares that art and science are both dangerous. "Truth's a menace." In *1984* the Party imposes an epistemology that rejects reason and the evidence of the senses. *Doublethink* is a system of mental cheating. Reality is subjective. The individual mind knows nothing; only the Party knows. A member of the opposition in Ayn Rand's antiutopia remarks: "You know, I think that the only real moral crime that one man can commit against another is the attempt to create, by his words or actions, an impression of the contradictory, the impossible, the irrational, and thus shake the concept of rationality in his victim."[73] Poor Huxley, determined to discredit Christianity by every possible means, nevertheless filled his utopia with Christian virtues, including the fruits of reason. His imagination failed him, apparently, inasmuch as he could find no

---

[72]The argument is drawn from Lewis, *They Asked for a Paper,* pp. 154ff., 162ff. "If minds are wholly dependent on brains and brains on biochemistry, and biochemistry (in the long run) on the meaningless flux of the atoms, I cannot understand how the thought of those minds should have any more significance than the sound of the wind in the trees." *Ibid.,* pp. 164f.

[73]Aldous Huxley, *Brave New World* (New York: Harper Colophon Books, 1960), pp. 173, 175, 182; George Orwell, *1984* (New York: New American Library Signet, 1961 [1949]), pp. 69, 177f., 205; Ayn Rand, *Atlas Shrugged* (New York: Random House, 1957), p. 488.

way to import those virtues into his pantheist heaven of the East except from the West; the utopia's founder arrived on site with a medical degree earned in a nation of Presbyterians! All of Huxley's ingenuity proved incapable of deriving the benefits of science and of service to others except from the principles of transcendence that he hated so passionately.

The sands of Kantian rationality are running out in the West. People who depend on the human mind to shape nature's configuration are in an unenviable position when they come to believe, after decades of being taught otherwise, that reason is a weak and uncertain reed on which to lean. If everything depends on rationality and reason is dead, then there is only chance. That is when Tyche, the goddess of fortune, comes into her own. Daniel Bell is on the right track in seeing tychism—a reality dominated by unknown forces—making a resurgence. "When life has grown arbitrary one becomes obsessed with, and prays to, chance."[74]

The Cult of Narcissism

In a society that shifts its attention from phenomena to noumena, reason to unreason, material to spiritual, the individual is likely also to change his views concerning himself and his relationship to the world. Eastern religion seems to denigrate the self in preaching the annihilation of the ego. Cox accepts this at face value, but that is an error. In the Eastern utopia, declares Huxley, people worship "their own suchness visualized as God." As Needleman says with sympathy, self-centeredness is a feature common to all the religions of Asia. Chesterton concluded that the most horrible religions are those that encourage self-worship. "That Jones shall worship the god within him turns out ultimately to mean that Jones shall worship Jones." Thus, we are back to humanism. This is not far different from the divine spark theories that periodically invade Christianity through mysticisms of one kind or another or that blossomed in other guises during and after the Enlightenment. People who accept humanism in other forms find it only a gentle transition to accept it in this form. The individual and all that he feels, does, and says are lifted to ultimacy. Thus the turn to the East is a fitting end for individualism in the West.

The cult of self-expression, with all its excrescences, has become so pervasive that society is often said to have fallen into narcissism. The

---

[74]Daniel Bell, *The Cultural Contradictions of Capitalism* (New York: Basic Books, 1976), pp. 150f.

individual believes himself to be the measure of both reality and moral principle. Thus, there are no standards, no belief in eternal truth, no objective measure of right and wrong; norms are delusions, and self-discipline serves no purpose. As Harvard's Irving Babbitt put it in an earlier period, "every ass that's romantic thinks he's inspired."

Narcissism flourishes under the cloak of psychological theories of personal growth. Underneath the superficial optimism, despair lies concealed. As Christopher Lasch says, ". . . It is the faith of those without faith."[75] New York University psychologist Paul Vitz also considers this genre of psychology, represented by such scholars as Erich Fromm, Carl Rogers, Abraham Maslow, and Rollo May, a form of narcissism. He believes it teaches self-worship and is in fact a religion posing as a science.[76]

Psychologies of narcissism fall into the mainstream of the new American society in stressing the importance of the *experiences* of life. As materialism gives way to the new spiritualism, what is possessed seems less important than what is experienced. People would rather save for a luxurious vacation than a luxurious car. Experience is important because it is composed of sensations, and sensations are all that is left of man after the reductionisms of both behaviorism and pantheism destroy his being. For both behaviorists and pantheists human life consists of a succession of sensations inhering in nothing. Without experiencing sensations, then, man loses his identity, even his existence.

Fromm, for example, considers the question of how we are to deal with the sense of impotence and desperation that results from the dissolution of the old bonds that once sustained society. He finds his answer in spontaneity. Spontaneous action "affirms the individuality of the self and at the same time it unites the self with man and nature." By spontaneous action he "realizes his self." It is as if man creates himself by spontaneous activity; without it he would not exist. He must *experience* to be himself, to be alive. So vapid is this conception that when Fromm tries to tell us what life is, he can only lapse into tautology: the only meaning life has, he says, is living itself.[77]

Charles Reich, the legal scholar who left the Yale faculty to join the homosexual culture of San Francisco, asks what we lost when society turned on evil ways in the 1960s. His answer is a long list of personal ex-

---

[75]Christopher Lasch, *The Culture of Narcissism: American Life in an Age of Diminishing Expectations* (New York: Norton, 1978), p. 51.

[76]Vitz, *Psychology as Religion,* pp. 32,80,105.

[77]Fromm, *Escape from Freedom,* pp. 256–63.

periences that he said could no longer be his.[78] The straight life was evil because it declined to give him the experiences he craved, and therefore—to use Fromm's formulation—withheld from him life itself. The talk about "justice" sprinkled throughout his book is pure moonshine, for an ethic as egoistic as his must be at war with justice. The demand for personal experience is completely self-centered, capable of being fully as costly as the demand for things. When it is driven by the religious need to validate life itself, it is incapable of considering any form of justice that may conflict with self-interest.

Delving into the self in search of ultimate significance has serious consequences, as do all forms of egoism. One of these is the increase of sentimentality. This destructive impulse, often highly regarded as somehow being "idealistic," is self-regarding, concerned with feeling good rather than doing good, and thrives on the falsehood that feelings are interchangeable with external realities. Historian Henry May examined its increasing force early in the twentieth century and concluded that it is inseparable from naturalism.[79] The callousness of sentimentality is beyond dispute. There is no incongruity in weeping over the beauty of a flower or a Mozart concerto in between tours of duty in the torture chamber. The sentimentality of some of the most vicious members of the Nazi hierarchy is almost legendary. Solzhenitsyn noticed the same thing in the Soviet concentration camps.[80] In *1984,* the state music department programs a machine to write sentimental songs that it uses as an anodyne, so that the masses will be less able to understand what is being done to them.

The affinities between pantheism and selfist psychology are so apparent that we are not surprised to find Cox reporting that many psychologists are becoming enamored of Eastern religion. Nor is it surprising that the result of this is the transformation of therapist into priest. Swiss psychiatrist Paul Tournier writes that when the psychological counselor passes from diagnosis to recommendations on moral behavior, he becomes a soul-healer. His recommendation is necessarily based on a the-

---

[78]Charles A. Reich, *The Greening of America* (New York: Random House, 1970), pp. 152-55.

[79]Henry F. May, *The End of American Innocence: A Study of the First Years of Our Own Time* (New York: Knopf, 1959), p. 73.

[80]An Estonian named Arnold Susi, flung into a cramped cell with Solzhenitsyn, explained it in this way: "Cruelty is invariably accompanied by sentimentality. It is the law of complementarities." Aleksandr I. Solzhenitsyn, *The Gulag Archipelago, 1918-1956: An Experiment in Literary Investigation,* trans. Thomas P. Whitney (New York: Harper and Row, 1973), vol. 1, p. 202.

ology, whether conscious or otherwise.[81] Vitz gives numerous examples of selfist psychology's destructive influence in almost every area of life. Its intense egoism destroys the capacity for love and encourages the breakup of community and of family. Inasmuch as it dominates the helping professions and government agencies, it receives not only the aura of an official stamp of approval and massive funding but also the impetus of coercion.

A World Become Spooky

This chapter has sought to demonstrate that the idolatries based on nature, whether coming in secular guise or as overtly religious, are founded on presuppositions that are religious in nature. It accepts the wisdom in Toynbee's vision of the ubiquity of religious ideas, even where they are denied. All observers of the human scene are theologians, he said, for "theology is an incubus that a [student of human affairs] can never shake off. . . . Theology is inescapable, and it is dynamite. It will betray its identity through the camouflage by exploding in the end."[82] In our age, the camouflage of which Toynbee speaks has consisted largely of the myths of secularity that people have wrapped around academic disciplines. With their roots in a civilization founded on biblical understandings, these disciplines valued the rational, and they benefited from the ability to study a natural world that was demystified. The doctrine of creation meant that there was nothing of the divine in a rock, a plant, or a human body, permitting them to be studied rather than feared or worshiped. Clearing the world of spooks made it possible for us to learn about it.

Now the spooks are back, and that is the explosion Toynbee warned about. Secularizing intellectuals thought they were ridding the house of the noumenal by sweeping religion out the door, but while they were at it, the spirits flew in the window. We have completed the pilgrimage from studying nature, to believing that nature was all there is, to idolizing it. Expelling the biblical presuppositions that were the only ones that could provide a foundation for rationality, we unwittingly invited the irrational to join us. When irrationalities based on the phenomenal proved to be thin gruel, we called for the noumenal to provide nourishment. With all the nonsense that has been written about the generation

---

[81]Paul Tournier, *The Meaning of Persons* (New York: Harper and Brothers, 1957), p. 110.

[82]Arnold Toynbee, *Reconsiderations,* vol. 12 of *A Study of History* (New York: Oxford Univ. Press, 1961), p. 67.

gap, this remains. Many older people are materialists while their children have become spiritualists. We should not be so foolish as to think that our fate lies in having to choose between those two manifestations of the idolatry of nature.

The Second Face of Janus

Idolizing nature has serious consequences. Early in the century, when some of them were becoming visible, a group of intellectuals led by Irving Babbitt, Paul Elmer More, and Stuart P. Sherman, known collectively as the "new humanists," made pariahs of themselves by warning about the effects of naturalism. They thought society was entering a new barbarism because it was destroying the influences that reined in human appetites. They were distressed at the materialism, the hatred for tradition, the glorification of what was useful, the extreme individualism and egoism, and the growing inability to make moral judgments.[83] Babbitt and his friends were witnessing the triumph of nature in its phenomenal manifestation, which in the United States came perhaps a generation after it had reached its apogee in Europe. It was not until after World War II that the cracks in it became obvious enough for more than the occasional prophet to worry about, and its decline, which Harvey Cox at first mistook for its triumph, came in the 1960s.

Richard Neuhaus has rightly called attention to the irony in the fact that people now wish to counter the dangers of scientism by appealing to nature.[84] That is to appeal from one face of Janus to the other. Now that nature is no longer to be exploited, it is ready to be worshiped. It is still the whole show and we are still part of it, but now being part of it means that we no longer recognize anything that transcends it. For this mentality, the closer we are to nature and the further from civilization, the better off we are. The extreme hatred for human beings and corresponding love for animals that fills the satires of Jonathan Swift is coming into vogue. That is the perspective informing Lewis Mumford's notion that Western civilization saved itself only by bringing into its festering impurities the wisdom of those who, by living close to nature, remained unspoiled.[85] Pure nature, hateful mankind. Belgian anthropologist

---

[83]See J. David Hoeveler, Jr., *The New Humanism: A Critique of Modern America: 1900–1940* (Charlottesville: Univ. of Virginia Press, 1977), p. 63.

[84]Richard John Neuhaus, *Time Toward Home: The American Experiment as Revelation* (New York: Seabury, 1975), p. 106.

[85]Lewis Mumford, *The Transformations of Man* (New York: Harper and Brothers, 1956), p. 68. Cf. Crane Brinton, *A History of Western Morals* (New York: Harcourt,

Claude Lévi-Strauss wrote volumes glorifying the savage mind as superior to the civilized mind. He thought that primitive magic was equal in its way to the science of the West. There are many manifestations of this in the arts, where we find the glorification of the primitive and coarse over the refined and civilized; the rhythmic over the melodic.

Nature in Control

When humanity is not distinguished from nature, there is almost no limit to the extent of its abasement. The fact that homosexuals once had to remain in the closet was a sign of sanity in the society. Now that sexual perversion is being touted as an alternative life-style, and politicians in some jurisdictions cater to it, we must wonder if the pit has any bottom. We are now publishing serious treatises arguing for the benefits of incest. The naturalist assumptions that remove sexual practices from the realm of morality remove everything from the realm of morality. Animals do not act morally or immorally; they only act naturally. A system of ethics that says human beings ought to base their behavior on nature therefore justifies any behavior, because nature knows no ethic. If naturalism rules, it means there is no bar to adultery, which is all right with many naturalists, but it also means there is no bar to murder. Naturalism in ethics moves persistently to fulfill the logical mandate of its assumptions. If man is only one of the animals, it makes no sense to grant him a privileged position over the other animals. It is by a logical inference that some are now proclaiming the rights of animals and proposing vegetarianism as a moral imperative. To say that man is qualitatively superior to animals is to be guilty of the sin of "speciesism."[86]

The hostility between nature and history is sharpened when the governing metaphysic has no way to reconcile them. Skinner ridicules history as being unfit for any purpose except entertainment, insists that its validity is spurious and that it has no real facts. His naturalism stands to science in the same way historicism stands to history. Because they require experience as a metaphysical imperative affirming existence, the

---

Brace, and World, 1959), p. 313: "For those American primitivists of our own day the only prospect that can please is one with no trace of humankind at all. The great hope in mankind for them has ended—and not only for them, if we may judge from the intellectual temper of our age—in the great disgust, a disgust so universal as to have little consoling power."

[86]See, for example, Stephen R.L. Clark, *The Moral Status of Animals* (Oxford: Clarendon, 1977); also Peter Singer, "Animal Liberation," *New York Review of Books,* April 5, 1973, pp. 17–21.

selfist psychologists exalt change as the source of value, just as histori-cists do. Carl Rogers deprecates any kind of stability in favor of move-ment, "from fixity to changingness, from rigid structure to flow, from stasis to process."[87]

With nature in control, untrammeled by mind, will, or value, dehu-manization is complete. Anything we do or fail to do, all evidence of so-cial or personal dysfunction, is said to stem from the environment. There is no freedom, no personal responsibility, and therefore no reason to regard human beings as anything but another of nature's products. Skinner's endorsement of the platitudes of Humanist Manifesto II can be nothing but a grotesque mystification or a cynical deception. *Beyond Freedom and Dignity* is as furious an attack on the "high" view of human-ity as we shall find. The differences between maggots and men, on this showing, are only quantitative and relative. Naturalism therefore con-firms Lewis's judgment of it. "Man's conquest of Nature turns out, in the moment of its consummation, to be Nature's conquest of man."[88]

If moral values and reason are no more than epiphenomena of natural origin, where can the line be drawn between acceptable and unaccept-able behavior? There is no answer to that except a pragmatic one. But the pragmatic answer, as the pragmatist will agree, disappears into smoke when the circumstances change. If there may be said to be any un-changing norms they will be drawn from nature where, it is plain, per-sonal relations are red in tooth and claw.

Determinism makes the box tighter, because even if there were in na-turalism a rationally inferred morality it could not be followed. Even if by mystification we erect an ideal, like love of one's neighbor, the deter-minist denies that one is free to obey or disobey it. The Marquis de Sade, who was a chemical determinist, was far more consistent than Skinner in devising the system of ethics that we call sadism. Modern determin-ists may not like the details of his ethic, but they cannot refute him within the bounds of their system, so well does he fit it. This is a system bound with iron, leaving no hope that the sinner will repent, because the sinner cannot help what he is doing; environmental contingencies brought about his behavior. Although the determinist sees no point in admonish-ing the sinner, Chesterton pointed out, he can put him in boiling oil, which is, after all, an environment. Irrationality and sentimentality, frustrated at their inevitable failures and bound by nothing that tran-scends nature, can hardly be expected to forgo violence.

---

[87] Quoted in Vitz, *Psychology as Religion*, p. 21.

[88] Lewis, *Abolition of Man*, pp. 42f.

Huxley could not make his *Island* a utopia without loading it with the Christian virtues, which, although he could not admit this, were all that made it attractive. That fact is so evident that he must have been aware of it, at least subconsciously. Perhaps this fundamental contradiction, along with a certain artistic honesty, accounts for the pessimism that caused him to end the utopia with a military take-over engineered by the neighboring island.

Absence of freedom in the individual is the microcosm for the entire society. To speak of corporate freedom is absurd if the individual is purely a part of the natural environment and determined by it. That is why Skinner says that those who choose freedom as a value are on a quixotic pursuit of the impossible. (He also writes of the emotional instability, fanaticism, and psychotic responses of those who believe in freedom!) In *Walden Two,* utopia's members quietly vote as the controller, Frazier, instructs them. He affirms the legitimacy of using despotic government in order to better the lot of everyone. Democracy is "scientifically invalid" because "in the long run man is determined by the state." All the determinisms, in practice, result in the domination of an elite. Everyone is determined by what lies outside him: by environment, by natural forces, by circumstances, by social class, and by economic interest. The logical inference from this view is fatalism or resignation. But the determinist avoids that conclusion, as we have seen, by discovering that he is exempt from determinism. Whether a sociologist arriving at a "value-free" theory, a member of the vanguard able to direct the revolution, a controller who somehow can plan in a way that is not determined, mystification allows him to rule the masses, who cannot escape the exceedingly fine net of determinism. Thus the reductionism that makes human beings automata, if it is not accompanied by nihilism, always draws in its train a mystification that allows the elite (planner, psychologist, social theorist, controller, analyst) to escape determinism's iron grip and so qualify to play god, or at least nature's high priest.

The heaving sea of naturalism therefore casts up onto the shore two odd fish. One is he of whom Charles Reich is the exemplar: noumenal man, with a dreamy irresponsibility repudiating the rationality that makes possible what he values as well as what he hates, glorifying sensual experiences, and exalting attitudes and values that, widespread enough, would make it impossible for society to persist. Here is an antinomian egoism that by some miracle is expected to result in love and justice. The other is he heralded by the Galbraiths and the Skinners: phenomenal man, exalting rationality with a philosophy that makes reason impossible, submerging man into a nature that binds him irretrievably, giving him the status of brute or machine and, finally, taking charge in the name of survival. The phenomenal man is the one who kills Reich as a parasite who reduces the chance of survival. We have had prophets warning us about both specimens since early in the century, and we do not yet know which is the greater danger or which will gain ascendancy.

The Riddle of the One and the Many

Metaphysical monisms are attractive because they cut through Gordian knots that otherwise might drive us to consternation. If we say that all is mind or all is matter, we need no longer consider the relationship between mind and matter. It is much like the Copernican revolution that relieved an earlier generation of the necessity for solving the riddle of epicycles. But what is legitimate in one sphere is not necessarily legitimate in the analogue. The relief we experience in rejecting dualism is that of an "aha" experience. It is a blinding flash of what we think is enlightenment that allows us to build fruitfully and disastrously on a false foundation. The basic problem is solved and we move ahead, now believing with the physicists that all is mind or with the psychologists that all is matter. This sets us up to support one set of idolatries or the other.

The errors of metaphysical monisms are related to those of epistemological dualisms. For in adopting the Kantian schema, we divide the objects of sensation and those that lie beyond sensation into categories that are mutually impermeable, making it impossible for meaning to penetrate one of them and for perception to penetrate the other. This results in the phenomenal world being trivialized into mere factuality, since meaning can be found only in the sphere that the Kantian system renders unknowable. Meanwhile the noumenal world gives rise to irrational mysticisms, since dualism cuts it off from the correcting influence of the sensible world.

In a debate with the new humanists, T. S. Eliot argued that they were mistaken to think that naturalism could be refuted without a transcendent principle upon which nature was dependent. "Either everything in man can be traced as a development from below or something must come from above." He maintained, therefore, that the only alternative to naturalism is supernaturalism. Eliot's position has been confirmed by succeeding events, for Babbitt's stand was flattened by the naturalist steamroller. Babbitt himself ended up in the miasma of Buddhism, which is only another form of the naturalism he detested.

Prolegomena to Any Christian Epistemology

In considering the relationship between man and nature, the important theological question is not monotheism and polytheism but rather immanence and transcendence. For if deity is identified with nature or any part of nature—sun, moon, sea, winds, earth, grain—it does not matter much whether there are one, ten, or a million gods, since they are bound up in natural processes. The creation myths of antiquity, so many of which have been thought to be mere variants of the Genesis account, are really quite the opposite. Those myths portray the visible universe as in some way identified with deity. The universe is eternal, and the god emerges from it. Or a deity is manipulated in some way so that the elements of the universe are created out of its being. The head of the Babylonian pantheon, Marduk, for example, created the earth and sky from the two halves of Tiamat, the personification of evil, after a ferocious battle. The Judeo-Christian conception is radically different, for in it God is, as the Schoolmen said, *totaliter oliter*—wholly other than the universe. Therefore he must not be identified with it or any part of it. Being free of it, he is *free,* and those who are created in his image are also free. Materialism and pantheism, whatever their differences, share immanence, the identification of ultimacy with the creation. They must therefore end up deterministic, fatalistic, and pessimistic, or else cover up their logical conclusions with mystification.

What the doctrine of creation does with the metaphysical problem, incarnation does with the epistemological one. Although we no longer read Kant, we are part of an intellectual world that has been shaped by the responses to his teaching that there is an unbridgeable gulf between matter and spirit. How can we observe the facts directly, that is, sensibly, and thus come to know phenomena, and yet at the same time understand their meaning? How can objectivity and subjectivity be comprehended together? How can transcendence and immanence be understood as inhering in the same being at the same time? Those who believe in the Christian doctrine of incarnation do not need to make choices between fact and meaning because there is an archetype for understanding how the world of flesh and the world of spirit make contact. For if God was in Christ, and if the way to the Father is through the Son, then there is no need to accept a formulation that erects an unbridgeable gulf between the sensible and rational, object and subject, matter and mind. We do not need to choose between brute factuality and mystical derangement.

The answer to the antinomies of the ancient Greek philosophies, as the philosophers taught, was a conception called *logos.* That is the clue to understanding the antinomies of modern life and philosophy as well. "In the beginning was the *Logos,* and the *Logos* was with God, and the *Logos* was God. He was in the beginning with God; all things were made through him, and without him was not anything made that was made" (John 1:1–3). Thus do creation and incarnation come together. Thus does nature spring from its creator while remaining separate from him and dependent upon him. Thus do we understand a world that is demystified and also know a creator that is beyond the creation. On this showing, nature, as Chesterton said, is not our mother, but our sister, and we do not need to bow down before her. The nature gods for us are just ordinary trees and stars, and therefore good; we do not divinize them and turn them into something evil. At the same time both spirit and matter inhabit the universe and both are knowable. Therefore we do not think that the objects of our senses constitute all that is. And we do not erect a wall of hostility between the two aspects under which we comprehend the creation: history and nature.

Most importantly, we recognize in human beings that which is created in the image of God and is therefore higher than nature. There is no other principle which can erect a permanent bar against treating them like animals or rocks.

Idols of Power

The Creation of Leviathan

PERHAPS the most characteristic feature of modern history, one which impinges upon virtually every area of life, has been the development of the nation-state. So pervasive is its influence, so "normal" do its vast powers seem, that to read a document that seeks to limit severely the scope of those powers—even so recent a one as the Constitution of the United States—evokes a sense of great antiquity and strangeness.

The long and difficult process, filled with odd turnings and retrogressions, by which the central authority came to dominate the entire society may be traced from the days when the early medieval monarch sought to become something more than *primus inter pares*. His enemy was the nobility, ensconced in quasi-independent estates but fortified by the interlocking loyalties that were the essence of feudalism. His ally was the rising middle class, emancipated from serfdom on the estates of the nobility, and recreating prosperity in the eleventh century through the rise of towns and the revival of commerce that signaled a new civilization. This alliance of the middle class with the central authority against the centrifugal interests of the nobility flowered spectacularly during the reign of Louis XIV in late seventeenth-century France. One hundred years later the middle class took over the state *in toto*, the culmination of an eight-hundred-year process.

Those eight centuries were filled with endless examples of the striving for power and wealth that we expect in political struggles, but the

French Revolution added to them the powerful forces of nationalism. The peasant's grandfather thought of himself primarily as a native of Brittany, France being a shadowy conception represented chiefly by the king. Now, the peasant knew himself as a *Frenchman,* and his chief loyalty was France. This dramatic change permitted patriotic public figures like Victor Hugo and Charles Maurras to speak of the "goddess France."[1] It meant that those who fought for France were no longer simply doing a job for which they were paid, but were patriots rendering due obeisance to a deity. For them, to do their duty was to do their *sacred* duty, language that has remained part of the liturgy of patriotism to the present, even in officially atheistic countries like the Soviet Union.

God Marching on Earth

Hegel was an enthusiastic observer of the French Revolution, and in his mature philosophy he contributed to the development of the centralized state a reasoned panegyric to justify it. The state for him was not something to be defended on pragmatic grounds but was the supreme institution brought into being by the inexorable forces of history. The historicist system we associate with his name conferred qualities of inevitability and moral value on it, and his descriptions gave it the aura of divinity.

> The Universal is to be found in the State. . . . The State is the Divine Idea as it exists on earth. . . . We must therefore worship the State as the manifestation of the Divine on earth, and consider that, if it is difficult to comprehend Nature, it is harder to grasp the Essence of the State. . . . the State is the march of God through the world. . . .[2]

One would have to search hard to find a modern social theorist acknowledging that Hegel was right to say that the state is God marching on earth, but at every turn we stumble over those who advocate actions that can be logical inferences only from such a position. For them the state is the only savior we can expect on earth. Salvation is to be found in the messianic state, or it is to be found nowhere. Therefore, the only branch of human endeavor that can save us is politics. "The resolution of the crises thrust upon us," says Robert Heilbroner, "can only be

---

[1]For the early development of nationalism in Europe see Geoffrey Bruun, *Europe and the French Imperium: 1799-1814* (New York: Harper and Brothers, 1938), ch. 8.

[2]The quotations from Hegel were compiled by Karl R. Popper, *The Open Society and Its Enemies,* 4th ed., 2 vols. (Princeton: Princeton Univ. Press, 1963), vol. 2, p. 31.

found through political action.''[3] Arthur Schlesinger tells us why that is so. We need a complete reconsideration of the whole panoply of social and economic policies under which we live, he says, even though prosperity has given most Americans enough of the material things in life. (This was written in 1962, before the effects of social democracy had destroyed the confidence people had in the economic system.) Affluence is not enough because it does not touch the qualitative aspects of life. That leaves us with a sense of "spiritual disquietude." It is only the action of the state, says Schlesinger, that can solve our spiritual problem and lead us to "the promised land."[4]

We should not make the mistake of thinking that the religious language is purely a literary form. The state, for these devotees, is messianic in all its essentials, and their politics are directed toward religious ends. The state will provide for us whatever prosperity could not, because it has replaced God. In the hands of theologians of political redemption, therefore, the state is an idol.

The conjunction between historicism and statism that we find in Hegel has been a recurrent one since his time. Karl Mannheim says that the technological transformation of society makes state planning of the economy essential. As much as he would prefer to live in a free society, he has no choice but to accept a social order in which some people "force [their] conception of 'the good life' " on others. We must resign ourselves to the inevitable because "we have no power to choose."[5] University of Chicago sociologist Morris Janowitz has recently asserted the historical principle that coercion has brought into human experience immeasurable suffering but that this was necessary for the achievement of progress.[6]

When Christian images are merged with Marxist conceptions, there

---

[3]Robert L. Heilbroner, *An Inquiry into the Human Prospect* (New York: Norton, 1974), p. 100.

[4]Arthur Schlesinger, Jr., *The Vital Center: The Politics of Freedom* (Cambridge, Mass.: Riverside, 1962 [1949]), p. xiv.

[5]Karl Mannheim, *Man and Society: In an Age of Reconstruction,* trans. Edward Shils (London: Kegan Paul, Trench, Trubner, 1940), p. 6. Apart from the issue of historicism, Mannheim assumes that a high degree of technology requires central planning. He nowhere shows why we should accept that, nor does he show any correlation between technological efficiency and central planning, a correlation that his conclusion requires. He ignores the fact that statism is found in all kinds of societies from the most primitive to the most complex.

[6]Morris Janowitz, *The Last Half-Century: Societal Change and Politics in America* (Chicago: Univ. of Chicago Press, 1978), p. 13. Janowitz does not identify the historians he says have made the principle clear, much less provide any evidence for the conclusion.

is no depth to which the theoretician will not descend. John MacMurray, who thought he had discovered the clue to history, said that the kingdom of God would automatically come into existence even where the state supplants the church. In common with so many intellectuals during the 1930s, he contended that such was being accomplished in the Soviet Union, even though Communism is "unconscious of its historic continuity with its Christian origin."[7] Marxist theologian José Míguez Bonino acknowledges the unfortunate fact that there has been a loss of liberty in Communist nations and also a "liquidation" of large numbers of people, but on the other hand, he wishes us to consider the fact that Marxism has proved to be a "powerful and efficient motor of social change."[8] Thus history marches on, and one can do nothing about the wreckage left in its trail.

Only the State Can Save Us

People who have experienced liberty often require strong motivation to give it up. Those who wish to impose state power on them provide the strongest reason of all for doing so: salvation from disaster, named or unnamed. The word "survival" is never far from the lips of such theorists. B. F. Skinner, as we have seen, says repeatedly that we cannot be saved without turning ourselves over to controllers who will condition us to act in ways that are conducive to survival. Mannheim tells us that the only alternative to a planned society is chaos. Schlesinger's *Vital Center* was a defense of the thesis that only a powerful central state had saved us from communism in the 1930s, with the unsubtle implication that the same would be true in the future. In 1980 he wrote that "affirmative government" was not only necessary, but inevitable, because such problems as energy shortages and inflation (the causes of which completely eluded him) make it "a technical imperative." Heilbroner says that only obedience to the political powers can save us. The second Humanist Manifesto declares that we cannot survive without "bold and daring" measures, by which it means collectivist ones.

Those who can be convinced that survival is at stake are likely to agree

---

[7]John MacMurray, *The Clue to History* (New York: Harper and Brothers, 1939), p. 206. This was the same mentality that led Auguste Comte to advocate "resignation" to things as they are since there is in any case nothing that can be done to deflect the march of history. See George L. Mosse, *The Culture of Western Europe: The Nineteenth and Twentieth Centuries* (n.p.: Rand McNally, 1961), pp. 198-201.

[8]José Míguez Bonino, *Christians and Marxists* (Grand Rapids: Eerdmans, 1976), p. 88.

to almost any remedy, since extinction seems worse than all the alternatives. If placing extraordinary powers in the hands of political leaders will truly stave off the ultimate disaster, then those who demur can be made to appear as enemies of the human race. That is why arguments based on survival are so effective in persuading people to permit actions that violate their moral code.

A Moral Revolution

The constant exhortations to allow the state to relieve us of our difficulties run counter to older injunctions to beware the power of the state because it robs us of our liberties. This new dependence on the state reveals a dramatic change in the entire moral fabric. British historian E.H. Carr embraces this change and identifies it as one of realism, belonging to the tradition of Hegel and Marx. A realist, says Carr, "makes morality a function of politics" and "cannot logically accept any standard of value save that of fact." Thus, the historicist confusion of fact and value is made to serve the omnipotent state and to justify whatever pragmatic measures will further the values of the authorities. Since this is the position Carr—along with many others—calls "realist," those who disagree are burdened with the task of showing that they are not living in a dream world.

Equalitarianism uses a similar moral inversion. It once was considered immoral to take a person's property for the benefit of others by threatening the use of force, but now inequality is advanced as a greater evil than theft. Since this is incontestably a fact, those who agree with Carr that value can proceed only from fact have no choice but to be equalitarians. Joseph Fletcher has proceeded in the same direction from a theological perspective. Someone who observes a person in need and gives his property to help is practicing "microethics." Much better, he says, to practice "macroethics," which would support increased taxation in order to see that the needy are helped. This would have the advantage of insuring "a wholesome investment balance and socially sensitive social balance."[9] This reversal of ethical thinking makes voluntary sacrifice for the good of others an example of "petty moralism," while it advances state confiscation to the pinnacle of moral rectitude. As is his custom, Fletcher obscures the revolutionary nature of his position with

---

[9]Joseph Fletcher, *Moral Responsibility: Situation Ethics at Work* (Philadelphia: Westminster, 1967), pp. 198-202; for an exposition of the relationship between equalitarianism and despotism see Robert Nisbet, *Twilight of Authority* (London: Heinemann, 1976), ch. 4.

meaningless phrases about wholesomeness, sensitivity, and balance. It was just this perspective that led Reinhold Niebuhr in the early 1930s to believe that because of its march toward collectivism, Germany was "where all the social and political forces of modern civilization have reached their most advanced form."[10]

It is ironic that Niebuhr (who wrote a great deal about irony) should have made such a remark, since he knew so much about the propensity of the professors of morality to do evil. (He often complained that his students misused his brand of realism to justify the abuse of power.) Solzhenitsyn has written that the villains of the classical literatures were pale versions of their counterparts in the real life of modernity. The reason for that is that the villains of literature were purposely and self-consciously evil. Today ideology provides the driving force for evil, convincing the malefactor that what he is doing is good, strengthening his determination. Not that this is strictly a modern phenomenon; Jesus told his followers that their persecutors would think they were serving God (John 16:2).

Idolatry also serves as a set of blinders. Solzhenitsyn tells of Eleanor Roosevelt's visit to the labor camp where he was incarcerated. She reported that it was a humane institution for curing criminals. At the very time Stalin was murdering millions of Soviet citizens, John MacMurray published the glad tidings that this regime presided over "the nearest approach to the realization of the Christian intention that the world has yet seen. . . . It expresses the continuity of the Christian intention in an explicit and practical form, and thus makes an immense human advance in the process that Jesus began."[11]

Some of those who have remained closest to the biblical tradition have been the most perceptive in explaining the affinity evil has with professions of good. In a play entitled *Devil to Pay,* Dorothy Sayers portrayed an anguished Faustus who allied himself with spiritual evil in order to destroy human suffering. That was the pattern, she believed, followed by the builders of earthly utopias.[12] C. S. Lewis, in an essay he called "Lilies that Fester," argued that the more pretentious the visions of rulers, the more defiling the rule is likely to be. In other words, "Lilies that fester smell worse than weeds."[13] Such is the nature of the moral

---

[10]Quoted in Friedrich A. Hayek, *The Road to Serfdom* (Chicago: Univ. of Chicago Press, 1944), p. 46.

[11]MacMurray, *Clue to History,* p. 206.

[12]Dorothy L. Sayers, *Christian Letters to a Post-Christian World,* ed. Roderick Jellema (Grand Rapids: Eerdmans, 1969), p. 233.

[13]C.S. Lewis, *They Asked for a Paper* (London: Geoffrey Bles, 1962), p. 118.

inversions that accompany ideologies professing to save humanity.

Hayek has written that in the last generation there has been a revolution in the way the political left understands its mission. He thinks that future historians will interpret the hundred years following 1848 as the century of socialism, and that it was terminated by the Soviet example and by the obvious losses of both liberty and productivity in Western countries. The welfare state then moved in to fill the vacuum left by socialism's failure.[14] Similarly, University of Rochester economist W. Allen Wallis interprets the Galbraithian arguments about "public squalor" as a major shift. It departs from the intellectual bankruptcy of calls for socializing the means of production to the still-respectable cry for socializing the results of production.[15]

Our Father, the State

When Diocletian published his draconian Edict of 301, destroying the few remaining liberties of the old republic, he justified it by referring to himself and his associates as "the watchful parents of the whole human race." Rulers have ever been tempted to play the rôle of father to their people. In his justification for state direction of the national economy, A. P. Lerner defended rationing "as a form of guardianship" that the state should exercise over the population in order "to prevent foolish spending."[16] The state that acts as a wise parent instead of a vindictive judge has been an attractive image to many people. They include ecclesiastical authorities who have completely missed the point of the gospel warning to "call no man your father on earth, for you have one Father, who is in heaven" (Matt. 23:9). The father is the symbol not only of authority but also of provision. "Our Father who art in heaven. . . . Give us this day our daily bread" (Matt. 6:9,11). Looking to the state for sustenance is a cultic act; we rightly learn to expect food from parents, and when we regard the state as the source of physical provision we render to it the obeisance of idolatry. The crowds who had fed on the multiplied loaves and fishes were ready to receive Christ as their ruler, not because of who he was but because of the provision. John Howard Yoder has rightly interpreted that scene: "The distribution of bread moved the crowd to acclaim Jesus as the New Moses, the provider, the Welfare King whom they had been waiting for."[17]

---

[14]Friedrich A. Hayek, *The Constitution of Liberty* (Chicago: Univ. of Chicago Press, 1960), ch. 17.

[15]W. Allen Wallis, *An Overgoverned Society* (New York: Free Press, 1976), p. 235.

[16]Abba P. Lerner, *The Economics of Control* (New York: Macmillan, 1944), p. 52.

[17]John Howard Yoder, *The Politics of Jesus: Vicit Agnus Noster* (Grand Rapids: Eerdmans, 1972), p. 42.

The paternal state not only feeds its children, but nurtures, educates, comforts, and disciplines them, providing all they need for their security. This appears to be a mildly insulting way to treat adults, but it is really a great crime because it transforms the state from being a gift of God, given to protect us against violence, into an idol. It supplies us with all blessings, and we look to it for all our needs. Once we sink to that level, as Lewis says, there is no point in telling state officials to mind their own business. "Our whole lives *are* their business."[18] The paternalism of the state is that of the bad parent who wants his children dependent on him forever. That is an evil impulse. The good parent prepares his children for independence, trains them to make responsible decisions, knows that he harms them by not helping them to break loose. The paternal state thrives on dependency. When the dependents free themselves, it loses power. It is, therefore, parasitic on the very persons whom it turns into parasites. Thus, the state and its dependents march symbiotically to destruction.

When the provision of paternal security replaces the provision of justice as the function of the state, the state stops providing justice. The ersatz parent ceases executing judgment against those who violate the law, and the nation begins losing the benefits of justice. Those who are concerned about the chaos into which the criminal justice system has fallen should consider what the state's function has become. Because the state can only be a bad imitation of a father, as a dancing bear act is of a ballerina, the protection of this Leviathan of a father turns out to be a bear hug.

The State as Idol

Hegel's idea that the state is God walking on earth is a frank statement of a belief with ancient roots that has never, perhaps, been more widespread than today. It is the conviction, as Ellul says, that the state "is the ultimate value which gives everything its meaning."

> It is a providence of which everything is expected, a supreme power which pronounces truth and justice and has the power of life and death over its members. It is an arbiter which . . . declares the law, the supreme objective code on which the whole game of society depends.[19]

---

[18]C.S. Lewis, *God in the Dock,* ed. Walter Hooper (Grand Rapids: Eerdmans, 1970), p. 314.

[19]Jacques Ellul, *The New Demons,* trans. C. Edward Hopkin (New York: Seabury, 1975), p. 80; see also pp. 81ff., 170ff.

Deifying rulers has always been a means of legitimizing their rule. The imperial cult at Rome began as early as the first century and was intended to solidify the hold of the emperors and establish their legitimacy. At first the republican traditions died hard, and when Gaius (A.D. 37–41) spoke openly about being a god, there was considerable opposition. By the time of Domitian (81–96), it had become common to address him as *dominus et deus,* "my Lord and God." The religious language of patriotism is a similar attempt to lend sacred aura to the mundane. Even officially atheist regimes speak about the sacredness of the motherland and of the cause of communism. So intent was Hobbes to elevate the prerogatives of even the infidel king, that he insisted that for the Christian to disobey him is to disobey the voice of God.[20]

The idol state uses the language of compassion because its intention is a messianic one. It finds the masses harassed and helpless, like sheep without a shepherd, needing a savior. Proponents of such a conception are as impatient with government inefficiency as any libertarian; more so, because the libertarian has no divine expectations from the state. Daniel Moynihan, social scientist and U.S. Senator, is furious about the "inexcusably sloppy work" done by federal officials working in the antipoverty program but is content with their efforts to play God.[21]

Conde Pallen's utopian novel only makes explicit the catechism that the deified state implies:

Q. By whom were you begotten?
A. By the Sovereign State.
Q. Why were you begotten?
A. That I might know, love, and serve the Sovereign State always.
Q. What is the Sovereign State?
A. The Sovereign State is humanity in composite and perfect being.
Q. Why is the State supreme?
A. The State is supreme because it is my Creator and Conserver in which I am and move and have my being and without which I am nothing.
Q. What is the individual?
A. The individual is only a part of the whole, and made for the whole, and finds his complete and perfect expression in the Sovereign State.

---

[20]Thomas Hobbes, *Leviathan* (London: J.M. Dent and Sons, 1914), pt. 3, ch. 43, p. 329.

[21]Daniel P. Moynihan, *Maximum Feasible Misunderstanding: Community Action in the War on Poverty* (New York: Free Press, 1969), p. 168: "If administrators and politicians are going to play God with other persons' lives (and still other persons' money), they ought at least to get clear what the divine intention is to be."

> Individuals are made for cooperation only, like feet, like hands, like eyelids, like the rows of the upper and lower teeth.[22]

When Galbraith says that in the power of the state lies our only chance for salvation, he gives us a premier example of what Ellul calls "the new soteriology."[23] The Chinese once worshiped the same god, who was expected to save them from all problems. A common proverb was, "We must study the works of Chairman Mao each day. If we miss only one day the problems pile up. If we miss two days we fall back. If we miss three days we can no longer live." Whether salvation is to be found in the chairman or in the phalanx of experts who direct the machinery, it is only through the application of state wisdom and power that we can be delivered.

Modern messianism resembles the millennial movements that were common in the Middle Ages and into the early modern period. But most of those movements were connected with traditional Christianity and thus never lost the bounded view of humanity that alone can prevent the deification of human institutions. They tended to form sects that were voluntary and communal. In the eighteenth century, however, messianism became revolutionary, seeking salvation in the complete overturn of society. Since the afterlife was considered a superstitious remnant of more primitive times, secular messianism required that all accounts be settled in the here and now. As Lenin said, the struggle of the proletariat is "to set up heaven on earth."[24] This return to a pagan conception is prefigured by the apocalyptic vision of the New Testament, which describes as satanic the totalitarian state claiming to bring salvation (Rev. 13).

The oft-quoted injunction to render unto Caesar the things of Caesar and unto God the things of God (Matt. 22:21) has lost its edge through repetition. The Pharisees to whom it was addressed were staggered by it because it contradicted one of the assumptions that was basic to the ancient world: the all-encompassing nature of state power. Even Athens at

---

[22]Conde Pallen, *Crucible Island* (New York, 1919), quoted in Thomas Molnar, *Utopia: The Perennial Heresy* (New York: Sheed and Ward, 1967), p. 186.

[23]John Kenneth Galbraith, *The New Industrial State* (Boston: Houghton Mifflin, 1969), p. 399; Ellul, *The New Demons,* p. 200.

[24]J.L. Talmon, *The Origins of Totalitarian Democracy* (New York: Praeger, 1960), pp. 9f.; F.A. Voigt, *Unto Caesar* (New York: Putnam's, 1938), pp. 14, 54; for a biblically based critique of the messianic pretensions of the modern state see Oscar Cullmann, *The State in the New Testament* (New York: Scribner's, 1956), pp. 75-83 and *passim.*

its height conceived of its people as appendages of the state.[25] When the crowd urged the fearful Pilate to execute Jesus, they said: "If you release this man, you are not Caesar's friend." That was perfectly true, for Caesar demanded all that a person had; but the belief that there were some things that belonged to God instead brought the sword to such pretensions. That is why the persecution of Christians was inevitable as long as the state was thought to be all-inclusive.

In the United States, federal tax policy illustrates the government's unconscious rush to be the god of its citizens. When a provision in the tax laws permits the taxpayer to keep a portion of his money, the Internal Revenue Service calls this a "tax expenditure," or an "implicit government grant." This is not tax money that the state has collected and expended but money it has allowed the citizen to keep by not taking it.[26] In other words any money the citizen is permitted to keep is regarded as if the state had graciously given it to him. Everything we have is from the state, to which we owe gratitude. In fact, we are the property of the state, which therefore has the right to the fruit of our labor.

Fletcher comes close to making this point explicitly. In saying that "taxation is stewardship," he uses, but departs from, the biblical idea that God is the owner of all property, and the putative owners under statutory law are really stewards who have the responsibility to exercise control as the owner wishes. His position makes sense only if the state is the lord who is the real owner of everything. The offering formula

---

[25]Cf. George W. Botsford and Charles A. Robinson, Jr., *Hellenic History,* 4th ed. (New York: Macmillan, 1956), p. 237: The culture of Athens "rested on belief in the all-comprehensive perfection of the state, to whose good the citizens were to subordinate their individual interests and devote their lives alike in war and peace." See also Herman Dooyeweerd, *The Christian Idea of the State* (Nutley, N. J.: Craig Press, 1968), ch. 5.

[26]Kenneth E. Boulding and Martin Pfaff, eds., *Redistribution to the Rich and the Poor: The Grants Economics of Income Distribution* (Belmont, Calif.: Wadsworth, 1972), pp.169, 174; Gabriel G. Rudney, "Implicit Public Grants Under the Tax System: Some Implications of Federal Tax Aids Accounting," in *Ibid.,* p.175: "The Treasury currently prefers to identify these implicit grants as tax aids in order to have this designation consistent with the standard federal budget practice of identifying explicit government subsidies as public aids." Martin and Anita Pfaff, "How Equitable are Implicit Public Grants? The Case of the Individual Income Tax," in *Ibid.,* p. 201: "Under present law implicit public grants provide a vehicle of redistribution to the wealthy." What the Pfaffs mean is that since the wealthy have more to be taxed and since they are taxed at higher rates under the progressive tax system, loopholes must benefit them more. It is not that the money of other people is given to them, but that less of theirs is taken away. This objection makes sense only under the assumption that everything belongs to the state and an injustice is committed in permitting the prosperous to keep some of what they think is their property.

prayer, "We give thee but thine own," is a declaration that the steward is only rendering to God what he already possesses legally. The steward is declaring recognition of his stewardship and affirming that his relationship with God is as steward to lord. But to say that taxation is stewardship is to affirm that the state is the lord to which everything has the status of property. The citizen is transformed thus into servant, supplicant, worshiper.

Creating Utopia

The planning of grandiose schemes for the creation of ideal societies, as Toynbee observed, does not come in the flush of triumph but rather in the desperation that accompanies decline. It stems from a desire to peg society at the level to which it has been degraded rather than allowing it to decline further. There is, unfortunately, a widespread impression that utopias are the work of impractical dreamers and have little significance in the real world. Thomas More originated the use of the term *utopia*—which means "nowhere"—in the sixteenth century, and afterwards it came to be used generically for any imaginary society that illustrated and promoted a perfect form of social organization. Far from being harmless, utopias are drawn up and pursued by serious people erecting idols empowered by the state and impelled by intellectually and emotionally attractive ideologies.

Our own age propagates utopian ideologies in part because people have high expectations for technology. George Kateb, among the most honest and perceptive of utopia's modern defenders, argues that technology now makes utopia both possible and inviting, whereas earlier it was unattractive.[27]

---

[27]George Kateb, *Utopia and Its Enemies* (Glencoe, Ill.: Free Press, 1963), p. 15; also p. 108: ". . . technology still is what gives credibility to utopian speculation, that which alone makes interesting and relevant the utopian hope in the twentieth century." There is also an antitechnological utopian position, exemplified by Lewis Mumford who hopes that utopia will produce the kind of person who will counter the present reliance on machinery. Lewis Mumford, *The Transformations of Man* (New York: Harper and Brothers, 1956), p. 179. Ellul opposes utopias in part *because* they are technological, a trait which for him is enough to condemn almost anything. See Jacques Ellul, *The Betrayal of the West,* trans. Matthew J. O'Connell (New York: Seabury, 1978), pp. 151-63; also Jacques Ellul, *The Technological Society,* trans. John Wilkinson (New York: Knopf, 1964), *passim;* Harvey Cox, because he does not know where to look, believes that utopian thinking has largely disappeared in the West. And because he misconstrues the significance of utopias, he thinks this is a pity. See Cox, *The Feast of Fools: A Theological Essay on Festivity and Fantasy* (Cambridge: Harvard Univ. Press, 1969), p. 84.

The high-blown language of moral fervor that dominates modern justifications of utopia makes it clear that we are dealing with a religious phenomenon. Mumford's "new world" civilization is to be a place where the ecological patterns constitute "moral atonement" for what people have done in the past. His title, *The Transformations of Man,* expresses that aspect of utopias which makes them so beguiling. Our principal task, he said, is "to create a new self."[28] Sir Richard Acland acknowledged that he was describing the new order in terms that showed a different kind of man than his readers were accustomed to. Why should we expect people to behave in such constructive ways? Because they will be new men, said Acland, transformed by the power of "many forms of education, preaching and propaganda."[29] Kateb, too, describes utopias as having a common cluster of characteristics that add up to a new kind of man. The social democrats who have molded Swedish society for the better part of two generations have taken it as an article of faith that they could create new people by manipulating the environment.[30] Charles Reich's *Consciousness III* is intended to produce "a 'new head'—a new way of living—a new man."[31]

One of the most influential of utopias was portrayed in Edward Bellamy's novel *Looking Backward,* published nearly a century ago. It was attractive enough to have inspired the formation of hundreds of Bellamy clubs, yet the society depicted was in many ways drab and uninviting. Diversity, for Bellamy, must have seemed something akin to original sin. The stores, the clothing, the residences, and the incomes were all the same, made uniform by the governance of bureaucrats. The real attraction in this society was the people, who were all educated, courteous,

---

[28]Mumford, *The Transformations of Man,* p. 179. See also p. 251: "Emerson well said in his essay on Man the Reformer that it was stupid to expect any real or permanent change from any social program which was unable to regenerate or convert—these are religious phrases for a common psychological phenomenon—the people who are to engineer it and carry it through."

[29]Sir Richard Acland, "What Shall the New Order Be? The Case for Common Ownership," in *Towards a Christian Order* (no editor) (London: Eyre and Spottiswoode, 1942), pp. 152-55.

[30]Roland Huntford, *The New Totalitarians* (New York: Stein and Day, 1972), pp. 66f.; cf. P.T. Bauer, *Dissent on Development: Studies and Debates in Development Economics* (London: Weidenfeld and Nicolson, 1971), pp. 73f.: "[Gunnar Myrdal] envisages planning as a wholesale transformation of people's attitudes, values and institutions, by compulsion if necessary. This reinterpretation of the concept envisages the policy not as state control of the economy but as attempted remoulding of man and society."

[31]Charles A. Reich, *The Greening of America* (New York: Random House, 1970), p. 5. For a good discussion of various current movements that claim to be producing new men, see James W. Sire, *The Universe Next Door* (Downers Grove, Ill.: InterVarsity Press, 1976), ch. 8.

cultured, and loving. Strife was unknown in this land full of paragons. There was no crime, greed, laziness, or lying. Bellamy's message was unmistakable, especially since he repeatedly interrupted the flow of the novel to preach: human nature is naturally good and people are "god-like in aspirations . . . with divinest impulses of tenderness and self-sacrifice." Therefore, once external conditions are made acceptable, the Ten Commandments become "well-nigh obsolete," bringing us a "second birth of the human race."[32]

In Karl Mannheim we have alternate displays of realism and phantasm, the latter manifestation appearing to be an updated version of Bellamy. Mannheim tells us first that social engineering schemes requiring a new kind of man for their functioning are utopian, by which he means they partake of fantasy and are unscientific. Sixty pages later he advocates the harnessing of "planned persuasion," not to foment strife as the Nazis did, but to encourage constructive behavior. He goes on to say that education can so change human nature as to make for the reign of peace and decency. Even in the international realm, he writes, it should be possible to "coordinate education and propaganda" so as to extend decency and morality around the world.[33] The naiveté is breath-taking, but this is what Mannheim considers to be "scientific sociology."

Kateb, with extraordinary honesty—although one might wish that he had been willing to pursue the matter more rigorously—acknowledges the difficulty he has in common with all these utopians: the doctrine of sin. He thinks the realities of life in the twentieth century have made belief in that doctrine virtually a sign of maturity. How, then, can the problem of human nature be resolved by utopian planners? "We cannot answer this question; that is beyond us. We can only ask it, in perplexity and alarm." But he goes on to "assume . . . that the difficulty we have just mentioned did not exist." Kateb's deliberate refusal to face the reality that would destroy his position is reminiscent of John Rawls's presumption that envy does not exist in society because it is irrational, and his admission that if this assumption is incorrect, his entire equalitarian argument is without foundation. Self-delusion about human nature is the reef waiting to make a wreck out of ideologies that wander out of a narrow channel. "It is because we rejected the doctrine

---

[32]Edward Bellamy, *Looking Backward: 2000-1887* (New York: New American Library, 1960 [1888]), pp. 191,194, *passim.*

[33]Mannheim, *Man and Society,* pp. 200,260f.

of original sin," C. E. M. Joad contended, "that we on the Left were always being disappointed."[34]

The obvious response to critiques of utopia is to differentiate between good and bad utopias. Kateb thinks *Brave New World* portrays a benevolent society and *1984* a malevolent one. But this is a false distinction, based in part on Kateb's perception of the authors' intentions, which he misconstrues. Orwell purposely gave the game away by having O'Brien reveal that the real motivation of the inner party is the exercise of power, while Huxley was more subtle in keeping the mask of benevolence intact. The message of both authors is the same: externally Big Brother (or the controller) is looking out for you, while, in the courts of power, destruction lurks. But the utopians fail to recognize these realities. Every society on the way to utopia has Big Brother up front with sweet talk and O'Brien in the back office pulling strings.

Although utopian thinking finds its way into the churches, as do the other idolatries, it is fundamentally hostile to Christian faith. It wishes to build a spurious kingdom of God on earth wholly out of manmade materials. Frazier says to Burris of *Walden Two*: "Turn your face on Heaven." Later on, Burris, who by then has been converted to the utopian faith, describes the community as "essentially a religious movement freed of any dallying with the supernatural and inspired by a determination to build heaven on earth."[35]

Raymond Aron has seen clearly that ultimate lawlessness, the eradication of the boundaries of human power, not only make all actions morally permissible but also appear to open up all possibilities for accomplishment. "That God is dead means not just 'Everything is permitted' but also, and especially, 'Everything is possible.' "[36] Reinhold Niebuhr said much the same when he concluded that cynicism and nihilism have played less a role in the history of modern political disaster than has utopian thinking, which is incapable of recognizing the effect of sin on hu-

---

[34]C.E.M. Joad, *The Recovery of Belief: A Restatement of Christian Philosophy* (London: Faber and Faber, 1952), p. 82.

[35]B.F. Skinner, *Walden Two* (New York: Macmillan, 1947), pp. 208,256. Cf. Nicholas Berdyaev, *The Meaning of History*, trans. George Reavey (New York: Scribner's, 1936), p. 191: "The Utopia of terrestrial paradise and beatitudes . . . is nothing more than a perversion and distortion of the religious faith in the coming of the kingdom of God on earth. The grotesque rationalization of an unconscious millenarianism."

[36]Raymond Aron, "On the Proper Use of Ideologies," *Culture and Its Creators: Essays in Honor of Edward Shils*, eds. Joseph Ben-David and Terry Nichols Clark (Chicago: Univ. of Chicago Press, 1977), p. 11.

man action.[37] Vladimir Bukovsky learned that lesson as he read the socialist utopias and discovered, to his amazement, that all of them had actually been realized—in the Soviet Union.[38]

The Rule of the Elite

Reminiscing about his youth as a socialist, Irving Kristol recalled that he and his friends never denounced anybody for being elitist. "The elite was us—the 'happy few' who had been chosen by History to guide our fellow creatures toward a secular redemption."[39] As with Kristol and his comrades, so with the legions of political saviors who have infested the West for nearly two centuries. The essence of revolutionary movements is the succession of elites through the process of violence. It is a mistake to think this is the product of a modern personality cult, as if before there were mass media the situation were fundamentally different. Political rivalry has always turned on the gaining and keeping of power.[40]

Pursuing power would be pointless for many and futile for all in the absence of ideological spurs to action. People serve movements for which they feel loyalty. And they are able to win adherents only to the extent they are able to transmit that feeling. No matter how evil the movement, almost invariably it calls attention to its virtue and seeks to attract support on that basis. "Power always thinks it has a great soul and vast views beyond the comprehension of the weak," wrote John Adams to Thomas Jefferson, "and that it is doing God's service when it is violat-

---

[37]Reinhold Niebuhr, "The Pope's Christmas Message," *Christianity and Society,* Winter, 1942, reprinted in Reinhold Niebuhr, *Essays in Applied Christianity,* ed. D.B. Robertson (New York: Meridian, Living Age, 1959), p. 214. Malcolm Muggeridge made the same point in saying that the great liberal statesmen had done more harm than had Stalin, Hitler, and Mussolini because, not having died in ignominy, their work in the destruction of art, politics, and society continues, undiscredited. See Malcolm Muggeridge, "The Great Liberal Death-Wish," *The New Statesman,* March 11, 1966, p. 331.

[38]Vladimir Bukovsky, *To Build a Castle: My Life as a Dissenter,* trans. Michael Scammell (New York: Viking, 1978), p. 105.

[39]Quoted in Peter Steinfels, *The Neo-Conservatives: The Men Who Are Changing America's Politics* (New York: Simon and Schuster, 1979), p. 82.

[40]Cf. Yoder, *Politics of Jesus,* p. 245: ". . . the real uniqueness of each of these positions is only that it identifies differently the particular moral elite which it holds to be worthy of guiding its society from the top. . . . But what modern man finds himself practically incapable of challenging is that the social problem can be solved by determining which aristocrats are morally justified, by virtue of their better ideology, to use the power of society from the top so as to lead all men in their direction."

ing all His laws.''[41] The greater the pretensions to righteousness, it sometimes seems, the greater the potential for evil. Mircea Eliade has interpreted Marx's work as a continuation of the mythic Asiatic redeemer stories. The proletariat are the innocents who suffer in order to redeem the world. Thus, Marx, hostile to the entire religious tradition in his conscious secularity, was also squarely within it.[42]

People who attach themselves to ideologies often accept willingly the blinders that serve as a badge of membership. When Galbraith says that the "only reality is the right social purpose," he tells us frankly that *will* is the only definer of reality. It does not matter what might be there objectively for the eyes to see, since the disciple determines his perception by means of an interior quality, much in the way the mind determines the configuration of the natural world in Kant's philosophy. Only some such process can account for the naive assessments of totalitarian regimes that have come from intellectuals visiting them. Such regimes always preside over huge Potemkin villages, created to impress visitors, but how is it that the visitors so often fail to peer behind the building fronts and see that what is advertised is not there? During the 1930s large numbers of Western intellectuals visited the Soviet Union at a time when millions of Soviet citizens were starving and millions more were being killed and imprisoned by the regime. Yet many of them, especially those who used Marxist "science" as a tool of evaluation, reported that they had seen the future and that it worked! Especially gullible were the British Fabians such as Beatrice and Sidney Webb and George Bernard Shaw. They had the same "social purpose" as Galbraith, so we may assume that they apprehended the only reality that could exist for them. The same is true of recent visitors to China and Cuba.[43]

---

[41]Quoted in Reinhold Niebuhr, *The Irony of American History* (New York: Scribner's, 1952), p. 21.

[42]Mircea Eliade, *The Sacred and the Profane,* trans. Willard R. Trask (New York: Harcourt, Brace, 1959), p. 207, quoted in Andrew M. Greeley, *Unsecular Man: The Persistence of Religion* (New York: Schocken Books, 1972), p. 109. Greeley adds that after Eliade wrote that, Chairman Mao assumed the position of "The Marduk of the Contemporary Chinese."

[43]For examples see Ellul, *The Betrayal of the West,* p. 102; Aleksandr Solzhenitsyn, *Warning to the West* (New York: Farrar, Straus, and Giroux, 1976), p. 133. British dramatist Tom Stoppard wrote in 1980 that the clever are often the most easily fooled. "For example, if one were to say to an intelligent child the following: 'Life in East Germany is very agreeable, and there's a wall around it to keep people in,' the child would say, 'There's something wrong here.' But if you said it to a professor of political science or of political history, you'd have a much better chance of persuading him that what you said isn't nonsensical."

Niebuhr had earlier reached a conclusion similar to Galbraith's with respect to the all-encompassing importance of social purpose. He said that coercion—and by implication virtually any political action—is justified if it is done "in the service of a rationally acceptable social end."[44] This assigns to reason the task of determining value, one that it never accomplishes on its own, and blesses any means claiming to be directed toward an approved end. Niebuhr was reluctant to give full credit to the fact that value-defining is a suprarational act. Galbraith shows the same reticence in identifying his value judgments for what they are, and that apparently is why Kristol refers to him as a "reluctant rabbi" rather than an economist.[45] For his insistence that he knows better than ordinary people what should be done with their property and his desire that he and his fellow experts should have the power to dispose of it mark him as something more than a purveyor of technical expertise.

Galbraith's rabbinical position is common enough, but it has been obscured by another, which received the added patina of presidential proclamation. In a press conference of May 1962, President Kennedy explained that the viewpoints to which we assign the common political labels no longer conform to modern realities. Rather than becoming impassioned partisans of the liberal, conservative, Democratic, or Republican positions, he said, we must recognize that the problems we face are technical ones. This means that they are "beyond the comprehension of most men." Galbraith could have written that himself. The ordinary citizen who accepts it understands that there is no point trying to fathom the intricacies of correlating the growth of the monetary base with that of M1, but fails to understand that if he accepts passively Galbraith's expertise he is also accepting his values. *There is no value-free expertise.* The end-of-ideology position made popular in the late 1950s by Daniel Bell, Raymond Aron, and others should not have been taken to mean that objectivity has replaced ideology.

The New Gnosticism

Combining social purpose with expertise sets the stage for a gnosticism in which only the special few have the key to the secrets of the universe. This is not something that can simply be learned from books, although the *cognoscenti* are almost invariably well-educated. They must also have the requisite "social purpose," for the knowledge required to

---

[44]Reinhold Niebuhr, *Moral Man and Immoral Society: A Study in Ethics and Politics* (New York: Scribner's, 1952 [1932]), p. 234.

[45]Irving Kristol, *Two Cheers for Capitalism* (New York: Basic Books, 1978), pp. 60f.

run society cannot simply be communicated rationally. They are like the Pharisees who taught that God gave Moses not only a written law but also an oral one, handed down through the generations to only the privileged few. This was the key to the power of the Pharisees: they had the knowledge to unlock the meaning of the Pentateuch, to be the recipients of wisdom had by no others. Not possessing esoteric knowledge, the masses have no choice but to turn their lives over to the elite to be managed. Never ask the enlightened ones about their track record, which is a series of disguised disasters; just accept on faith that they have the secret to life.

That is why Bishop Robinson hopes for the salvation of the masses through the interposition of a "revolutionary elite," for it is only through their "education and intelligence" that we can be saved.[46] The antiutopias are far closer to the mark in identifying those elites as the plague from which we need to be saved. Ayn Rand's is superior in one respect at least to those of Huxley and Orwell: she portrays the elite as made up of weak and frightened men who are unable to cope with the destruction wrought by their own folly.

Those who seek salvation in the elite characteristically place their hopes in knowledge. Thus Mumford considered the difficulties in enforcing prohibition and concluded not that the state had no right to use compulsion in such a matter but that there was insufficient scientific knowledge to warrant banning the use of alcohol.[47] The more comprehensive the hopes for the elite, the more complete must be the knowledge possessed by them. For Mannheim, planning society's future means attacking maladjustments "on the basis of a *thorough knowledge of the whole* mechanism of society and the way in which it works. It is not the treatment of symptoms but an attack on the strategic points, *fully realizing the results.*"[48] They know it all!

But there is more, for if intelligence and knowledge were the only requisites, the gnostic vision would be lost, and mere book-learning would be sufficient to direct society. Mannheim, assuming that society resembles an organism that must undergo central direction, asks who should be permitted to provide that direction. "Is it to be those human groups in which traces of primitiveness—the 'old Adam'—operate without re-

[46]John A.T. Robinson, *Christian Freedom in a Permissive Society* (London: SCM Press, 1970), p. 93. Curiously, the terrible fate from which the masses are to be saved is that they "are being subverted and pulped by the mass media." The bishop somehow expects that the propaganda experts will save us from propaganda.

[47]Lewis Mumford, *The Story of Utopias* (New York: Boni and Liveright, 1922), p. 257.

[48]Mannheim, *Man and Society,* p. 114. Emphasis added.

straint or those which have, through gradual education, developed their rational and moral capacities so far that they can act not only for a limited group, but also for the whole of society, and bear the responsibility for it?'' Here we have the masses sunk in original sin, and the elite not only made smart but also transfigured so that their moral being is redeemed from perdition. A fitting preparation for saviorhood. Mannheim also reveals here what we seldom see so plainly; the sociology of knowledge mystification that permits the elite to rise above their conditioning—''they can act not only for a limited group, but also for the whole society''—has its roots in a religious vision, the redeemer class achieving the salvation of society. Those divine pretensions, as Talmon has said, form the basis for the imposition of force. For if the people resist the selfless wisdom of the enlightened ones, then the vanguard, ''acting as the trustee of posterity, is fully justified in using force and intimidation, in ignoring the apparent wishes of the people'' without providing any occasion for complaints about the violation of liberty.[49]

Warnings about the rule of intellectuals come mainly from intellectuals. (Perhaps because once one has attended a faculty meeting, it is much harder to imagine that the participants possess the secrets of divine wisdom and objectivity.) Popper thinks that Plato exercises such fascination in part because he ''charmed all intellectuals with his brilliance, flattering and thrilling them by his demand that the learned should rule.'' Francis Bacon's *New Atlantis* (1627) portrayed a utopia in which the elite was composed of scientists who were higher than the state and kept officialdom ignorant of any knowledge with which it did not believe they could be trusted.

But if the elite has the knowledge to be the power behind the throne, then it has the knowledge to make it worthwhile for the throne to coopt it. In 1870, Emil de Bois-Reymond, one of Germany's most eminent scientists, publicly boasted that the University of Berlin was ''the intellectual bodyguard of the House of Hohenzollern.'' Ludwig von Mises considered that this placement of scholarship in the service of power was the beginning of doom for German culture, which could only end in the triumph of barbarism.[50] Bertrand de Jouvenel is frightened by the intellectuals who perform studies about proposed courses of action by the state, because he considers it impossible for them to retain objectivity.

---

[49]J.L. Talmon, *Political Messianism: The Romantic Phase* (London: Secker and Warburg, 1960), p. 20.

[50]Ludwig von Mises, *Omnipotent Government* (New York: Arlington House, 1969 [New Haven: Yale Univ. Press, 1944]), p. 14.

He thinks it inconceivable that studies should be commissioned and paid for if they arrive at conclusions conflicting with what the officials wish to do.[51] Insofar as the studies reflect the homogenized idolatries that characterize the academic enterprise, they can be expected to support the expansion of state power and the corresponding diminution of civil liberties. To the extent that they are successful in portraying the expansion of public powers as progressive or enlightened, they will tend to make intellectual work an efficient abettor of the idol state. But it should go without saying that there is nothing scientific, compassionate, or rational in this process.

The Apotheosis of Power

Once the illusions of compassion and rationality are stripped away from the exercise of state power, there is nothing left to see but power itself. As O'Brien tells the hapless Winston Smith in *1984*, "Power is not a means; it is an end." Later on, Smith shows that he finally understands when he painfully writes: "GOD IS POWER." Solzhenitsyn tells with feeling of how hard it is to part with power. He longed, as a former officer, to be chosen as a group leader by the administration of the transient prison camp. Silently he pleaded, "Me, me, pick me!," and then experienced the pain of having to remain one of the anonymous souls taking orders in the ranks. Power, however, is not only a personal goal, since it functions also as the bringer of salvation. French historian Elie Halevy recalls Sidney Webb's explaining to him that "the future belonged to the great administrative nations where the officials govern and the police keep order." This propensity for power exists where we might expect it least. Such prominent pacifists as Charles Beard, Stuart Chase, and George Soule looked back with longing from the 1930s to the wartime economy where they could find order.

If power does not exist for the enlightened ones to take over, then it must be created. Galbraith became known as an advocate of what he

---

[51]Bertrand de Jouvenel, "Intellectuals and Power," *The Center Magazine*, vol. 6, no.1, Jan.-Feb., 1973, pp. 52ff.; cf. Niebuhr, *Moral Man and Immoral Society*, p. 214: ". . . the expert is quite capable of giving any previously determined tendency both rational justification and efficient detailed application." Also Edward C. Banfield, *The Unheavenly City Revisited* (Boston: Little, Brown, 1974), p. 286: ". . . as the technician comes to play a more important part in policy-making he is bound to come more and more under the discipline of large organizations, especially foundations and government agencies, whose maintenance and enhancement depend in some way upon the elaboration of an alarmist, or at any rate expansionist, public definition of the situation."

called countervailing power, by which he meant the augmentation of state authority to counteract the supposedly overwhelming nature of corporate power. But as often as his thesis has been repeated, the documentation of that corporate power has remained terribly weak. If it is acknowledged that even without state power the individual is virtually helpless against corporate manipulation, there is no argument left against the state's moving in to provide protection. "Once it is agreed that the individual is subject to management," Galbraith said in one of his later works, *The New Industrial State,* "the case for leaving him free from (say) government interference evaporates." He thus shifts the question away from whether or not the citizen should be controlled—that presumably having been settled—to the question of who should control him. Yet elsewhere he admits that the consumer is perfectly capable of resisting corporate blandishments to buy its goods. Galbraith seeks to avoid the implications of this admission by drawing a false distinction: "The management of demand . . . works not on the individual but on the mass."

The same deliberate overstatement of the power of others is evident in international organizations and for the same purpose. In recent years the director general of UNESCO has been assisting Third-World attempts to curb a free press by complaining that journalists have the power to control people and nations. Magnifying the power of the press becomes the pretext and the prelude for the assumption of control by national and international politicians. Now that the power of the state has become supreme, we no longer hear from Galbraith anything of countervailing power.

Scholars-on-Pension

What Galbraith does tell us is the identity of those who ought to exercise control. They should be those people upon whom the "technostructure" is dependent for a trained workforce. Since this elite "holds the critical cards," it stands a good chance of gaining power. Such people, we are not surprised to learn, resemble Galbraith and his friends; the political revolution will be led by intellectuals. No wonder this conception has received such a warm welcome on the campuses. Apparently there is no fear in the academy that professors will be as unable to handle the responsibilities of power as are the business executives. "There seems to be a touching belief among certain Ph.D.'s in sociology," Huxley remarked, "that Ph.D.'s in sociology will never be corrupted by power."[52]

Intellectuals without class allegiances or pecuniary ambitions have become a favorite invention of the twentieth century. They are to function much as the priesthood in the Middle Ages did, who served a higher cause without the impediments of wife and family that tugged on lesser men. People like Harold Ickes, Stuart Chase, Rexford Guy Tugwell, John Dewey, A. A. Berle, Gardner Means, George Soule, intellectuals all, many with close ties to the powers in Washington, exemplified and also advanced the interests of those who were thought to have no interests except for those of the republic. They were a class without class allegiances, because they stood above them.[53]

This conception is wholly illusory. When we read a manifesto like *The New Industrial State* we shall deceive ourselves entirely if we do not regard it as we would a document from the Republican National Committee or the Fabian Society or the Communist Party of the Soviet Union. It is a political tract from a scholar-on-pension whose pension does not begin until we give him the power for which he is pleading.

It is not an exaggeration to say that the intellectuals who exercise or aspire to exercise the dominant influence on the state constitute a class. Kristol has popularized the expression "the new class," and M.I.T. linguist Noam Chomsky coined the appellation "the new mandarins" in reference to them. Chomsky documents case after case in which the intellectual elite justify policies with intellectual dishonesty, immoral sacrifices to pragmatic ends, and outright lies.[54] Kristol distinguishes the new class from the bureaucrats who, by and large, are timid and conservative, content to draw salaries without taking risks. The new class, in contrast, is made up of crusaders who consider it squalid to earn a living in commercial activity, who think that "private" is demeaning and "public" ennobling, and whose every word on capitalism is intended to convey the impression of exploitation and injustice.

It is not likely that the line between the bureaucracy and the new class can be drawn as finely as Kristol thinks. Both prosper as the private sector declines and as the state absorbs and expends a greater proportion of

---

[52]Aldous Huxley, *Brave New World Revisited* (New York: Harper Colophon Books, 1960), p. 22.

[53]See James Gilbert, "James Burnham: Radical of the 1930s," *A New History of Leviathan: Essays in the Rise of the American Corporate State,* ed. Ronald Radosh and Murray Rothbard (New York: Dutton, 1972), pp. 210-12.

[54]Noam Chomsky, *American Power and the New Mandarins* (New York: Pantheon Books, 1967).

the national wealth. In the redistributory society, the main redistribution that takes place is the flow of power from the periphery to the center where the new class awaits. The despoiled are the possessors of private power, against whom the elite still warn us, while they quietly accrue that power to themselves. But the former power was decentralized and to some extent self-neutralizing, because competitive. Power that is concentrated is to a much greater extent inescapable.

The preference for power to the exclusion of wealth in the new class is also exaggerated. Even in the officially equalitarian societies, those who have won power manage to live more affluently than ordinary citizens. In the Soviet Union the elite are given large apartments in segregated areas, shop in special stores, receive treatment in designated hospitals, and now are able to pass those privileges on to their children. An article appearing in a philosophical journal in 1972 argues that these hereditary arrangements increase the welfare of all social groups. In 1960, the income differential between the highest-paid and the lowest was 40:1, about four times the difference in most Western nations. And the income tax did not exceed 13 percent regardless of how high the salary.[55] Thomas Sowell, a black economist, has shown how some black leaders have feathered their own nests by supporting labor and government officials in the promotion of policies that increase the unemployment of black youths. They have been coopted into the elite.

As their policies intensify hardships, the elite act just as the Soviet leaders do: they take action that removes from themselves the difficulties caused by government policy. When President Carter ordered public buildings to set air conditioning thermostats no lower than 80 degrees, federal judges enjoined the government from enforcing the order *in their own buildings*. Congress has protected itself (and the federal bureaucracy) by exempting themselves from the Social Security program and giving themselves a pension system that is adjusted for inflation. Thus, they saddle the citizens with the money they are depreciating while shielding themselves from its effects.

Bukovsky described a bureaucratic struggle between two rival Soviet psychiatrists in a way that could be used in any country.

It was a pitched battle between two mafias for key posts, the management of clinics, dissertations, fat salaries, titles, private cars, and personal pen-

---

[55]Alex Inkeles, *Social Change in Soviet Russia* (Cambridge, Mass., 1968), cited in Helmut Schoeck, *Envy: A Theory of Social Behavior,* trans. Michael Glenny and Betty Ross (London: Secker and Warburg, 1969); see also Daniel Bell, *The Coming of Post-Industrial Society: A Venture in Social Forecasting* (New York: Basic Books, 1973), p. 456, n. 111.

sions. The ultimate judges in this conflict were the Party authorities, who controlled the distribution of life's limited blessings; whoever was best at dressing up the Party's will in scholarly clothing would come out on top.[56]

Thus do the elite disgrace themselves and their respective callings by engaging in the struggle for power through the state apparatus.

The Shepherds and the Sheep

A class that is able to distribute life's blessings exercises a godlike power. Other ruling elites owed their powers to their ability to read and figure, but this one acts through a sacerdotal quality. Members of the new class have not only skills that are above the ordinary but also moral purity and exalted levels of wisdom and disinterestedness. Of the old economic elite they can say: "They pursue filthy lucre while we seek the welfare of society." It is only through such pretensions that the corresponding powers can be justified. Mannheim allows that social planning "need not necessarily be used to create human sheep," but he makes it virtually unimaginable how his vision can be put into effect without doing so. He says frankly that such institutions as family, school, work, and leisure are "instruments under our control. . . . Whether they are used to produce uniformity or a many-sided individuality depends on the will of the planner." By and large the leaders of the American elite are not honest enough to say that for them, too, social planning means that our most private preserves are fit instruments to be placed under their control. But that is the direction in which we are moving.

The distance between social democracy and totalitarianism is very short, largely because the latter is implied in the former. Daniel Bell thinks that the "public household," which is his version of social democracy, properly has the task of adjudicating between all the claims of rival groups in the society, of distinguishing not only what is right from what is wrong but also what is more right from what is less right, of adjusting the claims of individuals against those of groups, of balancing the advantages of liberty against those of equality, and of weighing equity against efficiency.[57] Where can he find a mortal sufficiently wise and disinterested to tackle that agenda? He will never do it. When Dio-

---

[56]Bukovsky, *To Build a Castle*, p. 389.

[57]Daniel Bell, *The Cultural Contradictions of Capitalism* (New York: Basic Books, 1976), p. 26. Bell's basic assumption on this matter is that all resources belong to the state; once that is granted it is futile to deny the state the right to apportion them.

cletian decided to control everything in an empire in the process of disintegration, he did what Bell and his friends will have to do: he declared himself a god!

There is no arena in society in which the elite are able to acknowledge themselves unfit to govern. Galbraith, for example, believes that the state should set the standards for architecture, his own preference in this field favoring "the taste of talented despots." Those who disagree with this he labels "advocates of environmental disorder." Orwell's genius was his ability to show that the passion for power animating such visions of the new class leads to the society of *1984*.

> The new aristocracy was made up for the most part of bureaucrats, experts, sociologists, teachers, journalists, and professional politicians. These people, whose origins lay in the salaried middle class and the upper grades of the working class, had been shaped and brought together by the barren world of monopoly, industry and centralized government. As compared with their opposite numbers in past ages, they were less avaricious, less tempted by luxury, hungrier for pure power, and, above all, more conscious of what they were doing and more intent on crushing opposition. This last difference was cardinal.[58]

Modern visions of salvation by state direction are incompatible with freedom. In a clumsy metaphor, Bellamy had his hero awaken in the nineteenth century, after spending time in the future utopia. Dispirited, he saw a regiment of soldiers marching past and was once again inspired. "Here at last were order and reason, an exhibition of what intelligent cooperation can accomplish." Galbraith might have derived his conception of architectural order from this passage, since Bellamy intended us to see that a good society was one that was patterned after the orderly regiment, that people should live and work in the same way they go to war. That is no doubt why so many of the American elite admire the social democratic society of Sweden. For it is highly regimented, centrally directed, provides complete welfare services, discourages individuality, provides universities that are run like bureaus of the state, monopolizes theater, radio, and television, plans architectural styles, dominates the publishing industry, and officially discourages individual residences. What is attractive about all this is that the Swedish elite control it all.

Where do these dreams of power end? E. H. Carr, serving as chair-

---

[58]George Orwell, *1984* (New York: New American Library Signet, 1961 [1949]), p. 169.

man of the UNESCO committee on human rights, explained that no society could provide the humanitarian benefits his committee was advocating, unless "it has the right to call upon and direct the productive capacities of the individuals enjoying them."[59] Muggeridge recalls Beatrice Webb, to whom he was related by marriage, saying wistfully that in the Soviet Union people *disappear,* apparently thinking of good candidates for the same fate in Britain.

Bureaucrats, Politicians, and the Exercise of Power

State power can be applied only because there exist administrative organs that translate the wishes of political authorities into action. It is commonly supposed that political and bureaucratic functions are sharply divided and that the latter are able to act only insofar as they are given commands by the former, being themselves impotent to decide on policy. Only some such conception can legitimate the enormous powers that the bureaucracies exercise. This is the "ideal type" conception of bureaucracy that was systematized into a coherent theory by Max Weber.[60]

But the faceless bureaucrat silently obeying orders, completely dependent upon the hierarchical configuration of administrative and political authorities, is a textbook pattern that does not describe what actually happens in bureaucratic organizations. A truer description will be found in the novels of C. P. Snow, which depict the struggle for power that is at the heart of all those relationships. Snow's novels have the ring of truth because he spent his whole adult life in the bureaucracies of academia, the civil service establishment, and Parliament, and he knew how they functioned.

The power of the bureaucracy is the reason presidents have complained so vociferously that they cannot get their orders executed. Political scientist Richard Neustadt described the presidency as a "clerkship" that gives the incumbent the right to persuade his subordinates to do his bidding. A strong president is one who can get the government to follow his orders.[61] The bureaucracy is unmanageable. Galbraith says that when he was the federal government's chief price controller during World War II he had no control over what happened. Decisions were

---

[59]Quoted in Friedrich A. Hayek, *The Mirage of Social Justice,* vol. 2 of *Law, Legislation and Liberty* (Chicago: Univ. of Chicago Press, 1976), p. 184.

[60]H.H. Gerth and C. Wright Mills, trans. and eds., *From Max Weber: Essays in Sociology* (New York: Oxford Univ. Press, 1958 [1948]), ch. 8.

[61]Richard E. Neustadt, *Presidential Power: The Politics of Leadership* (New York: New American Library, 1964 [New York: Wiley, 1960]).

made by technocrats on committees—lawyers, accountants, economists, specialists of all kinds—and he was "nearly helpless" to do anything but ratify them. After two years of the same kind of experience, President Carter's attorney general, Griffin Bell, said in a speech that bureaucracy is "more than a painful nuisance. It is a prescription for societal suicide." The independence of the bureaucracy from political authority means that bureaucrats do not merely enforce law or administer it: they make the law. They *are* the law, and the old ideal of having a government of laws rather than of men can no longer be realized. The new class has found a vehicle for giving its values the force of law without bothering to take over the political authority of the state. That is one reason nothing seems to change much in social democracies when voters throw one party out of office in favor of another.

Harold Laski of the London School of Economics argued that replacing political action by administrative fiat was virtually the only way England would bring the socialist vision into being. He called for a "wholesale system of delegated legislation," and thought it "inevitable if the process of socialisation is not to be wrecked by the normal methods of obstruction which existing parliamentary procedure sanctions."[62] The political process, which for most citizens is all that legitimates the exercise of state power, is for the new class a restraint on their ability to impose their will on others. The immense bulk of the *Federal Register* gives sufficient testimony of the extent to which the bureaucracy has supplanted the constitutional prerogatives of the Congress. Aubrey Jones, a highly experienced politician and bureaucrat in the United Kingdom, believes that Britain's two major parties are sufficiently similar that many issues are being "hived off" into nonpartisan administrative offices where they are resolved without respect to the outcome of elections. He does not object to this, and views with equanimity the likelihood that this practice will increase.[63] He is not alone in welcoming the increasing irrelevance of elections to what the government actually does.

The effect of this is to make legislators out of the bureaucrats of the new class. They do not merely regulate industries, disburse funds, and enforce laws. They determine the interest that is received on savings, the accessories that may be placed on cars, the kind of house that may be lived in, the material that may be worn, the medicine that may be taken,

---

[62]Harold J. Laski, "Labour and the Constitution," *New Statesman and Nation,* no. 81 (new ser.), Sept. 10, 1932, p. 277, quoted in Friedrich A. Hayek, *The Road to Serfdom,* (Chicago: Univ. of Chicago Press, 1944), p. 63.

[63]Aubrey Jones, *The New Inflation* (London: Andre Deutsch, 1973), p. 175.

and so on. In other words, bureaucrats shuffle not papers, but people. As one congressman exclaimed to the chairman of the Consumer Product Safety Commission: "You've got so much power here it's unbelievable. . . . You've got life or death over whether consumers have anything to consume."[64] The Soviets, before they decided to become respectable, called bureaucrats commissars, and this was a more honest expression, because it recognized that the administration of laws in modern states carries with it political power. We expect bureaucrats to protect us from all of life's contingencies, which they cannot do, and we leave ourselves defenseless against our protectors. Could we find a better description of a protection racket?

Khadi Law and the End of Justice

Iconographic representations of justice invariably show her to be blind. True justice does not distinguish between people on the basis of appearance, wealth, position, religion, or social status. The blindness of justice means that it cannot see any of those characteristics and therefore renders judgment only on the basis of law and the facts in the case. Yet, conceptions of law exist that require that justice remove her blindfold.

Max Weber's legal typology identified two basic types of law. The first is formal law, in which general rules specify what kinds of conduct are prohibited but which does not concern itself with the outcome of social and economic arrangements. Adjudication is a matter of comparing the facts of the case as they are ascertained with the rules as provided in the statutes. Formal law permits the citizens to know in advance what the law prohibits, because it is dependent on written rules that can be learned easily. This characteristic makes it an abomination to authoritarian regimes of all types, inasmuch as it reduces their ability to make arbitrary judgments. Formal law's clear revelation of its provisions makes it difficult for the authorities to decide the outcomes to which it is pleased to award the appellation "just."

The second type of law is substantive law, which is very much concerned with the outcome of the social relationships that issue from the case. Weber called this arrangement khadi-type justice because of its resemblance to the kind of judgment rendered under Islamic law. It is concerned not with setting forth rules of conduct and making judgments in

---

[64] Quoted in Murray L. Weidenbaum, *Government-Mandated Price Increases: A Neglected Aspect of Inflation* (Washington, D.C.: American Enterprise Institute for Public Policy Research, 1975), p. 31.

accordance with expectations that the rules be followed, but rather with expedients that will make the outcome consonant with what the judge believes is just, according to the religious, political, or ethical values that inform him. Substantive law may be used by any form of government but normally will be in force where the widest powers of discretion are to be reserved for administrative and judicial officials.[65] These ideas are defended in the West as "positivist law," by which is meant that the validity of the law is dependent entirely on the fact of enactment; it does not have any force prior to that, nor may its validity be questioned after it is enacted by the constituted powers.[66]

Substantive law is compatible with democratic regimes as well as other kinds, in spite of the fact that it minimizes the liberties of the citizens. Weber argued that democracy often rejects formal law because it is unwilling to allow its citizens to escape the arbitrary decisions of their peers, as transmitted through the legal system. This means that a democracy with a substantive legal system requires its citizens to meet the social requirements of the majority with all the exactitude possible in an aristocracy or monarchy. It was the Athenian democracy that killed Socrates. Hobbes saw no bar to a totalitarian state in the idea that a commonwealth might begin with a voluntary social compact. For once the compact is made, the people have no right to change it except with the agreement of the sovereign (pt. 2, ch. 8). That is why there is moral force behind the contention that the United States is not a democracy but a constitutional republic. The Constitution is to be a check not only on the arbitrary powers of officials defying the will of the majority but also on those who are only too willing to accede to a majority gone mad.

Substantive law rests on the principle of immanence; its legitimacy is found within itself, and it depends on nothing external. In practice, this means that the will of whoever is in authority constitutes the law. Hobbes denied that the laws of nature were laws, for if they were, that would hamper the sovereign by making his will subject to something external to himself. He said, rather, that they are moral virtues and a part of the civil law. Since the sovereign is identical to the law it would be absurd to say that he is subject to the law, because that would make him

---

[65]Max Weber, *Economy and Society: An Outline of Interpretative Sociology*, ed. Guenther Roth and Claus Wittich, trans. Ephraim Fishoff *et al.*, 3 vols. (New York: Bedminster Press, 1968), vol. 2, pp. 806, n. 40, 812ff.

[66]H.L.A. Hart, "Positivism and the Separation of Law and Morals," *Harvard Law Review*, vol. 71, no. 4, February, 1958, pp. 593-629. Hart points out in this defense of legal positivism that there was a reaction against it in Germany after World War II because it did not allow the individual conscience to oppose immoral laws.

subject to himself (pt. 2, chs. 26,29). If, on a particular matter of public concern, there is no statute, the sovereign may still judge as if there were one, said Hobbes. (pt. 2, ch. 18).

Thus immanent law, valid without reference to anything external to itself, is wholly arbitrary. That is the same thing as saying it is lawless. Hence, it is impossible to know beforehand what the sovereign—who believes himself equivalent to law—will decide. It is no wonder that for the seventy-five years prior to Hitler's rise in power the positivist philosophy of law achieved a standing in Germany that it had attained nowhere else. The German scholars considered it scientific, and thought that, in contrast, Anglo-Saxon law was a mess.[67]

People who thus view law find incomprehensible the psalmist's complaint about "wicked rulers . . . who frame mischief by statute" (Ps. 94:20). For if there are wicked statutes, it must mean that there is a law above the statutes by which their wickedness is identified and judged. There is a transcendent principle, a higher law, that relativizes all statutes and all sovereigns. And this is a law which says above all that the state is not God.

When the law is regarded wholly as the expression of state sovereignty, the citizen is ripe for manipulation. A reliable sign of this is the multiplication of laws and regulations covering all areas of life. Ayn Rand has portrayed the logic in besetting the citizen with so many rules that it is impossible to distinguish what is permitted from what is not. One of utopia's elite asks:

> Did you really think that we want those laws to be observed? . . . We *want* them broken. . . . There's no way to rule innocent men. The only power any government has is the power to crack down on criminals. Well, when there aren't enough criminals one *makes* them. One declares so many things to be a crime that it becomes impossible for men to live without breaking laws. Who wants a nation of law-abiding citizens? What's there in that for anyone? But just pass the kind of laws that can neither be observed nor enforced nor objectively interpreted—and you create a nation of lawbreakers—and then you cash in on guilt.[68]

If the judicial system dispenses khadi-type justice, there is no need even to pass laws in order to separate the innocent from the guilty. Supreme Court Justice William O. Douglas exemplifies the trend of recent

---

[67]Lon L. Fuller, "Positivism and Fidelity to Law—A Reply to Professor Hart," *Ibid.*, pp. 630-72; see also Hayek, *The Mirage of Social Justice*, pp. 44-56.

[68]Ayn Rand, *Atlas Shrugged* (New York: Random House, 1957), p. 436.

years for judges to become legislators. He records his shock when Chief Justice Hughes said to him: ''At the constitutional level where we work, ninety percent of any decision is emotional. The rational part of us supplies the reasons for supporting our predilections.'' He may have been shocked at such a frank statement, yet his support of sociological jurisprudence belies any impression that he was fundamentally opposed to it. Robert Bork of the Yale Law School, formerly solicitor general of the United States, comments on Douglas's statement that he and the Warren court ''demolished a restraining tradition and it is questionable whether it can be restored.'' The ''predilections'' of which Chief Justice Hughes spoke are the sentimental preferences of the judge who thereby becomes the embodiment of supreme law, the khadi-figure of the nation. Lawlessness and subjectivism triumph.

On this issue, as on so many others, we cannot hope to find satisfaction in one of the movements that dominate the American political scene. Shortly before World War I a conservative Supreme Court declared unconstitutional a variety of laws enacted to protect consumers and workers. It did this under the constitutional provision for a supposed ''right to contract,'' which, however, was nowhere to be found in the text of the Constitution. Fifty years later a court with a different ideological tinge invalidated anti-abortion laws in every state on the grounds of the constitutional right to privacy. The Court concluded that although the drafters had neglected to insert this right into the Constitution it nevertheless existed in the ''penumbra'' of the document. The Yale Law School's John Hart Ely, prominent as a defender of abortion on demand, attacked this shadowy judicial invention in an essay which became famous. He concluded that the decision was faulty, not because he disagreed with the judicial reasoning, but because it contained no judicial reasoning. ''It is a very bad decision, because it is bad constitutional law, or rather because it is *not* constitutional law, and gives almost no sense of an obligation to try to be.''

The Old Testament records numerous cases in which rulers adopted a theory that thousands of years later would be called substantive or positivist law. When that happened, a prophet stood ready to knock on the king's door and tell him that there was a law higher than himself, that he was the creature and not the creator. ''Hence the state does not decide what is good or what is law,'' says Ellul, ''but the good and the law determine the action of the state.''[69] Without recognizing that principle, all

---

[69]Jacques Ellul, *The Theological Foundation of Law,* trans. Marguerite Wieser (New York: Seabury, 1969 [New York: Doubleday, 1960]), p. 123.

the procedural safeguards in the administration of justice—constitutions, balloting, court systems, and the like—end up serving evil.

Power Through the Religion of the Schools

One of the most useful tools in the quest for power is the educational system. Galbraith regards it as the successor to land and capital as the most important determinant of who controls whom. Orwell must have had the same idea in mind when he put these words on O'Brien's lips: ''The Party is not interested in the overt act: The thought is all we care about. We do not merely destroy our enemies; we change them.'' That may be the best explanation for the progressive centralization of educational authority, first in the state bureaucracies and increasingly in Washington. Joel Spring's study of American educational policy after World War II found that it always served the goals of federal policy, notwithstanding the formally local character of its authority.[70] The same was true in the declining years of the Roman Empire. By the time the Principate ended, the extensive system of local public schools was firmly under control of the emperors. In our time power has similarly migrated from local boards to federal authority. Furthermore, the distinction between private and public schools is not being maintained. The IRS is harassing private schools by proposing stringent and arbitrary criteria for keeping their tax-exempt status. In higher education, the Education Commission of the States reports that by 1980, forty-six states provided direct or indirect operating funds for private colleges, up from thirty-one in 1972.

From the time they began in the United States, the public schools have been intended to be a social force. Beginning with Horace Mann, they were supposed to promote the socialization of diverse peoples, end crime and poverty, and in general solve the political, economic, and social problems of the entire society. Muggeridge recalls that his father's socialist vision included a society in which the population would be transformed through education. This process would change sports fans into enthusiasts of chamber music. In 1963, Dennis Gabor expressed the same illusion. Since 39 percent of young people were then going to college, he expected the next generation to be markedly different; good music, art, and literature would replace trash.[71] Galbraith, unhappy

---

[70]Joel Spring, *The Sorting Machine: National Educational Policy Since 1945* (New York: David McKay, 1976).

[71]Dennis Gabor, *Inventing the Future* (London: Secker and Warburg, 1963), p. 133.

that people in poor countries seem content with their poverty, hopes that education will increase their dissatisfaction.[72]

Although many of the most vociferous objections to any confusion of religion and state come from supporters of the public schools, no school of any kind can maintain such separation. Value-free education is a contradiction in terms, and any hierarchy of values constitutes a religious system. Hence, all education is fundamentally religious. Horace Mann, the father of compulsory state education in the United States, did not disguise this, but traded on it in order to gain adherents to his ideas: "But our system earnestly inculcates all Christian morals; it founds its morals on the basis of religion; it welcomes the religion of the Bible, it allows it to do what it is allowed to do in no other system, to speak for itself."[73] When Christianity ceased being the dominant religion, other religious ideas quite naturally replaced it in the schools. That is why Dewey, usually thought of as hostile to religion, also supported the public schools as "religious in substance" but in a way that did not come "at the expense of a state-consciousness."[74] He recognized that the formerly dominant Christianity placed limits on the loyalty that one could have toward the state, but that the new religion of the schools did not.

Education is a series of religious acts in part because the power of assumption is so great. Assumptions, in fact, are more powerful than assertions, because they bypass the critical faculty and thereby create prejudice. If someone argues the proposition that modern intellectual people do not believe in religious dogmas, I am able to judge whether his arguments are persuasive. The simple act of listening to an argument is almost enough to engage it. But if I listen to someone discourse on a related subject in a way that only *assumes* that modern intellectual people do not believe in religious dogmas, my mind tends to accept the assumption and bypasses it in order to engage the argument which, in fact, depends on it. That bypassed assumption is the pocket of enemy soldiers that was ignored in an effort to engage the main body of the adversary, and it lies in wait to strike from the rear. A false assumption can be combined with an unassailable argument, which then proves the truth of what is false. The false assumption is additionally beguiling because it

---

[72]John Kenneth Galbraith, *The Nature of Mass Poverty* (Cambridge: Harvard Univ. Press, 1979).

[73]Quoted in Paul Johnson, *Enemies of Society* (New York: Atheneum, 1977), p. 175.

[74]John Dewey, *Intelligence in the Modern World* (New York: Modern Liberty, 1939), pp. 707ff., quoted in Rousas John Rushdoony, *Politics of Guilt and Pity* (Fairfax, Va.: Thoburn Press, 1978 [1970]), p. 329.

often appeals to one of the worst instincts—the desire to be fashionable or at least to avoid being associated with the unfashionable or unpopular.

The assumptions of modern public education concerning the nature of man, the function of the state, the nature of truth, and so on are such as to inculcate a set of presuppositions that can only be called religious. Ivan Illich was perfectly justified in saying that the teacher is a font of moral instruction that substitutes for God, state, and parents, providing for his students the meaning of right and wrong. "He stands *in loco parentis* for each one and thus ensures that all feel themselves children of the same state."[75]

Individualism and Its Enemies

One of the bugbears faced by opponents of state power is the charge that they are advocates of individualism. Daniel Bell bemoans the loss of *civitas,* and the pursuit of private goals rather than public ones. This is a grievous fault for him, and he speaks of "vices" and "benefits" respectively when referring to the difference between private and public. For someone with this point of view, one who refuses to advance the causes of the state is presumed to be opposed to the welfare of society; all presumption of right is on the side of the collectivity. Social ethics for Bell are purely bipolar: individualistic (immoral) and collective (moral). A society cannot be considered liberal—that is cannot win Bell's approval—unless people "compromise" (by which he means "abandon") their values to those of the collective. Thus, to put anything before the collective is to advance blatant individualism and selfishness.

Apart from the value judgments, which Bell does not justify, the bipolar arrangement is without foundation. In fact, it is the most individualistic societies that are the most totalitarian and that by design of those who dominate the regimes. Totalitarian movements, as Hannah Arendt puts it, are "mass organizations of atomized, isolated individ-

---

[75]Ivan Illich, *Deschooling Society* (New York: Harper and Row, 1970), pp. 30f. Illich speculates that the school may represent the universal church which, in Toynbee's system, is the institution that survives the decay of a civilization. *Ibid.*, p. 43. Cf. G.K. Chesterton, *The Man Who Was Orthodox*, ed. A.L. Maycock (London: Dobson, 1963), p. 96: "Education is implication. It is not the things you say which children respect; when you say things they very commonly laugh and do the opposite. It is the things you assume that really sink into them. It is the things you forget even to teach that they learn. . . . There is no education that is not sectarian education." For examples that show how the religion of selfist psychologies is taught in all levels of education see Paul C. Vitz, *Psychology as Religion: The Cult of Self-Worship* (Grand Rapids: Eerdmans, 1977), pp. 10, 56, 110f.

uals.'' They demand the unquestioning loyalty of each individual in the society, and they can receive it only by completely isolating each person, so that his desire for belonging to something outside of himself can be met only by the party and state. In that sense the Bolsheviks in the U.S.S.R. have created a nation of individualists.[76]

Rulers who wish to attach the loyalty of the citizens unconditionally to the state apparatus do everything in their power to detach them from intermediate loyalties. They are abetted by one of the delusions of libertarianism, which often unwittingly aids the state in this aim. Thomas Szasz, for example, makes a case for recognizing the right of a child to "divorce" his parents and live with other people.[77] In the sixth century B.C., Solon attempted to strengthen his hold on the Athenians by weakening their ties with family and religious associations. Charles Reich justifies his social antinomianism, in part, by the notion that social institutions are "only another type of machinery," and therefore subject to supposed "laws of obsolescence." In asserting total autonomy in those ways, the individualist sets the stage for his complete loss of liberty, for there is nothing then to protect him from the idol state, which is only too happy to assist in the destruction of intermediate institutions.

Inferior Magistrates as Countervailing Powers

Hobbes strenuously opposed the dividing of sovereignty into different loci because he understood that to do so would destroy the unalloyed power that he believed the sovereign needed in order to rule (pt. 2, ch. 29). The course of modern history has gone pretty much in the direction Hobbes desired. The intermediate institutions, which formerly served to check the central power, have largely atrophied. When carried past a critical point, the result is what Soviet theorists call "democratic centralism." In its Western version, the phenomenon is moving in the same direction.

---

[76]Hannah Arendt, *The Origins of Totalitarianism,* new ed. (New York: Harcourt, Brace, and World, 1966), p. 323f. This argument has become a common one. Helmut Thielicke, *Nihilism: Its Origin and Nature with a Christian Answer,* trans. John W. Dobertstein (New York: Schocken Books, 1967 [1961]), p. 174, shows the instability of a nation of solipsists, which insures that individualism eventually ends up in a social contract theory of some sort.Molnar, *Utopia,* p. 21, describes the utopian pattern as transporting man from heteronomy to autonomy; but since that leads immediately to anarchy the individual must be delivered without delay to a collectivity which provides for and directs him. Talmon, *Political Messianism,* p. 186, calls attention to the French Revolution in which there was an easy passage from individualism to collectivist terror.

[77]Thomas Szasz, "The ACLU vs. Walter Polovchak," *Inquiry,* Oct. 27, 1980, p. 7.

The destruction of intermediate institutions accounts in part for the confusion that leads to equating "government" with the state. In his study of Puritan ideas, R. J. Rushdoony found that the Puritans considered the state (which they called "civil government") to be only one form of government. The individual exercising self-restraint is conducting governance, and so is the family, the church, the school, the guild, the profession, a rich variety of private associations, and finally, civil government.[78] All of them tend to limit the idolization and atomization of the self, and all act to prevent any single institution from exercising tyranny. Therefore, the contention that to limit state power invites anarchy or individualism cannot be sustained.

The most visible check on the arrogation of total power in the central government is a system of what political theorists used to call "inferior magistrates." The framers of the American Constitution were conscious of the excesses to which centralized political systems were prone, and their solution was to devise multiple levels of authority. The existence of states, cities, counties, townships, and independent taxing authorities, which, to apologists for the state, has been a messy derogation from beneficent centralized power,[79] has in truth saved us from some of the assaults on freedom that others have suffered.

When Theodore Roosevelt took over Herbert Croly's "new nationalism" he may not have realized he had the wave of the future in his hand. Introducing this idea to a Kansas crowd in 1910, he informed it that the fears and convictions that had motivated the framers of the Constitution were no longer to be operative. "The New Nationalism puts the national need before sectional or personal advantage. It is impatient of the utter confusion that results from local legislatures attempting to treat national issues as local issues. It is still more impatient of the impotence

---

[78]Rushdoony, *Politics of Guilt and Pity*, pp.331ff.

[79]For example, see Bell, *The Coming of Post-Industrial Society*, p. 320:"It should strike anyone, on momentary reflection, that in a society confronting the kind of problems we have, the existing organization of fifty states makes no economic, political, or social sense. . . . Under the Constitution, such concerns as education, welfare, local services, and the like are powers reserved to the states and municipalities. But these entities are no longer able to perform such services. Their tax bases are inadequate, their administrative structures archaic and inefficient." Here we have the unexamined assumption that the federal government is better suited to handle the problems of society than any other institution. There is no recognition of the federal role in causing those problems; no consideration of their increase in severity as correlative of the increase in federal power; no concept of countervailing power; no understanding of the ineffectiveness of federal interventions, even where they do not cause or exacerbate the problems; and no recognition of the inadequacy of local finances as a function of federal taxation.

which springs from overdivision of governmental powers.''[80] Roosevelt was only one in a long line of American politicians to express disapproval of local institutions and who insisted on treating all issues as requiring the application of federal power.

After three-quarters of a century, the new nationalism has borne bitter fruit. People who have despised the right of localities to govern themselves have delivered them into the hands of federal masters. Local politicians have acquiesed in the mugging of the provinces because in return for giving up political authority they have received monetary benefits. In effect they have sold their birthright for enough pottage to last another day. The chronic lack of discipline that keeps cities and states in financial decrepitude means that their ability to regain their rightful powers remains secondary to their need for a bailout. Freedom lies on the periphery, but cash beckons from the center. The politicians remain unchastened because the electorate does not demand that they act otherwise. "When a mayor says that his city is on the verge of bankruptcy," Edward Banfield writes,

> he means that when the time comes to run for re-election he wants to be able to claim credit for straightening out a mess that was left him by his predecessor. What he means when he says that his city *must* have state or federal aid to finance some improvements is (1) the taxpayers of the city (or some important group of them) would rather go without the improvement than pay for it themselves; or (2) although they would pay for it themselves if they had to, they would much prefer to have some other taxpayers pay for it.[81]

Therefore, the local government "crisis" is another example of the redistribution racket. It means, to quote Banfield again, that "people hate to pay taxes and that they think that by crying poverty they can shift some of the bill to someone else." But the lunch is not as free as it appears, the hidden bill being in the form of all the ills that issue forth from Washington: irrational rules, legislation, deficits, inflation.

There has been a flood of complaints from legislatures, governors, and mayors in recent years over the loss of control and the expense of complying with federal directives. It is no longer uncommon for local and state officials to take federal agencies to court for relief. In 1969 Milton Kotler thought he could detect a movement—he dared hope it might

---

[80]Quoted in Eric F. Goldman, *Rendezvous With Destiny: A History of Modern American Reform*, rev. ed. (New York: Vintage Books, 1956 [1952]), pp. 162.

[81]Banfield, *The Unheavenly City Revisited*, p. 7.

be a "revolution"—that would liberate even neighborhoods from the imperial domination of downtown powers, so powerfully was the passion for freedom from central control spreading.[82] But that revolution never happened, since local electorates have not been willing to send their money to Washington without receiving from the same source the taxes paid by other citizens. And in receiving money they accept strings, even in those programs that avowedly have none. Kotler seemed to realize his vision stood little chance of being realized since he presented an alternate scenario, one in which the local government would be thoroughly bureaucratized under federal control. "But this would . . . require the abolition of municipal autonomy."[83] Needless to say, there is little motivation for officials in Washington to initiate the revolution in apportioning power that local politicians lack the will to demand.[84]

The Family Under Attack

One of the primary bulwarks against both atomization and tyranny is the family, which therefore is a target of those who idolize the state. Ellen Richards, who founded the modern social work profession, treated children as social assets over which the state graciously allows parents to exercise stewardship. "In the social republic, the child as a future citizen is an asset of the state, not the property of its parents. Hence its welfare is a direct concern of the state."[85] In his review of the social science literature on the subject, Christopher Lasch found that the academic authors tend to support the process that brings the family under the domination of public institutions. Sociologists followed Emile Durk-

---

[82]Milton Kotler, *Neighborhood Government: The Local Foundations of Political Life* (Indianapolis: Bobbs-Merrill, 1969), pp. x-xiii.

[83]*Ibid.*, p. 26. Kotler's vision is flawed further in that he wants his autonomous neighborhoods to exercise the same kind of equalitarian domination that marks federal policy, with a whole panoply of economic controls. *Ibid.*, p. 56. Nisbet, *Twilight of Authority*, p. 246, points out that the impulse to decentralize may be either conservative (Burke) or radical (Proudhon, Kropotkin). In either case, "there is identical emphasis upon the values of localism, regionalism, voluntary association, decentralization of authority, and also identical fear of the political state, whether monarchical or republican in character."

[84]One exception is U.S. Senator Mark Hatfield, who advocates decentralization so that the federal government would give up powers to neighborhood and community governments. See Mark O. Hatfield, *Between a Rock and a Hard Place* (Waco, Tex.: Word, 1976), pp.178ff.

[85]Ellen H. Richards, *Euthenics: The Science of Controllable Environment* (Boston: Whitcomb and Barrows, 1910), p. 133, quoted in Christopher Lasch, *The Culture of Narcissism: American Life in an Age of Diminishing Expectations* (New York: Norton, 1978), p. 155. Lasch here quotes many additional experts to the effect that the state, and not the parents, is the final authority concerning children.

heim in viewing *society* as the entity that replaces the family. It was natural for practitioners of various kinds to adopt the same perspective. For educators and social reformers, the family was an obstacle to what they thought was social progress, and many of them wanted the state to take over the role of the family in raising children. When juvenile courts were set up, it was to serve as the protector of the children—from their parents.[86] Christopher Jencks is unhappy that the school is unable to overcome the influence of the family in resisting equalitarian doctrine. He thinks the answer may lie in transforming the schools so that they function like families.[87]

All this means that the state becomes the enforcer of virtue in the family. It protects children against their parents, teaching the citizens that their real security is to be found instead in government bureaucrats. This repeats the assumption behind the Nazi practice of inducing children to report the infractions of their parents to the state: the state is a higher loyalty than the family. We are approaching the excesses of the Swedish model, in which the directorate of social affairs may issue orders to remove any child from its parent to be reared wherever the directorate sees fit. Officials have the power to enter any home at will in order to investigate conditions. They may order the police to remove children forcibly and without court order. In 1968, this was done to twenty-one thousand children. These are not the actions of lunatics but rather follow logically from the idea that the state is lord of all and can tolerate no rivals. It, too, is a jealous god. When such a conception rules, the family is, as Daniel Berrigan put it, a "sitting duck for the state."[88]

The Attack on Economic Resistance to the State

Much of the hostility toward private wealth comes from the same impulse: hatred of its ability to insulate the citizen from the will of the state. Money empowers resistance; it gives one the ability to buy some gold coins, for example, and thereby hold a measure of independence from the monetary monopoly of the state; to send children to a private school and avoid the brainwashing of the public education monopoly; to open a

---

[86]Christopher Lasch, *Haven in a Heartless World: The Family Besieged* (New York: Basic Books, 1977), pp. 13ff., 103, 117.

[87]Christopher Jencks, *et al.*, *Inequality: A Reassessment of the Effect of Family and Schooling in America* (New York: Basic Books, 1972), pp. 255f.

[88]Quoted in Garry Wills, *Bare Ruined Choirs: Doubt, Prophecy and Radical Religion* (Garden City, N. Y.: Doubleday, 1972), p. 228. On this subject see Onalee McGraw, *The Family, Feminism and the Therapeutic State* (Washington, D.C.: The Heritage Foundation, 1980).

foreign bank account and provide oneself with protection against legal confiscation schemes. Propaganda alleging the immorality of inherited wealth is also a reflection of the assault on the family. Before he dropped into noumenal oblivion, Charles Reich wrote that private property "guards the troubled boundary between individual man and the state," but that there is a new wealth that has replaced it, one dispensed in myriad forms by the state. Increasingly, therefore, "Americans live on government largesse—allocated by government on its own terms, and held by recipients subject to conditions which express 'the public interest.' "[89] People who are thus described are more likely to be compliant servants of the authorities than are those who earn their living by giving value to private citizens who prize what they have to offer.

Big business often is said to be the enemy of government, but that is highly misleading. The robber barons were robbers because they bought off legislatures in order to further their economic interests at the expense of competitors and customers. Fundamental to the new nationalism was hatred for the Jeffersonian ideal of small businesses in competition with one another, a decentralized model that enhanced the preservation of liberty. Instead, it advocated the use of giant industrial concerns, with their efficiencies of scale and their potential for changing the social landscape of the nation. The public interest would be protected because the power of the state would supervise the whole affair. As tycoon Frank Munsey explained it to the old Rough Rider after he left office:

> . . . the state has got to . . . take on a more parental guardianship of the people . . . in their investments, their savings, their application of conservation. They need encouragement, the sustaining and guiding hand of the state. They need the German system of helping them to save money for their old age. It is the work of the state to think for the people and plan for the people—to teach them how to do, what to do, and sustain them in the doing.[90]

In the 1920s, supposedly the heyday of laissez faire, no less than after the New Deal had begun, big business proponents remained in control of the state and ensured that their interests were served above all. Some of the reformers who thought the country would collapse without federal domination were dismayed because they could find no way to give

---

[89]Charles Reich, "The New Property," *The Public Interest,* Spring, 1966, quoted in Bell, *The Coming of Post-Industrial Society,* p. 362.

[90]Quoted in Goldman, *Rendezvous With Destiny,* pp. 160f.

power to the state without at the same time giving it to the corporate interests they detested. "You see the dilemma in which I find myself," wrote literary scholar Vernon Louis Parrington to a friend. "We must have a political state powerful enough to deal with corporate wealth, but how are we going to keep that state with its augmenting power from being captured by the force we want it to control?" As long as he thought salvation could be found in the state, he could find no way out of his dilemma, for to augment the power of the state is to create a prize of great value, worth fighting for, and insuring that it goes to people who are able to mobilize wealth, or propaganda, or the power of mass envy to accomplish their will by grasping the reins of government.

Although he drew the wrong inferences, Galbraith was entirely correct in pointing out the manifold ways in which corporate and state officials interact to the advantage of both.[91] This is illustrated by the Swope plan, devised by the head of General Electric during the depression. It called for the compulsory cartellization of large businesses, using the trade association as a base for regulation, price controls and the federal determination of business practices. The federal government would exercise complete domination over industry. The U.S. Chamber of Commerce endorsed this plan, and the president of the National Association of Manufacturers wanted to go further and include even firms with fewer than fifty employees. Virgil Jordan, economist for the National Industrial Conference Board, said that American business people were ready for an "economic Mussolini."[92]

Thus, big business and big government are not enemies but friends, parasites feeding on the same victims. When they predicted the failure of President Carter's "voluntary" wage-price stabilization program, the editors of the *Wall Street Journal* expressed surprise that so many prominent executives were supporting it. Among the complaints registered against the newspaper's position was that of General Motors Chairman T. A. Murphy, who wrote several scathing letters to the editor defending the corporation against such criticism. The only puzzling feature in this episode was that the *Journal* should have been surprised that a de-

---

[91]Galbraith, *The New Industrial State*, chs. 26 and 27. Cf. Garry Wills, *Confessions of a Conservative* (Garden City, N. Y.: Doubleday, 1979), p. 125: "Nothing is more ludicrous than the big-businessman who laments the power of government. He gave it that power, and he uses it daily. Business and government grew big together, with business leading the way. They expanded by collusion, not by competition."

[92]Murray N. Rothbard, *America's Great Depression*, 2nd ed. (Los Angeles: Nash, 1972), pp. 245-48.

structive federal policy was embraced by big business, since it was simply the continuation of a pattern more than a century old.

Politicians known for the warmth with which they endorse state interventions now speak of a partnership between business and government as a way to "reindustrialize" the nation. They will not lack for corporate volunteers for this movement, for corporations and executives who go along with it can expect to be suitably rewarded. The potential for taxpayer-financed boondoggles is virtually without limit. Earlier in the twentieth century Italy pioneered a similar conception of the corporate state and called it fascism.

Regardless of what the social democracies do to the economic system, all its ills are laid at the door of capitalism. Jeremy Seabrook reports with sympathy the complaint of a British shop steward: "I think the welfare state is a wonderful concept, but like anything else it gets warped under capitalism."[93] The old socialists who looked forward with keen anticipation to the day that socialism would come are now bitter and disillusioned about the mess that life has become. Socialist Britain, with a full panoply of welfare services, with nearly 60 percent of its GNP in the hands of the state, is a hateful thing to them. Ridden by bureaucrats, the wealth of the nation destroyed as only socialism and war can do, it is defended in its present state by nobody. But the socialists blame *capitalism* for what has happened to their dream.

Such errors betray the common malady of confusing labels with the properties they are said to be describing. Irving Kristol, a leader of the neo-conservatives, whose devastating critiques of social democracy are among the most valuable of the current political commentaries we possess, thinks the solution is to create a conservative welfare state as Bismarck did. He would copy the liberals by giving handouts to natural supporters—old people, small businessmen, homeowners—rather than being parsimonious. The inventor of Parkinson's laws of bureaucratic behavior thinks the answer to the confusions of socialism is the spirit of nationalism. He calls for an "over-riding national purpose; one for which people might be willing to give their lives."[94] Thus, Parkinson decries statist policies but devises a solution that makes state policy more important than life itself. In the midst of hundreds of pages showing that statism destroys liberty, Karl Popper avers that it really is not so

---

[93] Jeremy Seabrook, *What Went Wrong? Why Hasn't Having More Made People Happier?* (New York: Pantheon Books, 1978), p. 192.

[94] C. Northcote Parkinson, *Left Luggage: A Caustic History of British Socialism from Marx to Wilson* (Boston: Houghton Mifflin, 1967), p. 200.

bad after all, providing it takes the form of "piecemeal engineering" rather than major planned reforms and providing that the limitations on freedom are imposed with equality.[95]

Garry Wills, in a book entitled *Confessions of a Conservative,* calls for socialized medicine, contends that only the Food and Drug Administration makes it possible for us to have wholesome food, and argues that a rapidly expanding bureaucracy is healthy because it "wants to share its privileges." It is no wonder that Wills thinks the American right wing is "an alliance caused by a common bugaboo: 'statism.' " That is like saying the Stalin-Hitler Pact was an alliance caused by a common bugaboo: concentration camps. George Will, stalwart conservative columnist, argues repeatedly that big government is good, being a surrogate for society. "Real conservatism requires strong government." Conservatives of practically all types, like Wills and Will, fall all over each other exalting the prerogatives of the idol state. That is why when they take power from avowed social democratic parties—as in Sweden, Britain and the United States—there are no fundamental changes. They go with the tide; an electorate that demands the property of other people will get it from their government no matter what the party in power calls itself. Hayek was right, and his critics wrong, in continually denying that he was ever a conservative.

Freedom as a Vice

It is no longer taken for granted, even in those countries where it has flourished, that freedom is a good thing. Erich Fromm taught that Protestantism and capitalism increased the freedom of individuals but alienated them from society, and therefore abandoned them to bewilderment and insecurity.[96] Mannheim wanted to provide for freedom in the planned society, but only within certain defined spheres he called "citadels." Outside the citadels, the planners can brook no interference from such institutions as the family, school, or employment. Where are the lines of the citadel to be drawn? That, too, depends on the will of the planner. Thus the citadel, whose only purpose can be to protect us against the planner, is itself designed by the planner. That is to give the fox charge over the security arrangements of the chicken coop. This is

---

[95]Popper, *Open Society and Its Enemies,* vol. 1, pp. 110, 157, 268, n. 4. See also Karl R. Popper, *The Poverty of Historicism,* 2nd ed. (London: Routledge and Kegan Paul, 1960), pp. 59-67.

[96]Erich Fromm, *Escape from Freedom* (New York: Holt, Rinehart, and Winston, 1963), p. 120.

Mannheim's explanation of how freedom is provided under central planning.

Political scientist Andrew Hacker has a similar perspective. He is distressed because the American people selfishly begrudge their government what it needs to solve all their problems. They refuse to be led.

> If government is to govern, it must be able to tell people they must stop doing things they are now doing; it must be able to curtail private activities and privileges so that society will be more orderly. Leadership is meaningless unless citizens are prepared to follow: to sacrifice individual pleasures and agree to redistributions in which they may be losers. To be a nation, in short, a society must have a citizenry willing to surrender a substantial portion of its freedom to public authority.[97]

One can only speculate with consternation what someone who could write those words in 1970 must mean by "orderly," "sacrifice," "surrender," and "authority." Perhaps he contemplated the vision of Sir Richard Acland, a member of parliament and one of the group of socialists around Archbishop Temple. He wrote that the community and not the individual should assume the responsibility for the earning of a living, with all shirkers sent to work camps. Hitler, Acland concluded in 1941, "has stumbled across . . . what will ultimately be required of humanity."[98]

Whether or not the state planner has a commitment to maintain a free citizenry does not much matter. He may make impassioned (and even sincere) promises to preserve the old liberties, but he is bound to be frustrated by them. There is no reason to expect that people will want what he has planned for them. The people will be obstreperous, elevating their desires above his. He really wants a laboratory, the craving that drove *Walden Two*'s Frazier. But a laboratory in which chemicals, rats, and Bunsen burners dictate matters to the experimenter is surrealistic madness. He will have to go for control. He may begin a democrat, but he will end up like Fromm, Hacker, and Acland. Or he will be like John Dewey, who continued to extol liberty but defined it as power.[99]

---

[97]Andrew Hacker, *The End of the American Era* (New York: Atheneum, 1970), pp. 126-31, 217; ch. 6.

[98]Sir Richard Acland, *The Forward March* (1941), quoted in Hayek, *Road to Serfdom*, p. 212, n. 3.

[99]John Dewey, "Liberty and Social Control," *Social Frontier*, Nov. 1935, p. 41, quoted in Hayek, *The Constitution of Liberty*, p. 17.

The Question of Totalitarianism

Once it is granted that state officials should have the right to determine the spheres in which they may exercise authority, or that liberty
has its ultimate meaning in power, we may ask where the lines are likely
to be drawn in the social democracies. In single-party regimes the question is irrelevant because the governing assumption is that the state is
properly in charge of everything—the totalitarian model. But where the
accepted theory *limits* state power, and especially where the competition
for power is considered legitimate, it is inevitably the case that the legitimacy of one action or another will come into question, and therefore the
drawing of lines is a perpetual issue.

We should understand totalitarianism to refer not to the severity of
the regime, its propensity to use such tools as terror and concentration
camps, but rather the scope of its purview. A totalitarian regime is one
that seeks to control every aspect of communal life, and to bring as much
of private life as possible into the sphere of the communal.

Considering this question in the early stages of the aggrandizement of
state power, Walter Lippmann thought that the devotees of collectivism
were deluding themselves in thinking that they would be able to avoid
absolutism. The problem is that there is nothing in their conception that
provides a place to stop, short of totalitarianism. "Their tastes and scruples are the sole checks on their principles, which in themselves are ab-
solutist."[100]

Substantive law is totalitarian by nature because it is teleologically
oriented, drawn by a vision of final ends with respect to the way people
live, and it seeks to impose that vision on the citizens. It is not an aberration, but normal, that khadi law judges and regulates what citizens may
eat, what medicines they may take, what wealth they may retain, what
risks they are permitted to run, and what prices they may pay or receive
for goods and services. Those who advocate substantive law think that
to allow the citizens to make their own decisions on such matters is to invite breakdown. Hobbes said that the sovereign must have the right to
dispose of the individual's property because to deny him that risks the
dissolution of the commonwealth (pt. 2, ch. 29).

Social democracy cannot be distinguished formally from totalitarianism, since it does not recognize in principle any limit to the purview of
state supervision. Before Mussolini allied himself with Hitler, both

---

[100]Walter Lippmann, *An Inquiry Into the Principles of the Good Society* (Boston: Little,
Brown, 1937), p. 52.

Franklin Roosevelt and Gunnar Myrdal were admirers of what he was accomplishing in Italy. New York University economist Melvyn Krauss has analyzed the National Industrial Recovery Act, declared unconstitutional by the Supreme Court in 1935, and found its provisions to be practically indistinguishable from those of the fascist corporate state. In Sweden, the national census requires considerable personal information, not for a data base, but for inclusion in government computers *by name*. If a person is unemployed, he is required to tell why. A central file on all citizens is kept for the use of financial institutions, police, and government bureaus.

The whole system is self-reinforcing. As Bror Rexed, director general of the Swedish Directorate of Social Affairs, put it: "Social welfare limits political action, because nobody will tolerate a threat to their benefits and the power of the Welfare State." Daniel Moynihan gave us an amazingly frank statement, perhaps because he had not yet realized how much he had to offer to his country in a political capacity, of the extent to which the democratic state exercises control over its citizens. Until recently, politics, says Moynihan, determined who got what, but now it has gone beyond that:

> It has become a process that also deliberately seeks to effect such outcomes as who *thinks* what, who *acts* when, who *lives* where, who *feels* how. That this description no more than defines a totalitarian society is obvious enough. But it has come to characterize democratic government as well. *I do not resist this development.* [101]

When they appear in the social democracies, policies of state supremacy are justified as being for the good of society and contrasted with individualism. That is, the state is confused with society. When society is said to require something, we find that the state is thereby given the right to accomplish it. Rexed put it this way: "The whole environment has to be arranged to bring the community into the Welfare State." [102] For Bell, the public household, which assumes the governance function, is a mystical entity. Not exactly the government, nor a public economic order, nor the domestic household, it is "prior" to them and "directive" of them. "It is the *polis* writ large." Thus we are not to be directed by a government, which we could oppose, but by a rule which somehow is identified with the whole society. To oppose such a rule, no doubt,

---

[101]Moynihan, *Maximum Feasible Misunderstanding,* p. xiii. Emphasis added to the final sentence only.

[102]Quoted in Huntford, *The New Totalitarians,* p. 262.

would be to risk identification with what those who created "newspeak" in *1984* called *ownlife*.

If the prospect of totalitarianism seems daunting to nations that still find freedom attractive, we are given to understand that it is nevertheless the only alternative to catastrophe. Robert Heilbroner says we are doomed to all the disasters that overpopulation can bring if we do not turn ourselves, body and soul, over to an iron government. If we do, however, that will bring "the resurrection of hope." For most capitalist nations "the required transformation will be likely to exceed the capabilities of representative democracy." In other words, in order to save us the controllers will have to do things to us to which we will not willingly agree. The entire "exhaustion-of-resources" syndrome is one huge apology for totalitarian control over the citizens.[103] "Survival" is also the watchword of the 1980 document *A Program for Survival,* produced under the chairmanship of Willy Brandt by European social democrats. This group would extend the controlled chaos of social democracy throughout the world in order to save us.

The Vision of Global Unity

In recent years, social democracy has concluded that the problems of society are so serious that they cannot be dealt with by individual countries. Making use of Buckminster Fuller's phrase "spaceship earth," many theorists conclude that in dealing with such issues as war, resource exhaustion, pollution, famine, and overpopulation—the "world problematique"—human beings must act as a single entity rather than having their actions fragmented in competitive or uncoordinated efforts.[104]

The interwar period was a fruitful time for theories of supranational sovereignty. World War I had wrought unprecedented devastation, and the rivalries of the twenties and thirties, along with the strengthening of repressive and expansionist regimes of the left and right, made it appear that a repeat performance was in the offing. In that context, Nicholas Berdyaev called for the national states to remain bearers of

---

[103]See, for example, Donella Meadows *et al., The Limits to Growth,* 2nd ed. (New York: Universe Books, 1974), pp. 163f., 179f., and *passim.* Raymond Aron, *In Defense of Decadent Europe,* trans. Stephen Cox (South Bend, Ind.: Regnery/Gateway, 1979), p. 170, characterizes the Meadows book, which reports studies commissioned by the Club of Rome, as "an almost ideal mode of pseudo-science."

[104]See, for example, Barbara Ward, *Spaceship Earth* (New York: Columbia Univ. Press, 1966).

culture, with sovereignty gradually being made to inhere in a world federation of national groups. After the next war and the following cold war, Humanist Manifesto II said that humanity would not survive without "bold and daring measures" that would have to include a worldwide legal system with a federal government girdling the entire planet. Others wanted a powerful central decision-making authority to which all international disputes must be submitted for arbitration. "There is but one sure way of ending war," Freud wrote in a letter to Einstein, "and that is the establishment by common consent of a central control which will have the last word in every conflict of interests."[105] On the occasion of the thirty-fourth anniversary of the founding of the United Nations in 1979, Secretary-General Kurt Waldheim prepared a statement for publication in *The Reader's Digest* in which he described the United Nations as the salvation of the world.

One of the most perceptive and honest of those who take the world-government position is the French commentator Jean-François Revel, who wants to see the world resources shared equally but says nothing can be accomplished, not even survival, without the establishment of a single governing power.[106] Lewis Mumford not only hopes for such a world government but says that it is "the destiny of mankind," thus adding historicist fatalism to the already potent attractions of unity. Along with such expressions has been a crescendo of attacks not only on patriotic excesses but also on all expressions of loyalty that elevate the particular over the universal.

In Toynbee we have a curious example of contradictory themes. On the one hand he repeatedly denounced the "parochial" evils of national sovereignty, which he portrayed as the foundation of many of our ills. He called for a supranational authority, perhaps patterned on the federal model of the United States, in order to make it easier for national states to give up their sovereignty.[107] On the other hand, he recognized that collective humanity is an idol fully as much as is the national state; he thought the world government would likely be dominated by either the United States or the U.S.S.R.; and he did not think that such a de-

---

[105]Quoted in Karl Menninger, *What Ever Became of Sin?* (New York: Hawthorn, 1973), p. 104.

[106]Jean-Francois Revel, *Without Marx or Jesus: The New American Revolution Has Begun,* trans. J.F. Bernard (Garden City, N.Y.: Doubleday, 1971); Jean-Francois Revel, *The Totalitarian Temptation* (Garden City, N. Y.: Doubleday, 1977).

[107]Arnold J. Toynbee, *A Study of History,* abridg. D.C. Somervell, 2 vols. (New York: Oxford Univ. Press, 1947, 57), vol. 1, pp. 317ff.; vol. 2, p. 276; Toynbee, *Reconsiderations,* vol. 12 of *A Study of History* (New York: Oxford Univ. Press, 1961), p. 619; Toynbee, *Experiences* (New York: Oxford Univ. Press, 1969), pp. 85, 377.

velopment would bring peace, because to think so would be to provide a technological solution to a theological problem.[108]

One of the recurring features Toynbee found in declining civilizations is their tendency to form universal states, entities that are not distinguishable from the supranational authority that he espoused for Western civilization. Moreover, the universal state normally is formed out of war, which Toynbee repeatedly described as the main scourge of humanity. It is founded, not at the height of the civilization's powers, but as a temporary arresting movement, a "rally" in its decline; it is not the summer but the Indian summer of the society. It is a "coma." Toynbee thought that the Egyptian and Sinic civilizations were sacrificed to "an oecumenical polity with an increasingly parasitic bureaucracy." In the same way, Eastern orthodoxy was squeezed by the strait jacket of a universal state, preventing elasticity, variety, and experimentation.

The wonder is that Toynbee as prophet was able continually to advocate as the answer to our deepest problems the institution that as historian he showed to have such profound defects. He failed to address this dilemma in his published works, and the probability is that he could think of no alternatives. The evils of the national state seemed so grave to him that the universal state could hardly help being an improvement.

It is perhaps not coincidental that visions of world unity should resurface at the same time that pantheism is enjoying so powerful a revival. Nationalism flourished during the period that phenomenalism held sway, lending to particularities an appearance of verisimilitude that it withheld from universality. The current vision apparently marks a reversal, a return to the idolatrous unity that characterized the cult of the Tower of Babel (Gen. 11:1–9).

Revel sees with rare clarity the avarice and stupidity of those who rule the nation-states. But by what miracle does he expect the species, insufficiently good and wise to rule the micro-jurisdictions, to obtain a new nature fitting them to rule the macro-jurisdiction? The ruler of this world state apparently is to be an Abraham Lincoln. But if he should turn out to be a Stalin—easy to imagine when we consider the identities of those who rule the mini-states of the present system—there might be two hundred million dead, instead of the twenty million who actually lost their lives in the Soviet Union. Leopold Kohr considered that the great advantage of small units over large ones was that the liability would be limited if the new order proved—as they generally do—to be harmful. "What would have happened if Hitler had succeeded in his

---

[108]Toynbee, A Study of History, vol. 2, pp. 290ff., 315, 329.

beer-hall putsch," he wondered, "and become a petty tyrant in Bavaria."[109]

Niebuhr thought there were at least two fallacies in the one-world arguments he had heard. The first is that there is never sufficient commonality of outlook to make them possible, and the second is that the creation of new institutions is never adequate to serve as an integrating force. What some people consider to be world anarchy, he believed to be preferable to world totalitarianism.[110]

The Irrationality of Statism

One of the barriers to comprehending the dangers of the aggrandizement of state power is the idea that however one might regret the loss of freedom, it will have to be borne in order to obtain benefits from the state that cannot otherwise be found. With all the evidence to the contrary, people are still persuaded that if state power should be diminished, society will be unorganized and anarchic. Galbraith, for example, thinks poor countries are disadvantaged in part because they lack sufficient administrators to staff government ministries and therefore are forced to rely on the market. Yet, some poor countries—including India, where Galbraith was United States ambassador—are overrun with university graduates, many with degrees from the West, unable to find employment consonant with their training. And elsewhere Galbraith described the effort to direct all of society from the central government as perhaps "the most uniformly dismal experiment of countries seeking economic development." It is only the blinding effects of a false dogma that prevent people from seeing that the same effort in the rich nations of the West is equally dismal.

The economic results of central direction must, by reason of the central direction alone, be unfavorable, because the system is formally irrational. It substitutes preferences of central planners for the estimations based on a price system that reflects both supply and demand. The system ignores the information contained in billions of decisions throughout the economy—information that finally is made available to everyone in the form of price—because the planner's will replaces the action

---

[109]Leopold Kohr, *The Breakdown of Nations* (London: Routledge and Kegan Paul, 1957), p. 70.

[110]Reinhold Niebuhr, *Christian Realism and World Problems* (New York: Scribner's, 1953), ch. 2. See also Niebuhr, *The Illusion of World Government* (Whitestone, N.Y.: The Graphics Group, 1949), p. 5, where he takes the position that the basic assumption of the world government movement is that the desirability of such a world order proves its attainability. This is a reprint of an article in *Foreign Affairs,* April 1949.

of the market, eradicating from the economy the rational use of supply and demand information provided by price fluctuations. Max Weber and Ludwig von Mises each arrived at this conclusion independently, and discussed it together shortly before Weber's death.[111] In 1982, Frank Morris, president of the Federal Reserve Bank of Boston, reluctantly admitted in a speech that the Federal Reserve System was unable to measure with sufficient precision even so basic a factor as the money supply of the nation.

In spite of all the evidence presented by recent revisionist scholarship that President Hoover instituted what amounted to a New Deal before President Roosevelt's time in office, and that government control *caused* the depression, apologists for the state still use the 1930s to argue that a powerful state is necessary to save us from such events. Joseph Schumpeter thought it completely evident that the New Deal inhibited recovery from the depression, something "the most ardent New Dealer must *and also can* admit."[112]

The Sacralization of Power

When Jesus spoke about the truth's making men free (John 8:32), it was in the context of faith and discipleship and had nothing to do with the reasons these words are inscribed on the lintels of twentieth-century American libraries. Christian freedom stems from the separation of the creation and Creator; from the repudiation of a demiurge that binds man to the ground of his being; from the rejection of determinisms and the affirmation of responsibility; and from the limitations on Caesar,

---

[111]Gary North, "Max Weber: Rationalism, Irrationalism and the Bureaucratic Cage," *Foundations of Christian Scholarship: Essays in the Van Til Perspective*, ed. Gary North (Vallecito, Calif.: Ross House, 1976), pp. 143f. North has a good discussion and considerable bibliographical help on this question.

[112]Joseph A. Schumpeter, *Capitalism, Socialism and Democracy*, 5th ed. (London: George Allen & Unwin, 1976), p. 64f. Schumpeter continues: "I for one do not see how it would otherwise be possible to account for the fact that this country which had the best chance of recovering quickly was precisely the one to experience the most unsatisfactory recovery." For an account of the depression that documents this thesis, see Murray N. Rothbard, *America's Great Depression*, 2nd ed. (Los Angeles: Nash, 1972). Rothbard demonstrates the fluctuation in the money supply that caused the expansion of the twenties, followed by the contraction of the next decade which the Federal Reserve Board was unable to reverse; the "Hoover New Deal"; the repudiation of laissez-faire long before the election of 1932; and the failure of all the efforts of the Roosevelt administration to end the depression. For an appreciation of the merits of the respective positions one should compare Rothbard's book with the flabby posturing of Arthur M. Schlesinger, Jr., *The Vital Center: The Politics of Freedom* (Boston: Houghton Mifflin, Sentry, 1962 [1949]).

the declaration that he is a creature, and the removal of the divine status that he continually seeks to acquire. Christian liberty rests on the foundation that man's responsibility to God may not be abridged or compromised by lesser loyalties. This is the conviction that made it possible for Peter to say that he would obey God rather than man, and thus relativizes all human powers. When loyalty to God disappears, there is no longer a barrier to an omnicompetent state. Social democracy makes society increasingly dependent upon the state for continued sustenance, thereby cementing its bondage. That is the wisdom in Chesterton's definition of a despotism as a "tired democracy."[113]

Daniel Bell has said that the central question before us is whether, with society's repudiation of Christian faith, culture can provide sufficient cohesion to prevent disintegration. His answer is that the state takes the place of the discarded religious tradition. But that cannot happen, says Ellul, until it is transformed into a cultic object. "It is not the state which enslaves us, not even a centralized police state. It is its sacral transfiguration . . . which makes us direct our worship to this conglomeration of offices."[114] The Enlightenment prepared the way for one manifestation of this worship, that which was directed toward the nation with its appurtenances of flag, army, anthem, and national glory. That has now been displaced by the state with its humanitarian ethic, its bureaucratic framework, its function as symbol of the aspirations of humanity. The state now fulfills the cultic function. J. L. Talmon's studies of secular messianism reveal this clearly. ". . . all Messianic trends considered Christianity . . . as the arch-enemy. Indeed they triumphantly proclaimed themselves substitutes for it. Their own message of salvation was utterly incompatible with the basic Christian doctrine . . . and its denial of man's power to attain salvation by his own exertions."[115] Redistribution takes its central meaning from this cultic function. The state giveth and the state taketh away. Blessed be the name of the state.

With a rough kind of honesty in his fiction that is absent from his philosophical writing, Skinner shows clearly that he understands his mis-

---

[113]G.K. Chesterton, *Everlasting Man* (New York: Dodd, Mead, 1926), p. 50.

[114]Ellul, *New Demons*, pp. 206f.

[115]J.L. Talmon, *Political Messianism*, p. 25; cf. *Ibid.*, p. 506: "Every one of the Messianic thinkers voiced the solemn conviction that his message was destined to supplant the Christian dispensation, undo the evil religion had engendered . . . and as it were start history upon its real course." Also Nisbet, *Twilight of Authority*, p. 88: "The Jacobin de-Christianization decrees at the height of the French Revolution, like the later Bolshevik assault on traditional Orthodoxy, sprang from a well-founded realization that power can become truly absolute only when an autonomous institutional religion has been displaced and succeeded by an increasingly sacralized government."

sion to be the bearer of salvation. He has Frazier comment upon his work as founder and leader of Walden Two, mimicking God's assessment of the Creation in Genesis. "I look upon my work and, behold, it is good." While he says this, he is lying on his back, with his arms stretched out to the side, his legs straight but crossed at the ankles, his head falling to one side, imitating the posture of crucifixion. Burris is startled to notice that he looks like Christ. In answer to Burris's question, Frazier refuses to admit that his power is less than God's. Later, he says: "I like to play God." Karl Barth saw these megalomaniacal visions of power as theocratic dreams that are discredited "when we discover that it is the Devil who approaches Jesus and offers Him all the Kingdoms of this world."[116]

It is those pretensions of divinity, whether conscious or not, that make the expansion of state power so pernicious. The impatience with the restricting influence of the Constitution, and the willingness of Congress and courts to nullify its restrictions through "interpretations," reveal the Khadi impulse, the desire to exercise full autonomy and thereby dominate the lives of the citizens. There is no better definition of lawlessness, even though people who act thus do so through the statutes and the legal apparatus. The only defense against this idolatry, as Jacques Maritain has said, is the New Testament's profanation of Caesar, which acts "by stripping the State of all sacred pretensions."[117]

In his defense of classical liberalism, Lippmann wrote that those who press for the expansion of state power do so because they have a doctrine that misery and disorder can be rectified by compulsion, that happiness comes from the state. When the application of that principle produces further disorder, they do not abandon the doctrine but rather call for the intensification of its application, since they have nothing else to recommend. Their irrationality is exemplified by Niebuhr who exalted the state even while admitting that it was a "new illusion" that "the collective life of mankind can achieve perfect justice." Only the madness generated by this illusion, he thought, could produce sufficient energy to sweep away the injustices of the old order. He acknowledged that the illusion was dangerous because it fostered "terrible fanaticisms," but thought it could be brought under the control of reason.[118] Niebuhr, of all people, should have known that fanatical illusions are not amenable to the correction of reason, especially when they are impelled by the driv-

---

[116]Barth, *Epistle to the Romans*, p. 407, quoted in Voigt, *Unto Caesar*, pp. 186f.

[117]Jacques Maritain, *Christianity and Democracy* (London: Geoffrey Bles, 1945), p. 24.

[118]Niebuhr, *Moral Man in Immoral Society*, p. 277.

ing force of idolatry. The madness of society may be judged by the identity of the fanatics, who happen to be respectable establishment people and not shadowy figures in robes. They tell us that "all modes of human association are affected with a public interest,"[119] thereby denying the existence of human action that may be said to be private. They think that only obedience to the political powers can save us, and we will render it because we crave strong leaders as an infant craves strong parents.[120] And they predict that the economic system will become "a detached and autonomous arm of the state."[121] And so shall we all, except that we shall find that arms of the state no longer possess anything that can be called detachment and autonomy. That is the spirit animating Senator Moynihan's assertion that he does not resist the development of totalitarianism in the United States.

The present statist orthodoxy is one of reactionary idealism, seeking to return us to a particularly virulent form of the mercantilism that the American Revolution was intended to deliver us from. Its special nastiness comes from its idolatry. For now the state is not only a means for the accumulation of power and wealth but also a means of salvation, the messianic hope, the deliverer of mankind.

Modern statism is the soured remnant of the Enlightenment idea of inevitable progress. This miserable wreckage, which once heralded joyfully the coming of the secular version of the kingdom of God, now hoarsely wheezes that if we worship it we shall receive salvation from extinction. The danger is not to be taken lightly. Woebegone as it is, with a record of fatuous incompetence, dishonesty, irrationality, and bloody repression almost beyond description, statism nevertheless boasts a hoard of fanatical adherents. Ignorant devotees or cunning and cynical hypocrites, they give it power and, equipped with modern technologies, make it a fierce and implacable enemy.

---

[119]John Dewey, *A Common Faith* (New Haven: Yale Univ. Press, 1934), p. 80.
[120]Heilbroner, *Inquiry into the Human Prospect,* pp. 102-10.
[121]Galbraith, *The New Industrial State,* p. 399.

CHAPTER SIX

Idols of Religion

Anticlericalism as a Biblical Theme

ANTICLERICALISM and antiecclesiasticism have long been associated with movements opposed to religious belief itself, and with good reason; but there is no necessary connection between them, for we find some of the most strident and sustained attacks on the religious establishment in the biblical literature. From the time that Aaron, the first high priest, acceded to the people's wish by casting a golden calf (Ex. 32), the religious leadership has always prepared the way for apostasy. The constant refrain of the prophetic message was that the priests, prophets and teachers had prostituted themselves and turned to the service of evil.

Both prophet and priest are ungodly; even in my house I have found their wickedness, says the LORD (Jer. 23:11).

Her priests have done violence to my law and have profaned my holy things (Ezek. 22:26).

I will stretch out my hand against Judah . . .
and I will cut off from this place the remnant of Baal
and the name of the idolatrous priests;
those who bow down on the roofs
to the host of the heavens;
those who bow down and swear to the LORD
and yet swear by Milcom (Zeph. 1:4,5).

But you [priests] have turned aside from the way; you have caused many to stumble by your instruction; you have corrupted the covenant of Levi, says the LORD of hosts (Mal. 2:8).

In the seventh century before Christ, the prophet Isaiah saw a paradoxical conjunction of conditions in the kingdom of Judah. The nation was sunk in corruption and oppression; bribery was rampant, and the legal system a tool of despoliation. Economic crime and murder abounded, and government officials committed criminal acts. Yet with all this, the official religion of the nation, the temple worship of the creator of the universe, flourished. People took part in the cultic observances of the God whose laws they had come to despise. The religious sacrifices, prayers, and festivals were especially revolting in those circumstances. "I cannot endure iniquity and solemn assembly" (Is. 1:13).

Any institution can become idolatrous, but it appears to be a particular hazard with institutions of religion. The charge to live righteously and speak the Word of God faithfully apparently provides fertile ground for the noxious weeds of self-righteousness, and they in turn render one impervious to the prophetic voice that demands repentance and restitution. From that low state, it is only a short step to the religious institution's becoming an active agent in the promotion of idolatry or even to become an idol itself as people confuse the means of worship with the object of worship.

In Isaiah's time the conversion of the temple's religious apparatus to the service of idolatry manifested itself in its support for the system of oppression that had gripped the kingdom. It departed from the ethical requirements of the law, while blithely carrying on the now meaningless and thoroughly hypocritical cultic practice, which had become nothing more than a hollow shell. Placed in the midst of a society sinking into desperate wickedness, the priests and teachers failed to sound the call to repentance and fell into the same low state as the community over which they were given charge. Thus the prophets were called to fulfill the role the religious establishment had spurned.

When Israel fell into idolatry, it did not openly renounce the worship of the God of Abraham, Isaac, and Jacob in order to bow before the pagan shrines. Rather, the nation combined the old rituals with what it knew of Canaanite religion. We can see this in the description of the religious revival under King Josiah (2 Kin. 23). The king commanded the priests to remove from the temple the vessels that had been introduced for the service of Baal and of the heavenly bodies; he deposed the priests who burned incense to the pagan deities; he scattered the cult prostitutes; he desecrated the altar at which the people had adopted the Canaanite practice of burning their children as offerings to Molech; he destroyed the high places, dedicated to Ashtoreth, which had existed since the time of Solomon. In turning away from God, the nation had not fallen into irreligion, but had combined the temple religion with the pagan beliefs and practices of the surrounding peoples. The worship of the God of the Exodus had been defiled by merging it with the worship of idols. When judgment finally came to the nation, it fell on this syncretistic perversion.

False Religion in the Early Church

In an effort to discredit Catholicism, Protestant church historians have often drawn a romanticized portrait of the early church, supposedly resplendent in the "purity" that preceded the dark night of Romanism. But the apostolic writings permit no such view as that. Descriptions of the church in the New Testament demonstrate that from the start it was plagued by serious distortions of doctrine and practice. The parable of the kingdom (Matt. 13:24-30) shows that it could never be otherwise. For the kingdom of God is said there to be like a field in which wheat and weeds grow together, so intermingled that nobody is able to pull the weeds without also destroying the crop. The good and the bad are to be separated at the final judgment; meanwhile the kingdom continues with both elements coexisting.

Therefore it is not surprising that descriptions of the early church, as well as warnings about its future, provide no hint of the perfection that later polemicists would profess to see there. It suffered from political rivalries that sometimes motivated religious zeal (Phil. 1:15), was plagued by false teachers (2 Pet. 2:1-3) and perverse and destructive leaders (Acts 20:29f., Jude 4), preached a false gospel (Gal. 1:6-9), practiced divisiveness (3 John 9,10), and harbored servants of Satan disguised as servants of Christ (2 Cor.11:13-15). In the apocalyptic vision, the church at Ephesus received praise for exposing false apostles, but those at Pergamum and Thyatira were condemned for tolerating false teaching, and the one at Sardis was said to be feigning life while in reality it was dead (Rev. 2,3). Moreover, the early writers did not expect that the situation would be very different throughout the whole existence of the church. Discussions of the last times repeat the themes of apostasy, clerical abandonment of the faith, and ecclesiastical fakery (1Tim. 4:1-5, 2 Tim. 3:1-5, Jude 18).

The biblical doctrine of the church, therefore, shows none of the unwarranted reverence we find in modern ecclesiastical boosters. Rather, it alerts us to the probability that the contemporary church is also mottled unpredictably. It exhibits, that is, confusing patterns of faithfulness and apostasy much in the way its primitive counterpart did.

Apostasy is described similarly in the New Testament as in the Old. As Israel became apostate, its practices were progressively less distinguishable from those of the Canaanites. Just as Israel was told repeatedly to separate itself from the immoralities of the pagan peoples it was displacing in Canaan, the early church was to separate itself from the beliefs and practices of the Hellenic civilization within which it existed. Christians were not to feel at home in the world but rather were to conduct themselves as strangers and exiles, without becoming conformed to the surrounding society (Heb. 11:13-16; Rom. 12:2).

The Conformity of American Religion

Ecclesiastical structures that depart from the faith do so by the loss of distinctiveness, the gradual conformation of their thought and life to that of the larger community. Sociological observations confirm that, by and large, the religious institutions of the United States do not teach values that are distinctive to their own traditions but rather use religious terminology that ratifies the values of the broader society. There is little to distinguish what the churches say from what other institutions teach, and we are left therefore with only an indistinctive religion-in-general. The public school, for example, will be found to be teaching little that is different from the ecclesiastical structure. Survey information suggests that people brought up in such churches, and the clergy trained to work in them, find that traditional Christian doctrines seem implausible. They are so accustomed to deferring to society's norms as *their* norms that anything else seems odd.[1]

Some of the most influential theological works of the twentieth century exhibit the domination of these outside norms. Paul Tillich and Rudolf Bultmann hoped to make theology conform to the requirements

---

[1]Peter L. Berger, *The Noise of Solemn Assemblies: Christian Commitment and the Religious Establishment in America* (Garden City, N.Y.: Doubleday, 1961), pp. 40f.; Jeffrey K. Hadden, *The Gathering Storm in the Churches* (Garden City, N.Y.: Doubleday, 1969), p. 221.

of philosophical truth which, for them, was the existentialism of Martin Heidegger. Tillich called this process "correlation." Others have chosen different systems, such as Jungian psychology, linguistic philosophy, popular sociology, and Marxist economics as models to which theology must conform. Crane Brinton, good disciple of the Enlightenment, concluded that mainline Protestant denominations had completed this process to such an extent that they had become indistinguishable from the Enlightenment orientation that has come to dominate American society.[2] Mortimer Adler puzzled over why Protestant theologians should have come to the position of atheism and decided that it was because they had committed themselves to the reigning views of naturalism and materialism. Once the norms of academic orthodoxy were accepted, it was only natural that its conclusions should be adopted as well.[3]

Even those parts of the church that have been most careful to maintain the integrity of their traditions against contamination have succumbed to some extent. Roman Catholicism and the evangelical wing of Protestantism, with their intellectuals increasingly trained in secular universities, have found it difficult to retain their distinctiveness and thus have had their walls breached from within.[4] This is the phenomenon that caused University of Chicago historian Martin Marty to speak despairingly of "the relevant reverends, the hip and swinging clerics, the secular clergy."[5]

Thus, the master of the American church is likely to be whatever cultural or intellectual fad has gained the ascendancy. Christology displays this tendency when the Gospels are used selectively to show that the "real Jesus" was an exemplar of the American middle class, or perhaps a guerrilla fighter, a social democrat, or a model of psychological fitness.[6] That is a recipe for intellectual and spiritual sterility, for by ac-

---

[2]Crane Brinton, *A History of Western Morals* (New York: Harcourt, Brace, and World, 1959), pp. 308, 471 and *passim*; also Brinton, *Ideas and Men: The Story of Western Thought* (New York: Prentice-Hall, 1950), p. 539.

[3]Mortimer J. Adler, *The Difference of Man and the Difference It Makes* (New York: Holt, Rinehart, and Winston, 1967), p. 283.

[4]On Catholicism see George A. Kelly, *The Battle for the American Church* (Garden City, N.Y.: Doubleday, 1979); on evangelicalism Richard Quebedeaux, *The Worldly Evangelicals* (San Francisco: Harper and Row, 1978).

[5]Martin E. Marty, *The Search for a Usable Future* (New York: Harper and Row, 1969), p. 144.

[6]Richard John Neuhaus, "Calling a Halt to Retreat, " in Peter L. Berger and Richard John Neuhaus, eds., *Against the World for the World* (New York: Seabury, 1976), p. 153.

cepting the dead end of the reigning assumption, the church absorbs whatever conclusions "enlightened" people consider current. In sociological terms, the church functions as just another means used by the political and social establishment to integrate society's values into the next generation. The support it receives depends on the extent to which it uncritically transmits values. Its passivity makes it acceptable and ensures its irrelevance. C. E. M. Joad saw the Church of England being transformed by this process into a "mere purveyor of vague ethico-religious uplift."[7]

Passively accepting domination by the outside culture is probably related to an implicit historicism into which the church intellectuals have fallen. The historicist mentality finds it difficult to consider the possibility that a dominant trend may be evil, and thus stands ready to embrace anything that will confer contemporaneity on itself. Brazilian Bishop Hélder Câmara thus put his blessing on virtually any activity that could be identified as progressive. Man is beginning to lose his childishness, said Câmara, and the church should recognize as "a positive force" the humanism that one finds in contemporary atheism. Man is now finishing the work of creation by taking command of history.[8] Likewise, Bishop Robinson denied that the new morality is a surrender to the spirit of the age, but he went on to plead that Christians should relate all moral decisions to the ethical norms that surround them. "We must embrace the relativities and not fear them."[9] Spanish theologian Alfredo Fierro insists that a theology is firmly grounded only "when it is in synchrony with its age."[10] Thus, in historicist perspective the prophetic thrust and the sharpness of the distinctive Christian witness are entirely lost.

We discover the same tendency in the church's acceptance of psychology. O. Hobart Mowrer, a University of Illinois psychologist, studied over a long period of time the relationship between academic psychology and the American churches. He found that psychology and psychiatry were beginning to discover the damage done by their naturalistic

---

[7]C.E.M. Joad, *The Recovery of Belief: A Restatement of Christian Philosophy* (London: Faber and Faber, 1952), pp. 237f.

[8]Hélder Câmara, *Revolution Through Peace* (New York: Harper and Row, 1971), pp. 25, 75. Câmara perceives this activity as the progressive deification of man. "We were born to be gods."

[9]John A. T. Robinson, *Christian Freedom in a Permissive Society* (London: SCM Press, 1970), pp. 10,17.

[10]Alfredo Fierro, *The Militant Gospel: A Critical Introduction to Political Ideologies,* trans. John Drury (Maryknoll, N.Y.: Orbis Books, 1977), p. 124.

assumptions, ideas that formerly were thought to be curative. On the other hand, much of the religious establishment had become so thoroughly imbued with the naturalistic assumptions that were inimical to its own traditions that it had serious difficulty shaking loose of their influences.[11] More recently, selfist psychologies have invaded the churches and replaced the timeless doctrines with encounter groups and transactional analysis. All the destructiveness inherent in these secularized religions are thus amalgamated into the gospel which, by its own claims, transcends the particularized religions of the surrounding cultures.[12]

Thus, the prophetic portrayal of the official religion of the Old Testament provides us with a paradigm of the institutional church of the late-twentieth century. As one leader of radical Christianity puts it, the old distinctions between left and right in the church have lost much of their meaning, for the institutions and leadership of both the conservatives and the mainline "liberal" Protestant denominations have simply turned their accession to wealth and prestige into passports to the establishment.[13] Harry Blamires, the English educator, began a book on the Christian message in the twentieth century by saying that his purpose was not, as many would suppose, to interpret the gospel to the world, but rather to deal with the opposite problem, that of keeping it uncontaminated from the accretions of the surrounding habits of thinking that are incompatible with it.[14] Just as the radical nature of what God had delivered through Moses was lost by merging it with the false religions of the surrounding society, so do we lose the radical nature of what God delivered through Jesus Christ. Protestantism has largely divested itself of the transcendent and has become almost indistinguishable from the surrounding culture.

In 1975 a group of Christian intellectuals issued what became known as the "Hartford Declaration." Originated by people of diverse organizational commitments—conservative evangelical, mainline Protestant, Eastern Orthodox and Roman Catholic—the appeal did not purport to defend one kind of theology against another but questioned the

---

[11]O. Hobart Mowrer, *The Crisis in Psychiatry and Religion* (Princeton: D. Van Nostrand, 1961).

[12]Paul C. Vitz, *Psychology as Religion: The Cult of Self-Worship* (Grand Rapids: Eerdmans, 1977), pp. 73f., 95, 111, 129. See also Karl Menninger, *What Ever Became of Sin?* (New York: Hawthorn, 1973).

[13]Jim Wallis, *Agenda for Biblical People* (New York: Harper and Row, 1976), p. 2.

[14]Harry Blamires, *The Faith and Modern Error: An Essay on the Christian Message in the Twentieth Century* (New York: Macmillan, 1956), p. ix.

direction of the whole religious enterprise in the United States. George Lindbeck of the Yale Divinity School said that at stake was "the possibility of theology, of distinctively Christian affirmations of any kind."[15] Religious syncretism means the submergence of any distinctive Christian positions under the weight of the dominant positions of the larger society.

Loss of Theological Underpinnings

Theological decrepitude seems to be the inescapable accompaniment to, if not a major cause of, ecclesiastical debasement. The religious revival under King Josiah came after the pentateuchal writings were recovered; thus the idolatry that preceded it occurred without the theological underpinnings that the law could have provided. The vacuity of the social gospel, which considered ameliorative action a fair exchange for theological understanding, almost ensured that humanitarian activity would become a substitute for what was peculiarly Christian. The intellectual leadership of the movement was unable to discern that that was so. To some extent the neoorthodox reaction to it repeated the same mistakes. Reinhold Niebuhr, whose criticisms of the liberalism that had informed the social gospel were as trenchant as any, repeatedly attacked the notion of absolute values that may be regarded as fixed and immutable. Any value, he said, "may, in a given instant, have to be sacrificed to some other value."[16] He failed to recognize that when we sacrifice that value, we are also sacrificing the people who are attached to it: the wife depending on some absolute value of faithfulness, the partner on honesty, the child on love, the comrade on courage.

Such errors set the stage for undermining the theological principles that bar the door to idolatry. For if theologically based values are to give way to pragmatic concerns, no ethical or theological principle can remain inviolate. In her defense of Christian socialism, Dorothy Sölle exemplifies this alliance between theological weakness and practical idolatry. She says that theology can only serve in a subordinate role. It is able to reflect on practical experience but cannot itself serve as the basis for action. This makes theology the handmaid of whatever political nostrum the theologian finds attractive. We are not surprised to learn that Sölle hearkens back to the Christian atheism movement of the

---

[15]George A. Lindbeck, "A Battle for Theology," in Berger and Neuhaus, eds., *Against the World for the World,* p. 30.

[16]Reinhold Niebuhr, *Moral Man and Immoral Society: A Study in Ethics and Politics* (New York: Scribner's , 1952 [1932]), p. 174.

1960s, and calls for a pantheism "in which we are all one with God."[17]

The doctrine of grace must also be found unacceptable by humanitarian-based theological pragmatists, because grace allows one to accept without guilt what is not deserved. To have something that another does not have, or to have something that is not earned, by inheritance, by "luck," by gift—in other words, by grace—is unsupportable for those theorists and requires the imputation of guilt. Only grace can expunge guilt. Social justice advocates are hostile toward Christianity precisely because the latter stands on grace, which the former hates. Christians taken in by the social justice argument have a social ethic at war with their deepest convictions and are, therefore, condemned to futility. The only theology consistent with humanitarianism is works-righteousness, or Pelagianism.

Humanism and the Church

Pondering the flirtation of the Christian clergy with humanism, biologist David Ehrenfeld wondered whether a person could unknowingly belong to one religion while imagining he is part of another. He concluded that such was indeed possible.[18] Humanists who have no special affinity for the message of the church nevertheless welcome whatever help they can get from religious organizations in furthering *their* ends. Karl Popper, for example, hopes that the Christian teaching of the fatherhood of God will assist humanism in securing the triumph of its goals.[19] Bishop Câmara promotes something he calls Christian humanism and wishes it to welcome every other kind of humanism, even the "one-sided and aggressive" atheistic variety.[20] Social ethics for clergy of this

[17]Dorothy Sölle, "Christians for Socialism," *Cross Currents,* vol. 25, no. 4, Winter, 1976, pp. 421ff. Hayek, who makes no claims of adherence to Christianity, commented on the propensity of those who lose their theological moorings to embrace the myths of humanitarian justice. Friedrich A. Hayek, *The Mirage of Social Justice,* vol. 2 of *Law, Legislation and Liberty* (Chicago: Univ. of Chicago Press, 1976), p. 66: "It seems in particular to have been embraced by a large section of the clergy of all Christian denominations, who, while increasingly losing their faith in a supernatural revelation, appear to have sought a refuge and consolation in a new 'social' religion which substitutes a temporal for a celestial promise of justice and who hope that they can thus continue their striving to do good."

[18]David Ehrenfeld, *The Arrogance of Humanism* (New York: Oxford Univ. Press, 1978), p. 3.

[19]Karl Popper, *The Open Society and Its Enemies,* 2 vols., 4th ed. (Princeton, N.J.: Princeton Univ. Press, 1963), vol. 2, p. 258.

[20]Câmara, *Revolution Through Peace,* p. 21. Câmara's vision for the future is one of ringing optimism, the kind that humanists in the industrialized countries have now largely abandoned.

persuasion are, unsurprisingly, humanitarian ethics. Archbishop Temple, describing the family as "the primary social unit" in Christian perspective, asked how it could be preserved. Only with decent housing, was the answer, and therefore the state must be made to ensure that that is what it has. The family cannot function without sufficient money either, so that is something else the state must see to. And because the personality must also be considered sacred, it would be a "national sin" for the state not to extend the age of free public education.[21]

Such pleas from within the church sound convincing because the humanitarian ethic of the broader society retains a residue of biblical teaching. This enables humanitarian apologists to seize the moral high ground. People who take seriously the biblical ethic and recognize the spurious nature of the humanitarian imitation cannot remain unaware of the problem. To protest what Ellul called the divinization of the poor or the creation and maintenance of dependency is to be thrown into conflict with those who cannot distinguish the real thing from the fake.

The War Against Economics

Examining the economic pronouncements of the church leaders, one is reminded of Chesterton's remark that the morality of most moralists has been "one solid and polished cataract of platitudes flowing forever and ever."[22] Having convinced themselves, rightly, that the biblical tradition has much to say about economics, the church intellectuals make theological statements serve as substitutes for economics. They enlist in what Mises referred to as the century-long battle against economics but without realizing what they are doing. Do church leaders who inveigh against "obscene profits" have any idea what would constitute adequate profit? Do they know the function of profit? Have they considered the ways in which profit is similar to and different from a salary? Is there lurking behind such statements a belief that any profit is wrong? Do they think that social service agencies, government bureaus, educational institutions, and church hierarchies are free of the competition that they believe constitutes the essence of profit-making businesses?

Early in his career, Niebuhr tried to make a case against capitalist enterprise by showing that businessmen were able to enrich themselves even while destroying the economic well-being of their employees. Writing during the depression, he created a hypothetical situation in which a

---

[21]William Temple, *Christianity and the Social Order* (London: Penguin, 1942), pp. 85–90.

[22]G.K. Chesterton, *Everlasting Man* (New York: Dodd, Mead, 1926), p. 230.

factory was on a two-day work week. It made such good profits that the owners decided to capitalize the income by selling three million dollars worth of stock. They pocketed this money, putting only a small portion of it into capital equipment. Thus, they became wealthy while their employees barely survived.[23] That some businessmen seek to profit at the expense of their employees—and everyone else—is incontestable. But nobody who thinks that a factory operating two days a week can make that kind of profit or easily find investors willing to buy its stock should say anything about economic matters.

Examples abound of such basic errors in economic thinking. One biblical scholar, unable to distinguish between a matter of fact and a matter of theology, concludes, because the prophetic writings of the Old Testament often described poverty as stemming from oppression, that oppression must always be the cause of poverty.[24] Another says that people in poor countries are poor *"because* we are rich."[25] A prominent Christian layman urges that we solve the problem of unemployment by shortening the work week without reducing wages. He wants to accompany this action by making it illegal for anyone to accept a second job.[26] Thus the fanning of guilt feelings combines with willful ignorance and contempt for any factual understanding of economic processes.

In case studies describing how middle class people, torn by guilt and contemptuous of free economic exchanges, help the poor, we can see more clearly the fruit of those delusions. One such report tells of truly wretched conditions in the slums of Washington, D.C., which were disintegrating because of lack of investment, leaving tenants increasingly demoralized. Yet, from the facts given in the report it is clear that the Christian workers trying to help the poor people had little understanding of the causes of the problem and could only make the situation worse. We learn there that something called a "D.C. Rental Accommodations Office," had to approve rent increases; that the tenants were able to gain political power by organizing with the help of their middle-class patrons; and that they were able to use the courts to force the landlords to accede to their demands. Given those realities, which the organizers thought were positive developments, the deterioration into slums was a

---

[23]Reinhold Niebuhr, "The Weakness of the Modern Church," *Christian Herald*, May, 1931, reprinted in *Essays in Applied Christianity*, ed. D.B. Robertson (New York: Meridian, Living Age, 1959), p. 72.

[24]Tom Hanks, "Why People Are Poor," *Sojourners*, January 1981, pp. 19–22.

[25]Wallis, *Agenda for Biblical People*, p. 84.

[26]William Stringfellow, *Dissenter in a Great Society: A Christian View of America in Crisis* (New York: Holt, Rinehart, and Winston, 1966), pp. 8f.

foregone conclusion. For the political pressures that initiate rent controls also keep rents too low to make investment rational. The landlord, who belatedly realizes that he has made a serious error investing in a rent-control environment, seeks to escape the situation with as much of his investment as he can salvage. Often, in the face of rising taxes and vandalism, he simply walks away from the property, preferring to lose everything rather than to remain tied to a hopeless situation. The organizers encourage the tenants to "demand their right to decent affordable housing," which means to saddle others with the responsibility of supporting them, and thereby help ensure their degradation.

That is how these advocates for the poor do their jobs. In this case, the organizers decided to have the tenants buy the property but discovered that to bring the apartments up to minimum standards would require an additional expenditure of ten thousand dollars for each one, an impossible sum for them. Where did they think the landlord was going to get the money for refurbishment when he had the tenants' agent—the rent controller—standing on his neck? The collapse of their efforts brought these Christian radicals to their old standby in time of crisis: guilt. They concluded, without any foundation whatever, that their problem was that they had retained too much of their middle-class orientation instead of becoming more like their clients. They should rather have dropped their insidious patronization and taught the poor people how to take responsibility for their own support, much as the patrons were doing.[27]

Churches of the Messianic State

This concern with the poor, which could have the healthy effect of sending the churches back to rediscover the biblical meaning of service and wealth, has instead all too often thrown them into the arms of the state. Theologians who exalt state power—Oscar Cullmann called them "collaborationist theological advisors"[28]—show themselves to have all the traits of the new class of the broader society. One of these, ironically exemplifying the title of his own book, *The Cultural Subversion of the Biblical Faith,* so defines freedom that to desire to be free of the domination of state officials is individualism and anarchy. The existence of

---

[27]See Perk Perkins and Jim Tamialis, "Euclid Street Journal," *Sojourners,* May 1980, pp. 18f.

[28]Oscar Cullmann, *The State in the New Testament* (New York: Scribner's, 1956), p. 56.

poverty, he avers, requires "even greater restrictions" by government masters.[29]

Ecclesiastical support for the state idolatry is unconsciously imitative of the temple religion that endorsed and undergirded the unjust rulers of Judah.[30] In this, the church intellectuals are doing just what Dorothy Sayers warned them against. She feared that the church, having long acquiesced in the control of one gang of exploiters, would simply transfer into a new alliance with its opponent. "If the churches make this mistake, they will again be merely following the shift of power from one class of the community to the other, and deserting the dying Caesar to enlist the support of his successor."[31]

In recent years even those whose traditional commitment has been to steer the churches away from too-easy accommodations with the surrounding society have discovered the state as an agency of Christian service. Awakening, finally, from their long misalliance with political conservatism, they begin to cooperate with something fully as bad, just as Sayers had feared. As usual, the intellectuals lead the way. A Christian sociologist says that to criticize the welfare state is "reactionary."[32] Another declares that opposition to the welfare state is led by selfish extremists, and that welfare programs "promote human dignity, self-respect, and happiness."[33] A historian contends that economic freedom "violates the basic ethical principles of Christianity."[34] Another historian, trying to persuade the evangelical movement that social democracy embodies a Christian ethic, says that personal charitable action is inferior to that undertaken by the state because it could lead to pride.[35] Billy Graham, finding that the Bible has numerous passages that urge helping the poor, joined the War on Poverty in 1967. He told an assem-

[29]James D. Smart, *The Cultural Subversion of the Biblical Faith* (Philadelphia: Westminster, 1977), pp. 93f.

[30]Cf. John Bright, *A History of Israel* (London: SCM Press, 1960 [1959]), p. 261: "Supported by the state and devoted to the interests of the state, [the temple religion] was in no position to criticize either the policies of the state or the conduct of the nobles who guided it."

[31]Dorothy L. Sayers, *Christian Letters to a Post-Christian World*, ed. Roderick Jellema (Grand Rapids, Mich.: Eerdmans, 1969), p. 156.

[32]Berger, *The Noise of Solemn Assemblies*, p. 142.

[33]David O. Moberg, *Inasmuch: Christian Social Responsibility in the Twentieth Century* (Grand Rapids, Mich.: Eerdmans, 1965), p. 107.

[34]Richard V. Pierard, *The Unequal Yoke: Evangelical Christianity and Political Conservatism* (Philadelphia: J. B. Lippincott, 1970), p. 73.

[35]Ronald J. Sider, "Ambulance Drivers or Tunnel Builders," a tract distributed by Evangelicals for Social Action. See also Sider's book *Rich Christians in an Age of Hunger: A Biblical Study* (Downers Grove, Ill.: InterVarsity Press, 1977), which oddly combines a

bly of congressmen that partisan politics should not be allowed to hinder welfare programs, thus elevating them to a moral absolute.[36] The Chicago Declaration, issued in 1973 by evangelical leaders attempting to bring a biblical understanding of justice into modern society, also shaded off into the confusions that encourage domination of society by the state.[37]

There is in all of this no appreciation of the devastating impact of the welfare system on its clients, and no understanding that supporting the system props up a network of evil institutions. With assumptions that are opposite those of humanists, these Christians arrive at identical political positions. Thus, it is hard to dispute the findings of survey reports that, despite the rhetoric about not being "of the world" that one hears from evangelicals, on the major political issues they cannot be distinguished from the rest of the population.[38]

Theology in the Service of Revolution

In the 1950s, Niebuhr considered it almost a waste of time to deal seriously with Marxism as an ideology, so completely had it discredited itself.[39] But that was overly optimistic, and all over the world learned people have become infatuated with this towering intellectual construct that claims to comprehend every action of corporate humanity. All over, that is, with the exception of the countries where Marxism has had an adequate chance to show what it is like in action. In the Soviet Union today, as Solzhenitsyn has said, it has become a joke. "No serious person in our country today . . . can talk about Marxism without a smile or a sneer."[40]

---

serious call for Christian discipleship with a panegyric for the movement with which it is incompatible: social democracy. In common with the evangelicals who support this position, Sider has not bothered to learn anything about the economic processes on which he expresses such strong positions.

[36]David O. Moberg, *The Great Reversal: Evangelism and Social Reform,* rev. ed. (Philadelphia: Lippincott, 1977), pp. 134f.

[37]Ronald J. Sider, ed., *The Chicago Declaration* (Carol Stream, Ill.: Creation House, 1974).

[38]Martin E. Marty, *A Nation of Behavers* (Chicago: Univ. of Chicago Press, 1976), p. 83.

[39]Reinhold Niebuhr, *Christian Realism and Political Problems* (New York: Scribner's, 1953), pp. 76f. Writing elsewhere in the same year, Niebuhr acknowledged that in his early writings he had been too uncritical of Marxism. See "Communism and the Clergy," *The Christian Century,* August 19, 1953, reprinted in *Essays in Applied Christianity,* p. 122. For an example of that early work, see *Moral Man and Immoral Society,* ch. 6.

[40]Aleksandr I. Solzhenitsyn, *Warning to the West* (New York: Farrar, Straus, and Giroux, 1976), p. 47. Cf. Vladimir Bukovsky, *To Build a Castle: My Life as a Dissenter,* trans. Michael Scammel (New York: Viking, 1978), p. 73: "From top to bottom, no one be-

Marxism may be impossible to take seriously where it is the official dogma, but many theologians in the West have rediscovered it as the map that points the way to the kingdom of God. Colin Morris believes that God is the "inspiration . . . behind all the revolutions of our time." Paul Lehmann sees revolution "in whatever form it takes" as the process by which God humanizes man.[41] More recently Marxist ideology has made inroads in such unlikely places as American evangelicalism and European Roman Catholicism.[42]

The focal point of what is now called liberation theology is Latin America.[43] There theologians and ecclesiastical authorities have sought to explain the religious meaning of social conditions by coalescing biblical and Marxist categories. Observing societies in which masses of poor people try desperately to earn a living while both political power and economic resources are controlled by small oligarchies, they describe the situation with the language of oppression common to both sources. Their task, then, becomes that of mixing the oil of Christianity with the water of Marxism.

Some, apparently recognizing the hopelessness of the task, resort frankly to mystification. "One is Christian and Marxist," says Dominican Laurence Bright, "because that's how things are."[44] Others seem to recognize that the purpose of any ethic at all is to show why one is not *anything* just because of the way things are. Alfredo Fierro, for ex-

---

lieves in Marxist dogma anymore, even though they continue to measure their actions by it, refer to it, and use it as a stick to beat one another with: It is both a proof of loyalty and a meal ticket."

[41]Quoted in Vernon C. Grounds, *Revolution and the Christian Faith* (Philadelphia: Lippincott, 1971), p. 202. Grounds's book is an excellent review of the literature of revolutionary theology through the late 1960s.

[42]Quebedeaux, *The Worldly Evangelicals,* p. 152. French Catholic layman Marcel Clement, *Christ and Revolution,* trans. Alice von Hildebrand with Marilyn Teicher (New Rochelle, N. Y.: Arlington House, 1974), p. 106, believes that Marxism has become a new theology spreading through the European church.

[43]Although liberation theology is prominently associated with Latin American theologians, their inspiration and instruction come from North America and Europe. Cambridge University historian Edward Norman, in *Christian Faith and the World Order* (Oxford: Oxford Univ. Press, 1979), pp. 46–70, traces the major influences. The thesis of Norman's book is that the great ecclesiastical bodies, national and international, have fallen under the domination of ecclesiastical naifs, are taken in by political nostrums, and suborn the political dimensions of biblical thinking to ideologies incompatible with it.

[44]Laurence Bright, "Christian and Marxist," in J. Klugmann and P. Oestreicher, eds., *What Kind of Revolution?: A Christian-Communist Dialogue* (London: Panther Books, 1968), pp. 124f., quoted in José Míguez Bonino, *Christians and Marxists* (Grand Rapids, Mich.: Eerdmans, 1976), p. 121.

ample, contends that the reason for being a Marxist that most such theologians, including himself, have adopted is that Marxist analysis of social and economic events is valid. In fact, he believes that the same philosophy underlies the thinking of many theologians who do not consider themselves Marxist, that it is becoming almost universal. How does theology relate to this Marxist assumption? Theology, Fierro's answer goes, may be considered valid insofar as it is a reflection "on the superstructural level of a specific situation at the level of the material infrastructure."[45] In other words theology is a pupil taking its lessons from the schoolmaster, which is Marxism. Christians are to be instructed only by what that stern teacher allows in the curriculum.

One of the results of such ideas is the increasing tendency of national and international ecclesiastical bodies to attach themselves to outside forces whose ideologies mimic biblical themes. The World Council of Churches, for example, has given money collected from constituent churches to guerrilla terrorists in Africa, some of whom claim responsibility for murdering missionaries. Terrorist groups expressing concern for the poor attract the attention of what Paul Ramsey of Princeton University has called the "social action curia," which then responds by supporting them. Common themes running through their work are the imposition of guilt on all who are not poor, praise for government ownership rather than private, and a preference for totalitarian regimes to democratic or authoritarian ones. The World Council tends to avert its eyes from the massive violations of rights in countries declaring themselves to be Marxist, while condemning trangressions in non-Marxist authoritarian ones.

Even though Marxism is meeting with unacknowledged repudiation even in post-Maoist China, the Latin American theologians who want to merge it with Christian faith are apparently gaining new strength. With the dominant oligarchies under increasing pressure from revolutionary forces, Marxism's uniform record of both brutal repression and economic failure seems to be overshadowed by its military and political successes.

One of the most influential Latin American theologians is José Míguez Bonino, who is also a vice-president of the World Council of Churches and one of the officials who have pushed that body into supporting terrorism as a means of Christian witness. Theology is virtually impotent, according to Míguez, unless it incorporates "a coherent

---

[45]Fierro, *The Militant Gospel*, pp. 114, 119, 124.

and all-embracing method of sociopolitical analysis."[46] That method is Marxism, which Míguez portrays as a neutral method of analysis that any fair-minded person can adopt. He deals with virtually nothing in the enormous corpus of literature that could have provided him with innumerable reasons why fair-minded persons should avoid evaluating anything with the Marxist method. More basically, no method of analysis is neutral; all contain presuppositions that are usually kept hidden, and that is especially true of Marxism. Although Míguez and many others call this system "scientific," he arrives at many of the same conclusions that social democracy does: rule by an elite; the primacy of the political dimension of social life; the new man created by social institutions; the necessity of a strong centralized state.

Perhaps the most perplexing difficulty the Marxist theologians have to deal with is the propensity of their favorite liberators to achieve the revolution with utter brutality. Their response to the problem is, generally, to thrash about in a bewildering combination of theory and pragmatism, but they never escape from the embarrassment. Míguez regrets the "liquidation" of so many people, and the wholesale loss of liberty but thinks this is more than compensated for by Marxism's ability to bring about social change. The Soviet Union "leaves a very painful impression" on him, but not because of the brutality. He is bothered mainly by the "hypocritical" retention of the material incentives provided by the remnants of a market economy (remnants which, in truth, are all that keep the socialist economy from collapse). The ethical problem has been clouded, he contends, by the propensity people have to impose on others unwarranted values, which he identifies as "abstract notions like freedom, truth or goodness." These he regards as sentimentalities with which Christians should not be bothered. The only criteria he will accept are those relating to how Marxists fulfill the "historical mission of the proletariat."[47]

---

[46]José Míguez Bonino, *Doing Theology in a Revolutionary Situation* (Philadelphia: Fortress, 1975), p. 147.

[47]Míguez, *Christians and Marxists,* pp. 87ff., 132. Cf. Raymond Aron, *The Opium of the Intellectuals,* trans. Terence Kilmartin (New York: Norton, 1962 [1955]), p. 156: "[The Marxist intellectual] protests against police brutality, the inhuman rhythm of industrial production, the severity of bourgeois courts, the execution of prisoners whose guilt has not been proved beyond doubt. Nothing, short of a total 'humanization,' can appease his hunger for justice. But as soon as he decides to give his allegiance to a party which is as implacably hostile as he is himself to the established disorder, we find him forgiving, in the name of the Revolution, everything he has hitherto relentlessly denounced. The revolutionary myth bridges the gap between moral intransigence and terrorism." Also Solzhenitsyn, *Warning to the West,* p. 103: "There is now a universal adulation of revolutionaries, the more so the more extreme they are! Similarly, before the

Since this imaginary historical mission is interpreted in whatever way suits the Marxist theoretician, the revolutionary ethic is its own justification. American theologian James Cone arrives at this conclusion using the antinomian ethical theory of the young Reinhold Niebuhr. The Christian cannot decide between good and evil, Cone says, but only between greater or lesser evils. Therefore, he must compare revolutionary violence with the evils of the dominant system to determine which is worse. "But if the system is evil, then revolutionary violence is both justified and necessary."[48] Bishop Câmara, who is widely regarded as a modern saint for his outspoken denunciations of the Brazilian oligarchy, has forcefully declared himself against violence, but only, apparently, on pragmatic grounds. Violence changes things too quickly, he says, so that the inner life cannot make a corresponding change.[49] Presumably if this deficiency should be eliminated by a technical innovation, violence would then be acceptable. The division into two airtight compartments of the theology of the church and the ethics of revolution has been characterized perfectly by one of Míguez's reviewers: "Jesus is Lord—in the Church; Marx is Lord in history."[50] Revolution thereby becomes the new god, lending to human action the transcendent ethic theologians formerly were inclined to ascribe to the divine commandments.

To speak regretfully of the excesses that have accompanied revolutions throughout the twentieth century, while affirming the need for more such revolutions, is to repeat the old aphorism that we cannot make omelets without breaking eggs. Even if one thinks that is a defensible ethical principle he should be clear about the identities hidden in the metaphor. The omelet is the revolutionary regime that decides who ends up where in the steeply ranked profile of the "classless" society— indeed who lives and who does not—and the eggs are the heads of those who get in the way of the emerging order. When the American black rev-

---

revolution, we had in Russia, if not a cult of terror, then a fierce defense of terrorists. People in good positions—intellectuals, professors, liberals—spent a great deal of effort, anger, and indignation in defending terrorists."

[48]James Cone, *Black Theology and Black Power,* quoted in Paul Johnson, *Enemies of Society* (New York: Atheneum, 1977), p. 245.

[49]Câmara, *Revolution Through Peace,* p. 37. Câmara's saintly reputation may be due in part to his naiveté. Míguez, *Doing Theology in a Revolutionary Situation,* p. 47, quotes him as saying: "I think we can avail ourselves of the Marxist method of analysis, which is still valid, leaving aside the materialist conception of life." This logical innovation may next bring us an advocacy movement in favor of vegetarianism which, however, leaves aside the prohibition against eating meat.

[50]David H. Chilton in *The Journal of Christian Reconstruction,* vol. 5, no. 1, Summer 1978, p. 193.

olutionary Eldridge Cleaver fled the United States he headed for Cuba, full of hope. Later he wrote of a regime that made a farce of its supposed principles and imposed on people extreme mental and spiritual suffering, as well as the kind of racism he had thought was an American monopoly. "My adult education began in prison and was ruefully completed in the prison that is called Marxist liberation."[51]

The theological defenders of revolution who reside in the target countries should consider where they are likely to be found once utopia comes into being. Revolutions typically start with relatively modest goals, in order to attract the widest support, and are guided by relatively moderate leaders. As power is accrued, moderate policies and those who espouse them are progressively discarded until those on the left fringe are in control. This sets the stage for the counter-revolution. We see finally a standard totalitarian regime of either left or right, which brooks no dissent. Along the way the relatively moderate leaders who began the revolution lose their lives.[52] That is why Richard Neuhaus has predicted that should the Marxist revolution come to the United States it would require the elimination of such persons as Galbraith, Michael Harrington, Caesar Chavez, and a large number of politicians on the American left. Should the revolution in Latin America succeed, Míguez and his friends will have to go. Their God-talk, however useful in this preparatory period, will prove too embarrassing to a regime that will be doing what revolutionary regimes do when they take power. Those theologians who declare that Marxism is a science will have no place among people who make revolution and not just propaganda, and they may have little time to consider what it is that they have delivered their compatriots into. As Crane Brinton discovered in creating his typology of revolution, the period between the overthrow of the moderate revolutionaries and "the full impact of the Terror" is usually short. Marx knew better than to think that his enemy was just nineteenth-century idealism, as Míguez believes.

Civil Religion and the Churches

Debates on the vitality of religion in modern life are often pointless because, using only quantitative data, they consider mere adhesion to various institutions without being able to evaluate fully the content of

---

[51]Eldridge Cleaver, *Soul on Fire* (Waco, Tex.: Word, 1978), pp. 98, 108, 143f.

[52]For the best exposition of this typology see Crane Brinton, *The Anatomy of Revolution*, rev. ed. (New York: Vintage, 1965), chs. 6–8.

what is believed or the commitment that accompanies it.[53] Adherence to religious institutions can encompass any content whatever, and religion can be made to serve any cause. One is reminded of President Eisenhower's oft-quoted remark that the American government makes no sense "unless it is founded in a deeply felt religious faith—and I don't care what it is." The revolutionary regime in France is noted for its repression of the Catholic church and indeed its hostility to all forms of Christianity, but few remember that Robespierre instituted the worship of God because he considered atheism to be a characteristic of the aristocracy.

Modern humanism exemplifies the more recent attempt to convert Christian institutions to the service of an inimical ideology. John Dewey, far from being hostile to the churches, wanted them to adopt a program congenial to the framers of the Humanist Manifesto. They should repudiate the supernatural, he thought, and adopt his definition of God as "a unification of ideal values," the "*active* relation between ideal and actual." This would enable them to join the crusade to solve social problems on which the humanists had embarked. Dewey believed that such a faith had always been implicit in human beings—hence his title *A Common Faith.* Now he wanted modern society "to make it explicit and militant."[54] Writing in the 1930s, he believed that the institutional church was on its last legs, split between an obscurantist fundamentalism and a reluctantly retreating liberalism, giving up one line of trenches after the other before the advance of science. Thus, as a generous offer designed to help a defeated enemy salvage some dignity out of his shame, Dewey invited what was left of the church to surrender and join the victorious march of humanism.

What Dewey was calling for was a revived civil religion that would ratify and further the aims of the humanist elite to which he belonged. That is a call that many echo today. Sociologist Robert Bellah believes that the death of American civil religion is the root cause of the nation's social disintegration.[55] Historian Sidney Mead, although not as pessimistic as Bellah—inasmuch as he thinks civil religion retains much of its old vitality—agrees that it has a redemptive quality, which demands

---

[53]For an example of this, see the work of the sociologist-priest Andrew Greeley, *Unsecular Man: The Persistence of Religion* (New York: Schocken Books, 1972).

[54]John Dewey, *A Common Faith* (New Haven, Conn.: Yale Univ. Press, 1934), pp. 43,51,87.

[55]Robert N. Bellah, *The Broken Covenant: American Civil Religion in Time of Trial* (New York: Seabury, 1975).

prophetically that the nation return to the ideals from which it is wont to depart.[56]

But civil religion can never fulfill those expectations because they mistake its function. The sociological function of such a religion, as Berger says, is "to maintain the social structure by integrating and sanctifying the commonly held values on which that structure rests."[57] When Will Herberg studied what appeared to be a religious revival in the 1950s, he concluded that it often consisted of "a religiousness without religion, a religiousness with almost any kind of content or none, a way of sociability or 'belonging' rather than a way of reorienting life to God."[58] Civil religion is capable of bringing some people to the highest level of society's expectations, but is incapable of calling those expectations into judgment. By its nature, it rises from the society; that is the meaning of the *civil* part of its name. One practices such a religion in his capacity as citizen.

A religious statement, on the other hand, which says "do not be conformed to the values of society" swings an axe at the trunk of civil religion. Civil religion eases tensions, where biblical religion creates them. Civil religion papers over the cracks of evil, and biblical religion strips away the covering, exposing the nasty places. Civil religion prescribes aspirin for cancer, and biblical religion insists on the knife.

Times of crisis produce surges of civil piety because religious observances are intended as propitiatory offerings to bring back good fortune and stability. When Augustus sought to restore peace after a long period of civil war, it was natural for him to turn to the imperial cult as one of his tools. Louis Schneider and Sanford Dornbusch analyzed forty-six books on inspirational religion published in the United States and found that what they all had in common was the conviction that religion or God or both were utilitarian instruments that could be manipulated to produce a better life for humanity.[59] Neuhaus refers to this process as one of *adhesion,* contrasting it with the biblical emphasis on *decision.* Religious adherence means that the local gods are patronized in the same way as any local institution, and to do so is an expression of belonging. There is thus no distinction between being religious and conforming to whatever society expects. Neuhaus paraphrases Rousseau: "Let a thousand gods

---

[56]Sidney E. Mead, *The Nation With the Soul of a Church* (New York: Harper and Row, 1975).

[57]Berger, *The Noise of Solemn Assemblies,* p. 72.

[58]Will Herberg, *Catholic-Protestant-Jew,* rev. ed. (Garden City, N.Y.: Doubleday Anchor, 1960 [1955]), p. 260.

[59]Johnson, *Enemies of Society,* p. 122.

blossom, so long as none of their cults interferes with the overarching devotion to the State."[60]

If the religious establishment will not consent willingly to being a civil religion, the authorities may force it to assume that role. In the 1930s the Russian Orthodox church cracked under the contrary pressures exerted by its ancient traditions on the one hand and the Soviet authorities on the other. One segment, which came to be known as the "Living Church," adapted itself to the state's direction and so enlisted in Stalin's campaign to bend the whole society to his will. Becoming the tool of a murderous regime, it discredited the entire church. In similar fashion, the German church split under the Nazi regime.[61]

But civil religion is not dependent upon ecclesiastical structures for its operation. Every cultural expression of our society—the state, class, national sentiment, educational institutions, the media, moral ideals—lends a sense of cohesion to countless people. Hendrik Berkhof has written that this is just what is wrong with our institutions. "They let us believe that we have found the meaning of existence, whereas they really estrange us from true meaning."[62] That is precisely the message of the prophets. John Bright interprets their call to the requirements of the Pentateuchal covenant as a rejection of the popular theology of the day, which is to say, its civil religion.

The Checkered Church

Establishment religion in the United States is fragmented in a way that is more fundamental than the familiar denominational mosaic. It displays a bewildering kaleidoscope of conflicting and shifting beliefs. To a large extent it reflects the diversity of American society, the nation's division into competing civil religions, as well as Christian faith. Wheat and many varieties of weeds flourish together. The remnant, under whatever guise it may appear, remains faithful, while in the same organization, society's chaplains bless whatever policy may issue from the civil establishment.

In the evil syncretism of the ancient kingdom of Judah, one of the reli-

---

[60]Richard John Neuhaus, *Time Toward Home: The American Experiment as Revelation* (New York: Seabury, 1975), pp. 198f.

[61]Wassilij Alexeev and Theofanis G. Stravrou, *The Great Revival: The Russian Church Under German Occupation* (Minneapolis: Burgess, 1976), pp. 15ff., 76f.; Franklin Hamlin Littell, *The German Phoenix: Men and Movements in the Church in Germany* (Garden City, N.Y.: Doubleday, 1960), ch. 1.

[62]Hendrik Berkhof, *Christ and the Powers,* trans. John Howard Yoder (Scottsdale, Penn.: Herald Press, 1962), pp. 25f.

gious ideas that took root was an early form of deism. " 'The Lord will not do good, nor will he do ill' " (Zeph. 1:12). The assumption was either that God was indifferent to the contempt for his law that was rampant in the nation, or that he was unable to do anything about it. The prophets thundered against that complacency, against the casual acceptance of idolatry. The early church, like the prophets, was extremely sensitive about the intrusion of idolatry. In fact, one of the main points of controversy within the early church was whether or not it was permissible to eat meat sold in the markets that had been sacrificed to idols. The writer of 1 John, after warning his readers of false teachers, concluded his epistle with the warning "keep yourselves from idols."

It is that sensitivity to the inroads of idolatry that the modern church has largely lost, and that is what marks its decline. French theologian Gabriel Vahanian, who has been on the faculty of Syracuse University for many years, argues that the contemporary church has lost its iconoclastic function, one that is essential to its nature, and that the ideologies have moved into the vacuum. Biblical iconoclasm directs itself against all human pretentions of divinity, something its imitators cannot do.[63]

Idols are hard to identify after they have been part of the society for a time. It became "normal" for the people of Jerusalem to worship Molech in the temple, and it seemed odd that people calling themselves prophets should denounce the practice. Molech was part of the establishment religious scene, one that had directed the national cult throughout living memory. The idol was supported by all the "best" elements of society, the political, economic, and religious power structure. The prophets therefore denounced the powerful, wealthy, and respectable, not because there is anything inherently wrong with those attributes, but because in that society people so described organized and validated a system of idol-worship and injustice. That is why the vocation of prophet is so unpopular and so hazardous. The contemporary church, in contrast, for the most part has made its peace with this society's "best." In a society in which idolatry runs rampant, a church that is not iconoclastic is a travesty. If it is not against the idols it is with them.

Alexander Schmemann, writing of the schizophrenia that characterizes American Christianity, says that people tend to be unaware that their Sunday worship service, from beginning to end, repudiates the

---

[63]Gabriel Vahanian, *Wait Without Idols* (New York: George Braziller, 1964), pp. x, 22-24.

culture that they daily uphold as their "way of life."[64] It is a paradox that the attempt to be contemporaneous, which is to say relevant, en-sures the irrelevance of theologies and churches. Taking their values and their epistemologies—indeed their gods—from whatever it is that history has brought to center stage, churches completely lose their func-tion. Instead of exposing the modern idols, they promote and serve them. They are the counterparts of the priestly servants of Molech in the temple at Jerusalem. Or of Roman Emperor Alexander Severus, who added Christ to the gods he worshiped in his private chapel.

Democratic Idolatry

The futility of the ecclesiastical establishment should not be taken to mean that the professionals who lead it are entirely responsible for the impotence of the laity. In this, as in so many other areas, the people get what they want. In their denunciations of the temple establishment, the prophets recognized that the false prophets and teachers prospered be-cause the people preferred them to the hearing of the truth. Evil pro-phets and priests abounded, said Jeremiah, because "my people love to have it so" (Jer. 5:31f.).[65] The New Testament warnings were similar: "For the time is coming when people will not endure sound teaching, but having itching ears they will accumulate for themselves teachers to suit their own likings, and will turn away from listening to the truth and wander into myths" (2 Tim. 4:3f.).

People desire false teaching because it enables them to absolutize con-tingent systems to which they have given allegiance. They seek religious leaders who will bless their idolization of the nation, or the state, or the unrestricted pursuit of wealth or power, or the acting out of their hatred and *ressentiment* through humanitarian policy. The "relevant" theol-ogies of both left and right confer the baptismal sprinkle on their respec-tive portions of the cultural and political spectrum. A sterile religious conservatism idolizes nineteenth-century culture in all its expressions:

---

[64]Alexander Schmemann, "The East and the West May Yet Meet," in Berger and Neuhaus, eds., *Against the World for the World*, pp. 135f. Schmemann here is speaking spe-cifically of the Eastern Orthodox churches in which he is a theologian, but the point is capable of wider application.

[65]Cf. Mic. 2:11: "If a man should go about and utter wind and lies, saying, 'I will preach to you of wine and strong drink,' he would be the preacher for this people!" Also Is. 30:9ff.: "For they are a rebellious people, lying sons, sons who will not hear the in-struction of the LORD; who say to the seers, 'See not,' and to the prophets, 'Prophesy not to us what is right; speak to us smooth things, prophesy illusions, leave the way, turn aside from the path, let us hear no more of the Holy One of Israel.' "

its hymns, its education, its enemies, its vocabulary, and that is why it sounds like a museum piece. A sterile liberalism idolizes the present, triumphantly brandishing its progressive credentials just as their destructiveness and vacuity are becoming evident even to many who once took them seriously. It only remains for some element in the church to baptize futurism, and thereby put the capstone on its folly. All these illegitimate associations serve to "civilize" Christianity and thereby make it fit for nothing the apostles would have recognized.

There are those who insist that the Christian gospel is a radical proclamation that relativizes all ideas and institutions, but it is difficult to find much coming from them that offers hope. One of them, for example, thinks that Christian radicalism "is perpetually in the position of complaining about the status quo, whatever it happens to be."[66] The prophetic voice, to this way of thinking, means constant bellyaching without any necessity for discrimination, reason, or knowledge. In general, the radical Christian left has been a shrill scream, indiscriminantly labeling everything it dislikes as idolatrous, and thus deservedly marshals small influence. Moreover, its hasty identification with the prophetic writings that denounce those who oppress the poor lead it to divinize the poor and to cooperate with the policies of social democracy that turn poverty into a permanent condition. Imposing helplessness on poor people, it works to ensure the triumph of humanitarian policies that condemn the poor to perpetual dependency. Having lost the power of discrimination, this type of radicalism mindlessly associates itself with any expression of antiestablishment feeling and so substitutes a shabby anti-Americanism for a truly radical gospel. Its denunciations of the establishment leadership coexist with steadfast support for the destructive humanitarian redistributive policies that mark the establishment for what it is.[67]

How do we account for the fact that the cults are flourishing at a time when the mainline Christian churches have turned from their historic mission and self-understanding? Daniel Bell writes that when the theology erodes and the institutional framework of the ecclesiastical organization weakens, it is only natural that people should search for direct

---

[66]William Stringfellow, *Dissenter in a Great Society*, p. 162.

[67]For examples of this, see any issue of *Sojourners* or *The Other Side*. The January 1981 issue of *Sojourners*, billed as an economic issue, illustrates the irresponsibility of much that passes for radicalism. It is informed by no serious economic analysis at all, but repeats the incessant complaints that one finds in every other issue. Devoid of serious consideration of economic realities, it ends up supporting the same destructive *ressentiment*-based policies that humanitarian theorists espouse.

religious experiences that do not depend on organization or intellectual categories. "What defines a cult . . . is its implicit emphasis on magic rather than theology, on the personal tie to a guru or to the group, rather than to an institution or a creed. Its hunger is a hunger for ritual, and myth."[68] When theology degenerates, we are given instead a modernized version of the old-time religion of emotional exhortation, with a little existential mystification for good measure.[69]

Sociological studies suggest that the clergy who are least comfortable with the traditional understanding of their roles tend to leave the parish ministry—to enter the ecclesiastical bureaucracies and influence them in "progressive" ways. This accounts for the common observation that the hierarchies do not have the confidence of the people in the denominations.[70] This element of the clergy may be most usefully regarded, therefore, as another manifestation of the new class of white collar communications professionals influencing the masses toward adopting the humanist vision of reality.[71]

The Kingdom Coopted

In serving as society's chaplains, the major denominations are only repeating the behavior of innumerable predecessors. When an evil king of Israel sought advice from the prophets, he had no trouble finding four hundred of them who were perfectly willing to tell him what he wanted to hear (1 Kin. 22:5f.). As the declining Roman Empire sank further into degradation, its thinly christianized emperors used the churches to prop up their sagging fortunes. "[W]hat they required of Christianity," Charles Cochrane has written, "was that it should subserve a de-

---

[68]Daniel Bell, *The Cultural Contradictions of Capitalism* (New York: Basic Books, 1976), p. 168.

[69]See, for example, Michael Novak, *A Theology for Radical Politics* (New York: Herder and Herder, 1969), p. 127f.: "The exit is to begin—one must begin for oneself, with no one else to say why or how; one must lift oneself by one's own bootstraps, in an act of gratuitous, creative freedom; one must create oneself out of nothingness. The exit is to begin to experience, to understand, to judge, to decide. For such acts, more than any others, enlarge the range of one's self and of one's world. One must begin . . . to feel, to intuit, to evaluate, to do."

[70]For the data see Jeffrey K. Hadden, *The Gathering Storm in the Churches, passim.* Hadden's assumption is that these clergy who run the church headquarters are in the right, which means that their main task is "winning the laity" (p. 232).

[71]Cf. Jacques Ellul, *False Presence of the Kingdom,* trans. C. Edward Hopkin (New York: Seabury, 1972), p. 39: "Belonging to the new social category known as 'the intellectual leaders,' [the clergy] adopt its imagery, vocabulary and newspapers."

finitely social and economic function."[72] Malcolm Muggeridge recalls that early in the century his father never lacked for a clergyman to add respectability to a socialist meeting by offering a prayer. The formula for this cooperation was "making the world a better place," and while they might differ on such minor issues as the existence of God and the nature of the universe, they could agree on the use of public funds for society's improvement. The socialist sponsors, mostly atheists, were, of course, utterly contemptuous of these clerical dupes.

A pluralistic society has many ways of coopting the churches. There was a time when the Protestant church was scathingly called the Republican Party at prayer, but depending on which element of it one is considering, it might as justly be called the Americans for Democratic Action at prayer, the Daughters of the American Revolution at prayer, Marxist revolutionaries at prayer, devotees of psychological uplift at prayer, seekers after mammon at prayer, and so on. The churches are useful adjuncts to a bewildering mélange of causes, out of which they create competing gospels.

If we consider churches in their role as institutions, they exemplify the common ailment of institutional failure in a declining society. Families fail to nurture, governments fail to provide justice, schools fail to educate, and so churches fail to represent Christ. Ecclesiastical failure is not a sudden event but, as in the case of those sister institutions, began long ago. The fact that the major denominations are being deserted by large numbers of people does not mean they have just now slipped. The grave weaknesses of intellectual power, of faith, of integrity, and of a sense of mission are only now becoming evident in the statistics. The mask has been taken away. Choosing to be relevant to society's illusions instead of to their historic mission, they join society in its degeneration.

Observing the relationship between American religious institutions and the larger society, the dominant image we find is convergence. Ellul believes that throughout the West the secular religions are insinuating themselves into the Christian churches, or else they are absorbing Christianity into themselves.[73] In that environment, Christians can find themselves coopted into any kind of movement if only they will "adapt" their beliefs to whatever subcultural element welcomes them. What ought to count for them is not their faithfulness to conservative, liberal, or radical shibboleths, but adherence to a standard.

---

[72]Charles N. Cochrane, *Christianity and Classical Culture: A Study of Thought and Action from Augustus to Augustine* (Oxford: Clarendon, 1940), p. 356.

[73]Jacques Ellul, *The New Demons*, trans. C. Edward Hopkin (New York: Seabury, 1975), p. 209.

To speak of a standard that should guide and animate the church is to say that the only hope for it to fulfill its true function is in a return to Christian orthodoxy, one that carries with it a determination to fulfill its heritage of doctrine, faith, and practice. This would not be satisfied with dogmatic utterances but would insist on the full application of the prophetic tradition, cutting radically through the idolatrous web of the larger society. It is not generally known that this kind of faith is what animated the remarkable burst of Christian social action that was a feature of American life for more than half a century until about the time of World War I.[74] Harvey Cox, who is no friend of such a faith, nevertheless is struck by the fact that many of those whose actions he most admires have been orthodox—people such as Dietrich Bonhoeffer, Dorothy Day, and Simone Weil. Orthodoxy, as Cox says, "can provide a more cutting, critical perspective on the world" than can a more accommodating position.[75]

Meanwhile, we are left with a church that to a large extent has chosen to befriend the powers that dominate the world instead of judging them. We should be reminded that the crucifixion of Christ was a joint production, instigated by religious authorities and then carried out by the state. When the state joins forces with historicism and humanism in forging the great brutalities of the future, we should not be surprised to find the representatives of the establishment churches, fuglemen for the idolatries, earnestly assuring us that God's will is being done.

---

[74]See the pioneering work of Timothy L. Smith, *Revivalism and Social Reform in Mid-Nineteenth-Century America* (New York: Abingdon, 1957); also Smith's student Norris Magnuson, *Salvation in the Slums: Evangelical Social Work, 1865-1920* (Metuchen, N.J.: Scarecrow Press, 1977).

[75]Harvey Cox, *Turning East: The Promise and Peril of the New Orientalism* (New York: Simon and Schuster, 1977), pp. 171f.

CHAPTER SEVEN

Consequences and Expectations

Understanding the Present and Forecasting the Future

Evaluating the current state and worth of a society from within and predicting its future is an extraordinarily difficult undertaking, one that has, in retrospect, made fools of countless people who have tried it. The two most eminent historians of ancient Greece were distraught over the state of Hellenic civilization at the very time that later observers were to regard as the Golden Age.[1] During Solomon's reign the Hebrew kingdom stood at its zenith, boasting the world's first standing army, a great building program, elaborate industrial and mercantile enterprises, and greatly expanded frontiers. Few of his contemporaries could have predicted that it was all to end soon. Yet, when Solomon died, a rebellion sundered the kingdom into two parts, and the former glory faded quickly. More recently, Walter Lippmann, in a striking miscalculation, thought that the 1930s were the last gasp of collectivism, which would be followed by a rebirth of his beloved classical liberalism.[2]

The well-known perils of prediction have not stopped others from trying their hand at this exercise. Anthony Burgess has attempted to bring *1984* up to date by undertaking a portrait of society only seven years in the future. His is a bleak forecast, including as it does runaway inflation

---

[1]Arnold J. Toynbee, *A Study of History,* abridg. D.C. Somervell, 2 vols. (New York: Oxford Univ. Press, 1947, 57), vol. 1, pp. 190f. Toynbee here provides quotations from Thucydides and Herodotus.

[2]Walter Lippmann, *An Inquiry into the Principles of the Good Society* (Boston: Little, Brown, 1937), p. 48.

produced by government printing presses; impotent leaders manipulated by pressure groups; an educational system practically destroyed by equalitarian ideology; a debased language; social disorder and mass conformity. Italian analyst Roberto Vacca thinks we are coming into a new dark age to be followed by a rebirth of glorious culture. He admits that the second part of this prediction is an assumption without evidence except for the "alternation" of historical events, apparently a version of the cycle theory of history. American Marxist historian L. S. Stavrianos also believes we are entering a dark age and he too, with a similar fit of wishful thinking, believes it will end in a glorious new civilization as the West comes to its senses and follows the trail blazed by Chairman Mao. Jean-François Revel thinks that the Watergate crisis was the end of a long era, and that henceforth the periphery of the United States will reassert its old predominance over Washington. Congressman Jack Kemp, perhaps as an introduction to his future presidential campaign, says that the new American revival is already under way. The American dream will be realized as more and more citizens make it to the consumer gravy train.[3]

History as a Moral Universe

In spite of the dubious example of all these prophets, it remains necessary to venture into the thickets of interpretation and prediction. The only alternative to some kind of "alternation" theory of history that assumes the hegemony of cycles is, apparently, a method that skirts dangerously close to the historicist projection of trends indefinitely into the future. Yet, we may be saved from this by recognizing and avoiding the assumption on which historicism rests, which is immanence. For if history is subject to principles and forces that lie outside itself, its course can be changed, even abruptly. We shall be painting a somber picture of the future of this society, but history is an open system. Just as the wicked generation that populated Nineveh was saved by repentance, so can any other.

Peter Drucker has written that there is only one possible cause of any revolution, and that is a fundamental change in values which radically alters the understanding people have of their own nature and where they

---

[3]Anthony Burgess, *1985* (Boston: Little, Brown, 1978); Roberto Vacca, *The Coming Dark Age,* trans. J.S. Whale (Garden City, N. Y.: Doubleday, 1973), p. 6; L.S. Stavrianos, *The Promise of the Coming Dark Age* (San Francisco: W.H. Freeman, 1976); Jean-Francois Revel, *The Totalitarian Temptation,* trans. David Hapgood (Garden City, N. Y.: Doubleday, 1977), p. 256; Jack Kemp, *An American Renaissance: A Strategy for the 1980s* (New York: Harper and Row, 1979), p. 1.

stand with respect to society and, indeed, the entire universe. Crane Brinton's interpretation of modern Western history was based on the same insight. He believed that when Enlightenment thinking began infiltrating European thought about three centuries ago, it profoundly altered the course of history. Since then the main influence on life and morals in the West has been the interaction and "mutual interpenetration" of the Christian world view and that of the Enlightenment.[4]

This may suggest to some that fundamental changes take place only over long periods of time, but that is not the case. Since such events are primarily moral, rather than material or technological, they can happen very quickly. In a brilliant analysis, French historian Paul Hazard examined the very phenomenon that so exercised Brinton's imagination: the beginning of the Enlightenment. He found that a rapid change in thought took place in the period roughly covered by the last two decades of the seventeenth century and the first fifteen years of the eighteenth. At the beginning of the period, the bishops were the major influence, but at the end, the Enlightenment philosophers. "One day, the French people, almost to a man, were thinking like Bossuet," wrote Hazard with some hyperbole. "The day after, they were thinking like Voltaire. No ordinary swing of the pendulum, that. It was a revolution."[5] The exaggeration in this interpretation largely concerns the identity of those who changed so much in such a short time. For it was the small number of the highly educated who joined Voltaire in the intellectual and moral revolution. The process in which ordinary people joined them has lasted almost three centuries; Brinton treated this phenomenon as the central feature of modern cultural history.

The displacement of the biblical faith that once informed Western society by the Enlightenment faith that is undermining it provides the unifying theme for the various idolatries that populate these pages. When Jesus said that false Christs would come to lead people astray (Matt. 24:24), he did not mean there would be lunatics thinking they were he, but rather that messianic figures and movements demanding ultimate allegiance would deceive people into following idols. The practice of idolatry has serious consequences, which the prophets of Israel identified as oppression, injustice, and bloodshed. That is why the ascendancy of Enlightenment faith to a position of dominance in recent dec-

---

[4]Peter Drucker, *The End of Economic Man* (London: William Heinemann, 1939), p. 10; Crane Brinton, *A History of Western Morals* (New York: Harcourt, Brace and World, 1959), p. 414, n. 1 and *passim.*

[5]Paul Hazard, *The European Mind (1680-1715)* (New Haven: Yale Univ. Press, 1952), p. xv.

ades has brought the pathologies of the West to a state of virulence.

To say that the spread of an idea throughout the population is pathological is to call into question the democratic faith. For in the form that democracy has gained popular currency, it is assumed that when the will of the majority is put into effect the result is beneficial. This has been congenial to the historicist faith that whatever history brings to the fore must be good.

But when the people turn to idolatries, and the outcome of *those* faiths become incarnated in society's institutions, the rot sets in. What happens in the future depends on the moral state of the people who decide to follow one course of action rather than another. This position is flatly opposed to the determinisms that are the natural outcome of Enlightenment materialism, and thus is unacceptable to the proponents of the religious ideas that have become dominant in the late-twentieth century.

Thus, we return the favor Marx did to Hegel and turn him upside down so that the moral, intellectual, and spiritual elements of humanity are recognized as the substructure, and the material events the superstructure. The disintegration of Western society, which is in the forefront of public discussion, then, is the embodiment of idolatries that are indigenous to the Enlightenment. None of them is new, of course, but their modern manifestations assume forms that are peculiar to the spiritual and material shape of the present age, and the combination of essence and accident that confronts us is unique, just as it has been for every other age.

Foul Is Useful and Fair Is Not

One of the dominant elements of that combination is the kind of pragmatism that shuns moral considerations or, recognizing them, deliberately contravenes them on the theory that success lies in doing so. Most of the alarmist cries about "survival" lead us in that direction. Robert Heilbroner, for example, insists that our condition is so perilous that we must willingly give up whatever values stand in the way of its amelioration.[6] That is a clear statement that means are superior to ends, technical considerations to moral principles. Ellul argues that this characteristic is the one that dominates our whole age, that it promotes the use of whatever techniques are available without consideration of their moral implications.[7] This is a modern version of Bernard de Mandeville's

---

[6]Robert L. Heilbroner, *An Inquiry into the Human Prospect* (New York: Norton, 1974), p. 26.

[7]Jacques Ellul, *The Technological Society*, trans. John Wilkinson (New York: Knopf, 1964), p. 99 and *passim*.

idea, now almost three centuries old, that public good arises from private evil, and when people stop practicing their vices, society will collapse.

Thus, we have a kind of moral alchemy: the base metal of evil actions is transformed into the gold of good outcomes; the wages of sin is life; what a man sows he will not reap. One of Shakespeare's most striking triumphs was his evocation of the depths of horror in *Macbeth* at the complete reversal of good and evil. The whole play embodies the witches' cry: "Fair is foul and foul is fair." And those are precisely the words that Lord Keynes used to persuade us that, although some day it may be possible to conduct economic affairs morally, for the next century our circumstances will be so grave as to make it impracticable.[8]

This denial of moral cause and physical effect has become commonplace, irrespective of the vision it accompanies. Roberto Vacca sees a dark age coming upon us because the complexity of our technological system is becoming too great to cope with the inevitable malfunctions, and therefore it must end in a complete breakdown. But he says nothing about the impulses that cause people to behave in certain ways, either in stable or catastrophic times, apparently assuming that that is irrelevant. Herman Kahn sees a golden age coming upon us, but in his schematic presentation of alternative views concerning such matters as resource availability, technology, capital, management effectiveness, and so on, he gives no hint that what people desire and purpose will have any bearing on the future.[9]

The great fallacy of our time, Malcolm Muggeridge has written, is the one that says that we may pursue collective virtue apart from personal behavior. Irving Kristol, who once criticized economists for being ignorant of the moral factors in economic life, afterwards abandoned that position and joined them in the beguiling chambers of pragmatism. One may lament the moral decrepitude that leads to destructive economic policies, he now says, but "such lamentations are for poets, not economists." The remedies for economic and social maladies, therefore, are to be sought in changing institutional arrangements. Jude Wanniski,

---

[8]"For at least another hundred years we must pretend to ourselves and to everyone that fair is foul and foul is fair; for foul is useful and fair is not. Avarice and usury and precaution must be our gods for a little longer still. For only they can lead us out of the tunnel of economic necessity into daylight." "Economic Possibilities for our Grandchildren," *Essays in Persuasion*, pp. 371f., quoted in Herman Kahn and Anthony J. Wiener, *The Year 2000: A Framework for Speculation on the Next Thirty-Three Years* (London: Macmillan, 1967), p. 215.

[9]Vacca, *The Coming Dark Age*, pp. 4ff.; Herman Kahn et al., *The Next Two Hundred Years: A Scenario for America and the World* (New York: William Morrow, 1976), pp. 10-16.

who championed the Laffer curve long before it became part of the Reagan presidential campaign, thinks that whenever rulers grasp that theory of taxation, golden ages ineluctably follow. Some of the most sensible work has been marred by the same hope placed in technical fixes. Ludwig von Mises, in the midst of a brilliant argument, expressed the conviction that common sense would be enough to save us from the fantasies and illusions that enhance the attractiveness of the idol state.[10] W. Allen Wallis, who understands better than most the political and economic degradation to which the nation has succumbed, nevertheless believes that a recovery can be expected from a revival of the educational system.

Moral Man and Immoral Society

The common tendency to seek technical solutions to societal problems is nothing more than the substitution of a technical-rational model for the older religious-moral one.[11] When social pathologies appear, we blame them on the "structures of society" (or if the religious establishment is speaking, our problem becomes "structural sin"). If the structures of society are guilty, and not we, then there is no possibility for personal repentance and no way to deal with guilt. We then do the irrational and destructive acts that maintain the systems of redistribution and humanitarianism, in a desperate and futile attempt to expunge guilt feelings by what seem to be good works. Doing as we please and blaming the result on structures is the moral equivalent of the free lunch. By-passing repentance and judgment, we try to arrest increasing chaos by adding a special investigative officer to the court, increasing a subsidy here or a dole there, implementing a halfway house here, a counseling service there. The diagnosis is wrong, and so the intended cure is futile.

After the deaths of some nine hundred people in James Jones's Guyana commune, psychiatrist Thomas Szasz searched the whole literature on the incident and found that universally the politicians, journalists, lawyers, psychiatrists, and other experts had concluded that Jones

---

[10]Ludwig von Mises, *Bureaucracy* (New Haven: Yale Univ. Press, 1946 [1944]), p. 125; but see his book *Omnipotent Government* (New York: Arlington House, 1969 [Yale Univ. Press, 1944]), p. 120: "There is no hope left for civilization when the masses favor harmful policies."

[11]The idea is taken from Robert N. Bellah, *The Broken Covenant: American Civil Religion in Time of Trial* (New York: Seabury, 1975), p. ix. Bellah goes on to say that this substitution is no advantage. "Indeed it only exacerbates tendencies that I think are at the heart of our problems. If our problems are . . . centrally moral and even religious, then the effort to sidestep them with purely technical organizational considerations can only worsen them."

was insane. New York *Times* columnist James Reston seemed to speak for everyone when he said that Jones was an "obviously demented man." Yet Szasz could find no evidence that anyone had doubted Jones's sanity before the incident. In fact, a gala fund-raising dinner in his honor, endorsed by seventy-five prominent leaders, was scheduled in San Francisco for December 2, 1978, and had to be cancelled after the massacre. Szasz's explanation makes more sense than that of the pundits and experts: "I think he was an evil man."[12] This is not simply a disagreement in which Szasz interpreted the evidence differently from the others. The significant point is that so many people concluded that a monstrous act like Jones's *had* to be an act of insanity; they no longer believed, if they ever had, that evil acts are done by evil people.

Moral failure has palpable consequences. As the ancient Greeks understood it, overweening pride would lead to downfall, *hubris* to *nemesis*. The modern habit of subsuming moral categories into material categories is a debunking process. The most sophisticated social thought places its emphasis not on one's obligations but on one's desires, although those are often dignified by being called "needs" or "rights." The moral foundation is thrown out the window and only the appetite is left. This may account for the fact that virtually every expression of modern idolatry is fatalistic. Moral action is inconceivable without freedom, and the various materialistic reductionisms are inconceivable with it. Marxism, behaviorism, evolutionism, astrology, and all the other environmentalisms insist that people do things only because external events compel them to do so. The real meaning of Erich Fromm's title *Escape from Freedom* is the flight from moral behavior. This fallacy is now part of the world view of educated people everywhere. Teachers, lawyers, government officials, journalists, social workers, artists— those who comprise the new class—"know" that environment produces character, that morality therefore is an epiphenomenon of material conditions and hence must be relative. If pressed to say *how* they know it, they may reply that social science has proved it, echoing Skinner's false dogma that to speak of freedom and dignity is prescientific.

Such ideas have been exported by the West to poor countries, many of whose leaders were educated in Paris, London, or New York. When Robert MacNamara left his post as president of the World Bank in 1980, it was with frustration and bitterness. Although he had transmitted untold billions from rich countries to poor, he saw his work as hardly begun and was weary of constantly trying to badger the donors to be

---

[12]Thomas Szasz, "The Freedom Abusers," *Inquiry,* February 5, 1979, pp. 4-6.

more generous. But it was impossible for the recipients, ruled by ideologues aping the worse of the Western idolatries, to have done more with the largesse of the West. There is no conceivable amount of money he could have given to them that would have changed things fundamentally. Materialist philosophies are unable to see that the form of capital that is indispensable is the moral and intellectual strength that creates abundance out of whatever is available. The West and its developing imitators, however, destroy what they have been given.

Materialist ideologies shatter any appeal to ethical limitations on the individual because they do not recognize transcendence, thus denying any reality that lies beyond the tangible and particular. The individual person becomes an island, a cancerous growth of egoism, because he rejects the transcendent, which is all that could teach him that it is not lawful for him to regard himself as the center and purpose of the universe, to whom all else must be subordinated. This cuts away the root and ground of all morality, leaving only vacuous moralisms, which are ignored because they are based wholly on pragmatism. Anyone saying that all moral principles derive from material conditions *except this one* is rightly hooted from the pulpit.

One of the chief errors in Ayn Rand's philosophy is her idea that the altruism of social democracy is the opposite of individualistic egoism. Seeing the destruction wrought by the former, she argues for the latter. But collectivism and egoism are both derived from immanence, both can live only when the limitations of transcendent law are overthrown, both are symptoms of the same disease. If it is lawful for the individual to do as he pleases, why should it not be lawful for the commissar to do as *he* pleases? If there is nothing to restrain one lawfully, then there is nothing to restrain the other.

Moralism and Guilt in the Absence of Morality

The crowning irony of this thoroughly immoral age is that more than perhaps any other it is incessantly and unapologetically moralistic. There is nothing so brutal that it cannot be defended with the joyous trumpeting of self-righteous satisfaction. An invasion is called an act of love; destroying a village is an act of salvation; reducing a poor man to perpetual dependence or killing an infant an act of compassion. There are few miserable little despots who do not use this language. No matter how vicious the action, the justification will be the promotion of equality, the helping of the poor, the protection against unfair competition, the extension of compassion, the defense against wicked imperialism or communism. Amid the declamations against Victorian "hypocrisy," exist also calls for the justifications of perversity. Envy, homosexuality, and state domination are prescribed as normative. The pathological becomes an "alternative lifestyle." The prophetic denunciations were not only of evil but of open proclamation of evil: " . . . they proclaim their sin like Sodom,/they do not hide it" (Is. 3:9).

Unadorned selfishness may be less harmful than the ersatz compassion that claims to be doing good for others, because it is less likely to infect the healthy tissue of society. It takes the money and runs without leaving behind the pernicious eggs of guilt feelings and *ressentiment* policy. In 1981, Joseph Savimbi, one of the leaders of the insurgency against the Marxist regime in Angola, commented in a television interview on what he saw happening in the social democracies of the West. "The great drama of the West in the modern era is its own guilt. Guilt is devouring the values of the West, and it is a tragedy to watch." People who reject the biblical doctrines of responsibility and sin do not thereby rid themselves of guilt, and so they feel guilty. They do, however, rid themselves of any way to handle their guilt, and that is why it breaks out so destructively. Responsibility denied is thrust upon a society anyway, but within the humanitarian context there is no way for it to repent and mend its ways.

When asked about Chesterton's famous remark that the United States was a nation with the soul of a church, Alistair Cooke replied: "That's true, but it also has the soul of a whorehouse."[13] Such is the way of moralism without morality.

Paganism Revisited: The Mimetic Inversion

The return of Western culture to its pagan past bears striking correspondence to the pattern of Toynbee's typology of mimesis. He was impressed by the universal tendency to pattern cultural and economic institutions after those of other peoples. The direction of this mimesis is crucial. In primitive societies it is directed uncritically toward elders and ancestors. When a civilization is being formed, the mimetic focus shifts to creative people who command a following by reason of their pioneering activities and their accomplishments.[14] One way to evaluate

---

[13]Quoted in Robert D. Linder and Richard V. Pierard, *Twilight of the Saints: Biblical Christianity and Civil Religion in America* (Downers Grove, Ill.: InterVarsity Press, 1978), p.164.

[14]On this and what follows see Toynbee, *A Study of History, passim,* especially vol. 1, pp. 49, 120, 245, 259f., 419, 455-66; vol. 2, pp. 98, 120, 347.

the future of a society is to determine the direction of mimesis. Who admires whom and on what grounds? Who seeks to be more like whom? Toynbee, among others, noted that the direction of mimesis has become such as to confirm other indications of decline. For as the proletariat in Western societies has become affluent, so the middle and upper classes have become proletarianized. Their attitudes toward time, work, and leisure have come to exhibit characteristics of the lower classes.

Toynbee was especially concerned that artistic standards were declining precipitously because of the acceptance as cultural norms of the patterns belonging to the proletariat, both those within and exterior to the West. In keeping with the dominance of naturalism, it is assumed that principles associated with civilization are decadent, and those that come from primitive cultures are more vital, a revival of an idea that became common among the eighteenth-century philosophers. At any rate, that is the direction of mimesis.[15]

At the same time the formerly-dominant civilization begins imitating the various proletariats, the latter cease to emulate those people they formerly regarded as their betters, and return to their own once-despised traditions. In the fourth century, when the barbarians in the Roman armies began keeping their own names instead of adopting those of the Romans, the Romans, including the imperial court, began aping barbarian manners, customs, and dress. Thus, Toynbee endorsed Christopher Dawson's observation that the mark of a culture's last stage is not decay but syncretism.[16] The advance into the established culture of the West of pagan and primitive modes of music and art should therefore not be regarded, as it so often is, as progress, but rather as a sign of decline. All this has a devastating impact on the life of the civilization.[17] What is sometimes interpreted as the conversion of the whole world to the ways of the West is, on this showing, something quite differ-

---

[15]Crane Brinton, who was not a Puritan, protested against the ignorant deprecation of the Puritan contribution to Western civilization in favor of the primitives. "They deserve better from us; we can perhaps learn from them almost as much as from the Zuni, the Hopi, or the Samoans." *A History of Western Morals,* p. 232. In 1977 Will Durant remarked to an interviewer that the upper classes have recently come to imitate proletarian speech, using "language that used to be confined to the gutter." Toynbee used similar illustrations.

[16]Arnold Toynbee, *Reconsiderations* (New York: Oxford Univ. Press, 1961), pp. 446f.

[17]Cf. John A. Lukacs, *The Passing of the Modern Age* (New York: Harper and Row, 1970), p. 129f.: "The vogue of what was called rock and roll was to signal the proletarian and barbarian advance of the coming Dark Ages. . . . The single cohesive symptom that was typical of all forms of art was a cult of ugliness." Also novelist and critic John Gardner, *On Moral Fiction* (New York: Basic Books, 1978), p. 16: "Most art these days is either trivial or false. There has always been bad art, but only when a culture's general world view and aesthetic theory have gone awry is bad art what most artists strive for, mistaking bad for good."

ent. It is, in Toynbee's words, a mass conscription "into the Western society's swollen internal proletariat."

As the dominant society continues its breakdown, the once-admiring external proletariat not only turn away their mimetic activity and admiration but also become hostile to the metropolitan center. At the same time, the disintegrating civilization turns against its own traditions and, in its admiration of the more primitive society, burns in self-hatred. In the past this process has often been accompanied by a *Völkerwanderung*, the physical entry into the declining civilization of the peoples of the external proletariat. It may be a modern manifestation of this that we see in the migration of people from the Third World to the West.

The Breakdown of Intellect

Such syncretism has profound cultural as well as material ramifications. The intellectual life of the society, in particular, undergoes a decline that is now becoming apparent in the West. For intellect, in the words of Columbia University historian Jacques Barzun, is "the capitalized and communal form of live intelligence; it is intelligence stored up and made into habits of discipline, signs and symbols of meaning, chains of reasoning and spurs to emotion." It is not only a large body of common knowledge but also the facility to bring to bear on an issue the appropriate portion of that knowledge. When college students are unable to identify Socrates, Hamlet, and Elijah, it is clear that the common cultural inheritance that once provided a measure of unity and mutual understanding has been fragmented. This is the failure, not of intelligence, but of its communal manifestation. Barzun believes that one reason intellect is collapsing is that it is hated, and hated because it is envied as a sign of superiority. Therefore, he expects that anti-intellectualism will increase apace with equalitarian sentiment. The fortunes of the common culture will fare poorly.[18]

Although intellect is not synonymous with reason, it is too much to expect that reason will flourish when intellect is despised. Daniel Bell has concluded that the West is undergoing an economic crisis from which it will not recover because it is forsaking rationality, the hallmark of bourgeois culture, in favor of "apocalyptic moods and anti-rational modes of behavior." Because of the disjunction between economic goals and the intellectual processes necessary to support them, "this cultural contra-

---

[18]Jacques Barzun, *The House of Intellect* (New York: Harper Torchbooks, 1961 [1959]), pp. 4-8

diction is in the longer run the most fateful division in the society."[19] Orwell had the good insight to realize that the future totalitarian regime could only flourish by battering the exercise of intellect and replacing it with something else. *Crimestop,* for the servants of Big Brother, is a means by which their minds refuse to grasp analogies or perceive logical errors or understand basic arguments if doing so would provide understanding inimical to the interests of the regime. It is, in short, "protective stupidity."

A similar process accompanies the various mystifications that populate the cultural landscape, combining moral fervor and intellectual confusion. A value considered to be of great importance, which cannot be realized or defended rationally with the available evidence, is seized upon through a leap of faith. Since people feel there is no hope without that value, it *has* to be judged both efficacious and realizable, even if there is objectively no reason to believe it is either. Mystification differs from faith partly in the unworthiness of its object, but more basically because it does not recognize what it is doing. Faith says boldly that there is a realm in which reason cannot determine reality, whereas mystification leaps to a conclusion its premises deny, in its confusion often remaining unaware of it. The early Christian church knew that irrationality and a dependence on instinct were the preludes to destruction (2 Pet. 2:12f.).

The breakdown of intellect is prerequisite to the creation of "mass man." Helmut Thielicke argues that as settled conviction and principles disappear in favor of irrational urges, people become completely susceptible to the moods generated by propaganda.[20] Norman Podhoretz, a certified member of the New York intellectual establishment until he adopted views unpopular in that rarified atmosphere, describes what happens to those who step out of line as a reign of terror. In a book appropriately entitled *Breaking Ranks,* he says that rather than thinking independently, the intellectuals tend either to allow themselves to be silenced or else completely change their views. [21] Solzhenitsyn makes the same point in remarking that although Western intellectuals are legally free, "they are hemmed in by the idols of the prevailing fad."[22]

---

[19]Daniel Bell, *The Cultural Contradictions of Capitalism* (New York: Basic Books, 1976), p. 84.

[20]Helmut Thielicke, *Nihilism: Its Origin and Nature with a Christian Answer,* trans. John W. Doberstein (New York: Schocken Books, 1969 [1961]), p. 151.

[21]Norman Podhoretz, *Breaking Ranks: A Political Memoir* (New York: Harper and Row, 1979).

[22]Aleksandr I. Solzhenitsyn, *A World Split Apart: A Commencement Address Delivered at Harvard University June 8, 1978* (New York: Harper and Row, 1979).

Such being the case, it is futile to expect that yet another reform of the educational system will bring us out of the slough onto high ground. It has become a *bon mot* to say that the purpose of a college education is to enable us to discover when someone is talking rot. But now rot is what is taught in many college classrooms: religious propaganda such as naturalism, historicism, and statism, covered in scientific garb. Students are left defenseless because they are untrained in discerning the religious assumptions that underlie what they are taught. They hear in lectures and read in history or economics books that it is inevitable that the excruciating problems we face be countered increasingly by state power to which we must give allegiance, and they see no alternative to accepting it. Then they graduate and teach it to children in the schools.

Perhaps the most damaging legacy to the next generation is moral relativism, clothed with suitable scientific coverings. For if to choose between two competing systems is purely an arbitrary act, then there is no such thing as objective truth, or at least no way to know it. People reaching that conclusion are ready for the degradation of reaching moral decisions on the basis of whatever sentiment happens to strike them at a particular time.

The entire scientific enterprise is vulnerable in this kind of environment, for it cannot easily withstand the impulse to shunt aside absolute standards of honesty in favor of the pragmatic buttressing of ideological ends. Max Scheler noticed that *ressentiment* sometimes operates in such a way that the scholar's entire world view may be falsified in order to degrade the objects of his hatred.[23] Whatever the motive, the acceptance of ideology as the governing force in scholarship is debilitating. Trinidadian novelist V. S. Naipul, speaking on American television in 1980, said that Third-World nations, fawned over by Western intellectuals, are deceived by that treatment. Uncritically laudatory of these countries, the scholars delude even their own citizens. He mentioned, for example, the puffery surrounding Ghana's "redeemer," Kwame Nkrumah. R. G. Collingwood, observing the extent to which irrationality was spreading into Western culture around the time of World War II, doubted that natural science would survive the attack.[24]

---

[23] Max Scheler, *Ressentiment*, ed. Lewis A. Coser, trans. William W. Holdheim (Glencoe, Ill.: Free Press, 1961 [1915]), p. 74.

[24] R.G. Collingwood, *The Idea of Nature* (New York: Oxford Univ. Press [Galaxy], 1960 [1945]), p. 175. For a chilling example of what Collingwood must have had in mind see Gunther S. Stent, *The Coming of the Golden Age: A View of the End of Progress* (Garden City, N. Y.: Natural History Press, 1969). Stent, a distinguished geneticist, is happy about the end of reason, which will no longer be needed because there will be nothing further to learn, so far have we advanced on the road to complete knowledge. "Mortal

Religious Secularity

Of all the misleading interpretations of this complex age, few are more so than the common one that secularism means the replacement of a world view that is religious with one that is not. This completely mistakes the meaning of religion. Max Weber rightly argued that each major aspect of human action is dependent on a distinctive set of religious attitudes. The religious outlook influences the institutions of society in ways that cannot simply be accounted for in material terms. Sociologist Gerhard Lenski's studies in American society confirm Weber's hypothesis. The religious character of human ideas and institutions is all-pervasive, even in nontheistic systems like Buddhism, communism, and humanism. All social phenomena, Lenski says, constitute systems of faith, not being based on logical or empirical demonstration, and all seek to respond to the most basic problems of human existence. Thus, all normal adults are religious. "Human existence *compels* men to act on unproven and unprovable assumptions, and it makes no exceptions."[25] One of Jacques Ellul's most important contributions has been to show that modern Western society is awash with religiosity, that the much-vaunted secularization process means the flourishing of anti-Christian religions.[26]

Humanism has become the most messianic of the idolatrous religions of the West. Anthropologist Margaret Mead included in her autobiography a frank acknowledgement that it was a religious belief and called urgently for its spread throughout the world. That is why Milton Friedman described Galbraith as "a missionary seeking converts." The same urge was behind Erich Fromm's *tour de force,* the transformation of the Old Testament into a defense of radical humanism.[27]

In some respects the cultural collapse of the West bears striking re-

---

men will soon live like gods, without sorrow of heart and remote from grief, as long as their pleasure centers are properly wired" (p. 73).

[25]Gerhard Lenski, *The Religious Factor: A Sociological Study of Religion's Impact on Politics, Economics and Family Life* (Garden City, N. Y.: Doubleday, 1961), pp. 298f., 322.

[26]This idea is expressed most clearly in *The New Demons,* trans. C. Edward Hopkin (New York: Seabury, 1975), *passim,* especially, pp.213-20. Cf. Will Herberg, *Protestant-Catholic-Jew,* rev. ed. (Garden City, N. Y.: Doubleday Anchor, 1960 [1955]), p. 271: "In the United States explicit secularism—hostility or demonstrative indifference to religion—is a minor and diminishing force; the secularism that permeates the American consciousness is to be found within the churches themselves and is expressed through men and women who are sincerely devoted to religion."

[27]Margaret Mead, *Blackberry Winter: My Earlier Years* (New York: Pocket Books, 1975 [New York: William Morrow, 1972]), p. 322; Milton Friedman, *Tax Limitation, Inflation and the Role of Government* (Dallas: The Fisher Institute, 1978), p. 61; Erich Fromm, *You Shall be as Gods: A Radical Interpretation of the Old Testament* (New York: Holt, Rinehart, and Winston, 1966).

semblance to that of earlier eras. The late-Roman Empire was full of deterministic philosophical and religious systems, such as Chaldaean astrology, binding people in an inexorable fate, making them automata. The search for some means of escape, a frantic desire for freedom, found expression in supernaturalisms of various sorts. The result was grotesque cosmologies and ethical systems, such as gnosticism.

Spengler and Weber, with remarkable prescience, foresaw that something similar would happen in the twentieth century. Spengler believed that the prevalent materialism would become unbearable and that people would therefore feel impelled to toy with weird cults as a means of escape. The final development of Caesarism, then, would be accompanied by this "second religiousness." Weber's expectations were not very different. He thought that phenomenal man, instituting a rationalized technological power structure intended to control life's contingencies, would collapse into emotionalism and irrationality and accelerate the increase of centralized political power. He expected that mysticism, high-blown claims to be acting out of "goodness," and the elevation of eroticism into an ethical principle would become dominant in the West.[28]

It appears that the noumenal is taking charge, as they expected. Fifty years ago it seemed that rationalism—the doctrine that says that reason is the way to all knowledge—was the enemy of Christian faith. Now it is irrationalism, the claim that reason leads to no knowledge, that seems more dangerous. Writing from the rarified air of Cambridge University in the late-1950s, C. S. Lewis could see around him no danger of Enlightenment rationalism, "but much of an immoral, naive and sentimental pantheism."[29] Arianna Stassinopoulos shows the effect of this. She does not see how far advanced pantheism has come in the West, even though she is one of its evangelists. She reinterprets the incarnation of Christ in pantheist fashion and says that the church has obscured its true meaning for two thousand years. It really means, she is convinced,

---

[28]Oswald Spengler, *The Decline of the West*, 2 vols., trans. Charles Francis Atkinson (New York: Knopf, 1926, 1928), vol. 2, p. 310; Max Weber, *Economy and Society: An Outline of Interpretative Sociology*, 3 vols., ed. Guenther Roth and Claus Wittich, trans. Ephraim Fishoff *et al.* (New York: Bedminster Press, 1968), vol. 2, p. 601.

[29]C.S. Lewis, *God in the Dock,* ed. Walter Hooper (Grand Rapids, Mich.: Eerdmans, 1970), p. 181; cf. William F. Albright, *From the Stone Age to Christianity: Monotheism and the Historical Process,* 2nd ed. (Garden City, N. Y.: Doubleday Anchor, 1957), p. 23: "Now again we see the religious world confronted by the imperious necessity of choosing between biblical theism and Eastern pantheism, which threatens to sweep away theistic faith as it is reinterpreted by neo-Gnostic religious thinkers of the contemporary West."

that every human being has the possibility of manifesting his own divine reality.[30] But the idolatries of spirit are no improvement over the idolatries of matter. A new morality stressing simplicity, poverty, and spirituality can have outcomes fully as evil as materialist morality.

It should be clear from all this that what is widely regarded as a struggle between the religious and the secular is really a struggle between religions. The current strife over such issues as abortion is perfectly in order, because it is an attempt by both sides to establish a rule of order in accordance with basic religious precepts. Man is the autonomous ruler of himself, able to define right and wrong and frame statutes according to whatever he defines as just. Or else man is created and sustained by a holy and just God who declares on matters of right and wrong in the form of law. Both are religious views held by faith. In the most basic sense there is no such thing as a secular culture. This is not a call for religious warfare; it is an assertion that religious warfare exists, and inevitably so if one religion does not simply surrender.

Manifestations of Religious Warfare

Numerous legislative and legal battles attest to the fact that religious warfare is taking place. In the aftermath of the Jonestown massacre came a congressional investigation of religious "sects." This establishes the principle that there is a legitimate federal interest in the classification of religious organizations. In California the state attorney general's office placed the assets of the Worldwide Church of God under receivership, using the argument that as a charitable organization, the church was only acting as the state's steward in disbursing funds. A federal appeals court ruled in 1981 that the Catholic church was subject to antitrust laws when it refused to approve the publication of a liturgy.

It is in the schools, however, that we are likely to see the struggle joined most fiercely. As Peter Berger, among others, has argued, the public schools are the principal agency in the United States for spreading the established cultural religion.[31] The burgeoning Christian school movement and the decline in public school enrollments have excited the alarm of many in the educational and political establishment who believe—with good reason—that the two are connected. Christian schools are potent alternatives to the established schools, because the intellectual decay and lack of discipline of the latter are related directly to the

---

[30] Arianna Stassinopoulos, *After Reason* (New York: Stein and Day, 1978), p. 170.

[31] Peter L. Berger, *The Noise of Solemn Assemblies: Christian Commitment and the Religious Establishment in America* (Garden City, N. Y.: Doubleday, 1961), p. 65.

humanist assumptions that inform them. The emotional intensity of the struggle is a direct function of its status as a form of religious warfare. In 1978 the Internal Revenue Service proposed to remove the tax-exempt status from private schools that could not demonstrate by a series of complicated measures that they did not practice racial discrimination. The burden of proof was placed on the schools rather than on the government, and the presence of minority students and faculty members was not sufficient to prove that racial discrimination was not in force. Only after an intense public relations campaign was the IRS proposal put on the shelf. Later on, after a serious miscalculation by the Reagan administration, pressures were brought to bear to enact legislation to accomplish the same ends: bringing private education under federal control, ostensibly to prevent racial discrimination.

At about the same time, Grove City College, affiliated with the Presbyterian church, was threatened with the loss of financial aid for its students. The college received no federal money directly, and the Department of Health, Education, and Welfare stipulated that it was making no charge of any kind of discrimination. The college, for its part, refused to sign any of the required HEW documents because it did not wish to acknowledge that the state had jurisdiction over a church college. It is just that contention that the keepers of American civil religion will not tolerate willingly.

As court cases remove from the schools the last vestiges that remain from the nation's Christian heritage, under the doctrine of the separation of church and state, it will throw into sharp relief the dogmas of the civil religion: materialist and selfist psychologies; relativist ethics; the policies of statism, and so on. The strategy is to brand as *religious* whatever remains of the old traditions while maintaining resolutely that everything in the dominant civil religion is really *secular* and thus inviolable. That is what is behind the outcry that the emergence from their long slumber in the 1980 elections of the conservative religious groups was a violation of the constitutional separation of church and state. The effrontery of the humanist religious establishment knows no bounds. In 1978 the American Civil Liberties Union entered a New York case and moved to have the court declare unconstitutional laws restricting abortion. It entered as evidence the fact that pro-life demonstrators were seen to carry rosaries, and it sent an agent to observe a United States congressman participating in a Catholic mass. Apparently citizen rights are suspended for anyone whose opinions can be shown to be connected with traditional religious beliefs while those who deny such beliefs have full rights.

Under the humanitarian reign, religious persecution may take on a benign appearance. Since there is a school of psychology that regards religion as a form of neurosis, C. S. Lewis expected that some day the state would find it necessary to treat such a disorder. The cure would have to be compulsory, but it would not be considered punishment. Treatment would be purely therapeutic and humanitarian.

As in so many other areas, Sweden may show us the way. Some years ago the only Roman Catholic church in Stockholm was demolished when a district was being redeveloped. Because of administrative delays and deliberate bureaucratic roadblocks, it could not be reconstructed elsewhere. Alva Myrdal, wife of Nobel prize winner Gunnar Myrdal and a formidable scholar and politician in her own right, was the government minister responsible at the time. Her explanation was remarkably frank: "We are dismantling the Church bit by bit. And where necessary we are using economic means to do so."[32]

The End of Prosperity

In 1966 the University of Minnesota's Walter Heller was invited to give the Godkin lectures at Harvard University. Fresh from a stint as chairman of President Johnson's Council of Economic Advisors, he delivered a song of triumph for the economics profession. We were living, he said, in "the age of the economist," and the years ahead would see an unprecedented economic expansion along with a tamed business cycle. This would all be the achievement of a sophisticated science of economics armed with a quiver full of the latest Keynesian tools.[33] Few disagreed with Heller at the time, but by 1974 multitudes were ready to smile ruefully at the Haynie cartoon that appeared in *Newsweek*. At a table bearing the sign "Government Economists," the Mad Hatter is saying to his colleagues Mickey Mouse, Snoopy, and Mad Magazine's Alfred E. Neuman: "As you perhaps know, some of our policies have been questioned of late." By then it was becoming apparent that the nation, far from being on the threshold of a fantastic period of prosperity, was on a plateau that would barely allow Americans to maintain their standard of living and from which finally they would gradually descend.

In retrospect it is clear that the economists expected results from their econometric models that could not be delivered, but that was not the main source of their errors. In common with other social scientists, they

---

[32]Quoted in Roland Huntford, *The New Totalitarians* (New York: Stein and Day, 1972), pp. 176ff.

[33]Walter W. Heller, *New Dimensions of Political Economy* (Cambridge: Harvard Univ. Press, 1966).

assumed that human behavior could be codified and manipulated as if it were the output of machinery. This made social problems seem amenable to technical fixes. The controllers had only to change the inputs, and the outputs would change correspondingly. Thus the moral dimension of economic life was lost. Policy based on such a model could not succeed.

That bias could not help but ensure that economic policy would be not only amoral, but eventually would become immoral. In his brilliant early work, Keynes understood that the money-printing policy he favored would eventually lead to economic collapse, and he struggled mightily to devise a way to prevent it. He settled finally on a capital levy, in which the state would confiscate part of its debt held by the citizens, because the effects of such a policy would be less detrimental than inflation would be.[34] He failed to see that one policy was as immoral as the other, and to the despoiled creditor the effects were identical. Seizing the money directly by repudiating the debt or indirectly by depreciating the purchasing power were two ways to skin the same cat.

Lewis Mumford takes Keynes's principle a step further. Not content to repudiate debt as a regrettable sacrifice of morality to expediency, he wishes to do it as a matter of principle. The "law of rent," which requires repayment of principal with interest, is too confining for him. He calls for a "continuing adjustment" of debt in such a way that maintains "balance" between conflicting needs, energies, and claims. This, he says, will avoid the old "superstitions" about honesty, and prepare the way for "new criteria" that will assure us of the "good life."[35] It is not difficult to predict where this will lead us: loans will cease to be made. Moreover, if the state withdraws from the administration of justice by refusing to enforce contracts of indebtedness, it will undermine the basis for the enforcement of all contracts. Economic transactions that depend on contracts will dry up in favor of those that can be consummated on the spot. Thus the propensity for short-term gains that is already present in a deteriorating economy is accentuated. The willingness to indulge in immoral acts for practical reasons is almost always impractical.

It is odd that the failures of both economists and those who despise economics stem from the same cause: hatred of a free-market economy. Classical economics focused its attention on incentives and the relation-

---

[34]John Maynard Keynes, *Monetary Reform* (New York: Harcourt, Brace, 1924), pp. 72ff.

[35]Lewis Mumford, *The Transformations of Man* (New York: Harper and Brothers, 1956), pp. 212f.

ship between price and supply and demand. Its governing assumption was that free people could make rational economic choices in keeping with their own values. Markets were important because they were where buyers and sellers met and traded, without coercion, on the basis of mutual satisfaction. Markets meant that people had to serve each other in order to satisfy their own economic needs.

Those who think that economics comprises the ultimate social reality—materialists like the Marxists—make classical economics impossible. Instead of a free people making their own choices, they erect a command economy as the alternative to markets. That destroys an economy in which people are forced to satisfy each other in the trading process and creates an environment that rewards people for manipulating the political process for their own benefit and at the expense of their fellow citizens. This means politics replaces economics. It is the system that the Germans call *Wehrwirtschaft*, the reorganization of the entire social and economic fabric of society along military lines.[36] This is a return to the basic assumption of mercantilism, which the American Revolution was fought to repudiate. Mercantilism was based on a zero-sum view of economics—gold in one person's pocket could not be in another person's—and it ensured that economic life would be filled with strife. One had to despoil someone else to get what he wanted. Modern statism is a return to mercantilism, to forcible impoverishment of some in order to benefit others, to zero-sum thinking.

One of the fondest delusions of the moralists of the American right is that if only conservatives are elected to power the slide can be reversed. But the unities of American political life are far more fundamental than the divisions. Economists Robert Bacon and Walter Eltis have highlighted the fact that in Britain governments of the right and those of the left pursue policies that are almost indistinguishable. In times of crisis especially (which means almost all the time in the social democracies), "the Left and Right positions can become so mixed up that it is difficult to tell which is which."[38] The same is true in the United States where ideological statements obscure the realities. Congressman Jack Kemp, one of the conservative hopes, bases his economic plan on the same redistributionary assumptions as his opponents, differing with them mainly on practical grounds. He recognizes the futility of killing the golden goose

---

[36]See the explanation of *Wehrwirtschaft* in Drucker, *The End of Economic Man,* p. 134 and *passim.*

[37]Robert Bacon and Walter Eltis, *Britain's Economic Problems: Too Few Producers,* 2nd ed. (London: Macmillan, 1978), p. 114.

by taxation and regulation, preferring to keep it alive so that it can still deliver in the redistributionary system. Conservatives like Kemp can be expected to keep intact the system that their opponents caused to flourish over the last few decades. But they will change the beneficiaries and the victims. Both sides will continue to make redistribution pay for themselves through the vote-buying process. That is the explanation for Ronald Reagan's discovery during the 1980 presidential campaign that New York City and Chrysler Corporation were worthy additions to the welfare economy. It is also the reason that the Thatcher government in Britain, despite its popular image, presided over enormous increases in taxation, government expenditure, and the money supply.

As early as its first year in office, the Reagan administration had continued the ignominious policies of its predecessors, although this was disguised by the rhetoric of both parties. A tax increase disguised as a tax cut, a budget increase disguised as a budget cut, and the continued policy of rewarding political friends from the public purse showed that there was no fundamental change. The much-vaunted balanced budget by 1984 became a joke after only a few months. Moral government does not come from an immoral people.

Meanwhile, American business, which has been on the federal gravy train for many decades, is, as always, ready to increase the take. Thornton Bradshaw, then president of Atlantic Richfield (and since made chairman of RCA), wrote in 1977 that American business does not operate as free enterprise but in partnership with government. He thought this was a fine idea. Bradshaw was formerly a member of the faculty of the Harvard Business School, and it does not take much imagination to guess what his students learned about the benefits of this partnership. In 1980 the Bethlehem Steel Corporation took out full-page advertisements in the *Wall Street Journal* calling for an end to "government bailouts." It did, however, reaffirm on the same page its need for federal protection from foreign competition. Business executives, as well as others, can always be expected to couple demands for parsimonious government with pleas for expanded favors for worthy recipients— themselves or their clients. There is sufficient evidence to suspect that, given the opportunity, big business would repeat its support given in the 1930s for compulsory cartellization. This "partnership" with the federal government would entirely wipe out the need to compete, and therefore remove the incentive to satisfy customers. The American economy, if they have their way, will become a collection of OPECs. Max Weber saw this taking place even in his own day. With the Christian ethic removed from capitalism, he said, it becomes a "nullity," an object of contempt.[38]

Using the power of the state to accomplish brigandage is an ancient practice, but it requires unusual decadence for an entire population to acquiesce in mutual pocket-picking, to allow itself, that is, to be bribed with its own money. The growing list of government dependents makes it less likely that we can reverse the trend. There are too many who have allowed themselves to become dependent on the dole in an endless variety of forms. Expenditure increases are built into federal legislation by formulas and are not subject to specific authorization. Thus the budgeting process is on automatic pilot and must accommodate itself continually to an ever higher base. Those "entitlements" are one reason that the budget is said to be out of control. If Congress approved no new programs, the future increases would still be forthcoming.

Should the redistributionary phenomenon continue, then the inflationary one will also persist. For in the absence of moral restraint, which would insist on paying for what one receives, the sums required to supply the wards of the state will not be covered by taxes and the balance will be provided by printing money. The debtor class, which has benefited from inflation, is so enormous and so influential that it is difficult to see how the political will could ever be summoned to stop the currency depreciation. Every time the recessionary part of the business cycle begins, the cries for more monetary expansion overwhelm the political system, as bankruptcies, defaults, foreclosures, and other evidences of overborrowing increase. People do not want to repay their debts in currency of the same value as they borrowed.

A Society Feeding on Its Future

Consuming capital is perhaps the clearest sign that greed has come to dominate our economic life. That is the moral meaning of such phenomena as pollution and the transformation of farming into a mining operation through the depletion of the topsoil and the draining of the underground reservoirs. A decline in wealth ought to mean that consumption diminishes, but a moral failure prevents that from happening. Instead, a way is found to continue consumption at its former levels: living on capital. Thus the capital stock is raided. Roads, bridges, and buildings deteriorate, long-term borrowing finances current consumption, and

---

[38]Max Weber, *The Protestant Ethic and the Spirit of Capitalism,* trans. Talcott Parsons (London: George Allen and Unwin, 1930), p. 182.

the industrial base falls into obsolescence. Paul McCracken of the University of Michigan calculates that the industrial capital stock is now falling instead of rising at its historic annual rate of 2.5 percent. We have hardly begun to pay for this in unemployment and reduced output. As more capital is destroyed by policies of taxation and inflation, people will remove it from uses that make it vulnerable. Saving will seem increasingly improvident, and more capital will either be consumed or placed into such unproductive forms as precious metals and collectables. In any case, funds will not be available to build factories, schools, and barns. As the capital stock continues to be consumed, the pauperization process feeds upon itself. People persist in maintaining their standard of living through more capital consumption and currency depreciation. The system eventually must collapse.

It is a mistake to think that the struggle we are describing is between the state and wealthy plutocrats, the usual equalitarian contention. We are witnessing a battle against all holders of capital, those who have savings accounts, stocks and bonds, annuities, insurance policies, and pension fund rights. Punitive taxation and inflation wreak havoc on all these investments. Thus, the entire middle class as well as many in what used to be called the working class are in the process of being expropriated. Those who prosper are speculators who realize what is happening and can take advantage of it and those who can manipulate the political process in such a way as to make themselves the beneficiaries of subsidies, grants, monopolies, tariffs, and other forms of political payoff.

The mistaken assumption of zero-sum economics is self-fulfilling. If people believe that their gain must come from someone else's loss, they seize what they are able; and if they can do it under cover of the law, they do it with impunity. A society imbued with this vision of economic life finds taking what others have to be more rational than producing what others need in return for fair payment. Thus, stagnation and injustice are reinforced.

Those who think that distribution can be separated from production lead us to the same place. "We produce plenty for everyone. We only need to redistribute it so that there is more equality." But redistribution changes production. People do not willingly produce goods they know will be seized for the benefit of others. The redistributors will find that there is less to redistribute, for a redistributory economy is less than zero sum. It is negative sum. Armed robberies are zero sum because their adventitious nature does not induce people to modify their behavior in anticipation of such an unlikely event. But the predictability of redistribution makes it sensible to reduce both investment and production in order to provide less for the tax collector. People consume more and hoard more, work less, save less, and invest less. Thus, redistribution is literally destructive of the nation's wealth, dismantling capital resources and providing disincentives to replace them.

As the social democracies sink into economic decrepitude, the neo-Malthusian laments seem to gain greater influence. We are becoming poor, they say, not because of what we are doing, but because the earth is becoming depleted, because there are too many people, because production cannot be increased without increasing pollution. Thus, we will need more state controls to save us. Since this mistakes the agent of decline for its remedy, it can only hasten the deterioration. The energy crises of the 1970s, almost wholly caused by federal price controls and allocation blunders, will likely be the paradigm of the entire economy for the remainder of the century.[39]

A Society Marked by Strife

Greed is not incompatible with peace provided it coincides with prosperity so that it can, in the short-term, find satisfaction. Economic decline is not incompatible with peace provided that it comes to a people who have not fallen into covetousness and are content to have less, even less than their neighbors. But the moral failures that ensure a declining economy also ensure that people will not be content with less. We can only expect social strife from this double failure. As long as social democracy declares redistribution to be a matter of moral rectitude, the misuse of the political process to gain what others have is inevitable. That is why we can no longer have our decennial census without a political uproar and court challenges. Estimates of the amount of money to be disbursed annually depending on the distribution of the population exceed fifty billion dollars. The size of the take dictates the forces to be used in securing title to it. Thus, the simple act of counting noses is now a part of the political process. It had to become that, once the political process became a means of redistributing wealth. The only surprise in this development is that politicians and analysts still are able to use the word

---

[39]Neil Goldschmidt, President Carter's secretary of transportation, admitted just before stepping out of office what innumerable economists had been saying for years: "The U.S. Government allowed us to go from a nation importing a third of its oil to one importing almost 50 percent because there wasn't the political courage to deregulate the price of oil." Yet, the political nature of our energy problems is much more profound than even this statement acknowledges.

"justice" to describe this process without entirely losing their credibility.

The effort to grasp for more of the declining wealth replaces some of the effort that formerly went into production, thereby accelerating the decline. The same circumstances took place as the Roman Empire disintegrated. The reforms of Diocletian and Constantine, M. I. Rostovtzeff has written, "by giving permanence to the policy of organized robbery on the part of the State, made all productive economic activity impossible." But fortunes continued to be made, Rostovtzeff continued, by using influence with political forces to secure favorable places at the public trough. "Thus, more than ever before, society was divided into two classes: those who become steadily poorer and more destitute, and those who built up their prosperity on the spoils of the ruined Empire."[40] The growing indications of a trade war, even among the putative allies of the West, is an international manifestation of the same phenomenon. Prosperity falls, and the response is to fight for a larger share of what remains.

What are the chances that society can continue in its present form while the economy deteriorates? Very small. Keynes, whose theories have been used to undergird the policies of inflation, warned that such a process was the surest means of tearing a society apart.[41] Not long ago people who interpreted current conditions as the prelude to disaster were considered to be on the far fringes of sanity. Now, respected establishment figures speak in those terms. Felix Rohatyn, chairman of New York City's Municipal Assistance Corporation, said in 1980 that the entire country was heading in the same direction as the City, toward bankruptcy and social and political upheavals. About the same time Roy Jenkins, veteran British politician and president of the European Common Market's executive commission, warned that the social and economic order in Europe was on the verge of breaking up. "If we don't change our ways while there is still time . . . our society will risk dislocation and eventual collapse."

Those who believe that redistribution by the state builds community where individualism would otherwise dominate have it completely re-

---

[40]M.I. Rostovtzeff, *The Social and Economic History of the Roman Empire,* 2nd ed., 2 vols. (Oxford: Clarendon, 1957 [1926]), vol. 1, pp. 530f.

[41]John Maynard Keynes, *The Economic Consequences of the Peace,* quoted in Paul Johnson, *Enemies of Society* (New York: Atheneum, 1977), p. 86: "There is no subtler, nor surer, means of overturning the existing basis of society than to debauch the currency. The process engages all the hidden forces of economic law on the side of destruction, and does it in a manner which not one man in a million is able to diagnose."

versed.[42] The urban disturbances of the 1960s were those of a people who were turned into dependents but whose desires were not met. We have had relative peace since then because we have bought it, with surpluses at first and then with capital withdrawals, continually redefining "need" so that all parts of society could take their places at the trough: individuals, businesses, cities. The tax revolt is a sign that it cannot continue, and the eighties and nineties may have new versions of the riots of the sixties. When professionals, union members, civil servants, and businessmen go on a rampage, the manifestations are different from when slum people do it, but they may not be preferable. One of Rostovtzeff's major theses was that the collapse of Roman society in the third century occurred when the imperial policies of inflation and punitive taxation destroyed the economy and set the stage for class warfare. That was the beginning of the end.

Social peace becomes harder to maintain in periods of disintegration because many people perceive themselves to be better off without it. We have already seen the horror with which debtors view the ending of inflation. Marxists have always lavished more invective on socialism than on capitalism because they fear that, if the population is mollified by concessions, it will be deflected from the charms of revolution. In the same way, those who wish to improve society incrementally are charged with "cooling out" the poor, buying them off with minor concessions that divert them from the goal of real equality. In her studies of European totalitarianism, Hannah Arendt found that numerous intellectuals, such as Nietzsche, Sorel, Pareto, T. E. Lawrence, and Brecht, desired passionately that the old culture should collapse utterly. Hitler sought the same end since that was all that could make him credible.[43] Daniel Moynihan has said that many of his fellow intellectuals desired the turmoil of the sixties to continue because their own ends were furthered by it.[44]

Antinomianism as an Accompaniment to Decline

Toynbee discovered a pattern of lawlessness, in theory and practice,

---

[42]That is the position, for example, of Kenneth Boulding, who associates the building of community with the grants economy. See Boulding, *The Economy of Love and Fear: A Preface to Grants Economics* (Belmont, Calif.: Wadsworth, 1973), pp. 112ff.

[43]Hannah Arendt, *The Origins of Totalitarianism*, new ed. (New York: Harcourt, Brace, and World, 1966), pp. 327ff.

[44]Daniel P. Moynihan, *Maximum Feasible Misunderstanding: Community Action in the War on Poverty* (New York: Free Press, 1969), pp. 180f. Also p. 179: "The reaction among many of the more activist social scientists . . . was not to be appalled by disorder, *but almost to welcome it.* How grand to live in interesting times!"

dominating civilizations in the process of decline. Falling into *abandon*, they lose the creative touch that characterized their period of vitality. He saw in the growing naturalism and antinomianism of the West unmistakable signs that the same process had come to our society.[45] Typically, antinomianism considers that law and freedom are opposed, that law is a restrictive mechanism, a product of a civilization and therefore opposed to the free exercise of natural instincts. That is why antinomianism and naturalism, as Toynbee pointed out, are twin manifestations of the same movement. The New Testament declares that this distaste for law will lead, not to the promised freedom, but to slavery. It associates lawlessness with idolatry, and one of the names it uses for the anti-Christ is "the lawless one" (2 Thess. 2:9; 1 Pet. 4:3; 2 Pet. 2:19).

Much of the current concern expressed about widespread contempt for the law falls short of understanding the basic problem because it puts the spotlight on private attitudes toward public authorities. This approach to analyzing the problem ignores the Khadi-impulse of the public authorities, their supposed right to declare by fiat what the law should be. The contemptuous attitude of many private citizens toward the statutes therefore mirrors that of the state officials toward the higher law they should be reflecting.

As the legislature exhibits divine pretensions in framing the laws, the judiciary begins playing the same role. Not content with declaring on the conformity of statutes with the Constitution, the judges rule on the wisdom of the constitutional provisions. One recent Chief Justice declared that the intentions of the framers of the Constitution were irrelevant to the current judicial responsibility, and that, consequently, the Supreme Court is to function as a "continuing constitutional convention."[46] If the law is what the judge says it is, then this Khadi-figure holds in his hands the destiny of each of us. The paradox is that disregarding the law strangles us with laws. That is why Solzhenitsyn, after a decade of being crushed by the heavy hand of the Soviet legal authorities, could say that the essence of the problem of justice in the Soviet Union is that the nation is lawless. Lacking the protection of law, the citizen is encompassed by the statutory constructions of lawless people

---

[45]Toynbee, *A Study of History,* vol. 1, pp. 440f. Because he was unable yet to discern a counter movement of asceticism, Toynbee speculated that the disintegration of the West might not be far advanced.

[46]Chief Justice Earl Warren, quoted in Raoul Berger, *Government by Judiciary: The Transformation of the Fourteenth Amendment* (Cambridge: Harvard Univ. Press, 1977), p. 408. Berger goes on to quote Justice Stone's famous remark of 1936 that "the only check upon our exercise of power is our own sense of self-restraint."

who wield power. "When you break the big laws," Chesterton warned, "you do not get liberty; you do not even get anarchy. You get the small laws."[47]

Ethics in a Post-Christian Society

What happens to ethics as humanists distance themselves further from the restraining influence of law? In a serious philosophical inquiry concerning the way in which various views of mankind influence ethics, Mortimer Adler concluded that the naturalism and materialism that inform humanist thought would destroy the humanitarian ethic. For without anything transcending the material, the love ethic is without foundation.[48] The action that despises the external restraint of law in favor of self-determination is one of self-deification. We can expect nothing from such a position but brutality. Describing the ferocity of the Chaldean hordes, one of the prophets put his finger on the source of their evil: "their justice and dignity proceed from themselves . . . guilty men, whose own might is their god" (Hab. 1:7,11).

While humanist sentimentality says that whatever is *felt* to be right is right, historicist fate says that whatever *is* is right. Unable to bring the historical fact into the judgment of a transcendent principle, it can only defend the historical trend it judges to be dominant, while deprecating dissent as the voice of the past, destined for the trash can of history.

Most attempts at evaluating society are materialist in orientation, considering economic and statistical data but not taking into account sufficiently the content of the belief systems that determine motivation. Gabriel Vahanian has written that there is a sense in which all Western thought, until recently, has been *christian* thought, even that which was consciously directed against Christianity. The entire context within which practically all debates were held was shaped by the presuppositions of a biblical world view and, to an outsider, were characterized more by unity than diversity.[49] The body of assumption that informed the ethic of society may be thought of as the moral capital that sustained it, gave it coherence, and kept it from disintegrating into barbarism. This capital is being consumed by the incessant attacks of the modern

---

[47]Solzhenitsyn, *A World Split Apart,* p. 17; G.K. Chesterton, *The Man Who Was Orthodox,* ed. A.L. Maycock (London: Dobson, 1963), p. 87.

[48]Mortimer J. Adler, *The Difference of Man and the Difference It Makes* (New York: Holt, Rinehart, and Winston, 1967), pp. 283f.

[49]Gabriel Vahanian, *Wait Without Idols* (New York: George Braziller, 1964), p. v.

ideologies. Its depletion means that it can no longer stand in the breech against the forces that exist to destroy the civilization.

People fail to appreciate the worth of society's Christian underpinnings because they are unconscious recipients of its blessings. The most vigorous atheist in the West has grown up in a world in which love and justice are ideals. But such ideals have no objective referent outside of the biblical accounts. That is why Philip Rieff has written that the old question about whether civilized man can be a believer is the wrong one. The real question is whether unbelieving man can be civilized.[50]

The interesting feature of Robert Heilbroner's neo-Malthusian vision of the future is that it requires great self-sacrifice on the part of the present generation in order for something to remain for future generations. But he can find no principle in his materialist world view that would give people any reason to sacrifice rather than have their last fling, one which sinks the world into environmental perdition. In desperation, finally, he decides that there will be a "saving element" that will be willing to sacrifice. But that is an imaginary creation that mystification has dredged up from a system which cannot produce it.

The irony of humanism is that it dehumanizes. Adler's examination of the consequences of naturalist thinking led him to conclude that if man is taken to be different from animals in degree only, and not radically in kind, then there is no logical reason to treat him differently from the animals. The exploitation or killing of people deemed to be inferior could not then be condemned any more than the killing of steers in a slaughterhouse. An altruism rooted in sentimentality is unstable and cannot withstand the testing that is inevitable in a civilization in the process of disintegration. That is why Ellul is right to say that the prevalence of torture in the twentieth century is not just a throwback to an earlier period but is a logical consequence of the West's denial of its Christian heritage.[51]

Once we reject absolute law and adopt theories that regard human beings as simply manifestations of natural forces, it only requires a serious crisis for those ideas to bear their evil fruit. That crisis is on the way. Accompanying the mining of the capital stock, and the consequent economic decline, are demographic events that are altering dramatically the profile of the population. The social security system, already enfeebled by the twin impulses to buy votes by granting benefits while defer-

---

[50]Philip Rieff, *The Triumph of the Therapeutic: Uses of Faith After Freud* (New York: Harper and Row, 1966), p. 4.

[51]Jacques Ellul, *The Betrayal of the West,* trans. Matthew J. O'Connell (New York: Seabury, 1978), p. 179.

ring tax increases, will be incapable of support by an aging population. In 1935, when the system was begun, there were eleven people in the labor force for every one that was more than sixty-five years of age. Now the figure is three to one. In forty years it will be two to one. It is inconceivable that people trained to regard themselves as the center of the universe will each agree to provide half the support needed by a retired person. In 1980 the Joint Economic Committee of the Congress warned: "This potential time bomb could explode."

The bomb is worse than the committee realized because it did not consider the intersection of demography and ideology. When there are too many people for the resources, an obvious solution is to reduce the number of people. As one British physician put it, when describing the deliberate withholding of care from newly born infants: "The death costs nothing; the life costs not only money but the preemption of precious medical, nursing, social, and educational resources."[52] Since the neo-Malthusian movement that has been gaining strength in recent years considers economic decline to be inescapable, it can be expected to join the call for the eradication of surplus persons. As the famous report to the Club of Rome explained it, the world's situation will worsen progressively with the rising population and will find relief only when the death rate increases.[53]

Death, then, is the answer to our economic problems. The elderly will be called selfish if they insist on living, and it will be a humanitarian deed and moral duty to see that they do not continue to live and so deprive others of the quality of life to which they aspire. Some day, perhaps, Francis Crick's call for a new ethic that would insist on mandatory death for all persons over eighty years of age will seem like a first hesitant step toward the brave new world that humanism is bringing into realization.

Pediatric surgeon C. Everett Koop, surgeon-general of the United States, has charged that increasingly the medical profession is purposely inflicting death on some classes of people—the very young, very old, and the disabled—by withholding care. A study done at the Yale medical school found that of 299 deaths in a special care nursery, 14 percent occurred after care was deliberately withheld. Early death became a "management option."[54] Two physicians at the University of Wash-

---

[52]Eliot Slater, "Health Service or Sickness Service," *British Medical Journal,* 1971, no. 4, p. 735.

[53]Donella Meadows, *et al., The Limits to Growth,* 2nd ed. (New York: Universe Books, 1974), p. 125.

[54]Raymond S. Duff and A.G.M. Campbell, "Moral and Ethical Dilemmas in the Special Care Nursery," *New England Journal of Medicine,* vol. 289, no. 17, Oct. 25, 1973, pp. 890ff.

ington medical school, Norman Brown and Donovan Thompson, investigated the deaths of 190 elderly patients who developed fevers, eighty-one of whom received no treatment. Forty-eight of those who went untreated died. Brown and Thompson concluded that those deaths stemmed from a deliberate plan by physicians and nurses to refrain from treating the patients.

We are being given philosophical justifications for the inflicting of death that treats such actions as enlightened and compassionate. One college ethics textbook argues that to kill a deformed infant or an incurably ill adult is to confer a blessing. Even defective children eight or ten years old would be better off dead and their parents even more so. The test is whether the sum of human welfare is increased. This utilitarian model determines good or evil under the schema of a supposed computation of plus and minus components. We should not pay attention to fears of murders and conspiracies, it says, because we can require concurrence from both physicians and officials of the state. And even if mistakes should be made, we would still be better off because of the benefits of ridding ourselves of those whose lives detract from the sum of happiness in the world. The bar to realizing such a happy state of affairs, according to this professor of ethics, is "the spell of the Jewish-Christian mores."[55]

Once we agree that we have the right to end the lives of those who are not sufficiently useful, we shall have to devise a hierarchy of usefulness. The aged, the infirm, deformed infants, infants of unreliable parents—the list goes on until it becomes clear that the injections will be given to all those not pleasing to the authorities. For if it is accepted as a moral principle that some people should die for the benefit of others, the identity of those to be sacrificed will be determined by pragmatic considerations, which is to say, power politics. Pull will be used to secure the ultimate political favor: that of being kept alive or having one's children and parents kept alive. Under those circumstances, political opposition will atrophy regardless of what democratic forms remain.

The biblical mores that so incensed our professor of ethics constitute the dam behind which the most destructive of humanitarian acts are chained. If the dam is breached there are no limits to what might be done.

The Drive for Power Accelerates

In its drive to engage in what it calls bettering the lot of its citizens, the

---

[55]Millard Spencer Everett, *Ideals of Life* (New York: Wiley, 1954), pp. 344-47.

state persistently expands its role. Now that it is fully immersed in economic life, it seeks further problems from which to protect the citizens. Angus Campbell, of the University of Michigan's Institute for Social Research, says that economic prosperity is accompanied by psychological deprivations—alienation, boredom, job dissatisfactions, and loneliness. Since economic needs are being met, he contends, it is essential that the state focus its attention on psychological needs. "A government that aspires to raise the national quality of life must concern itself with both." Senator Edward Kennedy's attempt to legislate a new criminal code is based in part on the same idea. He has proposed that the state be permitted to hospitalize without trial a defendant charged even with misdemeanors, if that is recommended by a psychiatric report. The institution would determine what treatment was necessary, and that could include drugs or electric shock. After thirty days, a judge could commit the accused for an additional year without trial.

When Jonathan Hughes published *The Governmental Habit* in 1977, the dust jacket bore the strong endorsement of John Kenneth Galbraith. Why would Galbraith praise a book which documented in excruciating detail the failure of the policies of government intervention with which his name had long been associated? The answer probably lies in Hughes's contention that the present system of federal control is only a "halfway house," with the benefits of neither a market economy nor a planned economy.[56] Galbraith had written earlier that the requirements of the industrial system ensure that the political institutions of the United States and the Soviet Union would converge.[57] His meaning was clear: the nation would have to move toward the command economy that the Marxist states had adopted. In the short time since then, we have accommodated his wish. He estimated in 1969 that perhaps 20-25 percent of total spending in the United States was done by the various levels of government. The present figure is more than 40 percent.

The persistent pattern is that the failures wrought by state intervention, rather than leading to a dismantling of the control system, serves as a pretext for further controls. Misfortune is taken as *prima facie* evidence that we can no longer afford the luxury of freedom. That is why the successes of the neo-Malthusian purveyors of doom presage the continued tightening of controls. Joseph Schumpeter made the same point in the notes prepared for his remarks before the American Economic Associa-

---

[56]Jonathan R.T. Hughes, *The Governmental Habit: Economic Controls from Colonial Times to the Present* (New York: Basic Books, 1977), p. 10.

[57]John Kenneth Galbraith, *The New Industrial State* (Boston: Houghton Mifflin, 1969), pp. 390ff.

tion, found after his death in 1949. He thought that the dislocations caused by inflation would be used to intensify the domination of the federal bureaucracy.[58] When Frederick Schultz ended his term as vice-chairman of the Federal Reserve Board in 1982, he said the same thing. Reflecting on the Board's failure to achieve monetary stability, he concluded that the result of inflation is "a loss of freedom and a change in the political system because . . . inflation makes the government take over more and more."

Now that the raiding of the capital stock is producing its inevitable results, the federal government has embarked on a program of "reindustrialization" to repair the damage. The ensuing partnership between government and industry will likely show the characteristics of both the abortive corporate state that almost came into being in the United States in the 1930s and the disasters that pass for planning in such places as Britain, Italy, and the Soviet Union. The resulting economic debacle will be widely cited to demonstrate the failure of capitalism. Already the system has resulted in what Amitai Etzioni—who coined the term reindustrialization—calls "lemon socialism." The state, says Etzioni, continues to encourage consumption rather than investment, and then bails out failing companies—the lemons. That is also the British pattern. Herbert Stein of the University of Virginia believes that this kind of structure will be supported by conservatives (as it was fifty years ago) because it will provide a means for big business to share power with government.

Poverty and Power

In the ancient kingdoms of Israel and Judah, government was perverted to the point that it ceased to serve the ends of justice. The prophets' denunciation was directed toward the misuse of the governmental and legal structures to enrich officeholders and their allies at the expense of those who were despoiled. Prophetic injunctions to rescue the poor and orphans were given in this context. The prophets did not say that poor people were morally superior to others but that the perverse use of legitimate institutions to rob a person and impoverish him was an injustice that would bring judgment upon the guilty ones. They were de-

---

[58]Joseph A. Schumpeter, *Capitalism, Socialism and Democracy,* 5th ed. (London: George Allen and Unwin, 1976), p. 430: "Perennial inflationary pressure can play an important part in the eventual conquest of the private enterprise system by the bureaucracy— the resultant frictions and deadlocks being attributed to private enterprise and used as arguments for further restrictions and regulations."

nouncing a redistributory system that used political power to take from one set of people to give to another. Unjust political authorities invariably accomplish the same ends. Modern ideologies tend to mask this reality by shielding the injustice with moral confusion. It was common in the nineteenth century to associate wealth with moral worth, thus implying that poverty came to the immoral. The perversions of the twentieth century more commonly aver that poverty is a sign of morality and wealth of immorality. In this way envy is covered by self-righteousness and turned into a virtue.

This reversal of the moral status of poverty accompanies a corresponding shift in the political alliances that embody the redistributive impulse. People find it difficult to believe that one can enrich himself unjustly by allying with the poor as easily as with the rich, but that is an ancient practice. Emperor Septimus Severus and his son Caracalla determined to consolidate their power by presenting themselves as champions of the lower classes against the higher. In the early third century Caracalla made no secret of that intention. He was openly contemptuous of the middle class and aristocracy. France in the old regime saw the monarchy adopt the same strategy. Louis XIV could become the Sun King because he promoted the middle class as a counterweight to the nobility that had always resisted the royal pretentions. Thus, there is considerable precedent to lend authority to Berdyaev's expectation that the coming epoch of Caesarism would be plebian in character.[59]

The Onset of Judgment

In the prophetic works of the Old Testament, which provide the model for the present study, judgment is inseparable from idolatry. Human actions have moral consequences. There is a principle of moral accountability in the universe. Idolatry destroys those who indulge themselves in it. One of the prophets of the northern kingdom put it this way: "With their silver and gold they made idols for their own destruction" (Hos. 8:4).

This connection between idolatry and retribution means that people who allow themselves to be seduced by idols seek to solve their problems by finding solutions in what will prove disastrous. Robert Heilbroner typifies the response of modern man to his situation. Drawing on the Greek myth of Prometheus, the Titan who rebelled against the gods, Heilbroner says that it was the Promethean spirit that empowered the

---

[59]Nicholas Berdyaev, *The Fate of Man in the Modern World,* trans. Donald A. Lawrie (London: Student Christian Movement Press, 1935), p. 105.

accomplishments of modern man and that that spirit can still save him in the future. But the ancient myth-makers knew reality better than do their modern successors. For the punishment meted out to Prometheus by Zeus can serve as the exemplar for what the biblical writers told us to expect. The Promethean act that brings upon us the judgment of God can be expunged not by repeating the offense but by repentance.

Judgment carries with it a certain inevitability because it is a consequence of man's attempt to live in a way inconsistent with his own nature. Cholera is a judgment on dirty living, not because God arbitrarily favors clean people but because of the structure of that element of the universe. Flood and famine are judgments on the avarice that causes people to destroy forests for the sake of short-term profit. Such human activities are not wrong because they do not pay. They do not pay because they are wrong.[60] Actions directed against the creation partake of the Promethean, inasmuch as they strike indirectly at the creator.

Another aspect to judgment, found throughout the Old Testament, was the disastrous punishment God would visit on those who defied him. People who should deign to despise the covenant with God were told that "the LORD will bring on you and your offspring extraordinary afflictions" (Deut. 28:58f.). Those disasters were then enumerated. They embraced almost every branch of human affairs: economic, medical, military, psychological, domestic, political, religious. This connection between idolatry and disaster was the constant message of the prophets as well. When the two kingdoms were successively carried off into captivity by the Assyrian and Babylonian empires, that was said to be the retribution that God had promised through Moses. It was judgment. Moreover, this judgment is continually described in personal terms. It is not a vague force that somehow brings retribution; it is the personal wrath of God in action. "Thou hatest those who pay regard to vain idols" (Ps. 31:6). The New Testament writers played on the same theme. One of them stressed that the word of judgment by which God would bring destruction on those who defied him was of the same character as the one by which he created the world (2 Pet. 3:5ff.).

It is only to be expected, therefore, that an idolatrous society should suffer the pain of judgment. Whether judgment is the virtually automatic consequence of contravening the naturally perceived realities of the world, or whether it is the divine wrath executed with purpose on those who persist in idolatry, there can be no escape from the consequences. That is why Herbert Butterfield warned against Christians' attaching

---

[60]Dorothy Sayers, *Creed or Chaos* (New York: Harcourt, Brace, 1949), p. 41.

too much value to the remnants of nineteenth century liberal culture in which Western society was still organized. The ruins of such systems have littered the halls of history, and to value them too highly is to make a profound mistake. The nation, the political and economic systems, the culture, all are transitory and must not be absolutized.[61]

There is a sense in which judgment that issues in catastrophe is the only way for good to come, inasmuch as it entails the erasure of evil. Niebuhr referred to the coming of catastrophe as the time when the idols fall, when human constructs are recognized for what they are in place of giving them the divine status their makers crave for them.[62] That is squarely in the biblical tradition. Only when judgment falls, said the prophet, will people "cast forth their idols of silver and their idols of gold" (Is. 2:20).

A Society Transformed

When a civilization turns idolatrous, its people are profoundly changed by that experience. In a kind of reverse sanctification, the idolater is transformed into the likeness of the object of his worship. Israel "went after worthlessness, and became worthless" (Jer. 2:5). As the psalmist put it,

Those who make [the idols] are like them;
so are all who trust in them (Ps. 115:8).

Bloodthirsty gods produce bloodthirsty people. If someone thinks that chance rules the universe, his actions are likely to appear random. If people increasingly think that malevolence rules, as do the growing legion of Satan-worshipers, we can expect more human sacrifice. If there is a decline in the number of people who believe that God is love, we can expect fewer who think that actions of love are moral imperatives. For any individual or society, therefore, the religious questions are the ultimate ones that govern human conduct, whether they believe it or not. That is what lies behind Butterfield's conclusion that for two thousand years ordinary Christian piety has made an enormous difference in

---

[61]Herbert Butterfield, *Christianity and History* (London: Collins, Fontana, 1957 [1949]), pp. 75f.

[62]Reinhold Niebuhr, *Faith and History: A Comparison of Christian and Modern Views of History* (New York: Scribner's, 1949), pp. 111, 153f.; Macaulay and Toynbee saw the termination of the decayed and putrifying Roman Empire as a "merciful release," a "happy ending." Toynbee, *A Study of History,* vol. 1, p. 362. On judgment as a manifestation of divine love, see above, ch. 1.

Western society, one that the historians, by and large, have missed entirely. The daily preaching of love and humility as virtues have made the moral landscape immeasurably different than it would have been otherwise, and we are now beginning to find out what life would have been like without it.

Thomas Jefferson, though a Deist, could write in the Declaration of Independence that "all men are created equal, that they are endowed by their Creator with certain unalienable rights" because biblical thinking underlay the fabric of the society in which he came to maturity. In a different context such ideas would have been far from "self-evident" truths. After biblical faith wanes, a people can maintain habits of thought and of self-restraint. The ethic remains after the faith that bore it departs. But eventually a generation arises that no longer has the habit, and that is when the behavior changes radically. When Israel began worshiping the Canaanite gods, it was only a matter of time before the nation began shedding innocent blood (Ps. 106:34–39). There is no protection against this in statutes or constitutions, which become scraps of paper when people come to despise the law that stands behind them. We learn historicist notions of destiny in the schools and find it hard to imagine the fragility of our institutions. They can survive the domination of wicked people in high places, and they often have; but they cannot long survive the people's insistence that wickedness be dominant, the continual boast that evil is good.

The generation now alive has remained true to many vestiges of the biblical faith. These remnants are the smile of the Cheshire cat, remaining for a time after the disappearance of the entity in which it was incarnated. Humanitarianism's preoccupation with helping acts would be inconceivable in a society with a different heritage. Solzhenitsyn speculates why, when as university students just before World War II began, he and some friends turned down an invitation to join the secret police, in spite of the benefits that would have accrued to them. "Without even knowing it ourselves, we were ransomed by the small change in copper that was left from the golden coins our great-grandfathers had expended, at a time when morality was not considered relative and when the distinction between good and evil was very simply perceived by the heart."[63] Eleanor Roosevelt, after she had gone on to become one of the most effective humanitarian leaders of her age, recalled that she grew up memorizing Bible verses and hymns as a daily practice. She thought it

---

[63]Aleksandr I. Solzhenitsyn, *The Gulag Archipelago, 1918-1956: An Experiment in Literary Investigation,* trans. Thomas P. Whitney (New York: Harper and Row, 1973), vol. 1, p. 161.

curious that even late in life, at crucial moments, the appropriate passages would come to mind to give her guidance.[64]

Thus, the remnant of health can remain for a time after the necessary conditions to sustain it have been removed. Before the capital stock of the old faith is completely exhausted, it still produces a little of its social income. A Faustian bargain has its attractions in the promise of short-term benefits, while the diabolic aspects lose some of their terror for their deferment to a distant future. The Indian summer of the Roman Empire, as Toynbee called it, was mistaken by Gibbon for the golden age. Toynbee used the term "breakdown" in a specialized sense to mean the termination of the growth period of a civilization, prior to its disintegration. During this phase, some of the most showy accomplishments appear, belying the fact that the end is approaching. That is why the breakdown is marked by verbal clashes between optimists and pessimists, both drawing on surface phenomena that give conflicting indications but fail to penetrate to the underlying pathology.

This asynchronous relationship between moral cause and material effect often frustrates our understanding and misinforms our expectations. Contrary to many historical accounts, radical changes can occur very quickly. This is often obscured by an unconscious Hegelianism that imposes on events a supposed necessity for "development," or else materialist assumptions that cannot understand the reality of radical moral change without finding first a material cause that accounts for it. Some such explanation must account for Huxley's error of 1931 in placing the *Brave New World* six centuries in the future. He recognized this afterwards, and by 1958 concluded ruefully that his worst fears were already upon us.[65]

Yet, there is nothing that has befallen us that is not remediable. If we are able to discern that we have brought our troubles upon ourselves, then repentance and faith can repair the damage. Otherwise, the future holds nothing but grim judgment. In that event, this society will likely follow the prophet's advice: "When you cry out, let your collection of idols deliver you!" (Is. 57:13).

---

[64]Anna Eleanor Roosevelt, "The Minorities Questions," *Christianity Takes a Stand: An Approach to the Issues of Today,* ed. William Scarlett (New York: Penguin, 1946), p. 72.

[65]Aldous Huxley, *Brave New World Revisited* (New York: Harper and Row, 1965 [1958]), p. 1. He still thought at that time that *Brave New World* was a far more likely outcome than Orwell's vision in *1984,* largely because of the ending of Stalinism in the USSR and because he believed that reinforcement is more efficacious than terror. Since his death in 1963, however, the intellectual bankruptcy of behaviorism and the resurgence of terrorism, both individual and governmental, have made Orwell more believable.

CHAPTER EIGHT

The New Community

*I*T remains for us to pass from our examination of pathology to consider how we might return to health. Exposing the idols of an age can only be a preliminary step. It enables us to direct our efforts away from the service of evil but is not sufficient to provide a strategy for action. We must consider further how to move toward bringing political, economic, and social life into conformity with the gospel. For if it is God's purpose "to reconcile to himself all things" (Col. 1:20), then we must not be content to accept compliantly the continuing growth of evil.

The Dual Vision of Righteousness

The message of the Old Testament prophets was twofold. Both tables of the law had been violated, that which permitted only God to be worshiped and that which regulated the relationships between human beings on the basis of justice. Israel's dual failing was the worship of false gods and the rejection of justice. That is apparently the invariable pattern.

Calls for the reformation of society that do not insist upon both orthodoxy and orthopraxy, therefore, are futile. A society that worships idols will come to demonstrate the brutality that derives from fealty to bloodthirsty gods. Yet orthodoxy is not enough, since faith without works is dead. That is why the prophets denounced religious observances by those who oppressed the weak. Bad faith and bad practice are equally defiant of the law.

Straight teaching combined with straight living, in the biblical vision, is to dominate all of life. There are no exempt corners in which one conducts business as usual while making perfunctory gestures toward religious observances. Much of the disagreement within Christendom has been between two half-gospels that have found no meeting ground. When the insistence of the Reformation that salvation was to be obtained by faith alone hardened into a new scholasticism, its adherents turned a deaf ear to the biblical teaching that the commitment of faith posed radical requirements on the way life is lived. It is extraordinary that those who have insisted that the Bible must provide the only authoritative guide for life should have been so prone to ignore the parts that judged their complacent acceptance of society's standards. That some of them proclaimed their "separation" by condemning superficial practices threw into sharp relief the unconscious assimilation of values they should have recognized as alien to the beliefs they professed.

At the same time the works-righteousness of popular religion departed from Christian foundations in other ways. Taking faith for granted, it identified it too readily with mental assent to dogmatic statements, rather than with the life commitment of which the Bible speaks. That makes it natural to focus on sacraments and moral injunctions as the two main axes of Christian life. But without a biblical understanding of faith, the sacraments degenerate into magic and moral principles into moralism.

Coexisting with these half-gospels has been a no-gospel that has captured much of American Protestantism. Functioning as weathervanes, these theologies point to the idols of the left or right, as the case may be, and seek their salvation in one version or another of the American Way of Life.

Such errors are avoidable. If we begin our examination with a clear understanding of how the idols have come to dominate our thinking, we can seek new paradigms. We can think of doing good without the humanitarian clichés coming to mind. Acts of love and mercy are integral with the biblical message, and their authentic expression will always be more powerful than the fakery of the idolatries.

Prolegomena to Any Christian Metaphysic

The dogmatic scientism that succeeded dogmatic religion as the foundation of Western thought has been superseded by a weary skepticism. Pontius Pilate's question, "What is truth?," is everywhere on the lips of relativists who do not believe there exists a principle which affords certainty for any kind of knowledge, factual or ethical. The descent into ir-rationality and barbarism that such skepticism engenders is avoidable only by returning to the theological certainties. Human rationality stems from the divine reason that preexisted human beings. Only the certainty that man was created in the image of God gives a solid founda-tion to reason and therefore to the possibility of human knowledge.

Ethical formulations from Genesis to Revelation have the same source. Love can resist being debased into sentimentality because it ex-isted absolutely in the creator prior to the creation. If God is love, then we have an objective referent for the law. For it is the law that provides the standard for making love concrete. A situation ethic that uses the language of love to circumvent law, on the other hand, justifies the doing of evil. Neither reason nor love can exist as an independent manifesta-tion of human autonomy. For being without foundation, except that im-parted to them by mystification, they inevitably deteriorate, as they are now doing.

To assert that truth is real, and objectively so, is to state a dogma that is contrary to the dominant position of our age. But the biblical writers commonly took positions that were contrary to the accepted wisdom of their ages. When the apostle Paul said that the wisdom of his age was rubbish (1 Cor. 2), he provided a model we should take more seriously than we are accustomed. At the same time, we do not oppose Christian faith to reason and science as such. All alternatives to Christian doc-trines are themselves grounded in unprovable assumptions, and in that sense cannot be distinguished from positions of faith. Dogma is inescap-able notwithstanding the failure of so many to recognize the pervasive-ness and fragility of their own belief systems.[1]

Christian faith is grounded in historical events. That is why the search for truth must drive us to the sources, to the collection of docu-ments we call the Bible. Only a framework that portrays God as the Lord of history provides us with a basis for transcending theories of imma-nence. It releases us from the domination of the standard visions of his-tory, which otherwise would leave us powerless before the myths of our society. Scripture destroys the myths of the age, any age.

Telling the truth is more fundamental than all other tasks. The Chris-

---

[1]Cf. Robert Nisbet, *The Degradation of the Academic Dogma: The University in America, 1945-1970* (New York: Basic Books, 1971), p. 22: "All major institutions are built around dogmas. So, for that matter, is social life generally. We could not live without dogma, which is no more than a system of principles or ideals widely believed to be not merely true or right but also beyond the necessity of the more or less constant verification we feel obliged to give so many other aspects of our lives."

tian writers who have made the greatest impact on the pagan world of the twentieth century—people like Chesterton, Weil, Lewis, and Sayers—were more than intelligent, able, and learned. They were bold. Rather than begging the world to believe, they told it the truth. Like that of Christ, their speech was full of "hard sayings." In contrast, defenses of the faith like Bishop Robinson's *Honest to God* worry that the world is no longer religious and think the solution is to change the gospel so that it is easier to believe. Instead they make it not worth believing. Apologetics should never be apologetic.

If our concern for truth is paramount, then we shall refuse to give sentiment the place accorded it by rival systems. The enthronement of emotional response as the center of human concern turns one inward. But introspection fails to stabilize the emotion. One becomes weary seeking replays of an emotional experience that returns only sporadically, if at all. Continued disappointment makes for cynicism.

Sentimentality destroys truth. It recognizes that truth is often hard, and therefore tries to soften it. Sentimentality rules many of the nineteenth-century hymns that predominate in so many twentieth-century hymnals. Sentimental lies deceive people about reality and induce guilt when hard times come, thereby weakening both faith and will. Christians must rid themselves, individually and corporately, of sentimentality because it refuses to see the truth. Corporate worship must be true to biblical statements and to observed reality or people will come to see, correctly, that the teachings of the church do not jibe with their experience, and so become disenchanted with them.

Anyone seeking to systematize knowledge on the basis of revelation will have to do it within a framework completely different from the common ones that have come to dominate Western philosophy. All of them exemplify the Kantian antinomies, being either idealisms that cannot account for the existence of the individual or material, or else materialisms that cannot account for mind, spirit, or collectivity. We are part of an intellectual world that has judged there to be an unbridgeable gulf between matter and spirit. But there is a different lesson in the incarnation. For if God was in Christ, and if the way to the Father is through the Son, then that gulf disappears. We must not accept any formulation that erects an impermeable barrier between the sensible and rational, object and subject, matter and mind.

Forty years ago Charles Cochrane wrote that Christ is the *logos* not only in the Christian sense but in the pagan sense as well. What the ancient philosophers sought was the answer to the impossible antinomies their thinking drove them to, much in the way Kantian dualism drives our contemporaries. They believed that the answer lay in a conception called *logos*.

Freedom and Responsibility

Arcane philosophical problems seem to be without practical effect, and many people dismiss them as unimportant. But that is a mistake. Monist metaphysical theories, whether materialist or idealist, are unable to account for human freedom, and hence construct social theories that dispense with it. Policy follows theory, and the conviction that human actions are the products of environment rather than personal volition issues forth in legislation that assumes that society is responsible for the individual's actions. Since freedom is assumed not to exist in the first place, there is little point in framing legislation in such a way as to maintain it. The progressive weakening of liberty in the United States, as in the other social democracies, is therefore a natural result of the false philosophies that have infected the West.

Biblical faith is the only apparent antidote to the determinisms that dominate the contemporary intellectual scene. Its serious consideration of history strikes at the naturalism that makes freedom impossible. If there really is such a thing as an order of reality called history, then matter is not all there is; freedom is possible, and the "science of behavior" is a sham. B. F. Skinner, in attacking history so venomously, instructively identified his major enemy. At the same time, the biblical doctrine of creation means that creator and creation are separate, giving to the latter the possibility of real freedom. This is perhaps the most basic philosophical difference between biblical religion and all rival systems.

Only that difference makes human responsibility possible. Moses' challenge to Israel as the Exodus drew to a close is fully as valid for us: "I have set before you life and death . . . therefore choose life" (Deut. 30:19). People following one course of action rather than another must not blame their choice on external contingencies. Those circumstances affect us all right, meaning that we cannot wall ourselves off from the environment. But we are not the passive victims of the interaction of the environmental stimulus with our past. Rather, that stimulus (temptation) finds in us, not a mechanical receptor and reactor, but a free moral agent willing or unwilling to do an evil act. Armed with that insight, there is no reason for Christians to adopt the prevalent doctrines that deny both freedom and responsibility.

Christ fulfilled the promise of liberty that the prophets had championed (Jer. 34:15ff.), just as he fulfilled so many other promises. The early church fought the influence of ideologies that sought to bring its people back into the subjection from which Christ delivered them (Gal. 4,5). Liberty in this sense is found only in the redemption provided by Christ; the fake redeemers must be avoided like the plagues they are. This means we begin by rejecting all the slave philosophies that promise freedom—Marxism, individualism, anarchism.

On this showing, liberty is rooted in the objective truth that is found in Christ. His words, "You shall know the truth and the truth shall make you free" (John 8:32), are found on library friezes across the land but not appropriately. They do not refer to the conflicting opinions of a multitude of books, but to the relationship that one has with the Father through the Son. This conception confounds the dominant ideas, because it says that freedom can be enjoyed regardless of the external condition and that it may be absent even where no sign of compulsion is present to an outside observer. The idolatries assume that the bars to freedom are all external. Erich Fromm said that freedom is possible only in the absence of economic scarcity[2] (which means it will never come) because he could not imagine how people could transcend their circumstances. Yet, that is precisely what biblical freedom means. It frees one from conformity to social and intellectual fads; from having to prove oneself; from the arbitrary and changing standards of society; from the need to demonstrate success; from the buffeting of every type of external pressure. This has nothing to do with the "self-actualization" of which selfist psychology is full, but rather recognizes that he who loses his life shall find it.

Since truth is what frees, Christians need to repudiate the alternative explanations that see freedom in such circumstances as the frontier origins of the nation, or in capitalism, in economic security, or in the overthrow of the obligations of traditional morality. If truth is what frees, then lies are what bind. Even in the first century it was clear to the church that those who promised freedom through the overthrow of the law and abandonment to the appetites were themselves slaves: "whatever overcomes a man, to that he is enslaved" (2 Pet. 2:19.)

Nobody can live in freedom if he is fearful of deprivation. That does not mean we need security and prosperity from society, as the dominant ideologies tell us, but rather we recognize that our security comes from God. In the list of the giants of biblical faith, Moses was said to be "not . . afraid of the anger of the king" (Heb. 11:27), and thus was free

---

[2]Erich Fromm, *Escape from Freedom* (New York: Holt, Rinehart, and Winston, 1963), p. 271.

to obey God. Nobody can live in freedom unless it is more important to him than competing values, such as prosperity and security. In many parts of the world one's own life must be of lower value than liberty.

The doctrine of personal responsibility is not the gloomy position it is often made out to be, but the only hopeful view. For it says that human misery is remediable, that it stems from causes that can be put right by repentance. We are not the passive victims of whatever external forces play upon us, nor of a sickness that forces us to act in destructive ways.

But to say that we are responsible for our own actions is not to say that on our shoulders rests the responsibility for everything that takes place in the world. We do not pretend that the fate of the world is in our hands. That way lies madness, being a burden that no human being can bear. Yet, we are not condemned to resignation and quietism, still less to despair. We are not the lords of history and do not control its outcome, but we have assurance that there is a lord of history and he controls its outcome. We need a theological interpretation of disaster, one that recognizes that God acts in such events as captivities, defeats, and crucifixions. The Bible can be interpreted as a string of God's triumphs disguised as disasters. Those events seemed to say not only that people and nations have failed but that God has failed. Only the prophetic word that both explained historical events and provided assurances that God is the lord of history could dispel the terror borne by such an appearance.

Prolegomena to Any Christian Ethic

Applying the prophetic insight is never to be done in a vacuum but must accompany an understanding of contemporary society that is true to the facts. It is an error to associate such regimes as those of the colonels of Latin America with capitalism. We ought rather to associate the repressive regimes of the right with the repressive regimes of the left. The rationalizations are different, but the realities are alike. It adds nothing to our understanding to say that the USSR is Marxist and Uruguay is capitalist. Both have regimes that rule for their respective oligarchies and their favored clients; the rest is window dressing. Latin American dictators claiming to be the last stand of free enterprise against the communist menace are playing to the gallery, and there is nobody in the gallery except American conservatives. The Soviets are doing the same thing, "protecting" the world against Western imperialism.

In the Holy Land two-and-one-half millenia ago, the main problem occupying the attention of the establishment was the threat of foreign domination. Israel was threatened in the late eighth century B.C. by the

Assyrian Empire, and a century after she had been swept away, Judah feared the onslaught of the Babylonian Empire. Those seemed to be straightforward balance-of-power problems, presenting no conceptual difficulty to the experienced strategists of the ancient world: They had to seek a foreign alliance to counterbalance the power that threatened them from the north and east. But the prophets told them that only disaster lay in that direction (Is. 30,31). They had completely mistaken the problem that was about to destroy them, and thus they looked in the wrong direction for its solution. The prophets told them if they repented and turned to God and thus solved the real problem, he would take care of the foreign powers. Those powers were not the forces of unmitigated evil, as they thought, but were the unwitting servants of God who was using them as the means of bringing judgment against a people who had turned away from him.

Those ancient societies had their analogue in early modern Europe where aristocrats dominated societies organized hierarchically and rigidly, with minimal social mobility. But our age is different. Here, an equalitarian society, beset with sins characteristic of democracies, caters to the demand of the envious of every status to possess the property belonging to others. This suggests that anyone using the prophetic writings has to use the *method* of the prophets rather than repeating their words thoughtlessly. That method was to begin by comparing the moral requirements of the law, which are fixed, with the practices of society, which are changing constantly.

At the same time, to support conservative causes that redirect the flow of public funds and implicit grants to the benefit of favored business interests, if it is not a purposeful favoring of injustice, betrays an ignorance of the meaning of American social and political institutions. On all sides of the political spectrum Christians are befuddled by the banalities of newspaper and textbook, both of which repeat the bland assurances that serve to lend credence to one kind of ideology or the other.

The difficulty lies in correlating the eternal aspects of divine law with the conflicting and misleading realities of the observable world. We have to avoid the practical atheism of interpreting events as if history were self-contained, without connection to anything beyond itself. At the same time we may not cut ourselves off from the phenomenal realities in order to float in some noumenal limbo of heavenly aspirations. This apparent dilemma lay at the heart of the celebrated controversy between Reinhold Niebuhr and Karl Barth. Barth's penchant for viewing everything under the aspect of eternity (*sub specie aeternitatis*) rendered many of his followers impotent to resist the Nazi regime until long after it had become obvious that there was a monstrous evil that had to be addressed; it also blunted their response to the evils of communism after the war. Niebuhr justly pointed out that the complete preoccupation with abstract theology exemplified by Barth could not deal with the concrete problems of bringing about justice. Yet Niebuhr's "Christian realism" left him vulnerable to the beguiling promises of pragmatism, and early in his career his willingness to compromise principle for results led him to help usher in the pretensions of the messianic state. Predictably, he won the applause of a generation of American intellectuals who otherwise had nothing good to say about theology or its practitioners.

This is another false dilemma. There is no necessity for us to ignore either events or principle. The prophets kept one eye firmly on the requirements of the law, and the other on the relationships and events of their own society. They dismissed the rationalizations and excuses offered by the political and religious establishment fronting for the idols and insisted that the nation return to the standards of God's law. That is the model the Christian church ought to be following now.

Calls for obedience to absolute law fall on deaf ears. Most people prefer to make of the statement that "God is love" an anemic sentimentality that justifies whatever is felt to be right.[3] Or they enthrone *change* as the normative principle of the universe, going with the flow of people and events in obedience to the historicist creed. This is an ethic that breaks the tension between what one wishes to do and what one knows to be right, collapsing the latter into the former. When Jacob Needleman began reading the Bible through the writings of the existentialist theologians, that tension dissolved for him in the conviction that human mortality meant that a man was to live only for the moment and that he was to find all meaning solely within himself. "In reading these ideas into our Bible," said Needleman, "I felt an immense sense of relief."[4] That relief has become commonplace in our generation. It comes to all who are able to dispense with the weight of absolute standards that they once were convinced placed obligations upon them.

---

[3]Sometimes those who recognize that morality is impossible without a higher law than the will of man mystify such law and rob it of its intended effect, because they are unwilling to say that it can only be rooted in the worship of an unchanging God. Cf. Walter Lippmann, *An Inquiry into the Principles of the Good Society* (Boston: Little, Brown, 1937), p. 347: "To those who ask where this higher law is to be found, the answer is that it is a progressive discovery of men striving to civilize themselves, and that its scope and implications are a gradual revelation that is by no means completed."

[4]Jacob Needleman, *The New Religions* (Garden City, N.Y.: Doubleday, 1970), p. 2.

Yet, there is a legitimate kind of relief that comes to those who accept the requirements of divine law. For them, many ethical difficulties are no longer difficult. What others call simplistic solutions to perplexing ethical dilemmas instead reduce those alleged dilemmas to their true simplicity. Murder, theft, lying, and adultery are declared to be what they are by virtue of renouncing the rationalizations that make them acceptable. One does not have to be a god any longer, which provides a relief that is rooted in the reality of the creation.

If the biblical ethic is thought to be too strict for the twentieth century, it is not because modern relativism has outmoded it. It was also too stringent to be comfortable to those who first heard it. Conventional morality is inadequate in the twentieth century just as it has been in every other century. The New Testament is full of plainly stated moral precepts that are spiritualized out of existence because they are supposedly impractical. Yet, if we want to maintain peace there is nothing more practical than to love our enemies and to return good for evil. When every slight or imagined slight is the occasion for damaging someone else, then mutual retaliation makes peace impossible. This may be thought of as the paradigm for all the hard sayings of the Bible.

The more that "practical" people despise these precepts, the clearer it becomes that pragmatism is the road to ruin. The idolatries have always been pursued by practical people. When Jeremiah upbraided the Judeans for worshiping a pagan goddess, they replied that all had been well with them when they pursued the pagan worship; it was only when they stopped those practices that misfortune visited them (Jer. 44:15ff.). Thus, idolatry is a practical matter. The false gods are to be propitiated, and then all will be well.

Idolatry and Injustice

The moral injunctions of the Sinaitic commandments immediately follow the commandments against idolatry. Actions cannot be separated from the belief that gives rise to it. When the prophets denounced idolatry, they also denounced injustice. Thus, the fruit of righteousness is not to be found on the vine of idol worship.

In the Christian era the idols have served the same purposes as in the preceding period. They provide the meaning to life, explain the universe, form the basis for personal security, and claim the whole being of those from whom they demand obeisance. The modern idolatries are as evil as those that required the worship of Baal, Molech, and Marduk. Indeed, they may be thought of as the old gods provided with newer identities, designed to appeal to modern sophisticates. This ubiquity of idolatry, underlying the changing appearances, explains why the New Testament writers warned about idols in the same manner as the ancient Hebrew prophets (1 Cor. 10:6-14; 1 John 5:21).

The idolatries are hostile to Christian faith, and with good reason. For tactical purposes they are happy to welcome a Red Dean of Canterbury or a liberation theologian into their midst, just as Muggeridge *père* did the trendy clergymen who lent respectability to his program to create a heaven on earth. But the biblical faith will not tolerate idols. That is the meaning of the repeated declarations that God is a jealous God. He does not permit rivals, and the idolatries instinctively recognize this.

Thus, Christians must learn to recognize when idolatry dons the guise of the Christian virtues. They must stop lauding the evil impulses of envy and hatred that often lurk behind such benign phrases as "social justice." Inevitably, this raises thorny issues that cause practical people to doubt whether stopping idolatry is feasible. There are always practical reasons to stay with whatever idol seems to bring results. If we no longer sacrifice children to Molech, what will that do to the unemployment rate in a few years? If we stop worshiping Marduk, who will protect us against the Babylonians? Paul found himself persecuted because of the economic dislocations that occurred when people turned away from idolatry to worship the true God (Acts 16,19). Once it is accepted that idolatry can be defended on practical grounds, there is no hope. It leads not to heaven on earth but to judgment.

One major function of the church is to unmask the idols and expose them for what they are. There is no basis for this to be done except the authority of the biblical witness. Unmasking the idols destroys their effectiveness, stripping from the false teachers their guise as angels of light. As Gabriel Vahanian puts it, Christian faith can be true to itself only if it is iconoclastic.[5] If it is to have any effectiveness, it must be actively engaged in breaking the idols.

We have reached a point in history in which it is essential to pay closer heed to the fourth Gospel and associated portions of the New Testa-

---

[5]Gabriel Vahanian, *No Other God* (New York: George Braziller, 1966), pp. 5ff.; cf. Jacques Ellul, *The New Demons,* trans. C. Edward Hopkin (New York: Seabury, 1975), p. 223: "The power to desacralize is solely and uniquely the power of the gospel." Hendrik Berkhof calls the process of stripping the false identities from the evil powers of idolatry de-deifying them. "When the Powers are unmasked, they lose their dominion over men's souls . . . . " *Christ and the Powers,* trans. John Howard Yoder (Scottsdale, Penn.: Herald Press, 1962), *passim*, especially pp. 36-46.

ment. There "the world" is identified as the system of political, cultural, and religious leadership that arrayed itself against God and refused to listen to the prophetic word that exposed its wrongdoings. It is that world which Jesus said "hates me because I testify of it that its works are evil" (John 7:7). The leadership of the early church recognized that the disciples were not different in that respect from their Lord. "Do you not know that friendship with the world is enmity with God?" (James 4:4). The Pauline summary for living an evil life was "Following the course of this world" (Eph. 2:2). A Polish bishop, afterwards known as Pope John Paul II, speaking in the United States in 1976, put it this way: "We are now facing the final confrontation between the Church and the anti-Church, of the Gospel versus the anti-Gospel."

Even when the lines are not drawn so clearly between the gospel and an idolatrous environment, an inevitable tension exists between Christian faith and society. Notwithstanding the uncritical acclaim sometimes accorded to Europe in the thirteenth century or New England in the seventeenth, it is questionable whether Christendom—the identity of the kingdom of God with any society—has ever existed. As long as the biblical world view is not identical with any other religious, cultural, or political system, attempts to relax the tension between them, to accommodate the church to the "best" of the surrounding society, surrenders the gospel to what will debase it. Theologies of peace that avoid conflict at any cost produce a tame church without offense, without effectiveness.

Such toothless theologies flourish when people do not take the New Testament seriously enough. Those documents appear dated because they cannot be reconciled with the prevailing wisdom. But it is easy to forget that they were always "dated," and for the same reason. The pathologies that required biblical texts to be written on the economic, social, familial, sexual, and legal aspects of life have always been there. Those texts cannot in fact become out-of-date because they rest on truths that come from outside of time and stand in judgment of all societies that contravene them.

Society and Its Dissenters

Those now living in a post-Christian world can find the New Testament especially meaningful because it was written in a pre-Christian world. We are in a position to read it with more comprehension, perhaps, than any generation of Western Christians in a millenium and a half. We can gain from it some of the peculiar understandings that Africans and Asians in the last few generations have been able to derive: the understanding of subversives in an alien culture. The invitation spoken at the inception of the Christian church has more meaning for us than for many millions of our predecessors: "Save yourselves from this crooked generation" (Acts 2:40).

The repeated New Testament call for separation demands that we refuse to think and act like those around us. Mass media have turned what otherwise would be a vast heterogeneous collection of subcultures into a homogeneous unity. Just as life in a small village squeezes its inhabitants into a common mold, so the pressures of the global village require a similar conformity. The drive for respectability, the concern not to be thought odd, makes us vulnerable to the errors of fashion, of snobbery, of servility, of hypocrisy.

Models to which one is expected to conform derive from particular visions of reality. In the *Brave New World,* the Bible and other Christian literature are declared to be pornographic, a monument of Huxley's extraordinary artistic vision. Once you believe that sensual happiness is ultimate, the literature that insists on truth for its own sake, on moral responsibility, and on renunciation of self for the sake of others must be seen as abnormal and subversive of your view of reality and, hence, normality. The main characteristic of the Savage in the novel, the trait that distinguishes him from his society and makes him fit only to be kept as a specimen in a zoo, is that he has a Christian conscience.

Society's most important institutions serve the socializing function, making people better balanced and adjusted to the way things are. And that is why they are so dangerous. All education is of necessity value-laden, and the public school is the most powerful of these instruments of conformity. Its goal is to instill society's norms and to discredit deviant ideas. The best elements of the Christian school movement—often dismissed as an expression of racism by the humanist defenders of the *status quo*—is a determined No! by parents to the homogenization of American life, a recognition that the model to which their children are intended to be conformed has become evil.

The bibilical norm requires that we renounce this kind of socialization. In the societies described in the Old Testament, the people of God who withdrew from the practices of an idolatrous society were called the remnant. In the New Testament the believers in Christ were urged to live as pilgrims, strangers, and exiles in the midst of an evil society (1Pet. 2:11; Heb. 11:13). Christians, thus, are to be subversives refusing to conform to the norms of their surroundings. Far from allying themselves with the "best" of the dominant culture, they must recognize that what is thought to be best is so only by comparison with a set of standards that is unacceptable. The appropriate response to the dominant culture, then, is to refuse subservience to it, to reject the domination of its norms, to withdraw support selectively from all institutions that base their activities on the idolatries that control American life. In short, to rebel.

In the apocalyptic vision, it is the kings of the earth that represent the ultimate evil (Rev. 18:9), and so it may be with authorities with which we have to deal. There is no official edict that cannot be abrogated by the refusal of people to obey it. This choice was faced and stated starkly by the early leaders of the church: "We must obey God rather than men" (Acts 5:29).

Defying Mammon

Materialism as an ethic has never been without its devotees, but it is especially virulent in the twentieth century because so many are metaphysical materialists. People who believe that all reality is material, with the intellectual and spiritual dimensions of life being mere epiphenomena, find it especially difficult to accept an ethic that says that material well-being is less important than other values. It is thus almost inevitable that people should regard the welfare state's creation of permanent dependency and helplessness in return for money as a beneficent tradeoff, an expression of humanitarian goodness (or of Christian love) in action.

Materialism, coupled with the productivity of machinery and electronics, has brought us to the universal expectation of More, first rising expectations and then rising entitlements. This is what the Bible refers to as covetousness, which is condemned from the original Ten Commandments through the whole biblical literature. The common observation that prosperity tends to bring spiritual complacency, pride, and moral decline goes back at least as far as the Pentateuch (Deut. 8:11-14). The wicked are identified as those who trust in riches rather than in God (Ps. 52:7).

The biblical outlook on wealth seems odd only because we have adopted as normal a way of life that is hopelessly unable to produce what it promises and has demonstrated that inability to almost everyone. As little children we learned that the doll or the game we invested with the aura of desire, and of which we thought we would never tire, inevitably palled on us after a time. The same is true of all the world's glittering satisfactions. What they have in common is that, after the initial flash of gratification, they fail to satisfy, leading us to seek further for the next bauble. We ought instead to reconsider the basic assumption. For if past acquisitions and attainments have not satisfied us, perhaps it is not in their nature to provide more than fleeting satisfactions. That is the insight that led the prophet to inquire: "Why do you spend your money for that which is not bread . . . ?" (Is. 55:2). For the greedy there is no conceivable level of wealth that would be enough, for greed is insatiable. That is why trying to satisfy it, giving in to the love of money, causes such intense suffering (1 Tim. 6:10). Chesterton put it this way:

> A man who is dependent upon the luxuries of this life is a corrupt man, spiritually corrupt, politically corrupt, financially corrupt. . . . Christ and all the Christian saints have said with a sort of savage monotony . . . that to be rich is to be in peculiar danger of moral wreck.[6]

He might have added that to covet wealth is no less debilitating. Greed is the governing emotion of those who desire to be rich, and contentment is that of those who refuse to enter the blind alley of the envious. "If we have food and clothing," declared the apostle, "with these we shall be content" (1 Tim. 6:8). But to preach this to the poor without taking it to heart oneself is to be accused, rightly, of hypocrisy. The injunction to be content, to avoid envy, is for all, irrespective of class or position.

Christians need to renounce the systems by which their fellow citizens plunder each other, either within or outside the law. They should earn their livings by providing goods and services to people who find them valuable enough to pay for them willingly. But in order to validate their contention that economics is not conterminous with life, they should also learn to give without receiving anything in return, reversing the process by which society is reducing itself to poverty. They should be wary of the temptation to have ever more of the world's goods, for that desire is what takes away personal freedom, delivering people into the clutches of those who want power. Covetousness is the weakness that induces them to give up what should not be for sale. The early Christians were said to have "joyfully accepted the plundering of [their] property" (Heb. 10:34); but this could only have happened to people who regarded themselves as pilgrims, content with whatever they had, having renounced the quest, on which their neighbors had embarked, for ever more goods to consume. For them the statement of net worth was valueless in determining human worth.

---

[6]G.K. Chesterton, *Orthodoxy* (London: Collins, Fontana, 1961 [1908]), p. 117.

Responsibilites of the Rich and the Poor

Our thinking on this subject tends to be muddled because we force the facts through a crude materialist filter that a degenerate Marxism has made part of the cultural environment. The constant biblical witness concerning poverty was directed toward those who had difficulty sustaining themselves with food and shelter (Lev. 25: 35ff.; James 2:15). It had nothing to do with ''poverty'' that is based on visions of affluence, the kind that has difficulty securing a car or television set, for that is a vision based upon envy. The Christian who is content with having enough to eat and drink, even if he happens to have more, will not sentimentalize those whom the state is pleased to classify as ''poor'' and thus baptize their envy. If they lack enough to eat and drink, he will see that they are provided what they need. To oppress the poor, in the biblical sense, does not mean to maintain a social system of inequality, but to despoil people and reduce them to poverty by means of false measures, oppressive laws, and corrupt judges.[7] On this showing, poverty is not a permanent condition, defining the essence of a person, but a circumstance to be assuaged by the restoration of justice or by charitable help until the poor person can resume his normal status in society, one in which he contributes rather than being the recipient of contributions.

Moral worth, then, has nothing whatever to do with wealth. The emphasis on wealth and poverty in some theological circles mirrors the monomania found in both social democratic and Marxist thinking. The old delusion that poverty is a sign of immoral living and wealth of moral worth is being replaced by one that says the opposite. God is said to be on the side of the poor, whereas in another age he was said to be on the side of the rich; that was how they got rich. Both conceptions are grotesque caricatures of biblical teaching. The biblical writers did not sentimentalize the poor, but recognized that they could be evil (Prov. 28:3). There was to be no partiality shown on the basis of wealth (James 2:1, 9). While most of the warnings in this respect were directed against those who were partial to the rich against the interests of the poor, it was also considered impermissible to favor the poor at the expense of justice (Ex. 23:3; Lev. 19:15). Rich people who oppressed the poor were condemned (James 2:6; 5:1ff.), but it was acknowledged that the rich could be righteous (Ps. 112; Job). There was to be a recognition that the amount of wealth was of little importance in assessing a person. ''Let the lowly brother boast in his exaltation, and the rich in his humiliation'' (James

---

[7]For numerous examples of this from the prophetic literature, see John Bright, *A History of Israel* (London: SCM Press, 1960 [1959]), *passim.,* especially pp. 241,261,273.

1:9f.). Thus, poverty and wealth are morally neutral: neither one is an evil to be ashamed of nor a sign of special worth or transcending glory. Both ideas are illusions shared by most of the idolatries.

Oppression of the poor has reached a new dimension in the social democracies. Humanitarianism imitates the prophetic voices that call for justice to the poor but, like all idolatries, prepares its charges for slaughter. Demoting them from human beings to the permanent status of victimhood, it explains away their faults as inevitable consequences of the environment and makes it virtually impossible for them ever to attain freedom. The humanitarian imitation of love assumes that man is a belly and so eradicates his human qualities. Christians who follow the humanitarian impulse describe their task as "serving the poor." But to serve them continually is to keep them dependent, complementing the humanitarian effort that turns them into servile creatures of the state. Some of the black population of the United States, first deprived of its full rights of citizenship, now has been reduced to servility and victimhood by this destructive combination of helpers.

No theory of helping the poor may be said to be Christian if it does not discriminate among the poor. The old distinction, now despised among social workers, between the deserving and undeserving poor is a reflection of a biblical theme. It has a sanctimonious ring to it because sanctimonious people have misused it, but that should not blind us to the soundness of its conception. When widows were enrolled in the distribution of charity, they had to be widows indeed, which is to say truly destitute, without family members able to care for them (1 Tim. 5:5). This was intended that the community's resources should not be wasted and that self-respect should not be destroyed by continued dependency.

The jubilee principle (Lev. 25) served the same purpose, although it is now sometimes misused to support modern redistributory policies. Promulgated at a time when land was the only form of productive capital, it required that land distributions should terminate every fifty years. At that time the land would revert to the family that originally owned it. Thus, no person or family could gain a permanent hold on the only kind of property that could produce income, and so reduce other families to permanent dependency. Land sales were to be priced in such a way as to take into consideration the time left before the jubilee. They were not sales as much as rentals. The buyer knew that at the end of, say, five years the land would revert to the seller, and he was therefore only obliged to pay for the value of its five potential harvests.

Christians ought not to support any policy toward the poor that does not seek to have them occupy the same high plane of useful existence that all of us are to exemplify. "Serving the poor" is a euphemism for destroying the poor unless it includes with it the intention of seeing the poor begin to serve others, and thereby validate the words of Jesus that it is better to give than to receive (Acts 20:35). Whereas humanitarian social policy keeps people helplessly dependent, Christians should seek to remove them from that status and return them to productive capacity. Serving is a higher calling than being served.

Among the early churches, those in the poor country of Macedonia perhaps best demonstrated that principle. Although suffering greatly, they refused to become dependent and instead became the servants of others. "For in a severe test of affliction, their abundance of joy and their extreme poverty have overflowed in a wealth of liberality on their part" (2 Cor. 8:2). They gave to benefit Christians they had never seen who were even poorer than they, and Paul used their example as a means of spurring greater generosity in churches that had more to share. Far from sentimentalizing the Macedonians and using their poverty as the occasion to dehumanize them, he urged them to work with their hands, to refuse to be dependent on anybody, and to admonish the idle (1 Thess. 4:11f.; 5:14). It is therefore ludicrous to use biblical teaching on the poor to support humanitarian social policy that assumes and ensures that the poor will always be helpless.

The biblical writers also struck blows against *ressentiment* attempts to use the poor against the rich. The exploited were to cry to God who would rescue them and take vengeance against their oppressors. Liberation theology to them meant that God would liberate the righteous and bring judgment on the wicked. Thus, the poor could rejoice even in bitter circumstances (Ex. 22:21ff.; Ps. 12:5; 34:6-18; 113:5ff.; 140:12f.; Hab. 3:17f.). This is regarded as a joke by modern materialists, or as a soporific to keep the masses in subjection, but it is difficult to see why it is ignored by many who profess to take seriously the biblical teaching concerning the poor.

Generous charitable giving was an imperative for both the prophets and the early church. The besetting sin of Sodom was not sexual perversion, according to one of the prophets, but rather unconcern for the destitute. "This was the guilt of your sister Sodom: she and her daughters had pride, surfeit of food, and prosperous ease, but did not aid the poor and needy" (Ezek. 16:49). To withhold tithes and offerings to be added to the storehouse was said to be the same as robbing God (Mal. 3:8ff.). Yet, the early church did not levy a tax to provide for the needy. It specified that all such giving be voluntary. The Corinthian Christians were asked to contribute "not as an exaction but as a willing gift" (2 Cor. 9:5). Thus, paradoxically, generous giving to the needy is both voluntary—that is, not a matter of compulsion—and obligatory.

Distributory justice, then, occurs when people redistribute their own property, not that of others. When they do this they can and ought to discern the difference between making someone a permanent dependent and helping him over a rough spot. Voluntary giving makes it possible to meet real needs and not the desires created by state definitions that bow to the force of envy and greed. Those who so help others can hope that in assuaging suffering they might in some small way decrease the effectiveness of humanitarianism's appeal to the guilt of the population at large.

Philosopher Richard Mouw has a modest proposal that he hopes will unite Christians otherwise disagreeing with each other in matters of social action. Let us all, he says, give generously to the truly needy, regardless of our political convictions, and so fulfill the biblical requirement.[8] Although Mouw's conception of the opposing forces is seriously flawed, his proposal is not. If more Christians would take it seriously, it might smoke out those who are using biblical themes only to protect their positions.

The Stewardship of Wealth

What to do with capital, as distinct from income, is a serious concern. The biblical response to the question has nothing to do with semi-Manichaean asceticisms any more than with hedonistic materialism. It deals, rather, with the principle of stewardship. A steward is the caretaker of property that belongs to another. The good steward husbands the property and causes it to produce its proper income. The bad steward mismanages the property so that it yields poorly, or he squanders it or, worse yet, regards it as his own. In the biblical view, God is the real owner of all that the earth contains (Lev. 25:23), and the putative owners are really the stewards whose job it is to manage the property in the interests of their creator.

Whatever privileges and rights legal ownership may confer, the obligations of stewardship are more fundamental. The Hebrew nation, in its debasement, thought that being a chosen people provided them rights and immunities that other nations did not have. But it actually

---

[8]Richard J. Mouw, "Jesus and the Poor: Unity in Christ in an Unjust World," *The Reformed Journal,* vol. 30, no. 5, May 1980, pp. 8–13.

made them stewards of a promise and a revelation—and thereby heirs of a responsibility that others did not have. What should have led them to gratitude and humility instead swelled them with pride. Being poor stewards, they were dispossessed.

Anyone who regards capital, in whatever form it is held, as a trust to be exercised in faithful stewardship for God has to conduct his affairs in a manner that is fundamentally at odds with that of contemporary society. This is so because society, as we argued earlier, is in the process of destroying its capital. Government levies and inflation convert capital into consumption and so dissipate it. In an effort to protect resources from the tax collector and from inflation, as well as to maintain their standard of living in a declining economy, people begin dipping into capital. This has always been folly, and the wisdom literature of the Old Testament branded it so: "Precious treasure remains in a wise man's dwelling, but a foolish man devours it" (Prov. 21:20). Capital, therefore, in contrast to income, should not be converted to consumption, should not be kept in forms that make it vulnerable to currency depreciation, and should be shielded from government confiscation, using all legal means. The innocence of doves must make way here for the wisdom of serpents.

If we understand capital, in the broadest sense, to be any asset—material or non-material—that produces continuing benefits of any kind, then its importance becomes clearer. With the biblical norms increasingly spurned by an idolatrous society, the family structure, the intellectual competence, the legal foundations, and the economic base—in other words, the capital—are all decaying. Therefore, the stability, peace, and prosperity they should be producing will increasingly be lacking.

This suggests that we ought to explore once again the meaning of the expression Jesus used in describing the function of Christians in their society: "You are the salt of the earth" (Matt. 5:13). When Roman civilization finally collapsed, it was the Christians who preserved what was best in it, and their descendants centuries later were able to build a new civilization using the building blocks they had saved. Capital of all kinds must be preserved to provide spiritual, psychic, and material income in a failing society. It is not only legitimate but imperative that Christians exercise stewardship in preserving the material, as well as the moral, capital with which they are entrusted. They should ensure that it produces income, but primarily that it is preserved so that it can be used in the service of its true owner.

One of the main uses of capital in a decaying society is to buffer its holders against the forces of disintegration. It makes it possible, for example, to resist the pressures for conformity that complete dependence on the economic system requires. It makes it possible to rescue children from the chief medium of state indoctrination by sending them to the right kind of Christian school. In general, it serves as a tool for the accomplishment of the preservation function that is the province of the worldwide body of Christians. It is essential, therefore, to resist the semi-Manichaean tendency that calls property evidence of injustice.

Beyond private economic morality to the larger issues, what should be the Christian response to the prevailing economic system? Is it permissible for Christians to favor capitalism? If by capitalism one means the present system of statist manipulation of resources and people for the benefit of those who run the political system and their adherents, the answer is no. If it means the free and responsible ownership of resources by all who give value for what they receive, without the application of coercive power, then the answer is yes. How can we accept great disparities of wealth? Largely because in the absence of force or the threat of force personal property reflects the worth of the goods and services an individual has given up for it; in a free economy value is received in return for value given. "Value" in this sense is subjectively ascertained by those who give and receive it and therefore is not to be overruled by authorities. There is, moreover, no way that an optimum distribution of wealth can be obtained except by giving some people the power to expropriate what others have, and this is not a power that can be given legitimately nor discharged responsibly. The very process of defining "optimum" is one that must engage every possible political strategem to protect one's property and obtain that of others. The current revulsion against capitalism, the widespread assumption that profit is tainted, is based on false reasoning and the deep immorality of envy, unable to tolerate that another should have more or be perceived as being in any way superior.

Unity Among the Faithful

None of the modern idolatries can give a satisfactory answer to the question of preserving the just prerogatives of both the individual and the collective. Statism, in its currently fashionable form, says that individualism allows the stronger to crush the weaker, and therefore the state must assume control over both. Individualism, in both classical liberal and modern libertarian forms, says that the state necessarily takes away liberty and must not be allowed to encroach on the individual, whose desires therefore are given the status of the rule of law. In practice, these antithetical positions are both given some freedom to maneuver in the context of an uneasy play of political forces whose hallmark is pragmatism.

Only the Christian gospel transcends these antitheses. The metaphor of the *body of Christ*, the New Testament's description of the Christian church, is the amazing answer in the sphere of human relations to the ancient conundrum of the One and the Many. It shows why we are not required to be either the isolated atoms of individualism, nor links in the great collectivist chain that is enslaving the world. If each of us is related to the whole of the community as, say, the eye is to the body, then the reason we cannot exist alone is clear; our needs, purposes, and functions must be related to those of the other members of the body. At the same time, the eye performs a vital function for the body and cannot be written off as unimportant or peripheral. "On the contrary, the parts of the body which seem to be weaker are indispensable" (1 Cor: 12:22). This is the only conception that makes feasible love as a practical expression of a social ethic. Under individualism love is debased to sentimentality; under statism, it is a cover for the exercise of power.

Christian faith therefore provides meaning for the individual within the context of a larger society. It is the analogue to the doctrine of the trinity, in which each manifestation of God retains clear identity and function without dissolving the unity into three gods. This is the truth in the often-expressed statement that there is no brotherhood of man without the fatherhood of God. (But this is bound to collapse if used in a purely pragmatic way: "Since we desire all men to be brothers, let us pretend that there is one God who is father of all.") Western individualism dissolves the unity to preserve the individuality. Utopian collectivisms and all pantheisms preserve the unity—at least in principle—while dissolving any basis for respecting the individual.

In the gospel, furthermore, lies the only true cosmopolitanism. Entering the midst of the deepest-seated national animosities, it transforms hatred into love. The apostle Peter was thunderstruck to be shown in a vision that he was to regard his erstwhile enemies as brothers. As he said to an officer in the army of occupation: "God has shown me that I should not call any man common or unclean. . . . Truly I perceive that God shows no partiality, but in every nation any one who fears him and does what is right is acceptable to him" (Acts 10:28, 34f.).

If reconciliation between people is to be more than a pious wish, then the body of Christ must become a living experience among Christians, actualized and made into a reality in the church. This has been done in every age, but its potential has rarely been fully realized. Reconciliation and then unity are the corporate aspects of justification. They mean that a new community is to be born out of the formerly isolated individuals, together becoming the new body of Christ.

Thus, self-sufficiency is swallowed up in mutual dependence. Marks of talent or genius are recognized as gifts to be used for mutual benefit. Self-indulgence is recognized as more than merely a general fault, being the specific betrayal of a portion of the body of Christ that needs the gifts a particular person has to offer it.

But the body of Christ is never coextensive with the visible church. In the history of Israel those faithful to God were the remnant, whose compliance with the forms of religious obedience was matched by inner faithfulness and obedience to God. The remnant was comprised of the few who recognized God as their Lord and followed him, even as the broader religious community committed greater or lesser forms of apostasy. The early Christians learned that under the new covenant a similar condition would obtain. In the parables of the kingdom of God, Jesus taught that the kingdom would resemble a field in which an enemy had sown weeds among the wheat. Not before the end of the age would it be possible to separate them out of the crop (Matt. 13:24-43). In the apocalyptic vision the church at Sardis, unfortunately a prototype of many to follow, contained only a few who remained faithful. In the main, it was dead (Rev. 3:1-6).

The forms taken by this new body of Christ are of less consequence than the extent to which it reflects the good grain in its membership, those who are part of God's new creation among human beings. For, although the idolatries celebrate their capacity to create "new men" out of the old, only this genuine reflection of God's creative power is able to embody new spiritual life. This makes the church's remnant a new community unlike every other in its potential for exemplifying corporate spiritual life in the midst of a decaying civilization.

Defying the Powers

One of the real contributions of the Christian radicals has been their insistence—indeed, their concrete demonstration—that a Christian community that is consciously modeled on the New Testament pattern is a powerful force.

The making of community is essentially a revolutionary act. It is revolutionary because it proposes to detach men and women from their dependence upon the dominant institutions, powers and idolatries of the world system over the lives of people.[9]

Richard Neuhaus has pointed to the paradoxical truth that the revolutionary act of abandoning the world in favor of the creation and maintenance of Christian community may, finally, render the greatest service to the world. It does this by witnessing to the judgment under which the present world order is condemned and by demonstrating the alternative that is available.[10] This suggests that the true Christian community will be what sociologists call a deviant subculture. In political terms, it may be regarded as subversive in the sense that it is radically and consciously attempting to subvert the values of society and the institutions that represent those values. Marching to a different drummer than their neighbors, these Christians are likely to appear threatening to many, and yet to some strangely attractive.

Dissident communities need to be more than collections of individuals if they are to avoid disintegration. If they are churches, they must exemplify the organic bond that can only be found in the body of Christ. That is a quality difficult to find in the typical American parish. An association that merely occupies its members for a few hours a week reinforces the fragmentation of the individual's life among numerous loyalties and makes it virtually impossible to build genuine community. The resulting privatized kind of religion tends to be completely ineffectual.

Deviant subcultures can survive only if they form permanent and effective communities to stand in opposition to the larger society. In sociological terms, they need to have "plausibility structures" that will support their deviance and that can only come from a close community of like-minded deviants. As sociologist Donald Kraybill says: "It is not psychologically healthy to be the only oddball around."[11] Vladimir Bukovsky, whose principled obstreperousness, both in and out of prison, nearly drove the Soviet authorities wild, acknowledged that without a closely knit band of like-minded partisans he could have accomplished nothing. The churches will be able to fashion effective groups of Chris-

---

[9]Jim Wallis, *Agenda for Biblical People* (New York: Harper and Row, 1976), p. 103.

[10]Richard John Neuhaus, *Time Toward Home: The American Experiment as Revelation* (New York: Seabury, 1975) p. 162.

[11]Donald B. Kraybill, *The Upside-Down Kingdom* (Scottsdale, Penn.: Herald Press, 1978), p. 305. See also the excellent discussion of this problem by Os Guinness, "The Problem of Modernity—and the Church," *Radix,* Nov.–Dec. 1978, pp. 8–13.

tians, living in community, only when they acknowledge the bankruptcy of the larger culture, just as the Soviet dissidents have done.

The Preservation of Intellect

Creating Christian culture can be accomplished only with the aid of a solid intellectual effort that takes seriously a responsibility to defend the truth. This requires a conscious departure from the debased norms that are gradually gaining predominance. Scholarship is neither to be feared nor its products given the exalted status of sacred texts. If the wisdom of the first century was "foolish" and "doomed to pass away" (1 Cor. 1, 2), so is what passes for wisdom in the present age. The New Testament writers were conscious that their teaching was despised by the cultured Greeks of the dominant civilization. The spirit of the age—any age—is always opposed to the spirit of Christ.

In their uncompromising determination to proclaim truth, Christians must avoid the intellectual flabbiness of the larger society. They must rally against the prevailing distrust of reason and the exaltation of the irrational. Emotional self-indulgence and irrationalities have always been the enemies of the gospel, and the apostles warned their followers against them (Col. 2:18).

Paramount among the difficulties in Christian thinking is the dominance of anti-Christian assumptions in the "best" of the surrounding culture. Those who think Christians can easily use the world's artifacts and methods in the creation of a new synthesis underestimate the all-pervasiveness and subtlety of alien and hostile influences. T. S. Eliot, who was much concerned about this problem, warned that "paganism holds all the most valuable advertising space." He feared that as long as Christians were a tolerated minority, the unconscious pressures of intellectual conformity would more gravely complicate their survival than would the plainly perceived dangers of active persecution.[12]

Since ours is not so much a pagan (which is to say a pre-Christian) society as it is a post-Christian one, the dangers are all the more serious. The forces of idolatry do not urge us to worship Zeus but rather use the language that for many centuries has been associated with the Christian church. Profound religious differences may on the surface appear trivial, and one who points to them runs the risk of being called a hair-splitter. Just as an observer in the seventh century before Christ would be

---

[12]T.S. Eliot, *The Idea of a Christian Society and Notes Toward the Definition of Culture* (New York: Harcourt, Brace, Harvest Books, 1940), p. 18.

hard-pressed to distinguish the altar of the Lord from one dedicated to Baal, so are we faced with similar confusion when devotees of the idol state use the language of Christian compassion in their evangelistic mission.

There is no defense against such perils without a vigorous intellectual effort that enables us to discriminate between the true and the bogus. What assumptions lie behind the standard appeals to security and prosperity, justice and equality? Whose ends are being served? Whose gods are being served? What are the consequences of the measures that this group would like to put into effect? We shall not be able to deal with questions like these until we prepare intellectuals who are able to penetrate with clarity the "advertising" that Eliot warned about, which permeates the output of all of our influential institutions. We have not yet devised a way to train them without making use of the major advertising agencies—the universities and seminaries of the reigning idolatries.

When the cultural life of antiquity collapsed with the Roman Empire, and a centuries-long era of darkness followed, it was a corps of Christian intellectuals who kept the manuscripts, and the skills to use them, from disappearing from the face of the earth. We cannot say how long or how serious the present decline will prove to be, but once again Christians can stand in the gap against barbarism. Just as the biblical doctrine of creation demystified the world and made science possible, so other aspects of the faith are needed to destroy the follies of the modern idolatries. We must demystify the nation so that patriotism does not serve as an excuse for killing people. We need to demystify the state so that it cannot do evil with impunity. We need to demystify wealth and poverty so that they do not remain principles of human worth.

None of this can be done without the intellectual sophistication to detect the special pleading and the false assumptions of the intellectual world arrayed against us. We need it to defend against tendentious proposals accompanied by "studies" that purport to buttress the most destructive utopia-mongering. Christian intellectuals need the courage and confidence to stand fast, if need be, against the near-unanimous weight of scholarly fashion.

Christ Against the World

To use the language of militance in describing Christian responsibility in the world is to advocate a view of societal relevance that is far from unanimously held. By and large, Calvinists of one kind or another have supported it. The Arminian and Pietist positions, on the other hand, are much more ones of withdrawal than of confrontation. John Howard Yoder, one of the more eloquent defenders of these positions, urges Christians to consider that they are not the guardians of history and thus should refrain from grasping for the levers by which they hope to move society in the desired direction.[13]

In some respects this disinclination to change society mirrors the early monastic movement, which recoiled in horror from the excesses of a disintegrating empire and resolved to remain unspotted. Many of the followers of Karl Barth, those who are determined to view temporal events *sub speciae aeternitatis,* have found themselves unable to make distinctions between competing claims for allegiance. Bemused by the call for putting spiritual values first, they are unable to move decisively in the struggles that mark modern life. This is another version of the neo-Kantian dualism, helpless to reconcile the worlds of matter and of spirit. It was no wonder that a number of Lutheran bishops supported Hitler in 1934; they had difficulty seeing how Christian faith could inform material action. Reinhold Niebuhr never tired of pointing out this persistent weakness in Barthian thinking.

Christians who resist acknowledging any close correspondence between their faith and the direction that history takes strangely echo the position taken by the reigning humanist establishment. As Richard Neuhaus has pointed out, their stand is precisely that of the modern secularists who wish to banish Christian ideas from influencing public policy. This understanding of Christian action aids its enemies by reinforcing the notion of the supposed irrelevance of Christian faith.

Biblical teaching, in contrast, insists that faith and works are inseparable, that the interior dimension, if it is not a sham, must have its effect on the external world. The "salt" of people changed by the gospel must change the world. In the prophetic tradition, turning away from false gods had to be accompanied by a resurgence in the doing of justice. At its better moments, the church has made enormous differences in the way society functioned. In the midst of Hitler's program to kill the incurably ill in 1941, Bishop Galen published a sermon that exposed the practice and caused widespread revulsion throughout Germany. Galen was spared only because propaganda chief Joseph Goebbels feared massive public reaction if he should be executed. Meanwhile, the government stopped the killings after seventy thousand people had lost their lives. Millard Everett showed good sense in blaming the biblical ethic for prej-

---

[13]John Howard Yoder, *The Politics of Jesus* (Grand Rapids, Mich: Eerdmans, 1972), pp. 234–38.

udicing people against the killing of infants who fail to meet whatever tests of perfection their elders desire to impose upon them. It is this continual willingness to stand against culturally approved evil in the name of Christ that makes of the church a revolutionary force.

Christian revolution begins with the individual and has its concrete effect in the culture. Whether or not it exercises control, it always takes its stand with the eternal requirements of God against the idolatrous attractions of the moment. This means that it may appear either backward- or forward-looking depending on the nature of the opposition. Its enemy at a given time may be an ideology that marshals ideas in order to preserve the current order or, at another time, a utopia that sacralizes a new order.[14] It may be subject, therefore, at any time to being attacked as either "liberal" or "conservative," but it can never be either. All orders, old and new, are subject to the same eternal law that the church serves, and therefore are judged by the same standard. If they are found wanting, it has nothing to do with their conformance to this or that tradition.

To expect a transformation of society that results from changed people is not an idealistic hope that can never come to pass; it is a matter of historical record. In the midst of the nature worship of the second millenium before Christ, Israel introduced the dynamism of a people who worshiped the God beyond nature. As long as Israel maintained the distinctiveness of this heritage, it alone among its neighbors built a society based on justice, one that recognized that there was an objectively understood ethic beyond the exigencies of power. Much later the new Christian church infused the Mediterranean world with the same vision. This social transformation made Western civilization what it was. Love became the central idea in the dominant ethic, so much so that idolatry adopted its language and actions and was thereby made tolerable for a time.

Contrary to the sense of affliction and defeat that marks so much of the contemporary church in the West, the tone in the New Testament was one of victory. If we turn away from the *Weltschmerz* adopted too uncritically from the larger society, and look instead at the emerging new churches of Asia, Africa, and Latin America, we see something akin to the first-century exemplars. Considered on a worldwide basis, the twentieth century is a great period of Christian expansion, and the

---

[14]"Ideology" and "utopia" here are used in the special sense found in Karl Mannheim, *Ideology and Utopia: Introduction to the Sociology of Knowledge*, trans. Louis Wirth and Edward Shils (London: Kegan Paul, Trench, Trubner, 1946 [1936]).

number of new converts to the faith has been estimated reliably as exceeding fifty thousand *per day*.[15] If current trends in East and West should continue, we may expect that some of what are now the poor, backward countries of the world will become the economic, political, and social leaders of the twenty-first century, while the neo-pagan West continues its slide into impotence.

Toward the Triumph of Justice

Few ironies are more bitter than the fact that the strongest declamations against injustice come from the apologists of Marxism, an ideology responsible for the death or enslavement of countless millions. The Christian churches of the West in recent years have addressed this issue largely from the perspective of the great depression of the 1930s. Reinhold Niebuhr in the United States and Archbishop William Temple in Great Britain, persuaded that the business cycle and the hardships of the thirties were caused by the unbridled play of market forces, led the movement to make state domination of the economy normative. This, they said, would bring into being the "just social order." Their vision for the messianic state was not far from what we have today. In this sense, if in no other, they may be said to have succeeded.

Notwithstanding the errors of some of the church's leaders in this respect, the doing of justice in society is one of the major themes in the biblical writings. How the weak are treated is a test for any society, because it requires self-restraint for the powerful to do justice. "If a king judges the poor with equity," declared the ancient wisdom literature, "his throne will be established forever" (Prov. 29:14). The king who does so does not make of the poor the arbiters of right and wrong, thus divinizing them, but refuses to sacrifice them to the interests of the rich or of himself.

Doing justice in this sense is *uniquely* the function of the state, one that it usually fails to perform. Within a religious federation Israel's twelve tribes functioned as a unified social structure. They found their principle of unity in the covenant with God. When the federated tribal structure broke down, the monarchy supplanted the law as the unifying structure of national life. The effect was the creation of a privileged class

---

[15]Cambridge University historian Edward Norman discussed this issue in the 1978 Reith Lectures, published as *Christianity and the World Order* (Oxford: Oxford Univ. Press, 1979).

and the destruction of justice.[16] That set the stage for the pattern of injustice that called forth the prophetic ministry of denunciation and ultimately led to the fall of the two monarchies.

Since injustice stems from the application of force or the threat of force against innocent persons, it is natural that those who seek to overthrow it should be active in political life. They should be working to stop the incessant looting taking place under the banner of redistribution, which at once makes dependents out of all its recipients and destroys the economy by removing the incentives for production. And it must insist that the criminal justice system, bemused by behaviorist contentions that criminals are victims, begin protecting the innocent against those who prey upon them. To take the position that faith should not be expected to affect corporate life is to acquiesce to the reigning order. For all its effect on the society, it is tantamount to saying that the rule of idolatry is legitimate. Or else it is to etherealize the faith by divorcing it from life. In either case, the injunction to act as salt in the world is robbed of half its meaning.

Questions about justice are fundamentally religious. This is naturally denied by those who think that the separation of church and state is a doctrine providing them with the means to structure the political order to the exclusion of Christian belief. But there is no such thing as law that does not assume a particular configuration to reality, which does not at least pretend to tell what kind of values are to be considered ultimate. That is why the establishment of justice as the aim of a biblical world view must encompass the changing of the political system. Justice means the ruling of society in conformance with the law of God.

If Barth and Niebuhr represent the Scylla and Charybdis of the eternity-time dichotomy, then an authentic biblical approach would be to reject the neo-Kantian split that can never seem to accommodate both eternity and time in the same system. We are not condemned to choose between a preoccupation with heavenly concerns that are completely irrelevant to earthly affairs and the kind of activism that can only worsen the conditions it seeks to ameliorate.

If we are to change the temporal in keeping with the eternal, then it will have to be done by changing the powers that control events. This means that we must work toward bringing the political, economic, and cultural landscape into conformity with the divine intention. That is

---

[16]This argument on the metamorphosis of Israel is taken from John Bright, *A History of Israel*, pp. 241f.

what the New Testament means when it speaks of Christ as the ruler of the kings of the earth (Rev. 1:5). The Lord of history is the rightful sovereign of events and institutions. There is a note of triumph in the writings left to us by the early church that breaks through the telling of manifold difficulties. It recognized that crucifixion was followed by resurrection. The current critique of "triumphalism" with its lachrymose dwelling on "brokenness" is the recipe for retreat and defeat, and presages the continued failure to change human institutions so that they conform to a view of justice consonant with God's law.

We should recognize that these powers exercise legitimate functions but refuse them the right to usurp others. They may, and must, punish murderers, but must not be permitted to order family life. Insofar as they do not confine themselves to their appointed tasks, Christians must be the disloyal opposition. We do not recognize their right to play god. Theologians have often lost the distinction between legitimate and illegitimate functions in urging Christians to support the powers without reservation. For we are enjoined to obey authorities that "punish those who do wrong and . . . praise those who do right" (1 Pet. 2:14), not those that foster evil. Religious traditions that advocate unquestioning loyalty to the powers make it almost certain that injustice will rule. The natural inclination people have toward misusing authority is encouraged when those who claim to follow a higher law than the statutes fail to act on that claim. Tolstoy was sympathetic with the Indians under colonial rule, but observing that thirty thousand British controlled two hundred million Indians, he concluded that the Indians had enslaved themselves. The passivity displayed by the Indians is properly a trait of pantheism, not of Christianity.

There is an almost infinite number of ways one can stand against the powers. We are not limited to either acquiescence or law-breaking. Once we reject passivity, we can consider how to carry on the struggle. There are speeches, demonstrations, petitions, withholding of services, letter-writing, marches, economic boycott, selective disobedience, refusal to serve the state, ignoring of government directives, stalling and obstruction, overloading the administrative system with excessive compliance, and so on.[17] Should the system worsen, of course, there is always the possibility of making oneself vulnerable to prosecution.

Prior to sabotaging the establishment, however, we should consider how to change its course. Perhaps we could turn the powers away from

---

[17]For the theory of nonviolent resistance, and scores of concrete strategies, see Gene Sharp, *The Politics of Non-Violent Action* (Boston: Porter Sargent, 1973).

idolatry and toward the establishment of the rule of justice. Proclaiming the gospel is fundamental to this. As the idolatries almost universally recognize, changing society without changing people is futile. The church's teaching function has to include a more biblical understanding of society if it is to influence the provision of justice.

In our effort to do this, is it possible to pursue wholeheartedly the program of one party or movement while recognizing its contingent nature? Not if "contingent" is understood to mean the opposite of "absolute." Inasmuch as these movements are driven by ideological forces that are to some degree in conflict with Christian faith, we are able to accord them at best only partial support. Our loyalty will always be suspect among those groups, and rightly so, for we are ready to change from support to opposition as soon as they depart from some approximation of justice by biblical standards. The danger in becoming "Christians for X," as Richard Neuhaus has well said, is that of becoming mere appendages to "Americans for X.'" This can only encourage millions of Christians, wary of being used by hostile forces, to turn away from their responsibility to work toward creating a just society.

The rival movements provide no help in understanding contemporary events. The common labels are as worthless now as they were a century ago when W. S. Gilbert lampooned them in *Iolanthe:*

> I often think it's comical
> How nature always does contrive
> That every boy and every gal,
> That's born into the world alive,
> Is either a little Liberal,
> Or else a little Conservative!

This is the dichotomous thinking that invites us to be part of any movement claiming to be "moral" or any movement that claims to favor the poor and oppressed. Such follies stem from blind submission to political symbols instead of seeing the realities hiding beyond them. To follow the modern ideologies, however disguised with biblical language, invites idolatry to set the agenda for the church. The early Christians, living among eastern Mediterranean populations divided into Jews and pagans, were called by the latter the "third race," and so called themselves. As long as they did not think of themselves as belonging to one branch or the other of a twofold division of the world, they could truly be Christian.[18] So it is now. Christians can be liberals if they wish, or con-

---

[18]See R. A. Markus, *Christianity in the Roman World* (New York: Scribner's, 1974), pp. 24ff.

servatives, or radicals, but not until they unmask those false images can they fulfill their real responsibilities.

It may be, then, that the only healthy relationship the church can have with the political parties is one of mutual suspicion, with a willingness to undertake short-term alliances of limited scope. Since each side is marching to a different drummer, it is difficult to see how the relationship can be any firmer, unless one or the other capitulates. Recent history is not encouraging about which side that would be. If we are successful, no party could lightly legislate or enforce the law in ways that are repugnant to Christians. They may finally do so, but only at political cost.

Representative government is worthy of support in principle because the biblical view of human nature concludes that all of us are flawed and unable to handle unlimited power without falling into pride and irresponsibility. Nevertheless, the ratification of law by majority vote does not validate it. To the democratic ideology, any action is just if it is approved by majority rule. To the libertarian ideology, any action is just if it is not coercive. Both are thus humanist to the core. In biblical perspective, right and wrong are not determined by the process leading up to their proclamation, but by the degree of conformity to the law of God. At the same time, most Christians have lived—and do live—under authoritarian or totalitarian regimes, and the kingdom of God is not thereby made of no effect. For Christians to remain faithful to their calling under regimes that are at once idolatrous and unrestrained in power is to invite persecution. These regimes seem to know instinctively that a church which has not been tamed is their most dangerous adversary.

One of the most serious dangers we face in seeking to influence the political sphere is that we, too, may succumb to the delusion that we possess the "solution" to the dilemmas of peace and justice, requiring only that we grasp the reins of power. If that should happen, we are only a step away from seeking to bring into being our own version of the messianic state. For it would imply that our salvation lies in yet another reformation of institutional arrangements. This society will have peace and justice when it repents and overthrows the idols, and not before.

Persecution

It is absurd that the name "Christian" should be taken by so many as synonymous with respectable, middle class, or conventional. It was first used to refer to *disciples*—those under discipline of the Master—and it was coined in the midst of persecution (Acts 11:26). Should we stop accommodating ourselves to the prevailing norms, we can expect to be treated in the same fashion. We have allowed ourselves to be bought off with our free education, prosperity, and tax deductions. The persecution may begin when we renounce all that and indeed become disciples. In fact, the disabilities brought upon the Christian school movement by officers of the state suggest that it has already begun.

Modern persecutions replicate the experience of the church from the beginning. While Christ was yet with his disciples, he warned them about what would take place. "If the world hates you, know that it has hated me before it hated you . . . . If they persecuted me, they will persecute you" (John 15:18ff.). One of the apostles later interpreted Cain's fratricide as the outcome of envy for his brother's righteousness and warned the followers of Christ that they could expect the world's enmity for the same reason (1 John 3:12ff.). The apostle James, initially attracted by what he thought was a gospel of success that would bring him political power, had to be told that he could not have what he craved. Later, he was killed by the state (Mark 10:35ff.; Acts 12:2). That pattern was repeated often for the church's first three centuries; the state wanted reverence that the Christians could not give without defying God.[19]

If the ancient precedents are repeated, we can expect the new persecution of Christians to be led by the social and religious elite, in conjunction with the authorities of the state. The warning of Christ was that those who were going to persecute his followers would think that by so doing they were serving God. This kind of persecution is extremely debilitating, because it induces in the victims doubt as to whether they are in the right, while convincing the guilty ones that they are. In the aftermath of the mass suicide in Guyana, reporters referred to James Jones's People's Temple as a manifestation of "radical Christianity." Had the political climate been different, the congressional investigation that followed could have resulted in legislation seriously restricting Christian groups that depart from establishment churches, and thus could be considered dangerous sects. Rousseau, who provided an ideology for modern totalitarianism, said that Christianity was of all things he knew the most contrary to the "social spirit." The state is never amused at being defied, and Christians who take their responsibilities seriously are not likely to remain within the pale of what its functionaries regard as socially responsible.

How should we react to the threat of persecution? Paul's famous pas-

---

[19]Ethelbert Stauffer, *Christ and the Caesars*, trans. K. and R. Gregor Smith (London: SCM Press, 1955).

sage on obeying rulers, so often misused to justify the domination of despots, offered a subsidiary reason for obedience: the maintenance of a clear conscience (Rom. 13:5). It is absurd to weaken oneself by violating the law for a trivial reason like evading taxes. The Christians of the first generation, undergoing severe persecution, "joyfully accepted the plundering of [their] property," and those who live now can do the same, rather than cheapening their resistance. Ayn Rand caught perfectly the power that a clear conscience gives one who is persecuted, in the words she put in the mouth of Dr. Ferris, a scientist who served the state in its quest for power:

> . . . there is no way to disarm any man except through guilt . . . . If there's not enough guilt in the world, we must create it. If we teach a man that it's evil to look at spring flowers and he believes and then does it—we'll be able to do whatever we please with him. He won't defend himself. He won't feel he's worth it. He won't fight. But save us from the man who lives up to his own standards. Save us from the man of clean conscience. He's the man who'll beat us.

One theme that emerges from the literature of resistance against the Soviet tyranny is that external power silences and conquers those who are willing to be conquered. Solzhenitsyn and Bukovsky give innumerable examples to show that submission is not a foregone conclusion in the face of inexorable force: it is an act that is engaged in willingly by those who could do otherwise. Political authorities whose final appeal is their ability to kill or imprison their opponents cannot easily cope with people who say that that is not the final appeal, but only one appeal among many. This appears on the surface to be courage, but it is really something much more profound and powerful. Faith makes it possible to be relatively indifferent to the secondary considerations while exercising supreme care about the main consideration.

In the midst of persecution, the community of believers is the main source of strength for Christians. Their unity is of capital importance, but this has nothing to do with the ecclesiastical gigantism that currently accompanies the great weakness of the churches. Organizational unity often serves as a pernicious substitute for the organic unity that ought to mark the body of Christ and has made it easier in the past for alien influences to subvert the church. The Living Church in the Soviet Union could be made a part of the state apparatus with little trouble once Stalin had moved his own people into the top leadership. The Nazi revolution similarly found the unified state church easy to take over, while the authorities could deal only with great difficulty with the lay-dominated decentralized churches.

Speculation on how best to meet the threat of disaster must be accompanied by a theology of disaster, and such a theology must center on the Christian virtue of hope. The apostle who suffered innumerable hardships, including beatings and imprisonment, wrote: "But thanks be to God, who in Christ always leads us in triumph" (2 Cor. 2:14). Hope is what enabled him to see the essence of the situation—triumph—beyond the accident of disaster. It is the quality of which optimism is the secularized and debased remnant. It is rooted in the faithfulness of God, the firmest of all foundations, instead of being a mere habit of thinking or, worse, the outcome of historicist or other theories of inevitable progress. Now that the prevailing fashion is to cry doom, it is needed all the more.

Embarking on the Great Adventure

Biblical faith finds great power—as does its imitator, Marxism—in the conviction that history is going its way. Or rather, that since Christ is the Lord of history, it is going history's way. Final victory is not dependent upon how well its work is done; rather it is assured regardless of all contingent factors. "Thy kingdom come, thy will be done on earth as it is in heaven," is not a pious wish, but a certainty. We do not question if we shall be able to bring such a happy state of affairs into being, but rather what our role should be in its inevitable fulfillment. Since the world's powers were "disarmed" in Christ (Col. 2:15) their might is limited, despite the illusions of invincibility they are able to project. The eschatology of victory is a principle theme of the New Testament.

Yet, we live in a world of phenomena as well as eschaton, and we must face the question of what good the gospel of Christ is in the here and now. Ironically, those who seek their ultimate value in the next world are the only ones able to do much good in this one. Those in love with this present world destroy it along with themselves. Charles Cochrane concluded his study of ancient Rome by affirming that Christianity was the synthesis that provided the only cohesion to the fragmenting culture of Hellenism. That may be the role it is presently preparing to assume again.

From the most homely of responsibilities to the most exalted, Christian faith has the capacity to infuse coherence and grace where disintegration now takes place. About seventy-five years ago French poet Charles Péguy declared that the true revolutionaries of the twentieth century would be the fathers of Christian families. He must have meant that the infusion of meaning and sanity into family nurture has enormous potential to thwart the march of the idolatries.

At the other end of the scale, it is getting ever more difficult to disguise the intellectual sterility of the modern movements that a century or two ago moved triumphantly away from their biblical underpinnings. Czech Marxist philosopher Milan Machovec has expressed frustration at theologians overly enamored of "dialogue" who fail to speak boldly enough about the distinctives of Christian faith. Although an atheist, he believes that the "dynamic" of the West lies in its allegiance to a transcendent God who relativizes present achievements. His goal is to find a secular equivalent for God, and thus rescue the moribund idolatries of communism from their predicament. Yet, the West itself has fallen victim to those idolatries, and only a return to the same transcendent God can rescue it.

In the New Testament, the metaphors commonly used to describe the church's external relations were those of war. The ethic of the early church made it inevitable that strife would come from its refusal to conform to the reigning idolatries. On the other hand, dialogue is for the church the great metaphor of decline and defeat, a dispirited acknowledgment that one does not have the truth. It is expressed on the popular level by the currently faddish emphasis on peace, security, and prosperity as the normal outcomes of Christian faith. This debased form of Christianity is unable to comprehend the contemporary meaning in the incident wherein Christ branded as satanic Peter's refusal to accept the reality of the coming crucifixion. The same idea is often found in the Pauline literature. "When people say, 'There is peace and security,' then sudden destruction will come upon them . . . and there will be no escape" (1 Thess. 5:3).

Their new-found minority status in a world headed for the brink of disaster holds the promise of providing more excitement than most Christians are expecting. Once again in the West we live under conditions the early church knew intimately, and perhaps we can understand better than most of our predecessors the meaning of passages in the New Testament dealing with these conditions.

One reason Chesterton's writings have been so challenging and hopeful to three generations of Christians is that he captured better than most the quality of adventure in Christian life. That is a quality of which we shall have more than enough if we are willing to accomplish the task that lies before us. For even the good kings of ancient Judah, who expelled the worship of the Baals from the temple, left the Asherim and their devotees undisturbed on the hills. So rooted in communal life had these deities become, that it was unthinkable to be rid of them. In the late twentieth century the West is similarly plagued with major and minor idols, some of them all but invisible. It is hard to imagine a more important or satisfying role than to embark on the spiritual, intellectual, and political adventure of working toward stripping them, root and branch, from the land.

Index